U.S.A. SIXTIES

Volume 1
AARON – CALLAS

GROLIER
EDUCATIONAL

Published 2001 by Grolier Educational
Sherman Turnpike
Danbury, Connecticut 06816

© 2001 Brown Partworks Ltd

Set ISBN: 0-7172-9503-6
Volume ISBN: 0-7172-9504-4

Library of Congress Cataloging-in-Publication Data
U.S.A. Sixties
    p. cm.
    Includes index
    Contents: v. 1. Aaron, Hank–Callas, Maria – v. 2. Capote,
Truman–Eichmann trial – v. 3. Eisenhower,
Dwight–Kennedy, Robert F. – v. 4. Kennedy assassination
(John F.)–Organization of American States – v. 5. Olympic
Games–Scientology – v. 6. SEATO–Yippies.
    ISBN 0-7172-9503-6 (set : alk. paper) – ISBN 0-7172-
9504-4 (v. 1. : alk. paper) – ISBN 0-7172-9505-2 (v. 2. :
alk. paper) – ISBN 0-7172-9506-0 (v. 3. : alk. paper) –
ISBN 0-7172-9507-9 (v. 4. : alk. paper) – ISBN 0-7172-
9508-7 (v. 5. : alk. paper) – ISBN 0-7172-9509-5 (v. 6. :
alk. paper)
    1. United States–Civilization–1945–Encyclopedias. 1.
Grolier Educational (Firm)

E169.12.U172000
973.92–dc21   00-023958

For information address the publisher:
Grolier Educational, Sherman Turnpike,
Danbury, Connecticut 06816

Printed and bound in Singapore

FOR BROWN PARTWORKS LTD.
Managing editor: Edward Horton
Project editor: Matthew Turner
Design: Ray Leaning
Picture research: Mirco Decet
Indexer: Kay Ollerenshaw
Project consultant: Professor Dana Ward, Pitzer College,
Claremont, California

Cover images: Robert Hunt Library

About this Book

This volume is one of a set about the events, personalities, and cultural forces that shaped Americans' lives in the most complex and fascinating period in the country's recent history. The decade began with the optimism of John F. Kennedy's inauguration and ended in the disillusion of the Seventies; in between it encompassed such major events as the civil rights campaign, the Vietnam War, the Cold War, the space program, and the Woodstock rock festival. The sixties were many things for many people, from hippies to Native Americans, civil rights protesters to the moral majority. *U.S.A. Sixties* explores the contradictions and complexities of the decade. Much of the agenda for today's United States was set at this time, when to the young anything seemed possible, and sometimes was.

The series is arranged as an easy-to-use A–Z. There are over 300 articles, each illustrated with images that capture the spirit of the era. Maps and charts back up important geographical and political concepts. There are also many boxed features where you will find specific information, such as biographies of important people or more detailed explanations about parts of larger subjects. Comprehensive cross-references appear at the end of every article to point you toward linked entries should you wish to research further into a topic.

At the end of the book is an extensive timeline, which places the events of the decade in their chronological context. There is also a list of further reading and useful websites for students who wish to explore deeper into specific subjects. Each volume also has a comprehensive set index that will help you find references to topics throughout the whole set.

CONTENTS

AARON, HANK 5

ABERNATHY, RALPH 6

ADVERTISING 7

AEROSPACE INDUSTRY 12

AGNEW, SPIRO 19

AGRICULTURE 20

AIR FORCE 27

AIR-TO-GROUND MISSILES 32

AIR TRAVEL 34

ALI, MUHAMMAD 38

ALLEN, WOODY 40

ALLIANCE FOR PROGRESS 41

ALTAMONT FESTIVAL 43

AMERICAN INDIAN MOVEMENT 45

ANTISMOKING CAMPAIGN 48

ANTIWAR MOVEMENT 50

APARTHEID 58

APOLLO PROGRAM 60

ARCHITECTURE 72

ARMS RACE 78

ARMSTRONG, LOUIS 84

ARMY 85

ASIMOV, ISAAC 89

AUTOMOBILE INDUSTRY 90

BABY-BOOM GENERATION 95

BAEZ, JOAN 101

BALDWIN, JAMES 102

BALLET 104

BARBIE DOLL 108

BARDOT, BRIGITTE 109

BASEBALL 110

BASKETBALL 115

BAY OF PIGS INVASION 120

BEACH BOYS 122

BEATLES 124

BELLOW, SAUL 128

BERKELEY FREE SPEECH MOVEMENT ..129

BERLIN WALL 131

BERNSTEIN, LEONARD 133

BIRTH-CONTROL PILL 134

BLACK PANTHER PARTY 136

BLACK POWER 138

BLACK STUDIES 143

BLACKOUT OF 1965 145

BLUES 146

BOOK PUBLISHING 150

BOXING 152

BRANDT, WILLY 156

BREZHNEV, LEONID 157

BRITISH INVASION 158

BROADWAY 162

BROWN, HELEN GURLEY 166

BROWN, JAMES 167

BROWN, JIM 168

BRUBECK, DAVE 169

BRUCE, LENNY 170

BUNDY, McGEORGE 171

BUNKER, ELLSWORTH 172

BUREAU OF INDIAN AFFAIRS 173

BURGER, WARREN 175

BURROUGHS, WILLIAM 176

BUSING 177

CALLAS, MARIA 180

FURTHER READING; PICTURE CREDITS   181

TIME LINE 182

SET INDEX 185

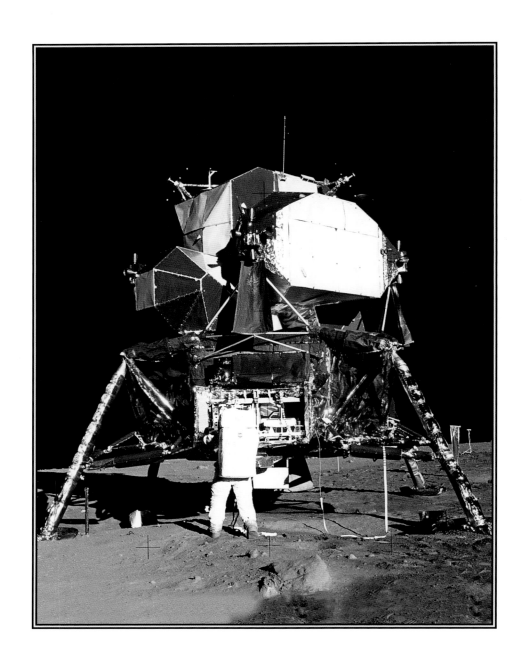

Volume 1

Aaron – Callas

HANK AARON b. 1934

During a glittering career that spanned three decades with the Milwaukee and Atlanta Braves, Hank Aaron broke one of baseball's most legendary records—Babe Ruth's career home-run total.

Hank Aaron arrived in the major leagues in 1954, and by the time he retired in 1976, he had become the greatest home-run hitter of all time, with 755. He broke the immortal Babe Ruth's record of 714 homers in April 1974 with a blast that also took him past Willie Mays's National League record of 2,062 runs scored. Almost all of Aaron's exceptionally long career was spent with one team, the Milwaukee and subsequently the Atlanta Braves (his last two seasons were with the Milwaukee Brewers of the American League).

Three times in the 1960s Aaron led the National League in home runs— 1963 (44), 1966 (44), and 1967 (39). He also won batting titles in 1956 (.328) and 1959 (.355) and finished with a lifetime average of .305. When he ended his playing days, Aaron also ranked first in lifetime RBIs, second in

▷ Aaron's right-handed swing was a model of power and consistency. In 1999 a new trophy was named after him and awarded to the major-league player with the season's best slugging percentage.

Aaron versus Ruth

Who was the greater hitter: Hank Aaron or Babe Ruth, whose home-run record he eclipsed? Fans of Aaron point out that Ruth never came up against the competition of star black players, that he did not have to face pitchers in night conditions, and that in his day fielders wore much smaller gloves (of significance in preventing runs, if not home runs). On the other hand, Ruth had to contend with spitballs. The question may have been settled by the statistician Ron Skrabacz, who has compared the batting records of every star player in 15 categories and then measured how each of them stood up against his contemporaries—the only possible standard of sporting supremacy. In Skrabacz's definitive analysis Aaron came out the fourth-best hitter of all time, behind the legendary Detroit star of the early 20th century Ty Cobb ranked first, Cardinal Stan Musial, and the Babe.

at-bats and runs scored, and third in games played and hits. Although not an outstandingly speedy outfielder, he stole 204 bases. Along with pitchers Warren Spahn and Lew Burdette, Aaron was the heart of the Milwaukee team that reached the World Series in 1957 and 1958, and in those series he batted .393 and .333.

Aaron rarely blasted the ball a tremendous distance—500 feet or more—and he lacked the charismatic appeal of a Mays or Mantle, but he impressed fans with his quiet modesty. One of the greatest players in the history of baseball, Aaron was inducted into the Hall of Fame in 1982. □

See Also: Baseball

RALPH ABERNATHY 1926–1990

Minister and activist Ralph Abernathy was Martin Luther King, Jr.'s principal associate during the long civil right struggle and his natural successor when King was assassinated in 1968.

△ **Ralph Abernathy holds an impromptu press conference from the inside of a police van after being arrested at the Capitol in January 1968.**

Ralph Abernathy first heard Martin Luther King, Jr., speak when he was a graduate student at Atlanta University in the early 1950s. The two men became firm friends when they were both pastors in Montgomery, Alabama, where, as a student, Abernathy had been the first black disk jockey on a white radio station. Their families dined together almost every night, and the two ministers regularly discussed ways to improve the lot of African Americans.

Together King and Abernathy organized the Montgomery bus boycott of 1955–1956, which resulted in the desegregation of public transportation in the city. King and Abernathy became respectively president and secretary-treasurer of the Southern Christian Leadership Conference (SCLC). While they were in Atlanta, setting up the SCLC in January 1957, Abernathy's home and church were bombed.

Civil rights tactician

When King moved to Atlanta in 1960, he persuaded Abernathy to follow him. Abernathy became pastor of Atlanta's West Hunter Street Baptist Church. "I realize the degree to which this move defined for Martin and me the strength and importance of our friendship," Abernathy recalled in his 1989 autobiography *And the Walls Came Tumbling Down*. "Abernathy was the glue for Martin's soul," said fellow civil rights worker David J. Garrow. "He gave him counsel, he gave him solace, he gave him perspective."

From there King and Abernathy organized protests across the South, with King as strategist and Abernathy as tactician. As a result, Abernathy was constantly at King's side, and they often shared a jail cell together.

In 1965 King named Abernathy his heir apparent. Some insist that Abernathy was jealous of King's fame and, especially, his Nobel Peace Prize. But King's wife Coretta pointed out that throughout it all, Abernathy was one of the "few people he could rely on." When King was shot in Memphis in 1968, Abernathy made the ambulance ride with him and shared his last moments. However, without King the SCLC became increasingly disorganized. Abernathy scored some minor successes in the form of legislation and the settlement of the hospital workers' strike in Charleston, South Carolina, in 1969. In the 1970s he bowed out of the civil rights movement, complaining that African Americans who "now occupy high positions made possible through our struggle... will not support the SCLC financially."

Looking back on his activist days, Abernathy acknowledged the debt he owed to King. "We were a team," he said, "and each of us was severely crippled without the other."

Abernathy's acclaimed autobiography was greeted with controversy. In it he revealed not only the inner workings of the civil rights movement but also King's extramarital affairs. He died in Atlanta in 1990. □

See Also: Civil Rights Movement; King; King Assassination; Segregation

ADVERTISING

As the consumer boom of the 1950s continued unbroken through the 1960s, it was fueled by an advertising industry that employed increasingly sophisticated techniques to make Americans buy.

Modern advertising, with its large all-purpose agencies and sophisticated research and marketing, was one of the leading growth industries in the boom years of the 1950s and 1960s. The United States, blessed with an enormous home market that provided the world's richest consumer base and a technology that produced the widest range of products, led the way. The center of New York's advertising industry, Madison Avenue, gave its name to the industry as a whole and was a byword for slick slogans and glossy images that persuaded people to buy more and more goods and services. Throughout the 1960s the world's 10 largest advertising agencies were all American or American-controlled multinationals.

In 1965 expenditure on advertising in the United States topped $15 billion, representing about 2.4 percent of the gross national product. By way of international comparison, the figure for the top-spending European country in 1966, West Germany, was 1.3 percent of GNP. One reason for American leadership in the field was that by 1960 there were TV sets in 90 percent of American homes. Thanks largely to television, the average American, according to 1965 estimates, was exposed to some 650 advertisements every day; some commentators put the figure as high as 1,500.

The power of advertising

Lacking a tradition of high-profile publicly funded television, program-makers in the United States were at the mercy of advertisers, who were able, as sponsors, to identify products with programs. For example, every Sunday night viewers were treated to the *Lipton Playhouse*, while the World Series was "brought" to sports fans by Gillette.

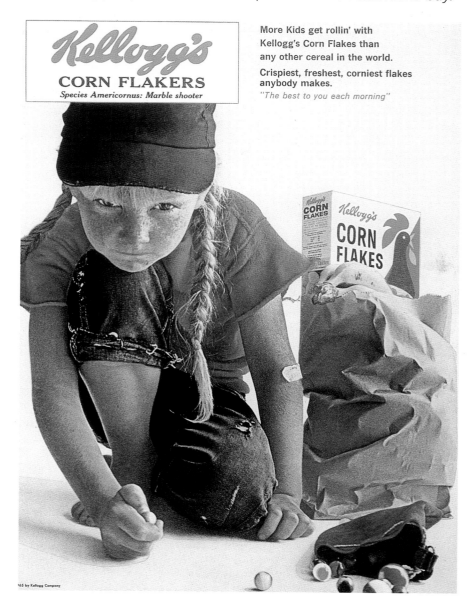

Kellogg's CORN FLAKERS
Species Americornus: Marble shooter

More Kids get rollin' with Kellogg's Corn Flakes than any other cereal in the world.
Crispiest, freshest, corniest flakes anybody makes.
"The best to you each morning"

△ Having established its famous slogan "The best to you each morning" by the 1960s, a manufacturer like Kellogg could reuse it with a variety of charming images.

Some commentators were disturbed by the pervasive influence of advertising and what they perceived as its wastefulness of economic resources. The 1960s opened with the industry under attack. Advertising's insidious appeal to "keep up with the Joneses" was condemned by critics as a blatant surrender to materialism. During the

1960 presidential election campaign Democratic candidate John F. Kennedy's two top aides, Arthur Schlesinger, Jr., and John Kenneth

Motivated to buy

Ernest Dichter's research into human motivation regularly landed him in controversy, especially since matters often came down to sex. An investigation for Chrysler yielded the finding that men viewed convertibles as they might a mistress, sedan cars more as wives. This may seem an unremarkable observation in an age when sexual symbolism is widely understood, but it was Dichter more than anyone else who made sexual allusion and symbolism a key element in advertising. Certainly the supposed association between convertible cars and glamorous women was relentlessly exploited in glossy advertisements.

Dichter did not always work on behalf of profit-seeking corporations. He advised the Red Cross on how to get more people to donate blood, and he worked on an antismoking campaign for the American Cancer Society. His advice on how to achieve world peace included the suggestion that the word "disarmament" should be dropped. "No one wants to be disarmed. Call it something else." To its advocates research alone could throw up such an insight into the emotive power of a word. Dichter had a reply to critics who charged that his research was never thorough and that his "findings" were little more than intuitive judgments. "I have an interviewing panel of between 2,500 and 3,000 in America, and I spend hundreds of thousands a year on research."

How to tell a real tiger from a pussycat:

Drive it.

Two seconds behind the wheel of a Pontiac and you know unquestionably you're in tiger country. You realize right away there's more to being a tiger than just bucket seats, carpeting, and sleek upholstery. There's Wide-Track handling, say. And availability of a six or two rambunctious V-8s in the LeMans. And a snarling 335-hp GTO or its 360-hp, slightly hairier, cousin. Get out and drive a tiger!

**Quick Wide-Track Tigers
Pontiac LeMans & GTO**

Pontiac Motor Division · General Motors Corporation

△ Dichter's research pinpointed the male association between glamorous convertible cars and sex, and advertisers were quick to exploit it with none-too-subtle campaigns.

Galbraith, openly asked whether advertising was swelling the coffers of the private sector of the economy at the expense of the public sector.

Public interest in advertising had been greatly stimulated by the publication in 1957 of Vance Packard's best-seller, *The Hidden Persuaders*. Attention was focused on Packard's exposure of "subliminal" advertising—the use, especially in TV commercials, of signals hidden to the viewer's conscious perception but registering at an unconscious level. The real importance of the book, however, was the prominence that it gave to the ideas of the motivational psychologist Ernest Dichter (*see box*). Packard's book was followed, in 1960, by Dichter's own publication, *The Strategy of Desire*.

The Austrian-born Dichter was the guru of "motivational research." His research centered on two questions: why do people behave as they do, and what motivates them? Advertisers who found answers to those questions could come up with effective selling copy and images. By the mid-1960s Dichter's Institute for Motivational Research was the leader in its field.

Partly as a result of Dichter's influence, advertising agencies became huge concerns, staffed with economic specialists and behavioral psychologists. Advertising agencies of the early 20th century had been little more than media brokers, selling space; they then switched sides and became representatives of companies who bought space.

▷▽ Two famous 1960s examples of the "creative" school of advertising. Such amusing self-deprecation raised the Avis and Volkswagen profiles.

When you're only No.2, you try harder. Or else.

Little fish have to keep moving all of the time. The big ones never stop picking on them.

Avis knows all about the problems of little fish.

We're only No.2 in rent a cars. We'd be swallowed up if we didn't try harder.

There's no rest for us.

We're always emptying ashtrays. Making sure gas tanks are full before we rent our cars. Seeing that the batteries are full of life. Checking our windshield wipers.

And the cars we rent out can't be anything less than lively new super-torque Fords.

And since we're not the big fish, you won't feel like a sardine when you come to our counter.

We're not jammed with customers.

Avis can't afford to relax.

Think small.

Our little car isn't so much of a novelty any more.

A couple of dozen college kids don't try to squeeze inside it.

The guy at the gas station doesn't ask where the gas goes.

Nobody even stares at our shape.

In fact, some people who drive our little flivver don't even think 32 miles to the gallon is going any great guns.

Or using five pints of oil instead of five quarts.

Or never needing anti-freeze.

Or racking up 40,000 miles on a set of tires.

That's because once you get used to some of our economies, you don't even think about them any more.

Except when you squeeze into a small parking spot. Or renew your small insurance. Or pay a small repair bill.

Or trade in your old VW for a new one.

Think it over.

▷ "The man in the Hathaway shirt" became one of the best-known advertising images of the decade. The eyepatch was a last-minute addition to an otherwise straightforward ad.

By the 1960s all-purpose agencies offered a full range of services, including research, media analysis and placement, graphic design, and advice on packaging and brand-naming—and even on product development. One innovative branch of research was undertaken by Sidney Weinstein, professor at the New York University of Clinical Medicine, who in 1969 began to make available to advertising agencies his analysis of brain-wave activity. Among other things, this helped advertisers under-stand how television images grabbed viewers' attention. General Electric, for one, was quick to explore the possibilities. GE's Dr. Herbert Krugman conducted laboratory experiments into brain-wave activity. He found that by adding clicks and flashes imperceptible to the viewer, the attention of the brain to what was being shown on the screen was heightened.

The target market

Advertisers beamed their messages almost exclusively at white middle-class families with expanding incomes. Although several liberation movements

Five ways to identify a Hathaway shirt—at a glance

IT'S AS EASY to recognize a Hathaway shirt as a Rolls Royce—if you know these subtle signs:

1. Notice how generously the shirt is cut. More cloth than you get in a mass-produced shirt. Ergo, more comfortable.

2. Look at the *buttons*. They are unusually large. And the *stitches*—unusually small.

More than 30,000 stitches in one shirt.

3. Now look at our *cuffs*. They have square corners. This applies to our French cuffs *and* to the kind you button.

4. Where the front tail joins the back tail, you always find our hallmark—the letter **H** discreetly embroidered in scarlet.

5. The men who wear HATHAWAY shirts are individualists, so they seldom wear *white* shirts.

The shirt illustrated above is a fine Karnac cotton from Egypt, woven for Hathaway in Wauregan. The rectangular checks are copied from a rare French original. Retails at $8.95. Write C. F. Hathaway, Waterville, Maine. In New York, call MUrray Hill 9-4157.

A silence broken only by the ticking of a clock

Car advertisements have produced many famous lines. "When better cars are built, Buick will build them" ran for decades; and there was Volkswagen's stark "This car is a lemon" boldly printed under the picture of a Beetle. One of the most memorable promotional lines ever used to sell a car appeared in 1958 and ran throughout the 1960s: "At 60 miles an hour the loudest noise in this new Rolls-Royce comes from the electric clock." The creation of David Ogilvy, it had a curious history. Far from being the brainchild of a copywriting genius, its origin lay simply in a remark made by an editor of *The Motor* magazine after testing the new Rolls-Royce Silver Cloud model. Ogilvy picked it up and presented it to Rolls-Royce executives in New York. Even then, it was hardly a new idea. In 1907 a review of the Rolls Royce Silver Ghost in *The Autocar* contained the observation that "at whatever speed the car is driven, the auditory nerves when driving are troubled by no fuller sound than emanates from the 8-day clock." At least Ogilvy's line was a little snappier! Although it originally appeared in only two newspapers and two magazines, the ad created such a stir that in the following year Ford based much of its advertising on the claim that its cars were even quieter than a Rolls. So a slogan written for the most exclusive car in the world was used to the advantage of an American top seller.

came to the fore in the 1960s, advertisers paid little attention to them. Black faces were hardly ever seen in commercials. The gay movement was not sufficiently advanced for advertisers to take account of what would later be called the "pink economy."

The advertisers' image of women as happy housewives, however, came under attack. In *The Feminine Mystique* (1963) Betty Friedan accused the advertising industry of encouraging women to equate satisfaction with a sex life plus the accumulation of consumer goods. Advertisers were "guilty of persuading housewives to stay at home mesmerized in front of a television set, their non-sexual human needs unnamed, unsatisfied, drained by the sexual sell into the buying of things."

Entertainment versus information

Throughout the 1960s there was a war of words between advocates of "creative" or "entertainment" advertising and defenders of a more traditional, direct "hard-sell" style. The rise of the creative advertiser, whose role it was to beguile consumers into paying attention to an ad, challenged the dominance of the account men in the upper echelons of

the advertising world. The leading creative firm was Doyle Dane Bernbach, whose president was William Bernbach. The fashion-setter in the entertainment school of advertising, Doyle Dane Bernbach produced famous ironic, apparently self-deprecating slogans such as "Think Small" for Volkswagen and "We're Only No. 2" for Avis car rentals.

The leading company among those that preferred to stick to more straightforward advertising, with lots of words and few gimmicks, was Ogilvy and Mather International, headed by the

British-born David Ogilvy. His firm rose rapidly up the ranks after its ad for Hathaway shirts in which, on a sudden whim of Ogilvy himself, the male model was given an eye-patch to wear. While "The Man in the Hathaway Shirt" was a representative of creative advertising, Ogilvy remained proud of producing ads that had line after line of copy with a daunting array of detailed information about the products.

American advertising agencies were also the first to exploit computers in a big way, since only the top American

▷ A billboard promoting right-wing Republican Barry Goldwater during the 1964 presidential campaign. Political advertising became big business during the 1960s.

firms were rich enough to afford the cost of buying and running one. Not only did computers greatly reduce labor costs, they enabled their owners to produce models of campaigns incorporating thousands of pieces of information.

One of the most famous of such models was the one created by the Simulmatics Corporation for Kennedy's 1960 presidential bid. The model showed Kennedy what issues voters were interested in and how he ought to present those issues. The 1960 presidential election was the first in which television advertising played an important role. In that year the two main parties spent $20 million on advertising during the presidential campaign. The figure rose to $25 million in 1964 and more than $35 million in 1968 (during a three-candidate race).

Negative persuasion

"Negative advertising" soon made its appearance. In 1964 the Democrats spent much energy and money depicting the Republican candidate, Barry Goldwater, as too trigger-happy to be trusted in a dangerous, nuclear-armed world. The most controversial of their ads showed a small girl picking petals from a daisy ("He loves me, he loves me not"); in the background a Russian voice sounded the countdown until, as the last petal dropped, the screen erupted into a nuclear explosion. The message? Goldwater endangered the future of America. As late as the 1968 campaign, however, only one negative political advertisement provoked serious protest, when the Democrats objected to a commercial showing presidential candidate Hubert Humphrey laughing amid pictures of war and urban rioting.

As advertising became an ever more pervasive element in daily life, questions were asked about its effects on people. Was advertising doing something more than simply providing the public with information? Were consumers being persuaded, almost despite themselves, to buy products they did not really want? If this was the effect of what Packard had called "hidden persuaders,"

was there a case for imposing outside regulation on an industry that had shown no inclination to regulate itself?

Regulating advertising

There had been attempts at regulation in the 1950s, but they had been difficult to enforce. For example, in New York State in 1963, 10 years after failing to persuade advertisers to comply with a law prohibiting billboards within a specified distance of the New York State Thruway, the authorities finally burned more than 50 of the most offensive of them to the ground. It also alarmed some commentators that in 1957 the car industry had simply abandoned an earlier agreement not to advertise speed.

The greatest battle was fought over tobacco advertising. The first real victory for the antismoking lobby over the tobacco companies came in 1965, when a federal law was passed requiring every cigarette pack to carry the words "Caution: Cigarette Smoking May Be Hazardous To Your Health." Congress also stepped in in 1968 with laws to enforce "truth in packaging" and "truth in advertising" on television, and "truth in lending" for finance companies. Enforcement lay with the Federal Trade Commission, which had authority to impose fines and other penalties. However, "truth" was not always easy to determine, and FTC investigations could take years to complete. □

Advertising facts and figures

In the 1960s the advertising industry grew considerably faster than the American economy as a whole. The tables below show, at the decade's midpoint, the breakdown of advertising revenues (up 50 percent since 1955) and the wide variation in the cost of advertising to the consumer.

ADVERTISING REVENUES BY MEDIA GROUP, 1965 [$000,000]

Medium	
Newspapers	4,435
Television (network)	2,497
Direct mail	2,271
Magazines	1,197
Outdoor sites	180
Radio (network)	889
Other (inc. trade papers and transit advertising)	3,649
Total	15,118

ADVERTISING EXPENDITURE AS A PERCENTAGE OF SALES, 1965

Company	Industry	Expenditure [$000,000]	% of sales
Proctor & Gamble	Soaps	245	10.9
General Motors	Automobiles	173	0.8
General Foods	Food	120	8.7
Bristol-Myers	Drugs, cosmetics	108	27.6
American Tobacco	Cigarettes	71	5.8
Goodyear	Tires	40	1.8
Schlitz	Beer	35	10.8
Standard Oil	Petroleum	23.5	0.8
Wrigley	Gum, candy	21	16.3

See Also: Automobile Industry; Consumer Society; Feminist Movement; Friedan; Housing; Magazine Publishing; Retailing Industry; Television

AEROSPACE INDUSTRY

Developed mainly in response to military needs, the U.S. aerospace industry in the 1960s grew to colossal size as the space program joined forces with the demand for military and civilian aircraft.

The successful moon landing in July 1969 was the American aerospace industry's most spectacular achievement of the 1960s. The triumph of the Apollo program stole the thunder of the Soviet Union, which had got a head start in the space race in the late 1950s and early 1960s. It was made possible by two related factors. First, the aerospace industry was able to draw on a vast pool of expertise that it possessed itself and could augment by tapping into the great American university research departments. Second, it had available to it enormous government-provided funds, which enabled it in just a few years to solve a bewildering array of technological problems. The aerospace industry was not a normal commercial operation like the automobile industry. There was no competitive market for moon rockets—just one buyer, the U.S. government.

From its very beginnings early in the century the aeronautics industry, fore-runner of aerospace, was not so much driven by any desire to find new and faster forms of passenger transport as by the importance of airplanes in wartime. The same was later true of the early research and development on rockets.

Military demands

Government backing for aeronautics took several forms. In 1925 the Post Office was made to contract all its air-mail services to commercial airlines. And the National Advisory Committee for Aeronautics (NACA)—set up in 1915 as part of the U.S. Navy budget—was given more and more funds to develop new kinds of aircraft. The military did not want to be left behind by European nations whose aeronautics industries were growing fast.

Based at Langley Field in Virginia, NACA employed at government expense mechanical and civil engineers who concentrated their efforts on improving aircraft design. Aircraft manufacturers did some research themselves, but much of the trailblazing theoretical work came from the universities and private foundations, the largest of which was the Guggenheim Fund for the Promotion of Aeronautics.

However, when the United States entered World War II in 1941, the Air Corps (still a branch of the U.S. Army) had very little in the way of military aircraft or personnel. It had only 800 modern planes in 1939. By 1943 there were two million workers in the aircraft industry, and one plant alone turned out 5,476 B-24 bombers in the final year of the war. When peace came in 1945, the American aircraft industry could turn out 110,000 planes a year. It was not just a question of quantity. NACA-Langley went from strength to strength and did much practical

▽ **Astronaut Pete Conrad, a member of the Apollo 12 mission, photographed on the lunar surface on November 19, 1969.**

△◁ **The design of the familiar Boeing 707 (above) was based on the USAF's Model 367–80 (left), a tanker and transport plane.**

John F. Kennedy and Lyndon Johnson. By the mid-1960s it was estimated that about 75 percent of all research and development taking place in aerospace was government-funded. For the big aircraft manufacturers that had built the aircraft for World War II—Boeing, Convair, Douglas, and Lockheed—the postwar conflicts ensured the Defense Department remained their biggest and most important customer.

Commercial consideration

The development of commercial passenger aircraft was almost an afterthought in the 1950s. A journalist once asked the president of Boeing: "What do you do between wars?"

The answer was that the big aircraft companies began, hesitantly at first, to experiment with converting military aircraft for civilian use. The luxurious Boeing 377 Stratocruiser of the 1950s was made up of various bits of the B-29 Superfortress bomber and military tankers. The Boeing 707, which ushered in the jet age for passenger travel, was based on Model 367-80, a tanker-cum-transport plane developed for the

research on engines. At the same time, a new center for aeronautical research staffed by scientists and engineers was set up—the Office of Scientific Research and Development (OSRD).

Almost all of this colossal industry, which combined the talents of academics, research scientists, the military, and manufacturers, was government funded, and it was almost exclusively concerned with making warplanes. It was an extraordinary organizational feat involving hundreds of thousands of people working in many different places toward a single end. It completely revolutionized the design of airplanes and their engines, developed radar, and laid the foundations for the jet age of the 1960s.

The demands of World War II created the modern aerospace industry.

The U.S. government spent an estimated $1 billion on research and development alone in the four years from 1941 to 1945. Even more money poured into aerospace as the Cold War set in. By the 1950s the government was spending $1 billion a year on research and development, including work on atomic weaponry; and when the Korean War broke out in 1950, the annual figure rose to $3.5 billion.

As his second term came to a close in January 1961, President Eisenhower drew attention to what he called the growing military-industrial complex that he thought unbalanced the American economy. Aerospace and the associated electronics industry were at the very heart of that complex. Eisenhower's misgivings, however, went unheeded by his Democrat successors,

The RAND Corporation

The origins and development of RAND, one of the foremost research institutions in the United States, illustrate the way in which aerospace research often spread over time into a wide range of fields. RAND was set up in 1948 at the instigation of what was then still the Army Air Force to bring together in peacetime some of the key figures in the development of aircraft during World War II. RAND is short for Research and Development. At first it was run as part of the Douglas Aircraft Corporation, but it was soon made into a nonprofit research organization.

Very early on RAND widened its brief to deal with a range of issues both social and scientific. During the 1960s RAND made significant contributions to the development of the space program and to digital computing and artificial intelligence, as well as in 1968 investigating reported UFO sightings.

Although it maintained its links with the USAF during the 1960s, RAND became well known for its reports on social and policy issues.

U.S. Air Force. Developing these new aircraft was very costly, but much of the expense could be offset by the money from military contracts. The same scientists and engineers who produced the planes that could carry atomic bombs to the Soviet Union could be employed on the technical problems of transatlantic air travel.

Defense budget money did not just go to the aircraft manufacturers in the 1950s and 1960s. Additional funding created a multitude of new research and development organizations. One of the more high-profile examples was the RAND Corporation, an off-shoot of the Douglas Aircraft Corporation set up in 1948 to carry out research for the

Air Force (*see box*). RAND continued to receive around $13 million a year in the 1960s from the USAF.

From laboratory to space

There were also lucrative contracts available in the universities for scientists and engineers working on various aspects of aerospace. Johns Hopkins Applied Physics Laboratory got defense contracts, and the California Institute of Technology ran the Army's Jet Propulsion Laboratory. The Air Force had also set up its own research and development centers such as the Aeronautical Engineering Development Center in Tullahoma, Tennessee.

In addition to this government-sponsored promotion of the aerospace industry, the beginnings of the space race gave it another massive boost. During and after World War II there had been a good deal of research into rockets, and after the war the U.S. had brought over from Germany Wernher

▽ **President Kennedy, photographed with Dr. Wernher von Braun, attended a NASA briefing on the Apollo program on November 16, 1963.**

von Braun, mastermind of the V2 missiles that had been fired with deadly effect against Antwerp in Belgium and London, England. Until the mid-1950s rocket research concentrated on firing missiles with nuclear warheads that would be able to hit the Soviet Union.

In 1955, however, a committee of scientists convinced Congress that the United States would gain great international prestige and demonstrate to the world its technological superiority over the Soviet Union if it put into orbit a satellite for the International Geophysical Year of 1957/58. But the Army, Navy, and Air Force squabbled over which should do the job, and the Soviet Sputnik beat them to it in 1957.

This triggered a renewed investment in aerospace. In 1958 the National Aerospace and Space Administration (NASA) replaced NACA and created new research stations concerned with space flight and the problems of putting a man into orbit. Whole new industries sprang up such as Aero Spacelines, created to carry large cargoes from one center to another.

Boom years

Within 10 years of the creation of NASA government expenditure on research and development in all aspects of aerospace and space flight went up four times, reaching $15 billion a year. Whole regions in the 1960s were dependent for their livelihood on defense budget spending. With the passing of the National Defense Education Act in the late 1950s, the science and engineering departments of American universities expanded so that from 1960 to 1967 doctorates in science and engineering went up from 6,000 to 13,000. Aeronautical engineering remained central, and by 1969 it was calculated that of the 132,000 graduate students in science and engineering, one-third were being funded by the federal government. And in the mid-1960s it was estimated that 60 percent of all scientists in these key fields were, effectively, government employees whether they worked in research facilities, industry, or universities.

Rockets and satellites

It was the involvement of aircraft makers such as Douglas and Boeing, as well a host of subsidiary companies, in the making of rockets that gave rise to the new term "aerospace industry." The term became common in the late 1950s as both the Army and the Navy were developing different kinds of rocketry to power missiles with nuclear warheads, and plans were laid for sending up the first satellites.

Although the development of rockets had orginally been entirely for military use, the prospect of space travel and the use of satellites to explore Earth's upper atmosphere had always been in the minds of such scientists as Wernher von Braun. It was his team, working at the Army Ballistic Missile Agency (AMBA), that developed the Jupiter C rocket which launched America's first satellite, Explorer 1, in 1958. A good deal of the development work on the rocket was done by the Jet Propulsion Laboratory, which was run from the California Institute of Technology.

The building and launching of rockets that carried satellites to examine solar winds, radiation belts, and interplanetary magnetic fields continued into the 1960s and made important discoveries that were essential to the future success of the space program.

Although the space program was behind so much of the activity in the fields of rocketry and satellites, the 1960s also saw a concerted effort to provide information about Earth itself and its weather systems. NASA's Tiros (Television and Infrared Observation Satellite) series, first launched in April 1960, revolutionized weather forecasting with its transmissions showing Earth's cloud cover on a global scale. At the same time, there were satellites monitoring military movements. The Samos (Satellite and Missile Observation System) satellite kept an eye on the entire planet, and Vela satellites launched in the mid-1960s could detect nuclear explosions in space.

▽ **Tiros II, the second successful weather meteorological satellite, was launched from Cape Canaveral in 1960 and is photographed here in a space environment.**

△ Douglas DC-9s being assembled at Long Beach, California, in 1968. Passenger jets were a big growth factor for the industry.

Recruiting the first astronauts

When the U.S. began its space program, it had to find from somewhere an entirely new kind of pilot—the astronaut. The National Aeronautics and Space Administration looked to the military to provide the pioneers when it first sought volunteers in 1959. At the time it seemed that the best apprenticeship for rocketing beyond Earth's atmosphere was experience of jet aircraft, and only military pilots had clocked up impressive flying times.

Would-be astronauts had to be under 40 years of age, in excellent physical condition, with a bachelor's degree in engineering, and a graduate of a test pilot school with at least 1,500 hours of flying time. They also had to be less than 5ft. 11in. tall because of the likely cramped conditions in spacecraft.

Although more than 500 men qualified, a great many dropped out after psychological and technical tests, and others were turned down. A shortlist was subjected to even tougher tests before the first American astronauts were chosen: three from the Navy (M. Scott Carpenter, Walter M. Schirra, Jr., and Alan B. Shepard, Jr.), Marine Lt. John H. Glenn, and three from the Air Force (L. Gordon Cooper, Jr., Virgil I. "Gus" Grissom, and Donald K. "Deke" Slayton). All except Slayton, who was revealed to have a heart condition, took an active role in the Mercury project.

As the space program progressed, NASA began to put more emphasis on educational qualifications rather than flight experience alone, and in 1964 the selection of astronauts was handed over to the National Academy of Sciences in Washington. By the late 1960s there were scientist as well as pilot astronauts training for space flight.

In 1967 aerospace was the biggest industrial employer in the U.S., with nearly 1.5 million employees, of whom over 800,000 were directly employed in the building of aircraft. Its total sales in that year were $27 billion, of which $15 billion was to the federal government. Total aircraft production had risen from 10,237 in 1960 to 18,660 in 1967. The most substantial rise in the period had been in the production of passenger airplanes, up from 8,181 to 14,660. Overall, however, government investment in the space program and the development of ever more sophisticated bombers and fighter planes remained a significant influence on the industry.

The demands of each section of this complex industry stimulated technological advance. For example, rocket power was employed by the Flight Research Center at Edwards Air Force Base to test the effects of very high speeds and altitudes on aircraft and spacecraft. A rocket-powered plane, the X-15, was flown by pilots at speeds of up to Mach 6.7—nearly seven times the speed of sound—and to altitudes of 67 miles. B-52 bombers were used to carry the X-15 for launching at several thousand feet. When the X-15 was at full speed the heat generated would turn some of its exterior a glowing red. Much was learned from these flights about the heat tolerance of metals and the gravitational forces that astronauts would experience. The tests began in 1960 and continued as the space program gathered pace. They provided valuable information on the use of alloys like titanium and the design of space suits for the Mercury and Gemini astronauts.

The growth of specialization

All this technology was provided by companies that had started out as aircraft and engine manufacturers and had had to learn new skills demanded by aerospace. Contracts for the space program were shared out. McDonnell, for example, was the main contractor for the Mercury and Gemini manned

▽ The rocket-powered X-15 was used to explore the effects of very high speeds and altitudes on both pilots and plane components.

orbiting vehicles. Boeing was the main contractor for the Saturn first-stage rocket, North American for the Saturn V third stage and the Apollo spacecraft, and Grumman for the lunar module.

Because individual defense and space contracts were so big, companies tended to specialize. McDonnell, for example, was involved only in the manufacture of military planes and equipment and parts of the space program, and was not involved in civil aircraft. Douglas, on the other hand, had a long and successful record in passenger aircraft going back to its legendary DC-3s of the 1930s, which were still flying worldwide in the 1960s and beyond.

Although the industry turned over vast amounts of money each year, its profits were often uncertain, for more and more money was being spent on research and development to stay ahead of the rapidly evolving technology, and profits were often low in relation to turnover. Reliance on military contracts was always risky, for the demands of the Air Force and the Navy were likely to change, and projects were frequently scrapped. To stay in business, the aerospace companies began to merge in the late 1960s. McDonnell joined forces with Douglas in 1967 to become a

giant of the industry. North American was acquired by the Rockwell-Standard company in the same year.

Questions of value

From the mid-1960s there was a rising tide of concern about the dependence of the aerospace companies on government funds, and the industry was accused of inefficiency. Contracts, it was said, were shared out rather than awarded to the best companies. There were opportunities for corruption since government officials were lobbied to favor the big contractors. The hazards of the military-industrial complex of which Eisenhower had warned were becoming apparent. At the close of the 1960s, with the Apollo program triumphant, there was a retreat from huge investment by government, and the wisdom of creating an industry so dependent on Cold War contracts was being challenged.

What did Americans gain from all this? It was a question that people began to ask with some urgency in the 1960s. Why put a man on the moon when you cannot solve the enduring problem of poverty at home or abroad? In part, the answer was secondary benefits or "spinoffs"—the application of all this scientific knowledge that

Size, space, and comfort

It was not clear in the late 1960s what the way forward would be for long-haul airliners. Was it greater speed and shorter journey times that would attract customers, or cheapness, convenience, and comfort? Research was underway in the United States, the Soviet Union, and Europe into the possibilities of supersonic passenger flight making use of technology developed for fighter planes. That was regarded at the time as one of the most exciting and difficult challenges for the aerospace industry.

In the United States, however, more research had gone into the possibility of building much larger passenger jets that gained in capacity and comfort what they conceded in speed. The results were revealed to the world on February 9, 1969, when a huge jet aircraft took off from an airfield at Everett, just north of Seattle, on its maiden flight. It was twice the weight of the trail-blazing Boeing 707. This was the first "jumbo jet"—the Boeing 747, which could carry more than 350 passengers.

While Britain and France continued developing their supersonic airliner Concorde, the U.S. aerospace industry surged ahead with the slower but commercially much more viable widebodied jumbo. There was great excitement when the first Pan Am Boeing 747, called *Clipper Young America*, roared off the runway at JFK Airport on January 21, 1970, bound for London. On its return to JFK crowds turned out to watch the giant airliner land. The following month TWA began its first jumbo service between New York and Los Angeles. Passengers were impressed by the space and comfort of the jumbos, which soon became a necessary addition to the fleets of leading airlines around the world.

Jumbo jets gave the U.S. aerospace industry a valuable lead on Europe, which was slow to compete in the widebodied market. Jumbos transformed the schedules of leading airlines and required airports all over the world to upgrade to handle the greatly increased flow of traffic.

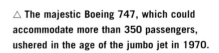

△ The majestic Boeing 747, which could accommodate more than 350 passengers, ushered in the age of the jumbo jet in 1970.

embraced not just the problems connected with flight itself, but the advances in electronics, computers, new kinds of materials, and so on.

The most obvious incidental benefit of the government sponsorship of aerospace for the military was the arrival of the jet age in passenger travel. But there have been many others that are not so obvious, which can be traced back directly to the huge effort and ingenuity that went into the development of aircraft and rocketry during the 1960s. A great many products such as radios, televisions, and calculators were improved with component parts developed by the aerospace industry (transistors and silicon chips). The space program produced new materials, for example, hard plastics of various kinds, and it also contributed to medical advances. Techniques developed to extract data from photographs of distant objects in space had important diagnostic applications, for instance.

Since the 1970s the role played by government in the funding of aerospace and other science and engineering research has shrunk, but the legacy is still there in many of the organizations that were set up during the boom years of the U.S. aerospace industry. □

See Also: Air Force; Apollo Program; Arms Race; Gemini Program; Mercury Program; Military-industrial Complex; NASA; Schools and Universities; Science and Technology; Space Race

SPIRO AGNEW 1918–1996

Although his tenure as vice president was cut short by revelations of past financial wrongdoing, Spiro Agnew's attacks on the media made him a high-profile figure in the Nixon administration.

Spiro Agnew was elected U.S. vice president on the Republican ticket headed by Richard M. Nixon in 1968. At the time Agnew was little known nationally, but he was not slow to make his mark. In 1969 he launched a ferocious attack on what he called political and cultural bias in the American media. By taking on such powerful institutions as the press and particularly television, Agnew made himself a figure of great controversy, which was unusual for a vice president.

Agnew was born in Baltimore in 1918 into a family of Greek immigrants. After service in the Army in Europe during World War II, he completed his law studies and became active in Baltimore politics. Agnew went on to win election as Republican governor of Maryland in 1966.

The vice president and the media

Agnew had been considered moderately progressive during his governorship, but the increasingly violent tempo of the anti-Vietnam War movement hardened his position. At the same time, he became convinced that the Nixon administration was the victim of bias in the media. In his view there was a concerted campaign led by television commentators to discredit the war effort—and by extension to undermine the government.

In November 1969 Agnew launched an onslaught on the media in general, his chief target being the TV networks. Only weeks before, President Nixon had appealed over the heads of the media to what he described as "the silent majority" in favor of the war and opposed to unruly dissent. Agnew went much further, pouring scorn on "an effete corps of impudent snobs" and, in another much-quoted phrase, "the nattering nabobs of negativism."

Agnew returned again and again to his theme, and his efforts seemed to bear some fruit. For example, the fall of 1969 was the high-water mark of the peace movement, with massive antiwar demonstrations in most major cities, including the largest of all when half a million demonstrators converged on Washington, D.C. Yet the national networks did not cover the event.

Agnew's efforts were rewarded when he was again chosen by Nixon as vice-presidential running mate in 1972 and duly reelected. The following year Agnew was confronted with charges

△ **Vice President Spiro Agnew took vehement exception to what he saw as media bias against the Nixon administration.**

that he had received kickbacks from contractors during his Maryland days. In what amounted to an admission of guilt, he pleaded "no contest" to a single charge of income tax evasion and resigned the vice presidency in disgrace. Agnew's unprecedented fall from high office was almost forgotten as the Watergate scandal swiftly engulfed the Nixon administration. He played no further part in public life. □

See Also: News and Current Affairs Programs; Nixon; Politics and Government; Republican Party

AGRICULTURE

Following the great leaps forward in postwar mechanization and agrichemical research, farming modernized aggressively through the 1960s and reached new heights of productivity.

In March 1967 many urban American television viewers were startled and angered to see newsreel pictures of dairy farmers pouring away thousands of gallons of milk into ditches and sewers. It was part of a protest in 25 states called for by the National Farmers Organization, which had been established during the mid-1950s in an attempt to draw public attention to the problems faced by the agricultural community. There were similar skirmishes with cattle and corn producers throughout the 1960s, as the dramatic rise in the output of America's farmers led to oversupply and in consequence steadily plunging prices.

Get bigger or get out!

This tension in the farming communities of America in the 1960s had been brewing for a long while. What tore them apart was the perennial and paradoxical dilemma of agriculture—the more efficient and productive it became, the lower prices fell as supply outstripped demand. The more successful farmers became in terms of the crops they hauled into town or to a packing plant, the poorer they were likely to be in the long run.

To ward off this squeeze on profits, farmers could only get bigger and compensate for falling prices by a bigger harvest. The slogan at the start of the 1960s in America's vast and sparsely populated rural regions was: "Get bigger, get better, or get out."

At the start of the 1960s there were still a few "two mule" farms in America, and the historic family farm was idealized in a romantic way by city folk. In its early days the United States had

◁ **The modern combine harvester enabled wheat farmers to exploit vast acreages with maximum efficiency and minimum labor.**

△ **New chemicals played an important part in the agricultural revolution. Here, longhorns are sprayed to keep grubs and worms at bay.**

prided itself on being a nation of farmers, with 80 percent of the population working the land. All that had changed with the growth of industrialism in the 19th century, and the flight from rural areas to the cities had continued ever since. In 1960 the farm population, according to Department of Agriculture estimates, made up only 11.5 percent of the national population.

Although there is a tendency to characterize regions of the United States as producing a single kind of crop—fruit in California, cotton in the South, corn in the Middle West, cattle on the Great Plains—the picture is forever shifting. Whereas in the 1950s the raising of livestock had been the largest single agricultural sector, by the end of the 1960s the growing of cash grain crops

Rural poverty

Although nearly a million U.S. farms disappeared between 1960 and 1970 (a fall from 3.7 million to 2.8 million), there remained in the rural regions a huge underclass of people living in poverty. A report by the President's National Advisory Committee on Rural Poverty in 1967, "The People Left Behind," estimated that 14 million Americans eked out a living in agricultural areas. Only a quarter of them possessed any kind of farm. The rest lived in shacks and broken-down homes out in the country, in villages, and in small towns.

These "forgotten people" got no benefits from government attempts to maintain farm incomes, nor were they given the attention of the poor in the cities. Eleven million of them were white, the remainder blacks, Mexican Americans, and Native peoples. Poverty was concentrated in the rural South, the Native American reservations, the upper Great Lakes region, New England, Appalachia, and the Southwest. Schooling and child care were far below the national norm, illiteracy far above.

Very many of these poor people were the casualties of the agricultural revolution that made farms so much more productive while greatly reducing the need for farm labor. Some were farmers who could not afford to mechanize and keep pace with the ever-increasing size of farms.

The Agricultural Act of 1965

The problem of food surpluses and the relatively low income of farmers—they always earned less than the national average wage—was a constant headache for government throughout the 1960s. Every year there was a new piece of legislation that attempted to find a compromise solution whereby farmers' earnings could be protected without encouraging them to plow up more acres and add to the food surpluses. From 1961 to 1963 attempts were made to trade off price support for farmers with control over how much they produced. But the farmers would not accept limits to their output.

The Agricultural Act of 1965 was a compromise that finally held, although in effect it did not solve the inherent problem of farming—supply always outrunning demand and driving prices down to levels where many farmers had to get big or get out. Government price supports for various commodities were fixed at what were called "world equilibrium levels." That stabilized prices but did nothing for farmers' incomes. To solve that problem, farmers were offered direct income payments on condition they accepted limits on production when surpluses were building up. And the government continued to hold stocks of surplus produce that it used to supply food programs at home and abroad. It cost a great deal of money and did little to raise farmers' incomes, but it did bring some stability to an industry that always threatened to rollercoaster out of control.

△ In 1966 this once-abandoned farm was a flourishing concern because of improved fertilizers and conservation techniques.

such as corn, wheat, and soybeans had overtaken it. Slightly over 30 percent of farms were engaged in this activity, just under 30 percent in livestock. There were relatively few of all other kinds of commercial farms specializing in growing tobacco, vegetables, fruit and nuts, or raising poultry—none making up more than 6 percent of the total.

The mechanization of the farming industry that the first tractors had begun in the 1920s was in full flood by the 1960s. New gasoline- and electric-powered machinery transformed farm work, replacing human labor and enabling a tiny workforce to plow and sow hundreds of acres.

At the same time, extensive research into the creation of highly productive hybrid plants, which had been going on since the 1930s, bore fruit in the 1960s

△ Modern equipment like this two-row harvester took the backbreaking drudgery and high labor costs out of cotton farming.

New methods for an old crop

Cotton-growing in the Deep South, which had once been sustained by slave labor, was by the late 1960s as highly mechanized as any sector of farming. Huge new machines drawn by 200-horsepower tractors had been manufactured with folding parts so that they could go from field to field by public road. A Louisiana cotton farmer around 1969 would put down selected and pretreated seed with a machine that could plant six rows at a time. He could take this machine across his fields at up to 10 miles an hour, which meant that in a single day he could plant up to 150 acres.

Pesticides applied at various times kept down weeds; chemical fertilizers ensured vigorous growth of the cotton; and when the bolls were almost ready, they would be prepared for picking by a defoliant that stripped off all the leaves as the plant was sprayed from an airplane. The bolls could then be harvested by machine. With all these new improvements at his disposal, the farmer could harvest up to four times as much cotton as could his father in pre-World War II days. There was government support at around 30–35 cents a pound, which easily covered the costs of mechanization while still affording a reasonable return.

In a way the life of the commercial farmer, whether his crop was cotton or corn or wheat, was more mechanized, enclosed, and air-conditioned than that of urban workers at the end of the 1960s. For long periods, whether spreading fertilizers or pesticides or planting or harvesting his crop, the farmer would be seated comfortably inside a huge machine where he could while away the time listening to the local radio station. Although there were those who argued that farmers had become too dependent on buying bigger and bigger machines, replacing 6-row with 8- or 10-row planters, it nearly always made economic sense. The quicker a crop could be planted and harvested, the more the farmer could take advantage of favorable weather and ensure a healthy crop.

so that the yields of crops like corn could be greatly increased. Industry began to supply farmers with chemical fertilizers that further pushed up the yields of such crops.

All these forces led to inevitable changes on the farm. The agricultural labor force had been falling steadily since the 1950s, when many workers left farms for better-paid jobs in industry. This trend continued in the 1960s, and the number of farmers fell steadily. Farms got larger and larger, the average size rising from 303 acres in 1960 to 390 acres by 1970.

Streamlining and profit-reaping

Because so much of the equipment and the fertilizers and insecticide and herbicide sprays were bought in by farmers, the whole business of agriculture grew

more commercialized. In the 1960s some of the bigger farms began to use computers to record stocks and output.

At the beginning of the 1960s the really big commercial operations—defined as those with cash income of over $40,000 a year—made up just under 3 percent of the 3.7 million farms in the U.S. By the end of the decade their numbers had doubled, and they made up 8 percent of all farms. Even more significantly this minority of farmers took more than half (55 percent) of all farmers' receipts.

In 1960 there were still 1,277,000 small farmers—a third of the total—earning between $2,500 and $9,999 a year. They took just over 20 percent of all farm receipts. Whereas the larger farmers were growing in numbers and importance, this poorest sector of the farming community was rapidly disappearing. By the mid-1970s more than half had gone out of business, and those who remained shared only 4 percent of the agricultural cake.

With their declining numbers farmers had begun to lose their traditional political power in the 1950s. Since the 1920s they had lobbied government for various kinds of financial support with considerable success: a whole series of initiatives had brought in price-fixing for key products and income support. In Congress there was a rough coalition of interests from key agricultural states known as "the farm bloc." In the 1930s it was believed that 300 out of 531 congressmen had to take note of farmers' interests for their political survival. At the end of the 1950s the farm bloc contingent was down to about a hundred congressmen. Even in Texas the farming community was a small minority by the 1960s.

Financial support

At the same time, there was growing resistance among urban consumers to the idea of keeping the price of farm produce high to protect farmers' incomes. In the boom period of the 1950s Americans spent proportionately less of their domestic budget on essentials such as food. Whereas at the end of World War II, 27 percent of weekly income was spent feeding the family, this was down to 21 percent by 1960. There was an expectation of cheap food leaving more money for other kinds of spending.

△ **High farm yields enabled the U.S. to export top-quality beef and dairy cattle, like these white-faced Herefords, to rebuild stocks in Latin America, Europe, Africa, and Asia.**

Traditional tolerance among Americans for federal support for farmers was severely strained by the beginning of the 1960s. Price-fixing encouraged the growing of far more corn, cotton, and other staple crops than could be sold on the market. The excess had to be bought up by the federal government and stored, creating great mountains of surplus produce. By 1960 farm programs were costing nearly $5 billion a year.

Despite continual complaints that support for farmers was costing too much and food prices were too high, no administration in the 1960s dared do what some had urged—leave agriculture to the forces of the marketplace. In 1971 Congress voted $8.1 billion for farm support, which included food stamps for the urban poor. The basis of the farmers' political power was shifting, but it was still formidable, and it was backed in the late 1960s by some wealthy agricultural enterprises.

Relying on immigrant labor

There were exceptions to the relentless mechanization of American farming in the 1960s, for not all produce could be harvested by the kind of huge machines that were used in the corn and wheat belts.

In 1965 one of the richest and most powerful farming regions in the U.S. was faced with a crisis. Since World War II California growers of strawberries and other fruits and vegetables such as lettuce had come to rely on immigrant labor from Mexico to harvest their crop. From 1942 the farmers had had great difficulty finding local labor as young men went off to war and others joined the munitions and other factories that paid better wages. To provide them with labor, the U.S. and Mexican governments set up what became known as the bracero program—braceros is the Mexican term for people who work with their hands.

This emergency measure was kept in place after the war, and every year hundreds of thousands of Mexicans crossed the border to harvest crops in California. Some too went to Texas and Arizona, where they became similarly indispensable. A survey in 1963 of some of the largest strawberry growers in California found that braceros filled 95 percent of the picking hours, and the proportion was almost as high a year later.

For the growers paying less than $1 an hour to a workforce that had no union and was desperate for work the bracero program ensured handsome profits. As one strawberry grower put it: "Braceros were here to make a living, not to make trouble. They were family men, not juvenile delinquents like you get today. We knew we could send them back if they complained, but we rarely had to. The bracero program helped everyone. Mexicans supported their families and Americans made money. It was the finest Peace Corps activity in reverse. Instead of us going to their country to teach them, they came up here to learn from us."

It was that kind of sentiment that was now being attacked by what one grower called "the bleeding hearts" in the 1960s, such as the civil rights and antipoverty movements. In California too there was a strengthening agricultural labor union movement that opposed the bracero program because it undercut wages. Faced with this pressure, the government brought the program to an end in December 1964.

Many predicted that this would be fatal for California agriculture. But ways around the problem were soon found. An Act of 1952 had created the noncitizen status of immigrant workers in the U.S. known as the "green card." Many Mexicans were recruited by California strawberry growers as "green carders." As many, or more, simply slipped across the border as illegal immigrants who would be given protection by their employers who desperately needed their labor. These workers had no documents at all and no rights in the U.S.

Research in the early 1970s suggested that about 95 percent of the coastal strawberry pickers in southern California were either "green carders" or illegal immigrants. Elsewhere they were a significant but smaller proportion of the labor force: 40 percent of the mushroom pickers in Monterey, 30 percent of the citrus-fruit workers in Ventura County, and so on.

▷ **Immigrant Mexican farmers, or braceros, harvest lettuces by hand on a U.S. farm.**

△ **This automated turkey farm in Peoria, Illinois, has an enormous poultry shed (the building on the left with ventilation shafts).**

were new markets, production was increased, supply outstripped demand, and prices tumbled. In 1971, with the government backing a great export drive, the price of wheat fell to $1.50 a bushel—the same price as in 1943. Despite the fall in prices, the American consumer—who was by the end of the 1960s spending only around 17 percent of disposable income on food—was complaining that exports were pushing up the prices paid at home. By the early 1970s there were clashes between labor unions in the cities and farmers over the price of food, when longshoremen held up the loading of American wheat destined for the Soviet Union.

Perhaps the most fitting epitaph for the American farmer of the 1960s was the rueful reply one gave to a reporter who asked him what he would do if he won a million dollars: "I guess I would go on farming until it was all gone." □

After the technological advances of the 1950s, the 1960s were a tough time for farmers. Despite all the federal aid, most struggled to make a living, which is why so many left the land.

Toward the end of the decade, however, an export market opened up that promised a new period of prosperity. In 1969 U.S. farmers sold a total of $5.7 billion worth of corn and other commodities abroad, much of it to Western Europe and Japan, and got paid in dollars. Although in the past much American produce had been sent overseas, it had usually been sold off at rock-bottom prices and paid for in weak currencies such as Indian rupees.

Despite this welcome development, the same old problems beset farming. As soon as it looked as though there

Agribusiness

An inevitable consequence of the growing size of farms, the mechanization of farm labor, the use of industrial fertilizers, and the "green revolution" of more productive hybrid crops, was the interest taken in agriculture by big businesses. In particular, those whose business was connected with farming output moved in on the farmers. This had happened in the 1950s in fruit production in Florida and California, and in poultry with the rise of intensively produced broiler chickens. The term "agribusiness" had in fact been coined in 1955 by John H. Davis, a former Assistant Secretary of Agriculture, to refer to "the sum total of all operations involved in the production and distribution of food and fiber."

The impact of "agribusiness" as it began to spread into corn and livestock became a big issue for farmers in the 1960s, and there were many protests and suggestions that it should be outlawed, for it threatened to eliminate the family farm altogether. In the fruit business and in poultry it had grown through "contract farming"—farmers did a deal with a producer of fruit juices or broiler chickens to buy their entire output at a fixed price. All the marketing was done by the contractor. In effect farmers became hired hands.

Not all agribusiness ventures were successful. One that failed was the attempt by the Gates Rubber Company in Colorado to establish a huge farming subsidiary raising corn, sugar beet, and hay along with 4,000 head of cattle on 10,400 acres in Yuma County. It invested heavily in machinery and employed a large staff. But it did not make a quick enough return for investors and closed down in 1971, only three years after it had begun. However, setbacks such as this did not reverse the trend toward agribusiness. By 1974 there were 28,000 farm corporations marketing 18 percent of American agricultural produce.

See Also: Environmental Movement; Green Revolution; Labor Relations; Science and Technology

AIR FORCE

During the 1960s the USAF was central to American military strategy—whether deployed to guard the U.S. and Western Europe from potential Soviet aggression or in action in the Vietnam War.

The 1960s were a highly eventful decade for the USAF. Heavily committed to the defense of Europe and North America, the service saw massive technological advances in terms of aircraft, weapon systems, and the development of intercontinental ballistic missiles (ICBMs). Almost all the USAF's training and operational activities were concentrated on being prepared for nuclear war against the Soviet-led Warsaw Pact. It was ironic, therefore, that the USAF's major combat role of the decade was over the jungles of Vietnam—a type of war for which the USAF was not prepared in terms of either tactics or training.

From the mid-1950s the cornerstone of U.S. defense policy was the USAF's capacity to deliver a devastating nuclear attack against the Soviet Union. This was the task of Strategic Air Command (SAC), which had more than 1,500 long-range bombers at its disposal in 1960, making it the most powerful strike force in the world.

In the event of Soviet aggression against Western Europe or an outright attack on the United States the strategy called for SAC to retaliate by dropping nuclear bombs on cities in the Soviet Union. The idea was that such a strategy, which was openly explained to the world, would deter any such aggression on the part of the Soviets. The primary aircraft tasked with carrying out such attacks was the mighty eight-engined Boeing B-52 Stratofortress.

△ **A B-52 Stratofortress prepares to land. Armed with nuclear bombs, B-52s were ready to retaliate against a Soviet strike at any time.**

Aided by air-to-air refueling, the B-52 was capable of delivering over 10 tons of thermonuclear weaponry to any point within the Soviet Union. By the end of 1961 a total of 744 B-52s had been delivered to the USAF. With tensions between the U.S. and the USSR often close to breaking point, SAC's massive force of bombers stood alert not only at their home bases but also in the air. B-52s were aloft 24 hours a day, with live nuclear bombs in their bays.

Only the most experienced crews flew these "Chrome Dome" missions (the nickname a reference to reflective

△ The XB-70 Valkyrie bomber could exceed 2,000 mph, but the project was canceled after a midair collision in 1966.

shields in the cockpit that would protect against the blinding flash of a nuclear explosion), and the safety of carrying such weapons on noncombat flights was taken for granted. This illusion was shattered in January 1966 when a B-52 collided during refueling from a KC-135 tanker aircraft. Both aircraft crashed off the coast of Spain. Radioactive material was released, and one of the bombs was not located for two months, despite an extensive search operation. However, such was the importance placed on "Chrome Dome" missions to ensure that an adequate number of aircraft would survive a surprise nuclear attack, that they continued for several more years.

The Soviets did not stand idly by while the U.S. enjoyed such a superior position in the skies. SAC's massive force of bombers was designed to strike in large numbers from high altitude. The Soviets therefore improved their ground intercept radar. This, combined with the rapid development of surface-to-air missiles capable of catching and destroying any high-flying bomber, ren-

dered the U.S. tactic questionable. The B-52s were therefore gradually reassigned to low level to stay hidden from Soviet radar. In the early 1960s the USAF, in conjunction with private development from the North American Company, began testing a new high-flying bomber capable of speeds of over 2,000 miles per hour. Named XB-70

Valkyrie, the aircraft began to demonstrate its awesome performance during test flights in 1964. These tests caused so much consternation within the Soviet military that the Soviets themselves immediately began work on a new fighter aircraft (the MiG-25 "Foxbat") that would be capable of catching and shooting down the Valkyrie.

Missile deterrents

By the end of the 1950s improvements in Soviet air defenses had led the USAF to reappraise the role of the bomber, and SAC was investing in a number of unmanned nuclear delivery systems. From 1957 to 1961 SAC deployed the SM-62 Snark—the only intercontinental cruise missile that has ever been deployed. Almost 70 feet in length, the Snark was larger than some bombers and had a range of 6,300 miles carrying a warhead with a 4-megaton yield. As a cruise missile, however, the Snark was vulnerable to counterattack in the course of its flight in the same way that an aircraft was vulnerable. It was therefore quickly outmoded by the introduction of the Atlas ICBM. Because its trajectory took the Atlas outside Earth's atmosphere before it dropped almost vertically on its target, it was impossible to intercept. The Atlas revolutionized the concept of nuclear warfare and spelled the end of the bomber as the primary delivery system. By 1964 the improved Minuteman ICBM was equipping SAC missile squadrons. Much more accurate than the Atlas, the Minuteman carried a warhead with an explosive power almost 100 times greater than that of the atomic bombs dropped on Japan in 1945.

In May 1966 tragedy stuck the U.S. project when the second test aircraft collided with a USAF fighter during a public relations flight for engine makers General Electric. Both aircraft were destroyed, and subsequently the project, which had cost the American taxpayer $500 million, was abandoned.

Deployment of ICBMs

It was increasingly clear that the bomber had become vulnerable to enemy defenses. This prompted SAC to research the potential of unmanned nuclear delivery systems. First, nuclear-tipped cruise missiles were developed. Basically pilotless aircraft, cruise missiles could be delivered in one of two ways. Hound Dog missiles were launched from B-52s and had a range of 500 miles, which meant that the B-52 could launch them while staying clear of concentrated enemy air defenses. Snark missiles were ground-launched, with a vastly greater range than Hound Dogs, but they were vulnerable in flight and were made obsolete by the ICBMs that became operational by 1960 (*see box p. 28*). Stockpiles of these new weapons were rapidly built up. Between 1960 and 1970 SAC's bomber fleet was cut by two-thirds (to just over 500), being replaced by more than

1,000 ICBMs. These ground-based ICBMs, the remaining long-range bombers, and the Navy's submarine-launched ICBMs would constitute the U.S. nuclear deterrent until the end of the Cold War and beyond.

Although the U.S. and the former USSR are perceived to be a long way apart, in fact, geographically, they are quite close neighbors across the Arctic Circle. To defend against a surprise attack by Soviet long-range bombers, the Distant Early Warning (DEW) Line was established in the late 1950s and early 1960s. Comprising a chain of early warning sites stretching thousands of miles from Alaska in the west through northern Canada to Greenland in the east, the DEW Line would give sufficient warning to allow interception of the enemy by fighter aircraft.

The defense system was later strengthened by the establishment of two further radar chains—the Mid-Canada Line and the Pine Tree Line on the U.S.-Canadian border. The primary defender against Soviet attack was the joint U.S.–Canadian North American Air Defense Command (NORAD). When NORAD was established in 1957, the USAF and Royal Canadian Air Force had more than 1,000 interceptors dedicated to air defense, a

figure that was maintained into the mid-1960s when it became acknowledged that the ICBM had largely supplanted the manned bomber.

Interceptor aircraft

On constant alert, the interceptors from the USAF's Air Defense Command (ADC) incessantly practiced interceptions aided by Ground Control Intercept radar, which could direct the aircraft straight to the target. The radar system used was known as SAGE (Semi-Automatic Ground Environment); it "flew" the interceptor to its target via an automatic pilot, the human pilot only taking control to fire the weapons.

In the 1960s ADC's frontline interceptors were the F-102A Delta Dagger, the F-106 Delta Dart, and the F-101B Voodoo. These fast and highly maneuverable aircraft were armed with air-to-air missiles, including the most powerful in the world, the AIR-2 Genie. Fitted with a 1.5-kiloton nuclear warhead, this weapon was designed to disrupt entire bomber formations and had a lethal blast radius of

▽ **The F-101B Voodoo, which could carry air-to-air missiles fitted with nuclear warheads, was a frontline interceptor during the 1960s.**

up to 2,000 feet. However, it did have a limited range of only six miles, so the launch aircraft had to pull a very tight turn after launch to escape the blast.

The USAF in Europe
From the mid-1950s the adversaries in the Cold War were neatly defined as NATO versus the Warsaw Pact, and these two came eyeball to eyeball at the European Central Front. By 1960 the rival alliances confronted each other with the most powerful concentration of military force ever seen. The greatest contribution to NATO's defense of Western Europe were the fighters, fighter-bombers, and reconnaissance aircraft of the United States Air Forces

△ The C-5A Galaxy was the largest aircraft in the world during the late 1960s and for years after, capable of carrying phenomenal loads.

Developing huge transport planes

In marked contrast to the isolationist foreign policy of the pre-World War II period, the United States entered the 1960s with widespread military commitments around the world. In order to prevent the spread of communism, it was considered essential that the U.S. military should have the ability to respond rapidly to a crisis anywhere in the world, and to achieve this goal, deployment and supply by air would be essential. At the start of the decade the USAF's heavyweight transport assets consisted of a substantial number of obsolescent propeller-driven aircraft which, although capable of handling large and bulky cargo, were slow, lacked range, and were hardly suitable to meet the new doctrine of "flexible response."

To fulfill this policy, it was apparent that a new long-range jet-powered airlifter was required, and in 1961 the Lockheed company was awarded the contract to produce such an aircraft. The resulting C-141 StarLifter was the world's first large jet aircraft to be designed specifically for the movement of freight. Its introduction into service in 1965 occurred just in time for the massive trans-Pacific resupply missions to Vietnam that would play such an important role in that conflict for the best part of a decade. The key to the StarLifter's design was the rear-loading doors that enabled the aircraft's vital supplies to be unloaded in under 15 minutes, so preventing valuable time from being wasted on the ground. In terms of productivity one C-141 could equal four of the propeller-driven aircraft it replaced.

Despite its great capacity, the StarLifter could not carry the largest and most bulky loads, which were still transported by older aircraft. This was addressed by developing the giant C-5A Galaxy, which, for well over a decade, was the largest airplane in the world. The mammoth Galaxy allowed the USAF for the first time to transport an enormous array of equipment. For example, in a single shipment it was possible to transport two M60 main battle tanks, sixteen 3/4-ton trucks, and three large Chinook helicopters or ten Pershing ballistic missiles with associated support equipment. Although the aircraft suffered from a number of teething troubles, the Galaxy would emerge during the Vietnam War as the king of heavyweight transports.

in Europe (USAFE). These aircraft were based in West Germany, France (until 1964), Italy, and Spain. They were backed up by longer-range nuclear bombers based in the United Kingdom. By the early 1960s USAFE had approximately 115,000 personnel and 1,500 aircraft assigned to the task.

Very large though this commitment was, it could not begin to match Soviet forces in terms of numbers. Nevertheless, the USAFE tactical aircraft were manned by well-trained and

Cold War reconnaissance

▽ The high-flying U-2 reconnaissance plane was able to penetrate deep within Soviet airspace in the late 1950s and early 1960s.

By 1960 the U.S. was becoming increasingly concerned about the growing nuclear and conventional capability of the Soviet Union's armed forces. Key to remaining ahead in the arms race was accurate intelligence on the state of these forces, and this became a priority. The CIA required accurate aerial reconnaissance, and the USAF operated the famous U-2 spy plane deep inside Soviet airspace. However, in May 1960 a U-2 piloted by Gary Powers was shot down over Soviet soil. Initial U.S. attempts to deny the incident proved embarrassing when the Soviets triumphantly produced the downed pilot before the world's media, and these flights were abruptly ended.

Nevertheless, USAF aircraft regularly made unofficial incursions over the border and constantly probed the peripheries of the Soviet Union. Moreover, reconnaissance was not limited to gathering photographic data. Electronic, communications, and radar information were extremely valuable, and aircraft such as the RB-57F flew high in the stratosphere gathering minute particles of fallout from Soviet and Chinese nuclear tests. Spy planes were also vital in analyzing the Soviet missile buildup in Cuba in 1962, which enabled President Kennedy to have a good picture of the situation during the Cuban Missile Crisis. Cold War spying missions were extremely perilous, and in 1960 an electronic-gathering USAF aircraft based in the UK was shot down by two MiG fighters over the Barents Sea. Over the next 10 years 29 aircraft were lost while employed in their dangerous task.

highly motivated crews, and the numerical inferiority of NATO's forces was judged to be offset by the quality of personnel and aircraft. USAFE forces were regularly bolstered by transatlantic deployments of American-based units. These "Reforger" (Reinforcement of Forces in Germany) exercises called. for a massive airlift of both equipment and manpower. In the event of Soviet aggression resupply by sea would be too slow, so the introduction of new transport aircraft was vital to ensure that an operational force could be deployed within hours of the call. The C-141 and especially the giant C-5A Galaxy could

carry engines, tanks, and even helicopters in their cavernous holds and were a vital cog in the air bridge across the Atlantic Ocean (*see box p. 30*). As well as in Europe the USAF maintained a substantial force in Asia, particularly in Japan, to ensure that any attack from China or the USSR could be repelled.

The challenge of Vietnam
Having trained for war against the Warsaw Pact, America was not prepared for Vietnam—a guerrilla war in jungle terrain for which tactics had not been established, and the use of nuclear weapons was militarily and politically

inappropriate. Nevertheless, the USAF played a crucial role in the Vietnam conflict. It was tasked with providing support for ground troops as well as conducting bombing operations against North Vietnamese supply routes and targets in North Vietnam itself.

The Vietnam War introduced a new combat role for the helicopter. When a USAF aircraft was downed, an HH-3E fitted with a winch flew behind enemy lines to rescue the crew. Nicknamed "Jolly Green Giants," these helicopters rescued hundreds of aircrews. So successful were they that they became a part of USAF deployment worldwide.

As the 1960s ended, the USAF was a critical factor in the Vietnam War, the defense of Europe, and the defense of North America. Never had the USAF had such wide-ranging commitments. In January 1960 it had had 16,230 operationally active aircraft with an average age of six years. By 1969 it had 10,230 active aircraft with an average age of six years. This shows that, through the decade, the USAF became a leaner, but more modern, force. □

See Also: Aerospace Industry; Air-to-ground Missiles; Arms Race; Cold War; Deterrence; Nuclear Weapons; Postwar World; U-2 Incident; Vietnam War; Warsaw Pact

AIR-TO-GROUND MISSILES

During the Vietnam War U.S. aircraft attacking targets in North Vietnam were vulnerable to counterattack by land-based missiles. AGMs effectively targeted these antiaircraft defenses.

Air-to-ground missiles (AGMs) were developed from the late 1950s as a means of hitting a target with pinpoint accuracy. Specifically, AGM targets were enemy surface-to-air missile batteries, and they were designed to lock on to those batteries' radar emissions. AGMs were first used during the Vietnam War, with notable success (*see box*).

Between March 1965 and November 1968 the United States Air Force and Navy conducted an intensive bombing offensive against North Vietnam. The air operation was designed to cripple North Vietnam's ability to wage war against South Vietnam and force it to reach a compromise settlement. U.S.

aircraft struck at many targets, including the Ho Chi Minh Trail along which supplies flowed to North Vietnam-backed guerrillas in South Vietnam, as well as ammunition and fuel depots, power and industrial sites, and various key bridges within North Vietnam itself.

The North Vietnamese reacted to the bombing offensive by vastly increasing their antiaircraft defenses, which grew to include 6,500 antiaircraft guns, 200 Soviet-built SA-2 Guideline surface-to-air missiles (SAMs), and 40 jet interceptors by the end of 1967. U.S. aircraft losses mounted alarmingly—some 455 were downed in the year after the opening of the offensive.

The Guideline missiles were the chief cause of concern, particularly during comparatively low-level precision attacks against individual targets. These missiles had a range of 30 miles and a top speed of Mach 3.5. The North Vietnamese Guideline batteries naturally tended to be clustered around the most "high-value" targets and, unlike the conventional antiaircraft guns and jet aircraft encountered by U.S. pilots, could not easily be either destroyed or avoided with the technology that was available. U.S. intelligence had identified 57 operational SAM sites in North Vietnam by the end of 1966.

Neutralizing the SAMs

To combat the Guideline sites, the U.S. forces initially used electronic countermeasures aircraft to jam the Guideline radars, so that the radar-directed missiles could not "lock on" to their targets. Such tactics did not destroy the surface-to-air-missiles, however. They just neutralized their immediate threat. The deployment of aircraft carrying both AGMs and sensor equipment that could home in on the guidance radar of the North Vietnamese Guideline launchers proved far more effective. The radar had to be switched on to acquire and track a target and then direct a Guideline to it. The AGM-armed aircraft carried receivers that gave warning of their illumination by a ground radar and identified its probable location. AGMs could then be fired against the radar site with a high probability of success.

The Wild Weasels

Such AGM missions against the North Vietnamese SAMs were code-named Iron Hand and mounted by specialized aircraft, usually modified F-100 Super Sabres, F-105 Thunderchiefs, and with particular success, F-4 Phantoms. These

Operation Rolling Thunder

Operation Rolling Thunder was the name given to some aspects of the U.S. bombing campaign against North Vietnam between 1965 and 1968. The operation, though it was massive in scale, was conducted in a tightly regulated manner. President Johnson had no wish to further antagonize China or the Soviet Union, both of which supported North Vietnam, by launching an all-out attack. His strategy was to avoid civilian casualties, strictly control the choice of targets, and prohibit the bombing of the Hanoi and Haiphong areas. Raids close to the Chinese border were also forbidden.

In the three years of Operation Rolling Thunder some 860,000 tons of bombs were dropped by U.S. aircraft, a total that was greater than the tonnage dropped on Japan during World War II. On paper at least, the results seemed impressive. For example, 77 percent of North Vietnam's ammunition dumps were destroyed, along with 59 percent of its power-generating facilities and 55 percent of its major bridges. Some 52,000 North Vietnamese civilians were killed, and 600,000 others had to be employed in repairing the damage or to operate antiaircraft defenses.

However, those bare figures can give a misleading impression of the effectiveness of the campaign in strategic terms. North Vietnam did not stop sending supplies and troops into South Vietnam. It is estimated that North Vietnamese troop levels in South Vietnam rose by 75 percent during Operation Rolling Thunder. Neither did civilian morale in the North collapse. It was not until President Johnson ended the aerial campaign that the North Vietnamese entered into negotiations with the United States.

△ An F-4 Phantom carrying air-to-ground missiles. Such AGM-armed "Wild Weasels" were able to protect U.S. aircraft by knocking out North Vietnamese SAM missile sites.

specialized aircraft were known as "Wild Weasels." By destroying the missile sites, the Wild Weasels ensured that the aircraft tasked with destroying a particular objective could reach their target without having to worry about counterattacks from ground-based SAMs.

Wild Weasel aircraft initially carried the AGM-12 Bullpup or AGM-78 Standard antiradiation missiles, and later the AGM-45 Shrike. The Bullpup, for example, which was fitted with either a 250-lb. or 1,000-lb. warhead, had a range of from six to 10 miles and a speed of up to Mach 2. When fired, the Bullpup was tracked visually by the Wild Weasel crew, who were able to steer the missile to its target via a radio command link.

AGMs made a significant contribution to the decline in the effectiveness of North Vietnam's missile defenses. In 1965 one aircraft was destroyed for every 17 SAM launches; by 1972 the figure was one aircraft lost for every 87 launches. During the bombing campaign U.S. planes flew 300,000 sorties and lost 938 aircraft. However, nearly half of these losses were incurred in the first year of the campaign before the full deployment of the air-to-ground missiles. □

See Also: Air Force; Vietnam War

AIR TRAVEL

The 1960s witnessed a revolution in the air. Once the preserve of the rich and famous, a trip by jet across America or beyond became affordable for the ordinary business traveler or vacationer.

A new term for the wealthiest and most glamorous Americans became fashionable at the start of the 1960s—the Jet Set. These were the people who in the 1950s might have crossed the country in the luxury of such propellered airplanes as the Stratocruiser, renowned for its cocktail bar and lavish sleeping berths. They would have taken the big ocean liners across the Atlantic, and then on by first-class rail to the French Riviera.

The coming of jet planes that could fly faster and farther and carry more passengers than the airliners of the 1950s revolutionized both domestic and international travel in America.

It all began on October 26, 1958, when Pan Am offered the first ever scheduled U.S. jet flight from New York to Paris. The plane was a Boeing 707. It carried 40 deluxe-class passengers and 71 in economy class, the largest number ever on a scheduled

flight to that time. The 707 took off from Idlewild (later Kennedy) Airport, refueled at Gander, and made Paris in the early morning. It took eight hours and 15 minutes. In deluxe class was a woman from Lake Forest, Illinois, who was having lunch in Paris and then flying straight back to New York.

▽ **Pan Am and United jet liners surround the John Rogers Terminal at Honolulu. The jet age brought the 50th state closer to the mainland.**

Passengers accustomed to the pro-pellered planes of the 1950s were impressed with how smooth and quiet the ride was on a jet. And it was so much faster, too. Speed, it turned out, was very much more in demand than Stratocruiser-type luxury. It became fashionable for a while for the well-to-do to fly to Paris just for the weekend, and one woman reportedly made the trip just to have her hair done for a high society event in New York.

Democracy in the air

For the Jet Set here was a new way of traveling the world. But they enjoyed only a brief period of isolation in the skies. Very rapidly the comfort and speed of jets attracted a wide spectrum of Americans. After 1961 big improve-

△ A sailor confirms his Eastern Airlines flight, 1967. With the bustle of passengers crowding the desks, it could almost be a scene from today—but for the absence of computers.

The executive jet

While business passengers were the first frequent fliers on the new jets of the 1960s, there was a demand from the big corporations for smaller planes they could afford to buy and fly themselves. Executive travelers, in fact, had a tremendous choice of small aircraft from the early 1960s. The leading company, Cessna, was constantly refining its models and brought out its first Skymaster in 1960. It was a four-seater twin-engined aircraft that cruised at 125 mph and proved popular with large-scale farmers and ranchers as well as big corporations. By 1966 Cessna had sold 11,000 of its 172/Skyhawk series.

Greater comfort in executive aircraft, with pressurized cabins and "club" seating arrangements, kept the demand high. But these were not jets, and though much speedier than any other form of individually owned transportation, they were slower than the big passenger planes that were establishing commuter services all over the United States.

The Lockheed Corporation produced the first commercial executive jet, which it sold to the Continental Can Company in 1961. It was the JetStar, which could cruise at over 500 mph and fly at 33,000 feet. But it was too expensive for the market at that time, and the price tag of more than $1.5 million led to disappointing sales—by the mid-1960s only 53 had been bought by commercial customers.

The big breakthrough that revolutionized business and corporate air travel came in 1964 with the first appearance of the Learjet. Just half the price of the JetStar, it cruised at over 500 mph and could carry two pilots and six passengers, and sold more than 100 in its first year of production. It was the brainchild of William P. Lear, who had made his name in aviation history in 1949 by developing the autopilot. Lear concentrated on developing aircraft for executive travel and while working in Switzerland in the 1950s came up with the first designs for the Learjet. Based on a Swiss fighter-bomber called the P-16, his sleek, swift plane ushered in the age of the executive jet.

ments in engine technology saved fuel, brought down ticket prices, and made for an even smoother ride, opening the way for mass air travel.

A measure of the way in which air travel boomed in the 1960s is the comparison of passenger-miles traveled on airlines, trains, and intercity buses. Whereas in the mid-1950s domestic airlines trailed in third place with 20 billion passenger-miles (trains and buses accounted for 23 billion and 22 billion respectively), by 1965 the air-lines were far in front with 52 billion. Buses were holding steady at about 23 billion, while trains had fallen back to 13 billion. These figures show a large increase in public transportation across the decade, all of it going to airlines, which were also replacing trains on long-distance journeys. This trend continued through the 1960s and beyond.

The commercial beneficiaries of the switch to air travel were the major American airlines: United, TWA, American, and Eastern were dominant in domestic operations, while Pan Am concentrated on the long-haul inter-continental market.

By far the largest contingent of fliers in the early days of jet travel were businessmen and women whose fares were on company expenses. Whereas others flew only occasionally, the business passenger was becoming a regular at the airports that grew up alongside the commercial and industrial centers. One estimate in 1964 was that more than 80 percent of all civilian air passengers were flying on business.

The popularity of jet travel for business people began to transform the executive way of life. Offices and hotels were sited near airports, which evolved huge parking lots. Overnight stays on away trips became less frequent—it was possible to hold a meeting at or near an airport and get home that same day.

Increased availability of flights and competition drove down prices, and airlines began selling spare capacity at a discount. This meant there were bargains on offer for those prepared to take a last-minute chance of getting on a flight, and young people in particular took up the opportunity enthusiastically. It was suddenly not all that expensive to get to Europe, and the number of American students going abroad rose one and a half times in the

Shuttle services

When the major airlines started buying the new jet aircraft, an older generation of serviceable planes came onto the market. These planes were ideal for short-haul trips. The first shuttle service was launched in April 1961 by Eastern Airlines, flying 95-seater Lockheed Constellations between New York and Boston and New York and Washington. It was billed as a "no frills" service for which passengers turned up at La Guardia 45 minutes before takeoff and took all their baggage with them onto the plane. No food or drink was served, and the price of the seats at $12 one-way to Boston and $14 one-way to Washington was just a dollar or so more than the rail fare.

early 1960s. At the same time, the "package vacation" came within reach of millions of Americans.

New vacation regions were opened up—especially in the Caribbean—and tourists started arriving in the U.S. from Europe and Japan in much greater numbers than ever before.

In-flight entertainment
After the first flush of excitement at the speed and comfort of jet air travel, passengers became bored on long-haul trips. To relieve the tedium, TWA and Inflight Services developed a system for projecting movies to keep travelers

entertained. The first film, *By Love Possessed*, starring Lana Turner, was shown in 1961. It was not the first time films had been screened: experiments had taken place as early as 1929, and TWA had shown a film called *Flying Hostess* in 1934. But it was during the 1960s that in-flight entertainment became a routine feature.

For passengers not interested in the movie, personal headsets were offered along with a menu of taped programs of music. Again, this was not entirely new, for in the 1930s some airlines had provided individual radio sets. They could be tuned in when the pilot gave wavelength settings for the various broadcasting stations over which the plane flew. But as with movies, the 1960s saw an improvement in the range and quality of audio entertainment.

Brought down to earth
The pace at which air travel increased had its price. Many airports were inadequate for the volume of traffic they were handling, and the development of automatic takeoff and landing mechanisms lagged behind (*see box p. 37*).

Safety became an issue as air traffic control struggled to keep track of all the planes crisscrossing the busiest routes. By the mid-1960s 2,000 of America's 3,200 publicly owned airports were in need of upgrading. The noise pollution

◁ **Cars crowd the Washington National Airport parking lot. Congestion and noise pollution around big airports came hand-in-hand with the growth in air travel.**

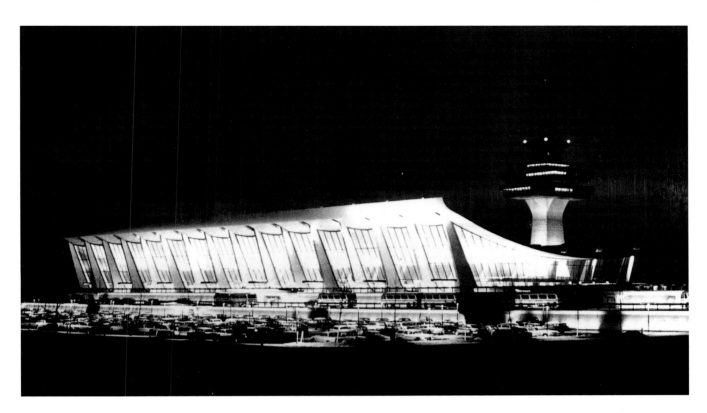

△ **Dulles Airport by night in the late 1960s. One of two sites serving the capital, it is a striking example of a modern jet-age airport.**

around airports, and the huge traffic jams that built up on approach roads, were already an issue in the 1960s.

The 1960s also witnessed the first ever skyjacking in America. In May 1961 a man calling himself El Pirato Corfrisi forced a National Airlines plane on a Miami–Key West flight to divert to Cuba. He threatened the pilot with a pistol and a knife, and got away with it, too, disappearing on landing at Havana. There followed a spate of skyjackings to Cuba. In the end security checks had to be brought in, adding a perception of risk as well as taking away some of the speed of jet travel.

In other ways, too, air travel was shedding some of its formerly free-and-easy image. In the 1960s pilots were told to stay in their cabin throughout the flight after a near-disaster in which a skipper who thought his autopilot was switched on fraternized with passengers until the jet started plunging earthward. He and the copilot leveled the plane at 6,000 feet.

After the first euphoric days enjoyed by the Jet Set, the problems inherent in rapid commercial growth took a lot of the glamor away from this new space-age way of traveling. Some even looked back nostalgically at prejet air travel.

But fast, inexpensive travel for the masses was here to stay, and it was left to the airports to modernize their infrastructures to meet the demand. By the end of the 1960s half of all Americans had flown at least once. □

Crowded skies

The tremendous success and popularity of air travel with the arrival of passenger jets in the 1960s very soon began to cause problems both in the air and on the ground. In 1965 there were already 2,389,000 aircraft movements in the heavily used New York hub of JFK, La Guardia, and Newark airports. More than 12 million passengers flew in and out in that year, and the numbers went on rising. Concern grew not only about congestion on the ground but in the air, for systems of air traffic control were under constant strain. By 1967 the air traffic controllers were handling 50 million operations a year. A Federal Aviation Authority (FAA) study in 1966 showed that 173,000 hours were lost at 304 terminals in America because of delays, most of which were caused by overloading of control systems.

The runways and taxiing areas of airports built in the 1950s were hopelessly inadequate for the jet age, and billions of dollars had to be spent upgrading them. Whenever plans for new out-of-town airports were put forward, local opposition was fierce. In fact, the advances of the aerospace industry in producing bigger, faster, more comfortable jets always outstripped the provision of airports. This remained the biggest constraint on the expansion of air travel in America during the 1960s.

See Also: Aerospace Industry; Leisure Industry; Science and Technology; Tourism; Transportation

MUHAMMAD ALI b. 1942

The bruising world of heavyweight boxing was captivated in the 1960s by an extraordinarily talented athlete who, in his own memorable phrase, could "float like a butterfly, sting like a bee."

Ali was born Cassius Marcellus Clay on January 17, 1942, in Louisville, Kentucky. He was raised in reasonably comfortable circumstances—unusual for a successful boxer of the time, especially for an African American boxer. He began boxing at school, and his early promise bore fruit at the 1960 Rome Olympic Games, where he won the gold medal at light heavyweight. Those who saw his performance were struck by his fleet footwork, which no one could recall having seen in a man of his size. This became even more remarkable when the young man quickly filled out to become a true heavyweight, with no apparent loss of speed.

When Clay returned in triumph from Rome, a syndicate of Louisville businessmen sponsored his swift entry into the professional heavyweight ranks. The syndicate hired Angelo Dundee as Clay's trainer, establishing a fruitful partnership that would last throughout the boxer's long career. Dundee would build on his protégé's natural gifts, adding toughness and punching power to his phenomenal speed and reflexes.

Rapid rise to the top

Clay's early progress through the heavyweight ranks was swift, but marked by controversy. He won every fight, often with contemptuous ease, mesmerizing his victims as well as his fans with the dizzying speed of his footwork and combination punching. But he was gaining detractors as quickly as admirers. He was outspoken in a way that challenged contemporary public expectations of African American sports figures, who were traditionally modest and dignified in their public utterances. Clay would have nothing to do with playing up to such a racial

△ Ali taunts ex-champion Sonny Liston, having felled him in round one of their rematch, on May 25, 1965. Liston was counted out.

stereotype and was gleefully vain and boastful. He delighted in predicting the round in which he would finish off each opponent, and he proved uncannily accurate most of the time. For example, in 1963 Clay fought the hard-punching British champion Henry Cooper in London and taunted the British press and public that their hero would fall in five. Clay's prediction appeared to have gone horribly wrong when Cooper flattened him with a left hook at the end of the fourth. But the bell came to Clay's rescue, he recovered his senses between rounds—and duly stopped Cooper in the fifth!

On February 25, 1964, the 22-year-old Clay got his big chance when he entered the ring to fight Sonny Liston for the heavyweight title. Liston had a fearsome reputation, and the odds of 7–1 against the challenger reflected the widespread belief that the "Louisville Lip" was about to get his comeuppance. In fact, Clay put on a dazzling display, hitting his opponent at will, taunting him by word and gesture, draining his immense strength and finally his will to

▷ **Standing out in a crowd in November 1970, Ali was now allowed to resume his career after his three-year absence from the ring.**

fight. Liston quit at the end of the sixth round, claiming a damaged shoulder. Suddenly, Clay's boast, "I am the greatest," did not appear so hollow.

Stripped of his title

The day after the fight the new champion shocked friend and foe alike by announcing that he had joined the Nation of Islam and that his name was now Muhammad Ali. For the remainder of the decade Ali would command as much attention for his controversial views as for his unbroken sequence of victories in the ring. In particular, his refusal to be inducted into the armed forces in 1967 at the height of the Vietnam War attracted widespread animosity, and he was stripped of his title and banned from fighting in the U.S. (*see box*).

Ali did not fight again during the 1960s, but a gradual relaxation of attitudes toward him as American public

Ali and the Vietnam War

On April 28, 1967, Ali refused to step forward when he was formally inducted into the U.S. Army, claiming conscientious objector status on the grounds that he was a minister of the religion of Islam. However, Ali was also a vociferous critic of the Vietnam War, and with his typical flair for expressing himself he encapsulated his objection in a memorable phrase: "I ain't got no quarrel with the Viet Cong."

A few days later Ali was indicted by a federal grand jury for draft evasion, convicted, and sentenced to five years' imprisonment plus a hefty fine. Ali appealed, and eventually in 1970 the conviction was overturned. But in the meantime his conviction meant that he could not leave the country, and he was banned from boxing. Instead, he turned to the college lecture circuit, where his antiwar stance had plenty of support.

Public reaction to Ali's action was polarized. Supporters of the Vietnam War scorned him as unpatriotic, many denouncing him as a traitor. Opponents of the war praised him for taking a principled stand—and for his willingness to pay such a heavy price for his beliefs. The erosion of support for the war during the late 1960s resulted in growing acceptance of Ali's sincerity; and when he was able to resume his boxing career in the 1970s, he found himself a far more popular figure than he had been during the 1960s. Afflicted in middle age by Parkinson's syndrome, almost certainly brought on by punishment sustained in the ring, Ali remains an unrivaled sporting icon.

opinion shifted against the war enabled him to pick up his boxing career in 1970. Despite the enforced layoff during his prime years, Ali went on to even greater glory in the ring during a series of epic clashes with all the best heavyweights of the time, most notably Joe Frazier and George Foreman. During the 1970s Ali regained, lost, and regained the heavyweight title, making him the only man ever to win the crown three times. In the course of doing so his claim to be "the greatest" gained wide acceptance, and he became as popular as he had once been reviled. In particular, he became—and remains—an inspirational figure within much of the Third World, whose interests he tirelessly championed. □

See Also: Antiwar Movement; Boxing; Draft; Nation of Islam

WOODY ALLEN b.1935

Having started out in the 1950s as a scriptwriter for TV comedians, at the beginning of the 1960s Woody Allen emerged as an original stand-up comic, and then as a highly individualistic filmmaker.

Woody Allen, whose real name is Allen Stewart Konigsberg, is one of the most productive writer-directors and actors of his generation. The Brooklyn-born natural comic has brought the self-analyzing, self-deprecating, and neurotic style of Jewish humor to the film world. His immediately recognizable and inimitable brand of comedy has established him as perhaps the most individual and independent, as well as the most self-centered, American filmmaker of recent decades.

Allen began learning his trade as a scriptwriter by preparing material for the television comedians Sid Caesar, Art Carney, and Buddy Hackett. In 1961 he set out on his own and began performing as a stand-up comedian in Manhattan nightclubs. It was in the clubs that Allen developed his unique brand of psychoanalytical humor. Much of the material was clearly autobiographical. Allen used introspection as a means to comic effect and to an exploration of the trials and tribulations of the misunderstood *schlemiel* who is consumed by the need to get his personal feelings and enervating "hang-ups" out into the open.

Comic becomes filmmaker

Allen's debut in the film world was as the writer of the screenplay for *What's New Pussy Cat?* in 1965. Despite a star-studded cast that included Peter O'Toole, Peter Sellers, and Ursula Andress, the film was not a critical success. It is remembered more for Tom Jones's recording of its title song than for the film itself. This movie did, however, provide two pointers to Allen's future career: he took a part in it himself, and his writing showed a talent for zany sex comedy mixed up with lots of ridiculous psychobabble.

See Also: Hollywood

△ **The youthful Woody Allen, who carried over his introspective style from the New York club scene to filmmaking. Allen's 1960s movies gained him a following, but limited success.**

Allen wrote, directed, and again appeared in his next film, *Take the Money and Run* (1969). The film was a parody of gangster movies, telling the story of a social misfit of a bank-robber so hilariously inept that he cannot even spell the words in the notes demanding money that he hands to cashiers.

Again, although neither a critical nor a commercial hit, the film was a foretaste of the parodic style that Allen was to use to telling effect in later films that he both wrote and directed, such as *Bananas* (1971), *Sleeper* (1973), and *Love and Death* (1975). It also gained some notoriety from the frequent use (for the time) of four-letter words. Part of the comic appeal of *Take the Money and Run* may derive from the spontaneity that Allen brought to its direction. He claimed that he did not "rehearse" the film in the conventional way, by which he meant that he never knew until it happened where in a scene he was going to put the camera. "Funniness is organic, like sitting around with a lot of people when something loopy happens. What you write is not what you shoot at all." □

ALLIANCE FOR PROGRESS

An early act of the Kennedy administration was to extend substantial economic aid to the nations of Latin America. But political and economic interests often clashed with humanitarian impulses.

Early in 1961, just a few weeks after his inauguration, President John F. Kennedy spoke privately to an advisor about an idea he had for a "club" of the Americas. Progressive Latin American leaders would meet regularly for more-or-less informal discussions at his father's house in Palm Beach, Florida. When Kennedy spoke to a group of Latin American diplomats on March 13, that idea had grown into an official proposal for "a new alliance for progress... a vast cooperative effort, unparalleled in magnitude and nobility of purpose, to satisfy the basic needs of the American people for home, work, land, health, and schools." By "American" Kennedy meant all the inhabitants of the Western Hemisphere south of the United States.

The idea was not new. A similar project, called Operation Pan America, had been suggested by the Brazilian president, Juscelino Kubitschek, two years earlier. At the same time, the Alliance for Progress was, from the point of view of the United States, a renewal of President Franklin Roosevelt's Good Neighbor Policy of the 1930s toward Latin America.

Joint interests and conflicts

One of the Alliance's merits was that it was in tune with the growing desire of Latin American nations for greater economic and political cooperation. In 1960 a free-trade treaty had been signed by the governments of Mexico and the 10 South American republics. Kennedy's proposal therefore fell on willing ears. On August 17, 1961, at a conference held at Punta del Este, Uruguay, every Latin American country except Cuba signed a treaty formally establishing the Alliance for Progress.

Cuba was the root concern that motivated U.S. policymakers. After the

△ **Alliance for Progress supplied the building material, local villagers the labor for this new health center in Colombia. Kennedy's stated purpose was to improve such fundamentals as healthcare in Latin America.**

overthrow of General Batista's government in 1959, the new Cuban leader Fidel Castro had nationalized U.S.-owned corporations on the island. President Eisenhower had responded by imposing economic sanctions, and that was followed by Castro's turning to the Soviet Union for economic assistance. Castro also began advocating Marxist revolution throughout Latin America.

When the Bay of Pigs invasion to overthrow Castro ended in abject failure in April 1961, the Alliance for Progress took on a deeper significance: to improve conditions for the people of Latin America and thereby render them less susceptible to communist propaganda. Though it was not publicly stated, the purpose was also to keep Latin America open to U.S. investors.

The members of the Alliance pledged to coordinate their economies and to initiate land and tax reforms in the interests of redistributing wealth from the rich to the poor. They aimed to achieve an annual rate of increase in income per capita of 2.5 percent. The envisioned cost of the project was $20 to $25 billion, most of it in long-term foreign loans at low rates of interest to provide better health and education, to facilitate rural resettlement and finance low-cost housing projects, and to assist economic development generally.

Specific targets included a minimum of six years of education for all children, the eradication of malaria, and the provision of pure drinking-water.

Short on delivery

Great fanfare attended the Alliance's inception. Over the following decade, however, only about $100 million was spent on the project (apart from loans), and 90 percent of that money was spent in the U.S. Few Latin American governments were progressive enough to carry through the land reforms that were essential if poverty was to be reduced. In Venezuela and Colombia, for example, agencies acquired large tracts of land, but they were mostly infertile and, in any case, were rarely redistributed to the poor. The size of small farms actually decreased, while those of rich landowners increased.

Overall, it is estimated that only $2 out of every $100 was used to help the poor. Nor was it easy to make headway toward economic integration when

CIA involvement

The effectiveness of the Alliance for Progress was undermined in part by the efforts of the Central Intelligence Agency to prevent left-wing governments from taking office in Latin America. What happened in Chile is instructive. Despite the injection of more than $1 billion in Alliance loans between 1962 and 1969, little money filtered through to the most needy members of the Chilean population. Powerful American corporations, such as the two copper giants, Anaconda and Kennecott, continued to play a dominant role in Chile's economy. Such companies were the target of radical left-wing movements that sought to establish Chileans' control over their own economic affairs and to redistribute wealth to the have-nots in their country. In the eyes of the CIA those left-wingers constituted a major threat to American investors and to the State Department's effort to minimize Soviet influence in Latin America.

The result was that at the same time as money was coming in from the Alliance for Progress, the CIA was deeply involved in training army and police forces in "counterinsurgency techniques" to stop left-wing guerrillas from achieving a socialist revolution in Chile. A U.S. Senate Select Committee admitted that there was "a vicious circle plaguing the logic" of the Alliance for Progress. "In order to eliminate the short-term danger of Communist subversion, it was often necessary to support Latin American armed forces, yet frequently it was those same armed forces who were helping to freeze the status quo which the Alliance sought to alter." In Chile the chief agency for social and economic reform was the Popular Unity party headed by Salvador Allende. Allende lost the 1964 presidential election to his right-wing opponent, who received $3 million from the CIA. However, Allende overcame the CIA's opposition to win the presidency in 1970. Three years later he was ousted, and killed, by a CIA-backed military coup.

local economies remained closely tied to developments in the international commodities markets. Countries with divergent economies failed to agree, for example, on joint programs for planned industrialization or on a common approach to foreign investment.

Of lasting significance, however, was that the Alliance for Progress resulted in the emergence of many new political parties throughout Latin America. These new parties stimulated political activism, and they were to play a major role in the upheavals of the 1970s and 1980s, particularly in Central America.

Resentment at the extent of U.S. control of the project was widespread

◁ **The Alliance for Progress helped fund this bridge over the Aysen River in Chile. Such projects boosted local economies as long as they involved Latin American industries.**

throughout Latin America. Capital equipment, available more cheaply elsewhere, had to be bought from the United States; grants were tied to U.S. investment. The cry of "Yankee imperialism" grew ever louder as the years passed, and Latin American countries fell far short of the financial contributions they were supposed to make from their own resources.

In the United States the Johnson and Nixon administrations faced the criticism that there had been no alliance and little progress. There were, of course, local successes, and the Alliance no doubt contributed to the improved performance of a number of Latin American economies in the 1970s. In the end, however, the venture failed to reach its targets. In 1974 the Alliance ceased to operate when U.S. funding was withdrawn. □

See Also: Bay of Pigs Invasion; Castro; CIA; Guevara; Kennedy, J. F.; Latin America; Organization of American States; U.S.–Mexican Relations

ALTAMONT FESTIVAL

Just four months after the hippie dream came to its full flowering at Woodstock, violent carnage disfigured an open-air concert at a speedway in California called Altamont.

△ **A hot-air balloon floats above the throng gathered at Altamont to enjoy a live performance by the Rolling Stones.**

The Rolling Stones did not appear at Woodstock in August 1969. But in November they were touring the U.S. to promote their new album *Let It Bleed*, a sarcastic reference to the Beatles' *Let It Be*. The tour was dogged with the threat of violence. Mick Jagger had once intimated his sympathy for the militant African American cause. The Black Panthers now demanded that he formally declare allegiance. When he did not comply, Jagger received death threats. Ike and Tina Turner, the Rolling Stones' warm-up act, also felt intimidated.

Stung by criticism of the high price of tickets to their concerts, Jagger let it slip at a press conference in New York that the band was planning to do a free concert in San Francisco on December 6. In fact no one had planned it.

It was assumed that the concert would be in the Golden Gate Park, but the Parks Department demanded a bond of $4 million against damage and cleanup costs. The manager of Sears Point Raceway offered his venue for free. Twenty-four hours before the concert was due to start, however, the corporate owners of the raceway demanded exclusive distribution rights for any film shot at the event or $1 million in cash, with another $1 million held in escrow against damage.

Attorney Melvin Belli, who had defended Jack Ruby over the shooting of Lee Harvey Oswald and was now involved in the high-profile Manson murder case, was called in. He arranged for the concert to be shifted to the Altamont Raceway, near Livermore, California, for just $5,000 cleanup costs plus a $1-million insurance policy against damage. Either Rock Scully, manager of the Grateful Dead, or Emmett Grogan of the Diggers suggested using the Hell's Angels as security. Hunter S. Thompson's 1967 book *Hell's Angels* had made the violent bikers' group seem fashionable.

From the first moment the Hell's Angels arrived, at 10 A.M. on December 6, at Altamont there was trouble.

△ **The aftermath of Altamont: as well as acres of litter, there were four fatalities to mark the night of mayhem.**

During the first set Angels pelted the band Santana with beer cans. Concert organizer Sam Cutler promptly paid them $500 for their remaining stocks, prompting the spurious legend that the Rolling Stones had hired the Angels for $500-worth of beer.

During Jefferson Airplane's set the Hell's Angels began assailing the crowd with weighted pool cues. When singer Marty Balin saw the Angels assaulting an African American man, he leaped off the stage to intervene, only to be knocked unconscious himself. Lead guitarist Paul Kantner tried to calm things down, but an Angel grabbed a microphone and abused him. During the Flying Burrito Brothers' set the Rolling Stones turned up. A teenage boy hit Jagger in the face and threatened to kill him. The Hell's Angels attacked the Stones' bodyguards but were called off by their leader Sonny Barger, since it was rumored that one of the guards, a small white man, was with the FBI.

While Crosby, Stills, Nash and Young played, the Angels charged the audience with pool cues. The atmosphere was now so filled with menace that when they had finished playing, the band ran for their helicopter without waiting for any applause.

The Stones then let the audience wait. Jagger wanted it to get dark so that his Satanic costume, created by British fashion designer Ossie Clark, would be seen to full effect in the stage lights. Meanwhile, the Angels drove their bikes through the audience to wall it off from the stage.

When the Stones began to play, the Angels went back to beating defenseless members of the audience. Jagger broke off from "Sympathy for the Devil," and he and guitarist Keith Richards begged the Angels to stop. They did not see, in the audience, 18-year-old African American Meredith Hunter being stabbed to death by a Hell's Angel. Three more people were killed that night. Two were run over by a car as they lay in their sleeping bags; the third, who was drunk, drowned in an irrigation ditch. It was a chilling finale to a decade of optimism. □

The killer walks free

On January 8, 1970, 22-year-old Hell's Angel Alan Passaro went on trial in Oakland, California, for the murder of Meredith Hunter. Arrested for a drug offense a few days after the concert, Passaro had been identified from *Gimme Shelter*, the movie of the tour that was playing coast to coast. The film clearly showed Passaro killing Hunter. Passaro admitted the killing, but claimed that Hunter had a gun that he fired. The Angels had already handed in Hunter's loaded gun to the California Highway Patrol, and the jury had no choice but to acquit.

See Also: Rock Music; Rolling Stones; Woodstock Festival

AMERICAN INDIAN MOVEMENT

Taking their cue from the Black Panther Party, in 1968 militant Native Americans formed the American Indian Movement (AIM) to spearhead their demands for improved status and the restoration of lost lands.

△ **Leaders of the American Indian Movement hold a press conference at occupied Alcatraz prison on Christmas Eve 1969.**

The American Indian Movement was formed in Minneapolis, Minnesota, in July 1968. It began as an offshoot of a Minneapolis Office of Economic Opportunity antipoverty program. Originally called Concerned Indian Americans, it quickly changed its name when it was pointed out that the initials spelled CIA! Its founders were Dennis Banks, Clyde Bellecourt, and George Mitchell, all Chippewa from Minnesota. Later, Russell Means, an Oglala Sioux, became a prominent spokesman for the movement. Banks and Bellecourt had worked under Minneapolis Black Panther leader Matthew Eubank at the city's Citizens' Community Center.

Modeling itself on the Black Panther Party, AIM set up "Survival Schools" and Indian Patrol, whose purpose was to help Indians (as Native Americans still called themselves) displaced from their reservations to urban ghettos by government programs. Church groups swelled AIM's coffers to $500,000, and members were taken on staff.

Red Power

AIM's banner featured a clenched fist. Its slogan was "United We Are One Powerful Fist—Dignity, Pride, Unity." Its colors were red, black, and yellow, for the oppressed peoples of the world, and green for the land. AIM was the zenith of the new militancy among Native Americans that followed the civil rights movement step by step through the 1960s. It had begun in June 1961, when 500 young Native Americans met at the University of Chicago and drew up "A Declaration of Indian Purpose." A militant element from that meeting formed themselves into the National Indian Youth Council (NIYC). It opposed the government-sanctioned National Congress of American Indians and the tribal leadership on the grounds that they represented white society more than the Indians themselves.

To draw attention to its grievances, the NIYC began deliberately flouting state fishing laws in well-publicized "fish-ins" in 1964. The NIYC borrowed its rhetoric from the civil rights movement. It talked of "Red Power," "Uncle Tomahawks," and "Apples"—Indians who were red on the outside, white on the inside. Their leader was Clyde Warrior, a Ponca from Oklahoma who had worked with the Student Nonviolent Coordinating Committee. Describing himself as an "academic aborigine," he denounced whites as racists, fascists, colonialists, and reactionaries.

President Johnson's War on Poverty took note. A special task force on the American Indian was formed, and the Office of Economic Opportunity devised community, training, and welfare programs for Native Americans. Despite this, in 1967 the mercurial Warrior resigned in protest. He accused the OEO of sucking Indians into the system rather than promoting self-determination. Within a year, however, Warrior died. In 1968 the National Council on Indian Opportunity, under Vice President Hubert Humphrey, was established to ensure Native Americans got their fair share of federal funds. At

△ A teepee erected on Alcatraz Island during the Native American occupation that began in 1969. After a prolonged stalemate U.S. marshals removed the last occupiers in 1971.

the same time, the Indian Civil Rights Act was passed. It repealed the hated Public Law 280, which gave the federal and state governments jurisdiction over Indian reservations without Indian consent. However, it also applied the provisions of the U.S. Constitution to Reservation Courts, which was bitterly opposed. Out of this opposition sprang the American Indian Movement.

AIM's goals eventually expanded to encompass economic independence, revitalization of traditional culture, and the restoration of lands that it believed had been illegally seized. The movement developed a strong following on the reservations, where the tribal leaders were seen as too conservative. AIM embarked on a number of highly publicized protests. It was one of the groups involved in the occupation of Alcatraz Island in 1969 by Indians of All Tribes (IAT), an *ad hoc* grouping led by Mohawk Richard Oaks and John Trudall, a Santee Dakota and AIM member. They demanded title to Alcatraz under the Act of 1882, which said that abandoned federal facilities—

The changing view

The 1960s witnessed a sea change in society's view of Native Americans—and in their view of themselves. New York radio reporter Stan Steiner broadcast a series of interviews with young militants on WBAI-FM. He published the interviews as *The New Indians* in 1968. The National Congress of American Indians followed this with *Custer Died for Your Sins: An Indian Manifesto* in 1969, which in turn was followed by Dee Alexander Brown's best-seller *Bury My Heart at Wounded Knee* (1970), a history of the West from the Native American perspective—or "How the West Was Lost."

Hollywood also viewed Native Americans sympathetically as an oppressed minority. But the key movies *Little Big Man*, *A Man Called Horse*, and *Soldier Blue* did not appear until 1970. Perhaps more influential was the low-budget hit *Billy Jack* (1971), which pitted the new liberalism, in the person of the half-Indian hero, against the redneck conservatives of a small western town.

such as a prison on an island—should be utilized for Indian schools. In addition they cited Title 25, U.S. Code 194, which stated: "In all trials about the right of property in which an Indian may be party on one side, and a white person on the other, the burden of proof shall rest upon the white person."

IAT said it intended to establish a Center for Native American Studies, an American Indian Spiritual Center, an Indian Center of Ecology, and an American Indian Museum on Alcatraz. It even offered to buy the island from the federal government, but on terms that reflected the way land had historically been acquired from their ancestors by the white man.

The Alcatraz demand

In formally stating its terms for Alcatraz, IAT displayed a gift for irony. "We, the native Americans, reclaim the land known as Alcatraz Island in the name of all American Indians by right of discovery," ran the statement. "We wish to be fair and honorable in our dealings with the Caucasian inhabitants of this land, and hereby offer the following treaty. We will purchase said Alcatraz for twenty-four (24) dollars in glass beads and red cloth, a precedent set by the white man's purchase of a similar island about 300 years ago. We know that $24 in trade goods for these 16 acres is more than was paid when Manhattan Island was sold [Manhattan being much larger than Alcatraz], but we know that land values have risen over the years. Our offer of $1.24 per acre is greater than the 47 cents per acre the white men are now paying the California Indians for their land [a deal recently arranged through the Indian Claims Commission]."

The occupation of Alcatraz Island attracted massive publicity, and Congress passed a House Joint Resolution asking President Nixon to "initiate immediate negotiations with the objective of transferring the unencumbered title" of Alcatraz Island to the American Indian community.

Nixon dispatched Robert Robertson, executive director of the National Council of Indian Opportunity, to Alcatraz. Robertson proposed that women and children be removed from the island, and the IAT contingent be reduced to five or 10 men, who would be placed on the federal payroll. IAT refused and promptly responded by seizing an unused section of the Fort Lawton military reservation near Seattle. Seventy-seven people were arrested for trespass and other offenses.

The government then proposed that Alcatraz become a National Park, with the occupiers being hired as park rangers. The answer, again, was no. Electricity and water supplies were cut. IAT prepared for a long siege. Meanwhile AIM staged two publicity coups, capturing the replica *Mayflower II* on Thanksgiving Day 1970 and briefly occupying Mount Rushmore.

By this time AIM was already subject to disruption by the FBI's covert COINTELPRO counterintelligence program. Finally, on June 14, 1971, a taskforce of U.S. marshals landed on Alcatraz Island and arrested and removed the remaining occupiers. □

See Also: Civil Rights Movement; FBI; Native Americans

ANTISMOKING CAMPAIGN

The pronouncement by the highest medical authority in the land that cigarettes were a grave health hazard came as a nasty shock to American smokers in the mid-1960s.

On Saturday, January 11, 1964, at 9 o'clock sharp, journalists were summoned to a State Department auditorium at the White House where they were handed a 387-page report. The report contained the findings of the U.S. Surgeon General's Advisory Committee on Smoking and Health. Locked in and without telephones, the press representatives were given 90 minutes to absorb the contents and to ask questions. Then they were released to tell the American people something they did not really want to know—that smoking cigarettes was ruining their health and killing them on a terrifying scale.

The end of a deadly love affair

The report came from Luther L. Terry, Surgeon General of the U.S. Public Health Service, and it compiled the findings of many medical investigations that had been made since the 1950s into the relationship between cigarette smoking and diseases such as lung cancer and bronchitis. Its conclusion was stark: "Cigarette smoking is a health hazard of sufficient importance in the United States to warrant appropriate remedial action."

It is hard now to appreciate what a shock the Smoking and Health report was for Americans in the 1960s. Smoking was an accepted fact of life. Nearly half of all adult Americans smoked, and the very act of lighting up was rich in symbolism.

▷ **Students in San Diego absorb the antismoking message as a demonstrator from the Health Education Club smokes a (nonhuman) lung over a barbeque.**

The 1950s had been the high point for a habit that had only begun in earnest at the turn of the century, with the mass production of cigarettes made from mild, flue-cured tobaccos. The convenient new cigarettes were cheaper and easier to inhale than cigars and pipes, and more socially acceptable than chewing tobacco. Cigarette advertising in magazines, newspapers, on radio, in the movies, and on television was inescapable. Movie stars not only smoked—the cigarette was a prop they could use to dramatic effect, stubbing it

out half-smoked to show anger, or blowing a long, slow stream of smoke to indicate disbelief. During World War II free cigarettes were issued to soldiers and became a standard part of their "survival rations."

As America entered the 1960s, the central place of cigarette smoking in national life was unchallenged, even though at a personal level many nonsmokers loathed the habit. Smokers puffed their way through more than 500 billion cigarettes a year. The industry itself was encouraged with grants to tobacco growers, while the federal government raked in $3 billion a year in tobacco taxes. It was for these reasons that the Surgeon General's devastating report in 1964 was delivered on a Saturday—to avoid an immediate share panic on Wall Street.

The antismoking campaign that began in 1964 in response to the Surgeon General's report had a monumental task. It had to overturn powerful cultural forces in an era when

personal liberation was keynote. To do that it had to challenge the immense power of the tobacco industry, which tried at every stage to refute the medical condemnation of smoking, and it had to persuade state and federal authorities to take some positive action.

Banning cigarette smoking outright was not contemplated. Progress would have to be made step by step. In 1964 a National Clearinghouse for Smoking and Health was formed to unite many agencies that were campaigning against smoking in colleges and the community. That year the American Medical Association declared for the first time that smoking was a health hazard, and the State Mutual Life Assurance Company became the first to offer lower rates for nonsmokers.

Americans did not suddenly stop smoking, but the habit that had been so deeply ingrained was undermined. By January 1, 1966, all cigarette packs carried a warning. The tar and nicotine yields of cigarettes were published by

the Federal Trade Commission from 1967. To counter such a negative image the tobacco companies emphasized low-tar tobaccos and filters—supposedly "safer" cigarettes. Smokers were quick to grab this mythical lifeline. Whereas a generation earlier filter cigarettes had been a rarity, by the end of the 1960s they accounted for two-thirds of consumption.

△ Daniel Horn of the National Clearinghouse for Smoking and Health displays the labels mandatory from 1966: "Cigarette smoking may be hazardous to your health."

Although there was a drop in the sale of cigarettes immediately following the publication of the Surgeon General's report, it proved temporary. Against a figure of 516 billion cigarettes bought in 1963, the figure for 1964 was 505 billion. But in 1965 it rose again to 521 billion and continued to climb until 1968, peaking at 540 billion. It then began falling, but there was a worrying increase in teenage smoking just as consumption overall began to reflect greater acceptance of the hazards. Overall, the proportion of adult smokers fell from about 41 percent to 37 percent by 1970.

The campaign heats up

By the late 1960s the antismoking lobby was well organized. All cigarette advertising on radio and television was banned in 1970, and the warnings on packs made stronger. The campaign gained momentum across the following decade. In the 1980s it really began to bite when the hidden dangers of passive smoking were recognized, and smoking bans became widespread on airlines and in public places. Cancer victims even started to file—and win—lawsuits against tobacco firms.

In retrospect the 1964 public health campaign against smoking was one of the most successful in history. □

Public awareness of the dangers

The fact that the Surgeon General's report was received as a bombshell in the U.S. did not by any means indicate that nobody had warned people before. As far back as 1954 the American Cancer Society (ACS) had issued a resolution warning the public against smoking. And in 1958 the ACS began a campaign to try to persuade teenagers not to take up smoking.

At this stage the main purpose of the ACS campaigns was not to get the government to take steps such as the banning of cigarette advertising on TV or putting warnings on packs. They were aimed at getting the health hazards of smoking across to the public. In that they were largely successful.

As early as 1957 a Gallup poll asked a sample of Americans: "Did you happen to hear or read about the recent report of the ACS reporting the results of a study on the effects of cigarette smoking?" More than three-quarters of people questioned said they did know about the report. In 1964 when another sample was asked if they had been told about the hazards of smoking, more than 76 percent said they were aware of the ACS antismoking publicity. In 1957 Gallup asked a sample of people if they thought smoking cigarettes caused lung cancer. Half said they did.

It is now generally agreed that the great significance of the 1964 Surgeon General's report was that it began a process whereby Americans started to believe not only that smoking was harmful, but that it was "antisocial," which made forcible controls on advertising acceptable to an ever-growing section of the population. However, except for the year in which it was published, numbers of smokers continued to rise throughout the decade.

See Also: Advertising Industry; Health and Healthcare

ANTIWAR MOVEMENT

In its early stages the U.S. involvement in Vietnam provoked little controversy, but from 1965 the escalation of the war was matched by mounting protests from Americans who opposed the war.

In April 1965 the student civil rights organization Students for a Democratic Society, under Tom Hayden, mobilized a 25,000-strong national march on Washington, D.C. The purpose of the march was to protest against the growing U.S involvement in the Vietnam conflict. What impact the march had was largely negative. In January 1965 a Harris poll had shown that 59 percent of Americans were cool toward the Johnson administration's policy in Vietnam. By the summer, in contrast, a solid two-thirds majority backed the administration.

There were a number of reasons for students taking a stand against the Vietnam War. One was that the young men who actually had to go and fight the war had good cause to question its purpose. Many were simply not convinced that a small civil war 8,000

miles away posed a threat to America or any major national interests. Right from the beginning, many of those in line for military service in Vietnam found ways to avoid it. Even many parents who supported the war in principle helped their sons avoid the draft.

From civil rights to Vietnam

On campus the civil rights movement had instilled in many students the idea that it was their duty to take a stand against injustice. It had also familiarized them with the effectiveness of protest. With the passage of the Voting Rights Act in August 1965 the civil rights protesters felt they had won the first round in the civil rights struggle. This left a large number of activists with a wealth of organizational ability and the feeling that with right on their side they could prevail against any opposition. Believing the U.S. involvement in Vietnam to be morally wrong, they focused their considerable energies on bringing it to a halt.

Many of the civil right leaders were committed pacifists. Martin Luther King, Jr., spoke out against the war, bringing to bear his enormous moral authority. The war itself was racially divisive. African Americans did not find it as easy as middle-class white youths to evade the draft. Indeed, President Johnson introduced a policy that drafted African Americans preferentially. He did this not for racist reasons, but because he felt that by putting black men in the armed services, he could provide them with improved health care and education, and promote their social advancement.

Many African Americans accepted this to start with. They saw fighting in the war as a chance to prove their worth to the country. Others thought that the war in Vietnam had nothing to do with them. The real enemy was back home. Al Harrison, civil rights organizer at Detroit's Wayne State University, said: "We got no business fighting a yellow man's war to save the white man."

▽ A bank of cameras greets veterans marching against the war at Washington's Lafayette Square on May 30, 1967.

African Americans seemed to be bearing a disproportionate burden of the war. While in 1965 eight percent of the military in Vietnam were black, African Americans made up some 23 percent of the enlisted soldiers killed in action. The growing feeling that African Americans were being unfairly sacrificed in a foreign war added to the list of grievances already exposed by the civil rights struggle. It was only after the beginning of the Vietnam War that rioting began to afflict the black ghettos of northern cities and the West Coast.

Antiwar activists tried to halt troop trains. In June 1965 protesters held up the 173d Airborne Brigade, which was en route to Saigon. Later that summer the Vietnam Day Committee, formed on the campus of the University of California at Berkeley that spring, organized further attempts to stop trains. They were unsuccessful. Only a handful of hard-core radicals were prepared to stand in front of a train full of armed troops. Most protesters would only picket local induction centers or march in demonstrations.

The March on Washington
On November 27, 1965, some 30,000 demonstrators came out on the streets in Washington, D.C. The protest was organized by SANE, the Committee for

a Sane Nuclear Policy. SANE's most famous member was child-care expert Dr. Benjamin Spock, whose presence was a significant boost to the antiwar movement's respectability in the public's eyes and attracted many other older liberals. More radical protesters who carried banners calling for the immediate withdrawal of U.S. troops from Vietnam were persuaded to keep a

△ One of the most popular of the antiwar slogans displayed outside the entrance to the Pentagon during the massive demonstration on October 21, 1967, when 50,000 protested.

low profile for the occasion. The march's leaders made speeches calling for an immediate end to the American troop buildup and condemning both sides for not making any serious effort to reach a negotiated settlement.

As they marched around the White House, their moderate banners called for a "Supervised Ceasefire" and claimed that "War Erodes the Great Society." President Johnson issued a statement the next day saying: "Dissent is a sign of political vigor." The vigor came, however, not so much from the liberals who protested outside the White House as from radicals across the country who had already adopted a new and dramatic form of protest.

Draft-card burning
In mid-October 1965 David Millar, a 22-year-old Jesuit charity worker in a Bowery soup kitchen, held up his draft card at an antiwar rally in New York City. "I believe the napalming of villages is an immoral act," he declared,

The ultimate protest

On April 21, 1965, a Buddhist monk publicly burned himself to death in Saigon in protest against the war. Television pictures of the ritual suicide were relayed around the world. Other monks and a young girl followed suit.

This potent form of protest was brought horrifyingly home to America on November 2, 1965, when Norman Morrison, a 31-year-old Quaker and father of three, burned himself to death outside the Pentagon. He was holding his three-year-old daughter when his clothes caught fire, but dropped her just in time. She was rescued unharmed by a passerby. A week later, on November 9, Roger Allen LaPorte of the Catholic Workers movement burned himself to death outside the United Nations building in New York.

The impact of these tragic events was enormous. Ninety-three percent of American homes had a TV and Americans could witness these self-immolations in their own living rooms. Fortunately, these public suicides did not start a trend. Mass protests, sit-ins, and, ultimately, full-scale riots proved to be more effective tactics in getting across the antiwar message.

holding a match to the corner of the card. "I hope this is a significant act—so here goes." He lit it and, at the end of October, became the first American to be arraigned under a new law that made draft-card burning a federal offense with maximum penalty of five years in jail and a $10,000 fine. Millar's hope was certainly fulfilled. His protest was without doubt a significant act. Draft-card burning became a regular feature of antiwar demonstrations and the nightly news. The cameras would also capture infuriated onlookers attacking the protesters or dousing the flames with water or fire extinguishers.

A fractured society

Clashes between antiwar demonstrators and their detractors became the norm. The leading ranks of a New York march were drenched with red paint. In Chicago and Oakland demonstrators were pelted with eggs. In Detroit marchers chanting "Hey, hey, LBJ! How many kids did you kill today?" were drowned out by prowar protesters singing "The Star Spangled Banner." When leading pacifist David Dellinger visited communist North Vietnam in 1966, he was denounced as a traitor.

Despite the opposition of a great many ordinary people, the protests continued. In New York and Chicago students seized university buildings. At New York University 130 students and members of the faculty walked out when Defense Secretary Robert McNamara turned up to collect an honorary degree.

By 1967 opposition to the war split American society. The antiwar movement now embraced a broad coalition. Antiwar intellectuals, notably Dr. Spock, the novelist Norman Mailer, and the world-famous linguistics professor Noam Chomsky, addressed "teach-ins" at colleges organized by Students for a Democratic Society. In 1967 they began to appear on televi-

△ Guards cordon off the Pentagon during the big demonstration on October 21, 1967. The confrontation ended in violence.

sion. Even on Johnny Carson's *Tonight Show*, guests openly expressed antiwar sentiments, though Carson kept his views to himself.

On the weekend of April 15–16, 1967, 125,000 antiwar demonstrators gathered in New York, with another 5,000 in San Francisco as part of the "Spring Mobilization to End the War in Vietnam." In Central Park protesters in bizarre costumes carried placards that said: "Draft beer, not boys," "I don't give a damn for Uncle Sam," and "No Viet Cong ever called me Nigger." Dr. King delivered a statement to the United Nations, accusing the U.S. of violating its charter. However, protesters outside the UN building still

The protest goes global

Protest against the Vietnam War spread around the world. Antiwar feeling ran particularly high in Britain. On July 4, 1965, a demonstration was held in London's Trafalgar Square. That night a homemade bomb exploded against the back door of the American Express offices in the Haymarket, less than half a mile away. In October two days of protest in London led to a march on the U.S. Embassy in Grosvenor Square, where 78 demonstrators were arrested. In 1968 the square was the scene of a full-scale riot. Three years earlier, in May 1965, 50 demonstrators were arrested in Sydney, Australia, just days after Australia had increased its contingent fighting in Vietnam to 1,300.

Whenever President Johnson traveled abroad, he was met with protest. There were more protests in Berlin, Paris, and Tokyo. When Johnson visited Australia in December 1967, the authorities were barely able to guarantee his safety. On one occasion his car was splashed with green paint. Violent antiwar demonstrations broke out when South Vietnam's President Ky visited Australia and New Zealand—which also sent troops to Vietnam—in January 1967. In Sweden the War Crimes Tribunal, backed financially by British philosopher Bertrand Russell, condemned the U.S. for war crimes.

Defense Secretary McNamara himself warned of the damage the war was doing to America's image abroad. In his resignation letter he wrote: "The picture of the world's greatest superpower killing or seriously injuring 1,000 noncombatants a week, while trying to pound a tiny backward nation into submission on an issue whose merits are hotly disputed is not a pretty one." It could have come straight from an antiwar leaflet.

had to be protected from prowar demonstrators by mounted policemen.

On October 21, 1967, some 50,000 demonstrators marched on the Pentagon. In a televised showdown they faced 10,000 U.S. Army troops and National Guardsmen drawn up to defend the building. The soldiers had rifles though no ammunition, but they were authorized to break up the demonstration by force if necessary. The confrontation was peaceful at first. Demonstrators came up to the soldiers and poked flowers down the barrels of their guns. Another group attempted to mystically levitate the building.

Violent confrontation

Eventually the demonstration was broken up with considerable brutality. Norman Mailer, who immortalized the event in *The Armies of the Night*, was

The view from Hanoi

It became apparent by the late 1960s that the North Vietnamese viewed the antiwar demonstrations in the streets of America and the relentless coverage of the war on U.S. television as part of their overall strategy to win the war.

One of the first men in Washington to realize this was Secretary of Defense Robert McNamara. A graduate of the Harvard Business School, he was a pragmatist and in 1967 instigated a detailed analysis of enemy engagements by the Defense Department's Systems Analysis Office.

The report stated that the North Vietnamese and their Viet Cong allies in the south "started the shooting in over 90 percent of company-sized firefights," and that "over 80 percent began with a well-organized enemy attack." It continued: "Since their losses rise—as in the first quarter of 1967—and fall—as they have done since—with their choice of whether to fight or not, they can probably hold their losses to about 2,000 a week regardless of our force level. If their strategy is to wait us out, they will control their losses to a level low enough to be sustained indefinitely, but high enough to tempt us to increase our forces to the point of U.S. public rejection."

Given the growing protests on the street, McNamara concluded the North Vietnamese strategy was working, and withdrawal was inevitable.

△ Burning a draft card, in Washington, D.C., in June 1968. This symbolic act could result in a heavy fine and imprisonment.

Why are we in Vietnam?

The novelist Norman Mailer had inherited the macho mantle of Ernest Hemingway. But instead of celebrating war, he became deeply pessimistic about it. In 1967 he published the novel *Why Are We in Vietnam?* Strangely, it is not set in Vietnam at all. The action takes place on a hunting trip in Alaska. However, the book explores men's quest to prove their masculinity and the relish that human beings take in killing—issues that seemed to be possessing America as a nation in its attitude to the war at the time.

In *The Armies of the Night*, published in 1968, Mailer took a more direct approach. The first half of the book records his firsthand experiences during the antiwar demonstration in Washington, D.C., in October 1967. The second half gives a detailed history of the origins and organization of the demonstration. Although this book could be dismissed as a piece of supercharged journalism, Mailer lent his intellectual authority to the fight against the war in the most public way he knew. But he was preaching to the converted. Mailer's influence extended only to the students and intellectuals who were already opposed to America's intervention in Vietnam. Support for the war came from blue-collar workers and Middle America, who neither read nor cared about the musings of Norman Mailer.

arrested (*see box*). Sporadic rioting continued for two days. TV viewers saw coverage of the 82d Airborne's action on the Potomac interspersed with the 1st Air Cavalry's action in Vietnam on the nightly news. Coverage of such demonstrations and the rioting in black ghettos of northern cities began to give the impression that America was becoming ungovernable. And the mounting losses after two years of hard fighting gave the impression that the war was unwinnable.

Although most people still condemned the antiwar protesters, the demonstrations began to have a political effect. Chairman of the Senate Foreign Relations Committee William Fulbright, Senator Robert Kennedy, and Senator Eugene McCarthy began to express their doubts about the war. President Johnson held firm, but Robert McNamara, who had been the chief architect of the war, began to turn against it. The commander on the ground in Vietnam, General William Westmoreland, said the war could not be won without a massive escalation, which would involve an extension of the already unpopular draft. With rioting on the streets, it seemed plain that this was an escalation that the country would not bear.

The Tet Offensive

There was a dramatic erosion in support for the war in the aftermath of the Tet Offensive in January 1968. During

Vietnam Veterans Against the War

One of the most powerful propaganda weapons the antiwar movement had was the group Vietnam Veterans Against the War. These men could hardly be accused of being cowards or communists—accusations regularly hurled at student protesters. They had served their country, been to Vietnam, and decided the war there was wrong.

They turned up to demonstrations in uniform, though they often threw away their medals. The injured—amputees and men in wheelchairs—added a powerful wordless protest to student chanting. They even defied a Supreme Court ban on demonstrating in Washington, D.C., with impunity.

On December 28, 1971, 16 Vietnam veterans occupied the Statue of Liberty, hung the Stars and Stripes upside down out of the observation platform, and sent an open letter to President Nixon, saying: "We can no longer tolerate the war in Southeast Asia regardless of the color of its dead or the method of its implementation."

◁ A protester wears antiradiation clothing at a student demonstration against both the war and nuclear weapons in November 1968.

Tet the communists moved into every major city in Vietnam, and TV viewers had to watch America's humiliation as the U.S. Embassy in Saigon was captured and held for six hours by 19 Viet Cong. It was a suicide mission, but nevertheless it showed the American people that after nearly three years of war, no progress had been made. People were particularly appalled when a Viet Cong suspect had his brains blown out on TV in a summary execution.

Tet convinced CBS anchorman Walter Cronkite—described as the most trusted man in America—that the war was hopeless (*see box p. 56*). When he said so on the nightly news, President Johnson said: "If I've lost Walter, I've lost Mr. Average Citizen."

He stopped the bombing of North Vietnam, authorized peace talks in Paris, and announced that he would not run again for the presidency.

Senator Eugene McCarthy, a virtual unknown running as a peace candidate, had already taken 42 percent of the poll in the New Hampshire primary. Four days later Senator Kennedy entered the Democratic race, also on an antiwar ticket. He was shot down in June 1968 before he could secure it.

Anchorman jumps ship

Walter Cronkite was a near-legendary figure in the United States during the 1960s, having become by far television's most famous anchorman. According to one politician, Cronkite could change the way thousands of Americans voted "by a mere inflection of his deep baritone voice, or by a lifting of his well-known bushy eyebrows."

From 1965 to 1968 Cronkite was evenhanded in his coverage of the Vietnam War; but when news of the Viet Cong's assault on the U.S. Embassy in Saigon on January 31 reached New York just before the evening news, Cronkite was outraged. "What the hell's going on?" he exploded. "I thought we were winning this war!"

Cronkite headed to Vietnam to see for himself. On February 27, 1968, he made a rare personal report on CBS, saying that it was now "more certain than ever that the bloody experience of Vietnam is to end in stalemate." He saw just one way out—negotiations with Hanoi.

Cronkite was reflecting public opinion rather than leading it. A week earlier, on February 20, the Senate Foreign Relations Committee had begun televised hearings that were openly critical of the war. Two days later the U.S. military authorities in Vietnam released the weekly total of American combat deaths—543, the highest ever. Public opinion would no longer tolerate that rate of loss after years of official propaganda that made out the enemy to be an ill-equipped peasant army, hanging on by its fingertips against the technologically superior U.S. forces.

The Democratic Party convention in Chicago in August 1968 turned into a full-scale riot with running battles between antiwar protesters and the police. Eyewitnesses claimed that it was the police who were responsible for instigating the violence, and the police behavior was denounced from the convention floor as "Gestapo tactics."

Hubert Humphrey, as expected, won the Democratic nomination to run against Republican Richard M. Nixon. As Johnson's vice president, however, Humphrey was tainted with his prowar policy. While postelection analysis showed that he was steadily gaining support in the final days of the campaign, the November election result was a victory for Nixon, who promised peace with honor.

It soon became clear, however, that rather than ending the war, Nixon was expanding it. In September 1969 a

▽ **A demonstration at Howard University on October 15, 1969. The civil rights movement provided many antiwar activists.**

former McCarthy campaign worker, Sam Brown, began the Vietnam Moratorium Committee to show that antiwar protest was not confined to students. The committee declared October 15, 1969, as National Moratorium Day, when 250,000 took to the streets of Washington, D.C. In November another 500,000 demonstrated in response to the committee's call.

The moratorium demonstrations had a great effect on Daniel Ellsberg, one of a group of defense analysts who had produced a massive report on the conduct of the war that became known as the *Pentagon Papers*. In June 1971 Ellsberg began leaking its contents to the *New York Times* (*see box*).

The protests began to take a more violent turn as the SDS grew increasingly militant. By 1969 it had split into

△ **The Confederate flag suggests mixed sentiments at an antiwar demonstration at Washington's Dupont Circle, November 1969.**

The Pentagon Papers

Although the publication of the *Pentagon Papers* and their effect on the war effort took place in the 1970s, the report was written in the 1960s. In June 1967, at the behest of Secretary of Defense Robert McNamara, 36 defense analysts began reviewing America's policy in Vietnam, beginning as far back as 1954. The resulting report took 18 months to compile. Called *The History of Decision Making Process on Vietnam*, it ran to 47 volumes, 7,100 pages in all, cataloging systematic government deception, cynicism, and incompetence in the handling of the war. Only 15 copies were printed. There were rumors that McNamara planned to leak the report to his friend Robert Kennedy to help him in his bid for the presidency.

Daniel Ellsberg, one of the analysts, had been a keen supporter of McNamara and U.S. involvement in Vietnam. But he was disillusioned by what he learned compiling the report. After the National Moratorium on October 15, 1969, he began secretly photocopying the study and passing pages to Senator William Fulbright, chairman of the Senate Foreign Relations Committee and a prominent critic of the war.

Ellsberg later sent copies to the *New York Times*, which began publication on June 13, 1971. President Nixon slapped an injunction on the *Times*, but then the *Washington Post* began printing more extracts. When the *Post* in turn was silenced by an injunction, other newspapers in Chicago, Los Angeles, St. Louis, and Boston took up the challenge. On June 30 the Supreme Court quashed the injunctions and strongly condemned the president's attempt to gag the press.

Meanwhile Ellsberg and another colleague Anthony J. Russo were indicted for theft. The charges were dropped in May 1973 after it was revealed that Nixon had authorized the burglary of the offices of Ellsberg's psychiatrist in an attempt to find evidence to smear him. The burglary was carried out by members of the White House staff, the so-called "plumbers."

several factions, the most notorious of which was the Weather Underground which began planting bombs. Over 5,000 bombs went off in all.

In May 1970 a protest against U.S. incursion into Vietnam's neighbor Cambodia at Kent State University ended in bloodshed when the Ohio National Guard opened fire on the protesters, leaving four dead. The killings shocked America. Although Nixon dismissed the protesters as bums, he was forced to withdraw American troops from Cambodia, and funding for the war was cut by Congress.

Ending the war

Protests continued. In May 1971 12,000 demonstrators were arrested in Washington, D.C. In November that year there were large-scale antiwar rallies in 16 cities. Opinion polls now revealed massive disillusionment with the war. A Gallup poll in April 1971 showed that 73 percent wanted U.S. troops out by the end of the year. Nixon concluded a negotiated settlement to the Vietnam War, which was signed in Paris in January 1973. □

See Also: Baby-boom Generation; Chicago Convention Riot; Counterculture; Johnson; Kennedy, R.; Mailer; McCarthy; McNamara; March on the Pentagon; Sit-ins; Students for a Democratic Society; Vietnam War

APARTHEID

One of the great international causes of the 1960s was a mounting revulsion against South Africa's policy of racial oppression—a sensitive issue for successive U.S. administrations.

In the decade that followed the election to power of the white National Party in 1948 a series of legislative enactments put in place in South Africa a rigid legal code of racial segregation known as apartheid (Afrikaans for "separateness"). Racial separation was more strictly enforced there than it had been even in the old days of the American South. Every citizen was classified in law as white, colored (of mixed descent), or black. Mixed marriages were banned; education was segregated; blacks were denied the vote. The Group

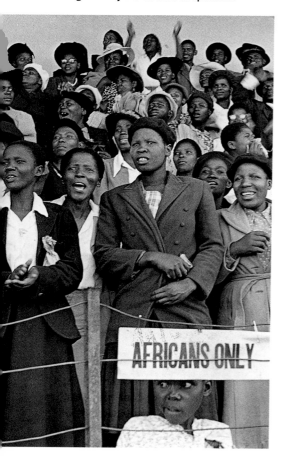

▽ **A soccer game, like virtually every aspect of public and private life in South Africa, was regulated by the dictates of apartheid.**

Areas Act laid down rules for strict segregation in property ownership, residential areas, employment, and trade. Most demeaning of all were the so-called "pass laws"—first introduced in the 18th century, but tightened up in the 1950s—which required blacks to carry identity cards at all times.

International pressure

Since blacks made up about 80 percent of the population, apartheid could be enforced only by turning South Africa into a police state. International hostility to the National Party's policy mounted with such intensity that in 1961 South Africa was compelled to withdraw from the Commonwealth of Nations (as the British Commonwealth had been renamed). In 1962 the United Nations General Assembly voted for economic sanctions against South Africa.

Although the campaign to apply economic sanctions against South Africa did not receive official American support in the 1960s, the White House openly condemned apartheid. In an age when major civil rights legislation was being enacted at home it could hardly do otherwise. Cold War considerations also came into play. Although South Africa was an important strategic ally of the West, the United States and its partners were frightened of driving the newly independent black nations of Africa into the Soviet camp.

The issue was highlighted in the early 1960s by the campaign to free South West Africa from the control of South Africa, mandated to rule it since 1920. The United States voted with the majority in the UN General Assembly to end the mandate in 1968 and to recognize SWA as the independent state of Namibia. South Africa, however, refused to withdraw its administrators, and the United States, like other leading

countries of the West, failed to insist that the UN resolutions be enforced.

The tepid U.S. opposition to apartheid was perhaps partly the result of a wish to keep the issue out of American politics. That was the view of leading black activist Malcolm X, who believed that the African American had been "brainwashed from ever seeing or thinking of himself as he should, as a part of the non-white peoples of the world." It followed, he argued, that "the first thing the American power structure doesn't want any Negroes to start is thinking internationally."

Large antiapartheid demonstrations of the kind that took place in Britain were not seen in the United States. Black civil rights leaders themselves directed little attention to apartheid. George Jackson, writing from Soledad prison to his lawyer in 1970, made passing, witty reference to the "Union of South Africa (U.S.A.!!)," but the issue received no mention in the autobiographies of Angela Davis, Huey Newton, and Malcolm X; nor did it find a place in the writings and speeches of Eldridge Cleaver. Black activists in the United States were far more interested in, and had more to learn from, places like Algeria, where insurrection had brought an end to the long rule of white European settlers.

Mandela and the ANC

The most effective organization struggling to liberate black South Africans from white rule and the long nightmare of apartheid was the African National Congress. Under the direction of Nelson Mandela and after his imprisonment for life in 1964 the ANC was happy for the United States to keep its distance from its affairs. Most ANC leaders were Marxist-Leninist in outlook, and the nationalist movement in

Massacre at Sharpeville

Early in 1960 the leaders of the Pan-African Congress called for a mass campaign of civil disobedience against South Africa's pass laws. Blacks were asked to report to police stations without their identity cards and request to be arrested. The object was to render the laws unenforcable. On the first day of the campaign, March 21, at the black township of Sharpeville in the Transvaal, protesters were disappointed when the police arrested only a few of their leaders. A crowd of 15,000 gathered around the station and, in their anger, began to hurl stones at police officers. The police opened fire, killing 56 people and injuring another 156. A similar confrontation cost seven lives at the Langa township outside Cape Town.

The United States joined the rest of the world in denouncing the South African police. Impervious to outside opinion, the South African government declared a state of emergency, called out the troops, and banned both the Pan-African Congress and the more militant African National Congress. Opposition to the ruling National Party was driven underground. Acts of sabotage followed—a favorite was blowing up electric-power towers—and the government response was the so-called Sabotage Act of 1962, which gave the police powers to place suspected subversives under house arrest without trial. Under the provisions of the Sabotage Act Nelson Mandela, whose very name became a symbol of the liberation struggle in South Africa, was sentenced in 1964 to life imprisonment on Robben Island.

△ The immediate aftermath of the Sharpeville Massacre in March 1960, in which 56 black South Africans were slain by the police. World opinion was outraged by the slaughter.

States had mounted a diplomatic offensive throughout Africa, and the State Department had established a new position of Deputy-Assistant Secretary for African Affairs. The United States had also established air bases in Morocco, Libya, and Liberia.

America's own unhappy history of race relations, moreover, hardly endeared it to black Africans. "The peoples of resurgent Africa," Mandela said in an address delivered in 1958, "are perfectly capable of deciding upon their own future form of government and discovering and themselves dealing with any dangers which may arise. They do not require any schooling from the U.S.A., which—to judge from events such as the Little Rock outrage and the activities of the Un-American Witch-hunting Committee [a reference to McCarthyism and the activities of the House Un-American Activities Committee]—should learn to put its own house in order before trying to teach everyone else." □

South Africa was assured of material support from the Soviet Union and other communist countries. Moreover, there were African armies prepared to provide military instructors in the techniques of guerrilla warfare. They in turn were supplemented by instructors from Eastern Europe, Cuba, and China to whom training bases were made available by South Africa's near neighbors, Tanzania and Zambia.

Before his imprisonment Mandela never ceased to remind his audiences that however much American propagandists might try to turn black Africans against communism and the Soviet Union, the idea of a communist bogeyman was an American creation designed to distract Africans' attention away from the real enemy, which was American economic imperialism. To this end, Mandela argued, the United

See Also: Cold War; Decolonization; Malcolm X; United Nations

APOLLO PROGRAM

President Kennedy's bold pledge in 1961 to put Americans on the moon by the end of the decade resulted in one of the greatest—and most expensive—technological feats ever achieved.

The most ambitious venture undertaken by the U.S. space program in the 1960s was the Apollo moon landing. The earlier space programs—Gemini and Mercury—had more limited goals, but they provided the necessary experience and expertise for the Apollo program.

As early as the 1920s scientists, fascinated by the developing rocket technology, had speculated on trips to the moon. The dream neared reality in the late 1950s when the National Aeronautics and Space Administration (NASA) proposed sending a manned spacecraft not to land on the moon but to orbit it before returning to Earth.

Soviets lead the way

That was the beginning of Apollo. President Eisenhower, however, was not an enthusiast for the space program. He concluded that a moonshot would have neither sufficient military nor scientific value to warrant the vast costs involved. Eisenhower publicly played down the rivalry with the Soviet Union over the launching of satellites. Referring to the Soviet Sputnik, the first satellite to orbit Earth in 1957, he drily remarked: "The Russians have only put one small ball in the air." Late in 1960 NASA's Apollo program was turned down.

The situation changed with the arrival of John F. Kennedy in the White House in 1961. Kennedy himself knew little about the huge aerospace industry that had grown up in America (and about which Eisenhower had expressed his unease). But Vice President Lyndon B. Johnson was a space enthusiast, and he claimed to have been deeply shocked

◁ **The Apollo program built on the success of its Gemini predecessor. Here, the first manned Gemini flight, Gemini 3, blasts off from Cape Canaveral on March 23, 1963.**

◁ An Apollo spacecraft verification vehicle is hoisted up to be mated to a Saturn rocket for testing, at Cape Kennedy in November 1965.

lenge is one that we are willing to accept, one we are unwilling to postpone, and one we intend to win." He could not have made it plainer that he was launching a space race with the Soviet Union, and that beating the Soviets to the moon was a matter of national prestige.

Though the political decision to back Apollo was thrilling for all those involved in the space program, it nevertheless left them with enormous challenges. At the time there was no rocket powerful enough to launch a spacecraft to the moon, and the whole of the Apollo enterprise would have to be on a much larger scale than existing space programs. As it turned out, the moonshot would require four new sites covering thousands of acres for the building of the rockets and shuttles as well as the testing equipment. All that infrastructure would have to be in place before the first launches. And there was precious little time to fulfill Kennedy's bold pledge to land men on the moon before the decade was out.

Base-building

Armed with what amounted to a blank check to get the moonshot underway, NASA set to work with a will. The rocket that would take astronauts to the moon would be much larger than any other and would have to be assembled away from the launchpad. Huge component parts would have to be moved from one site to another. Everything would be on a colossal scale.

NASA chose for the site of its "moonport" 125 square miles of land at Merritt Island, north of the existing rocket base of Cape Canaveral. Here NASA built the Vehicle Assembly Building, the largest structure of its kind in the world, with 130 million cubic feet of space—large enough to accommodate four moon rockets.

All of NASA's Apollo sites were in Texas or the Deep South, economically depressed regions that Kennedy wanted

by seeing among the stars of his Texas night sky the glinting of Sputnik.

Events conspired to push Kennedy toward a phenomenal commitment. On April 12, 1961, less than three months into Kennedy's presidency, the Soviets sent into orbit the first ever astronaut (the Soviet term was cosmonaut), Yuri Gagarin. Feverishly Kennedy consulted scientific advisors on the feasibility of the U.S. outdoing the Soviets in space. It had to be something spectacular, and he did not care about the cost. Within a few weeks the Eisenhower policy on Apollo was not only overturned—the project was given an even more ambitious goal than the original plan of orbiting the moon with a manned spacecraft.

On May 25, 1961, toward the end of a speech to Congress about "urgent national needs," Kennedy turned to his new theme: "Now is the time to take longer strides—time for a great new American enterprise—which in many ways may hold the key to our future on Earth... I believe that this nation should commit itself to achieving the goal, before the decade is out, of landing a man on the moon and returning him safely to Earth.... I believe we should go to the moon."

Space race

The following year in Houston, in the wake of the Cuban Missile Crisis of October 1962, Kennedy told a large audience that he had shifted the space program from "low to high gear" because that goal would serve to organize and measure the "best of our energies and skills, because that chal-

A

◁ A Saturn I rocket being prepared to launch a boilerplate (model) Apollo spacecraft into orbit in 1964. The purpose was to test the compatibility in flight of the two components.

The Mercury program had been based at NASA's Langley Research Center in Norfolk, Virginia, but Apollo required more space than could be found there to set up its organizational heart, the Manned Spacecraft Center. Humble Oil donated a site in Texas just outside Houston.

The new Apollo sites took time to become operational. In the meantime, existing space programs went ahead. In February 1962 Mercury astronaut John Glenn became the first American to orbit Earth, a great boost for NASA and an achievement that turned Glenn into an international star. The far greater technical problems of how to send a manned spacecraft to the moon, however, were nowhere near solved.

Rocket power

Back in the 1950s von Braun had assumed that a trip to the moon would require a much more powerful rocket than the biggest then in existence, the mighty Saturn developed by the military to carry nuclear warheads. On the drawing board was the even more powerful Nova; but when Kennedy gave the Apollo program the go-ahead, he allowed too little time for Nova's development. Von Braun therefore had to look for a way of building a super-Saturn rocket, Saturn V.

After much argument the Apollo program scientists decided that the best way of landing a man on the moon would be to launch a spacecraft with a three-stage Saturn rocket. Once it reached the moon's gravitational field, the spacecraft itself would go into orbit. A lunar module with its own rocket power would take the astronauts to the moon's surface and then back up to rendezvous with the spacecraft for the homeward journey.

The Saturn V rocket would have to lift an immense weight to escape Earth's gravity. Engine-testing and unmanned test flights began. Rehearsals for space

to support, and that had strong Democratic interests. The place chosen for the construction of the first stages of the project was an abandoned and rat-infested site near New Orleans called Michoud. It was named after a junk dealer who had owned it before the U.S. government took it over to build Liberty ships during World War II. The site was semiderelict, but it was readily available and had a roof of 1.8 million square feet, or enough to cover 1,000 suburban homes. And it was on the Mississippi, which meant that the huge

rocket parts could be moved from one site to another along the river.

Thirty-five miles from Michoud the eminent German rocket scientist Wernher von Braun found a site on the Pearl River for engine testing. It had to be remote because the noise of rocket testing was earsplitting, and what was called the Mississippi Test Facility was inhabited only by venomous snakes, mosquitoes, and a herd of wild hogs. A 400-foot-high test stand was built on new foundations, on pilings 100 feet long driven into Mississippi mud.

rendezvous techniques were carried out through the Gemini program, in which astronauts practiced leaving a spacecraft in the weightless conditions of space.

Political pressures

President Kennedy's commitment to the space program was already costing $1.2 billion in 1962, and a year later questions were being asked in Congress about its cost. Half-a-billion was cut from NASA's budget in 1963, and it looked as if the country might be having second thoughts about the wisdom of the president's enthusiasm for a moon landing.

The world had come to the brink of nuclear war at the time of the Cuban Missile Crisis in October 1962, but with that acute danger behind them Kennedy and Soviet Premier Nikita Khrushchev seemed to have come to a better understanding. It had been suggested at one point that the U.S. and the Soviet Union might cooperate in space as a mutual gesture of peaceful intentions. At the time Khrushchev had turned down the idea; but if the Cold War really began to thaw, perhaps it would resurface. Under less fraught circumstances perhaps Kennedy would not be so determined to press ahead with the space race.

The assassination of Kennedy in November 1963 put an abrupt end to any such speculation. His successor, Lyndon Johnson, was not only an enthusiast for space himself, but he was also determined that U.S. victory in the space race would be an epitaph for the slain president. By the mid-1960s the space program, the biggest part of which was Apollo, was costing $5.2 billion annually.

Superscale construction

Astronauts continued to train for the Apollo project, making excursions into space as part of the Gemini program so often that they became commonplace. Meanwhile the component parts of the

▷ Lunar Module 1 being prepared for the unmanned Apollo 5 mission in November 1967, which proved the module's viability.

constantly evolving Saturn rockets, the spacecraft, and the lunar module were taking shape. At the Vehicle Assembly Building stage one of Saturn V was in preparation. It would be moved out of the VAB on a huge platform through a doorway as high as a 45-story building.

Other components were being constructed at Michoud and by North American Aviation and Douglas Aircraft at Seal Beach and Huntington Beach, south of Los Angeles. All had to be transported to the Mississippi test facility. Douglas called on the 1950s luxury airliner the Stratocruiser, which was enlarged to provide a bulky hold to carry the rocket parts.

From Seal Beach stage-two Saturn components were hauled to a naval harbor and taken down the Pacific coast and through the Panama Canal up to the test facility, where engines

were tested and fired in the wild, alligator-infested landscape.

While work continued on Saturn V, the existing Saturn IB was suitable for Earth-orbiting missions, and by the beginning of 1967 everything was ready for the first launch of a manned Apollo spacecraft. The three astronauts selected were Gus Grissom, who had experience in both Gemini and Mercury, Ed White, who had completed a Gemini space walk, and a relative newcomer, Roger Chaffee. Everything was thoroughly tested before the launch was attempted.

Tragedy and triumph

To survive in the spacecraft the astronauts had to have a supply of oxygen, a relatively harmless gas in the weightless conditions in space but highly flammable at ground level. On January 27,

The tragedy of Apollo 1

The first Apollo astronauts scheduled to venture into space were Roger Chaffee, Gus Grissom, and Ed White. In January 1967 they were going through an extensive program of training on the ground in preparation for a launch the following month on February 21. At that time it looked as though the moon landing might be achieved by 1968, since unmanned flights carrying a full payload had been successful.

In the early evening of January 27 the three astronauts were lying on their backs in the spacecraft, watched by ground controllers on closed-circuit television. First Chaffee raised the alarm, and then White called: "Fire in the cockpit!" Ground control watched in horror as flames and then dense black smoke engulfed the cockpit of the spacecraft, and a ball of fire exploded through the side of the ship. Chaffee's last words were: "There's a bad fire, get us out of here!"

The spacecraft was 218 feet up on a launchpad at the Kennedy Space Center, and the explosion blew rescuers against the wall. It took five and a half minutes to reach the astronauts, by which time all three were dead, suffocated before the flames got to them.

Had the spacecraft had a quick-release escape hatch, the astronauts might have been saved. But escape hatches had been removed from spacecraft design because back in 1961 Grissom had accidentally blown his safety hatch open when he landed in the Atlantic after a Mercury flight. This had left him floundering in the sea as his craft sank.

After the fire on Apollo 1 safety hatches were reinstated. And there was much else to put right as well. The spacecraft was a firetrap. Nearly all the materials in it were flammable, and the atmosphere was 100 percent pure oxygen, so that the slightest spark would ignite instantly. Before the Apollo program could continue, a new spacecraft regime had to be put in place with nonflammable materials and a mixture of oxygen and nitrogen in the cabin, which was less explosive than pure oxygen. What had actually sparked the fire was never discovered.

◁ The burned-out shell of the Apollo 1 capsule after the fire that killed three astronauts on January 27, 1967. A complete overhaul of safety procedures followed the tragedy.

1967, the three Apollo astronauts were in the craft making checks with a high concentration of oxygen in the cabin. Suddenly Chaffee shouted: "Fire, I smell fire!" In a moment the spacecraft was engulfed in flames, and the three men perished before rescuers could get to them (*see box*).

Heads rolled after the tragedy. Harrison Storms, who was in charge of spacecraft development and had played a prominent role in popularizing the astronauts, was replaced. John Shea, manager of the Apollo program, also stepped down.

For months following the Apollo 1 tragedy NASA was understandably preoccupied with overhauling safety procedures, successfully so in that such a disaster did not recur. At the same time, the Saturn V rocket was finally completed ready for testing.

At 7 A.M. on November 9, 1967, the huge Saturn V blasted off from Cape Kennedy (as Cape Canaveral had been renamed in 1963). Although it was unmanned, it carried the payload for a fully operational moon landing with all three rocket stages as well as the command, service, and lunar modules. With its dramatic televised launch Americans saw plainly the magnitude of what the Apollo program entailed.

The numbering of Apollo flights can be confusing. After the tragic fire of January 1967 it was decided to call that failed mission Apollo 1. The successful testing of Saturn V in November 1967 was called Apollo 4 (*see box p. 65*), and Apollos 5 and 6 were similarly unmanned test flights. Apollo 7, launched on October 11, 1968, was the first successful manned flight; but because its mission was restricted to Earth orbit, it was launched with the smaller Saturn IB rocket. Apollo 7 orbited Earth 163 times while the command module was thoroughly tested.

First journey to the moon

With Kennedy's deadline of landing a man on the moon by the end of the decade fast approaching, the Apollo program took on a crammed series of trial runs. Apollo 8 was the first manned mission launched by the Saturn V. On December 21, 1968, Apollo 8 took off carrying television cameras and, for the first time, a crew heading for the moon.

Apollo 8 was the pivotal flight in the Apollo program. There was intense discussion about whether preparations were adequate for such a big step before it was approved. The commander of Apollo 8 was Frank Borman, and his fellow astronauts were Jim Lovell and Bill Anders. Mike Collins, who was to have been on the flight but had to pull out after surgery, was CapCom—in charge back on Earth.

Launching the Saturn V

The first successful launching of the massive Saturn V rocket was at Cape Kennedy on November 9, 1967. Although it was an unmanned flight, for those involved in the space program, and the vast army of assembled journalists, it was one of the most awe-inspiring and exciting moments in the whole Apollo program. The sheer size of this rocket was incredible. With the Apollo spacecraft on top it was fully 364 feet tall.

The Saturn V used three booster stages. The first, which would fire it out of Earth's gravitational force, was 138 feet high, with five F-1 rocket engines to power it. The fuel required for this stage alone took up 54 railroad tank cars filled with kerosene and liquid oxygen. Another 34 railroad carloads of hydrogen and oxygen were required for the second stage, which would carry the spacecraft and dummy module toward the moon.

At first the press and television site had been set up a mile from the launchpad, but the fear of an explosion if anything went wrong worried NASA, so they moved it back to three and a half miles. Even from this distance the gigantic force of the rocket startled reporters. They heard: "We have liftoff at 7 A.M. Eastern Standard Time," shouted by an over-excited Jack King of the public affairs office, then they felt the ground rumble beneath them. Seasoned pressmen began to shout: "Go! Go! Oh my God!"

Walter Cronkite's television studio began to fall in on him as he broadcast live for CBS Television. Reporters began to duck and dive as their specially built observation point vibrated frighteningly. Then the noise of the Saturn V's mighty engines reached them—a crackle that grew to a thunderous roar that observers could feel as a constant pressure on their faces. The success of this launch, in which the spacecraft and module were taken 11,234 miles before returning to Earth, put the Apollo project back on course after the tragic fire on Apollo 1. It also demonstrated to the world what awesome power was needed to take men to the moon.

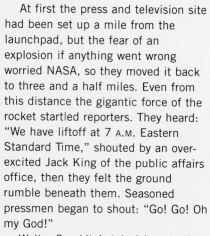

◁ **Apollo 4 at the moment of liftoff on November 9, 1967. This unmanned mission was the first to display the awesome power of the three-stage Saturn V rocket.**

△ Palms bow before the blast of the Saturn IB launching Apollo 7 from Cape Kennedy on October 11, 1968. Apollo 7 was the first successful manned fight of the program.

△ The control room at Kennedy Space Center during the Apollo 8 mission. On Christmas Eve 1968 the spacecraft disappeared from Earth's view—orbiting the dark side of the moon.

When the position of Apollo 8 had been thoroughly checked, Collins gave this brief instruction to the astronauts: "You are go for TLI." From the spacecraft Lovell replied: "Roger, understand. We are go for TLI." TLI was the jargon for translunar injection. The astronauts relit their S-1VB rocket and fired it for five minutes, increasing their speed from 25,000 to 33,500 feet per second. With the effect of a mighty slingshot, this thrust them out of Earth's gravitational field and pointed them toward the moon. It was the first time any human being had truly left planet Earth behind.

The spacecraft hurtled toward the moon, the astronauts looking back at Earth as a receding sphere. Although they were in constant radio contact with the scientists and engineers back at control, the onboard conversations of the astronauts were recorded and periodically beamed back to CapCom. On their first night the crew sent a message saying that someone should listen to what they had been saying. Worryingly, CapCom heard that Borman had suffered sickness and diarrhea. This problem was not made public at the time, but ground control was making plans to turn the spacecraft back if the other crew members were affected.

Into lunar orbit

Borman recovered quickly, but there were other worries. The power that would take the spacecraft into and out of lunar orbit came from the Service Propulsion System, or SPS. The SPS might also be needed to correct the

The lunar module

When Jim McDivitt, one of the astronauts assigned to Apollo 9, saw the LM—lunar module—for the first time, he exclaimed: "Holy Moses, we're really going to fly that thing?...If we're not careful, we could easily put a foot through it!" It was true that the lunar module was unlike anything else in the space program, as McDivitt put it, "like a tissue-paper spacecraft."

During the six years it took to design the LM those working on it were aware that it would only ever be used in conditions quite unlike those on Earth. The moon's gravitational pull was so much weaker than Earth's that the module could be built of relatively light materials. None of the rules governing the design of spacecraft applied. It could be any shape that suited because there was no need for it to be aerodynamic. One reason for the LM's makeshift appearance was the way it was wrapped in reflective foil to protect it from the unfiltered rays of the sun.

The lunar module was nicknamed "the bug," which gave the impression that it must be a little runaround thing much smaller than the command module. In fact, standing at 23 feet, the LM was more than twice the height of the command module. It weighed 16 tons and contained 18 engines, 8 radio systems, and a vast array of equipment, including life-support systems.

The LM was constructed in two parts. The upper section was where the astronauts lived on their way to the moon and back. In the lower section there were fuel tanks and storage areas for equipment. It was designed so that when the astronauts left the moon to return to the command module, the upper section broke away, leaving the lower section behind. Once the astronauts were back in the command module, the upper section of the LM was set adrift. In March 1969 Jim McDivitt and Rusty Schweickart of Apollo 9 tested LM-1 in Earth orbit. Ten weeks later Apollo 10 astronauts Tom Stafford and Gene Cernan tested LM-2 in orbit around the moon.

▷ **The lunar module LM-1 in Earth orbit, viewed from the command module of Apollo 9. This was the first manned test of the LM, and its subsequent successful testing with Apollo 10 in moon orbit was the final preparation for the Apollo 11 moon landing.**

course of the spacecraft en route to the moon. Tests had revealed a problem.

The SPS system had two channels for injecting fuel into the combustion chamber. The engine would work with just one, but for safety it was ruled that both must be functioning before the astronauts risked going into orbit around the moon. The problem engineers had discovered before the launch was that if both channels were fired together, there was a danger the engine might blow up. So the two channels—or "legs" as they were called—had to be tested separately. When the tests were carried out it was found that the engine was underperforming. But this was considered to be a problem associated only with short "burns" of the engine.

As Apollo 8 approached the moon, the scientists and mathematicians who had calculated the spacecraft's time and angle of entry into the moon's orbit were in a state of high tension. If they had made a mistake, the spacecraft might easily crash onto the surface.

Apollo 8 fired into lunar orbit on Christmas Eve 1968. A message went

The first moon landing

Four days after the Apollo 11 mission took off from Cape Kennedy on July 16, 1969, astronauts Neil Armstrong and "Buzz" Aldrin took their lunar module *Eagle* down toward the surface of the moon. The command module *Columbia* was held in orbit with Mike Collins on board. A message came from Houston: "If you read, you are go for powered descent." As always, major decisions were made not by the astronauts themselves but by the command center back in Houston.

As it happened, Armstrong and Aldrin did not "read" this message because they were out of radio alignment, and it was relayed to them by Collins. To regain contact, they had to realign the position of their module so that the antennae could pick up Houston. Aldrin fired *Eagle's* engine for the final descent, while Armstrong kept his eyes on the instrument panel, which told them how far they were from the moon's surface and where they would land.

As they descended, an alarm buzzed, and the computer signaled a fault 1202. Despite their extensive training, the astronauts did not know what it meant. Houston assured them it was nothing of significance and told them to continue with the descent. When they were only 3,000 feet

from the moon, another alarm went off. Once again they were assured that it was not serious and to keep going.

They had to avoid landing on rocky ground or in a crater, and Armstrong was scanning the moon's surface to look for a good place when he was told he had only 60 seconds of fuel remaining. A light came on in *Eagle* to indicate they were down. "Houston, Tranquillity Base here. The *Eagle* has landed."

Aldrin later expressed disappointment at not having being first to exit the lunar module, but the alignment of the astronauts in the module made it much easier for Armstrong to go first. He backed out of the module slowly and released a TV camera. This showed a fuzzy image in black and white, which was relayed to Earth. Armstrong could be seen climbing down a ladder, bouncing in the relative weightlessness of the moon's atmosphere. He put

△▽ A souvenir photograph of the Apollo 11 crew, Neil Armstrong (left), Mike Collins, and "Buzz" Aldrin, and a photograph of Aldrin working just outside the lunar module on the moon's surface, taken by Armstrong.

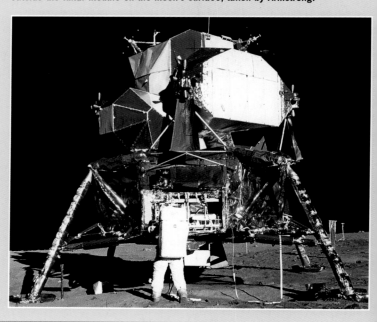

out to the crew: "Apollo 8, you are riding the best bird we can find." Jim Lovell called back: "Thanks a lot troops. We'll see you on the other side." With that the spacecraft disappeared behind the moon and out of all contact with Earth. In the control room they knew exactly when Apollo 8 ought to reappear if it had burned its SPS correctly. They waited in silence. The spacecraft reappeared exactly on time. Frank Borman read a prayer for the

congregation at St. Christopher's Episcopal Church in Houston, and the crew all read from Genesis.

Everyone at mission control knew that if anything went wrong with the SPS, the astronauts would end their days in lunar orbit, dying slowly as they ran out of oxygen. When the engine fired correctly and propelled them back toward Earth, a huge sigh of relief was breathed back at control. Interviewed later, many of those involved in the

Apollo program said this was the mission that was the most tense and exciting of all. As one put it, they had "stopped running around in circles. Apollo 8 went someplace."

The lunar module still required a manned testing, however. Apollo 9 was launched on March 3, 1969, so that astronauts could check out the LM while orbiting Earth (*see box p. 67*). With everything working satisfactorily, Apollo 10 set out for the moon on May

his left foot down first and delivered his memorable line, "That's one small step for [a] man... one giant leap for mankind." Back in Houston there were whoops of joy. Even a group of demonstrators who opposed Apollo because they felt the expense was not justified appeared to be as awestruck as the rest of the world by the achievement.

Armstrong and Aldrin spent 21 hours on the lunar surface before piloting *Eagle* back to the orbiting *Columbia* and the waiting Collins. On July 24 *Columbia* splashed down safely in the Pacific, 825 nautical miles southwest of Honolulu. With them the astronauts brought 46 pounds of moon rock. Behind they left an American flag and a plaque that read: "Here Men From Planet Earth First Set Foot Upon The Moon, July 1969 A.D. We Came In Peace For All Mankind."

△ Armstrong and Aldrin have a fascinating view of Earth rising above the moon as they approach *Columbia* on their return from the lunar surface in the lunar module *Eagle*.

18. While the command module remained in orbit, two astronauts left it in the lunar module and descended to within nine miles of the moon's surface before making a rendezvous with the spaceship and a safe return to Earth.

A man on the moon

Everything was now ready for the moon landing. It was to be attempted for the first time by Apollo 11. The Saturn V rose into the air above Cape Kennedy on July 16, 1969. On board were Neil Armstrong, Edwin "Buzz" Aldrin, and Michael Collins. They repeated the flight of Apollo 10, but this time they took the lunar module all the way down to the moon's surface, where they landed on July 20 (*see box above and p. 70*).

This crowning triumph of the U.S. Apollo program was viewed on television by 600 million people worldwide. But by that time such an achievement, with its accompanying propaganda value, was to some extent overshadowed by the televised horrors of the Vietnam War, then at its height. The world had changed since Kennedy's election, and the Apollo program seemed more in tune with the optimism of the earlier part of the decade.

The moon landing was by no means the end of the Apollo program, however. The program had a momentum of its own since it was, as one historian put it, the "largest single use of technological means to achieve a significant foreign policy goal in American history."

Ten more American astronauts were to land on the moon between 1969 and 1972, and there was both achievement and high drama in the later missions of the Apollo program. Apollo 12 made a second moon landing on November 19, 1969. This mission went much further than Apollo 11 in exploring the moon's surface. In the course of two moon walks that totaled nearly eight hours, an experimental unit was set up, and a wealth of photographs and more lunar samples were brought back to Earth.

Apollo 13—nobody thought to do away with this sinister number—followed a very different pattern after its launch on April 11, 1970.

Unlucky Apollo 13

It took more than two days to fly to the moon; and when Apollo 13 was about halfway there, an explosion shook the spacecraft and knocked out the power supply. The crew was unable to fire their main engine because there was no electricity, and they lost their main source of oxygen.

The world watched and waited as the astronauts, with tense-lipped advice from Houston, struggled to find a way of staying alive and harnessing the power needed to return them to Earth. Had the damage occurred when they were already in orbit around the moon, they would have been stranded, with no hope of getting home.

By using the firepower of the lunar module, shutting off items of equipment including their computer, and putting up with a cold and damp

Apollo 11 flight sequence

The Saturn V rocket operated in three stages. The first had to thrust the other two stages, the service module, the spacecraft *Columbia*, and the lunar module *Eagle* off the launchpad. To overcome the pull of Earth's gravity, its five F-1 engines burned for 2 min. 30 sec. Stage one completed its task 38 miles above Earth's surface, where it was jettisoned (**1**) and fell back to be burned up in Earth's atmosphere.

The second stage of the rocket then burned for six minutes, taking the astronauts to an altitude of 115 miles. It too was then jettisoned, and the third stage took over, powering the service module, command module, and lunar module into orbit around Earth in preparation for the departure to the moon (**2**). Fuel was reserved in the third stage to take the astronauts out of Earth's orbit toward their destination (**3**).

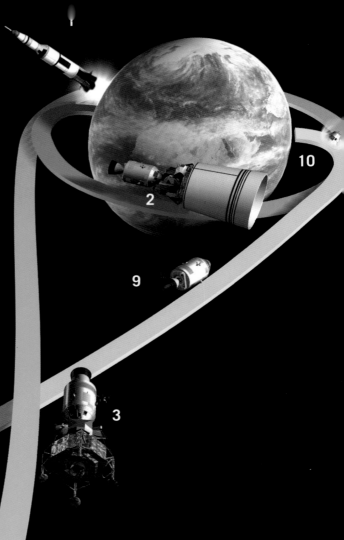

As the journey progressed, Earth's gravitational pull grew weaker as that of the moon grew stronger. At a prearranged time the service module, which had its own power, was detached from the third stage of the rocket, which was jettisoned. The service module, with *Columbia* and *Eagle*, then cruised into orbit around the moon. During this orbit Armstrong and Aldrin left *Columbia* in *Eagle*, which had sufficient power to descend to the moon and return to *Columbia* (**4, 5, 6**).

Once the astronauts were safely back in *Columbia* (**7**), the lunar module was jettisoned (**8**). Power from the service module then carried *Columbia* back toward Earth (**9**). Once the spacecraft was on course for reentry to Earth's atmosphere, the service module was jettisoned. *Columbia* then deployed parachutes to slow its entry into the atmosphere so that it would not burn up (**10**). *Columbia* splashed down safely in the Pacific.

△ A member of the recovery team shuts the Apollo 11 hatch, as the astronauts await helicopter pickup—and three weeks' isolation to guard against possible contamination.

The fear of contamination

There was a fear—understandable under the circumstances—that contact with the moon might in some way contaminate astronauts and their module, or that by taking microorganisms from Earth to the lunar surface, some unimaginable chain reaction might be triggered.

Accordingly, before each lunar mission there were strict decontamination procedures; and when the astronauts returned, they were kept isolated for 21 days while checks were made for any lifeforms that might prove harmful on Earth. Samples of lunar soil and rock were kept in quarantine for 50 to 80 days. As it happened, the moon proved to be lifeless—not a single microorganism was ever found.

atmosphere, they managed to steer their "lifeboat" back to Earth. There was plenty of oxygen in the lunar module, but they needed more lithium hydroxide, which absorbed the carbon dioxide they breathed out. When they tried to hook up supplies from the command module, they found to their dismay that the connectors were of different makes from different suppliers. However, with advice from ground control they managed to fashion a connector with bits of cardboard from their flight manual.

The final Apollo missions
The near disaster of Apollo 13 did not end the exploration of the moon, which continued until December 1972 with four more successful trips. Astronauts were able to stay longer, explore more extensively, and bring back more moon rock. With Apollo 15 in July 1971 the astronauts took an electric-powered moon buggy that allowed them to travel farther across the moon's surface.

By the early 1970s NASA's budgets and the Apollo program were being cut back. There were Saturn V rockets available for further trips to the moon, but they were canceled, and the last two became museum exhibits at Cape Canaveral (which reverted to its original name in 1973).

The success of the Apollo program capped an exceptional effort by NASA and the U.S. aerospace industry, backed by the necessary political will and financial commitment, to achieve the goal set by President Kennedy at the beginning of the decade. The first moon landing remains one of the defining events and images of the 1960s. □

See Also: Aerospace Industry; Gemini Program; Mercury Program; NASA; Rocket Technology; Space Race

ARCHITECTURE

In the 1960s modernism, or the International Style of architecture, was dominant, but some critics—as well as ordinary Americans—were beginning to question its merits.

△ **I. M. Pei's design for Boston City Hall incorporated Mediterranean themes such as an open piazza and stepped walkways—ambitious for winter conditions in New England.**

Between 1963 and 1973 nearly 20 million new homes were built in the United States, more than in any previous decade. However, there was a notable decline in single-family dwellings. In the cities more apartment blocks were built, and in the burgeoning suburbs developers employed architects to design groups of apartments or townhouses close together on a site, landscaping the remaining space for common use and providing facilities such as tennis courts, swimming pools, and artificial lakes. These developments often took Italian hill towns and New England villages as their models, and were self-consciously quaint and cloistered. However, in the 1960s as now, it was in the major buildings that make up the downtown areas of cities that architectural innovations were made and the results judged, by both architectural critics and the general public.

During the 1960s there was a huge shift in the public view of architecture. Since World War II the dominant ideas in American architecture had come from two Europeans, Mies van der Rohe and Walter Gropius. Having fled Nazi Germany in the 1930s, these major figures in architectural history had transformed American city centers with their rectangular towers of steel and glass. Despite having its origins in Germany as far back as the 1920s, the term modernism was still used to describe the style. During the 1960s disciples of modernism, notably the American Philip Johnson, continued to produce skyscrapers in what was also called the International Style because similar towers were springing up all over the world (*see box p. 73*). Every American city of any size, except Washington, D.C., and Philadelphia, was being transformed by such buildings. Many of these were built by the world's biggest architectural firm, Skidmore, Owings & Merrill (SOM), led by Philip Johnson and Gordon Bunshaft. However, younger architects were questioning their ideas. What had seemed revolutionary in the 1920s began to seem stale in 1960s America. People were finding modern blocks of steel and glass cold and sterile, and lacking in human scale.

Other imported European ideas fared little better. The idea of the open piazza worked well enough in sunny Italy, but it was not well suited to the climate of the northeastern United States. Boston's City Hall Plaza, Albany's Empire State Plaza, and the plaza at New York's Lincoln Center were all seen as failures. I. M. Pei's plan for Boston City Hall also borrowed from the medieval stepped streets of Sienna—but it had no relevance to a Bostonian who wanted to get a marriage license or a dog tag.

Modernism under attack

In 1962 three issues of the journal *Progressive Architecture* were given over to the question: Where is modern American architecture going? No clear

△ Albany's Empire State Plaza (later renamed in honor of Governor Nelson Rockefeller) is an example of the modernist design that came under attack during the 1960s.

answer emerged. But for the first time since World War II modernist ideas were being seriously questioned.

Some architects looked to the past for a clue. Edward Durrell Stone began to use curved lines, marble, and decoration in buildings such as his Huntington Hartford Gallery of Modern Art and his Kennedy Center in Washington. Minoru Yamasaki, noted for his uncompromising modernism, rediscovered the Gothic arch in his Science Pavilion at Seattle's 1962 World Fair. It was repeated in his work on the entranceways to the twin towers of New York's World Trade Center, which began construction in 1966. Although the square towers are made of steel, concrete, and glass—in other words, thoroughly modernist—the entranceways are reminiscent of the doorways of medieval European cathedrals.

The theorist of these new departures was Robert Venturi, who wrote "Complexity and Contradiction" in *Architect* in 1966. His Guild House in Philadelphia, completed in 1963, was seen as something of a shocker by the

An American modernist

Philip Johnson was the doyen of the International Style. With coauthor Henry Russell Hitchcock he had coined the term in an essay entitled "The International Style: Architecture since 1922," which served as the catalog for an architectural exhibition held at the New York Museum of Modern Art in 1932. Johnson had graduated from Harvard as a philosophy major in 1927, but returned in 1940 to study architecture under Marcel Breuer at the Graduate School of Design. Johnson's real master was, however, Mies van der Rohe, director of the Bauhaus school of art in Germany from 1930 until 1933, when the Nazis closed it. It was at the Bauhaus that the ideas behind modernism were developed. Together Mies van der Rohe and Johnson collaborated on New York's Seagrams Building, completed in 1958.

While he remained the champion of the modernist office block, in the 1960s Johnson was also responsible for the Sheldon Memorial Art Gallery at the University of Nebraska in Lincoln and the New York State Theater at Lincoln Center. These deviated from the principles of modernism, and critics began accusing him of losing his way. In 1982, following completion of New York's AT&T headquarters, whose top resembles an 18th-century Chippendale cabinet, Johnson was accused of abandoning modernism altogether.

△ New York's Lincoln Center, designed by Wallace K. Harrison, opened in 1966. The plaza drew criticism, but as a venue for the performing arts it is internationally acclaimed.

The father of the shopping mall

The man responsible for the modern shopping mall, Victor Gruen, was born in the Austrian capital of Vienna in 1903 and studied architecture there. After the Nazi takeover of Austria in 1938 he fled his homeland for the United States, becoming a U.S. citizen in 1943. In 1956 Gruen built the world's first multistoried, enclosed, climate-controlled shopping complex, the Southdale Center, outside Minneapolis. Others soon followed in Detroit, Indianapolis, San Francisco, and Los Angeles.

During the late 1950s and early 1960s Gruen applied the idea of the traffic-free suburban marketplace to the centers of aging American cities. In Fort Worth, Kalamazoo, Rochester, and Cincinnati he designed networks of "superblocks," or shopping areas. They were landscaped, traffic-free corridors of meandering walkways filled with public art, fountains, and benches, served by shuttle buses. Gruen also produced the master plan for the modern Iranian capital, Tehran. The thinking behind his urban renewal projects was outlined in his book *The Heart of Our Cities*, published in 1964.

In 1965 Gruen laid out the new city of Valencia in California and the following year built the Government Center in Boston. He retired in 1968 and moved back to Vienna, the city that had inspired many of his urban ideas. Gruen died in 1980.

architectural community at the time, although a survey in the 1970s showed that the people who lived in it were quite unaware of its significance. What was more, they liked living there—which was singularly unusual for project housing of the time.

The Venturi effect

The Guild House is a simple six-story, red-brick block providing low-cost housing in a semi-industrial neighborhood. What was revolutionary about the building was that it did not try to stand out. It was not raised above its neighbors on stilts, nor was it sleek and shiny. The main object of the building was to provide as many rooms as possible with a southern exposure, while

retaining a close relationship with the street. But it was unashamedly modern. Its entranceway was picked out with a shaft of highly polished black granite. Above it pop-art letters spelled out "Guild House."

Later, in "A Significance for A&P Parking Lots, or Learning from Las Vegas" Venturi argued that the modernists' humorless functionalism belonged to the gray days of the 1930s, and that architects should feel free to borrow from other styles they saw around them. One of Venturi's most praised buildings was the house he built for his mother at Chestnut Hill, Pennsylvania, which borrows from colonial architecture. However, his work drew criticism from Philip Johnson, who condemned his 1968 Brighton Beach housing project in Brooklyn as "ugly and ordinary."

Another architect who picked up on the playful hedonism of the decade was Charles Moore. His house in Orinda, California, completed in 1961, features prominently a sunken bathtub surrounded by columns.

In his Faculty Club at the University of California at Santa Barbara, com-

▷ **New York's Pan Am building, designed by the legendary Walter Gropius, presented a controversial new shape when it sprouted above Grand Central Station in 1963.**

The Pan Am building

In 1963 Walter Gropius completed one of his last great American projects, the Pan Am building in New York. From 1919 to 1928 Gropius was director of the influential Bauhaus school of art in Germany and in 1937 became professor of architecture at Harvard.

The Pan Am building is the culmination of the clean, uncluttered modernist style Gropius began with his design for the new Bauhaus building in Dessau in 1925 (the art school had originated in Weimar). It is a powerful and conspicuous edifice even for New York. Its 10-story base aligns with the cornice of Grand Central Station. The building does not occupy any real estate, only the airspace above the terminal. Above the base rises a 49-story lozenge-shaped tower. It changed the whole character of the 45th-Street area and dwarfed the genteel proportions of Park Avenue. For many it was seen as one step too far, but similar giant megaliths continued to be built in downtown areas across the United States.

pleted in 1969, Moore borrows from numerous styles. From the outside it looks like an angular version of the Spanish colonial revival style. However, its double walls filter the sunlight to create a glowing envelope around the softly lit interior, which features futurist bridges, stuffed heads, neon banners, and a gilded ceiling from newspaper tycoon William Randolph Hearst's grandiose castle at San Simeon.

Some architects became even more radical. Paolo Soleri, a former student of Frank Lloyd Wright, rejected the architect's traditional role. He dropped out of society completely and established a commune in the Arizona desert where those who shared his concept of the future paid to participate in his visionary work. Although Soleri's output was not prolific, his drawings inspired many. He became the role model for "alternative" builders and was influential with a new generation of community architects who hired themselves out to tenants' groups.

Saarinen's influence

Early in his career Venturi had worked with Eero Saarinen and Louis Kahn. Although Saarinen died in 1961, his legacy had already turned modernism

Expo '67

The great showcase for innovative architecture at the height of the 1960s was Expo '67 in Montreal. The U.S. Pavilion was built by the revolutionary engineer and architect Buckminster Fuller. It was a 200-foot-high geodesic dome, and visitors were moved through it by monorail, elevator, and escalator. With no internal structure, the dome was supported by an outer layer of triangular elements that overlaid an inner layer of hexagonal elements. The outside was then covered with a 141,000-square-foot skin of transparent plastic.

This imaginative lightweight structure did not go on to provide the low-cost housing many visionaries had hoped for. Instead, geodesic domes were used extensively by the U.S.

Defense Department to house its early-warning radar system. One of the other eye-catching experiments at Expo '67 was Moshe Safdie's Habitat. It used production-line techniques to produce a ziggurat of human-scale housing units. There were 158 apartments in all, although the original intention was to provide 1,000, made up of 15 different types of prefabricated units.

This bold experiment was a failure. Complete standardization of components was not possible since the units at the bottom of the building had to be strong enough to support those above. Traditional site-built, timber-framed houses were cheaper to construct. And when other Habitat-style buildings were constructed for longer-term use, they soon showed all the disadvantages of high-rise, system-built blocks—leaking joints, condensation, and ill-fitting doors and windows.

on its head. His TWA terminal at what was then Idlewild (now Kennedy) Airport, completed in 1962, was built in conventional materials—concrete, glass, steel—but it was shaped like an eagle in flight. His terminal building at Washington's Dulles Airport, also completed a year after Saarinen's death, resembles a wing ready for takeoff.

When Saarinen died, his practice was taken over by Paul Rudolph, who went on to design the Boston Government Services Center and the Architectural Faculty at Yale. Louis Kahn built the blank-faced extension to the Yale University Art Gallery. These men, with their use of aggressive, rough-hewn structures, were exponents of a style that came to be known as Brutalism. Although it has since come in for a great deal of criticism, not least because ugly expanses of weathered concrete make a tempting canvas for graffiti artists, it allowed architects to perfect a rounded sculptural style. Rudolph's open four-story parking garage in New Haven, Connecticut (1963), which contains no other element except formed concrete, has been copied the world over.

Bertrand Goldberg's Marina City in Chicago, built between 1964 and 1968, took this one step further with two circular towers that look like vertical flower stems. The 16 open automobile parking floors at the bottom are mirrored by the 40 floors of apartments with petallike balconies and are separated from them by a service floor.

The upward trend
Kevin Roche's 1967 Ford Foundation building brought a new kind of office block to New York. His brief was to create an environment in which the individual office worker or visitor could identify with "the aims and intentions of the group." The result was a modest 12-story block with a vertical conservatory rising the full height of the

building. Although influential, it did not reverse the general trend toward bigger and bigger. The mighty twin towers of the World Trade Center were already under construction.

In Chicago, the home of the skyscraper, bigger was always better. In 1968 Lake Point rose 645 feet over Navy Pier Park, containing 900 luxury apartments and two floors of offices. The gleaming tower was clover-shaped in plan, making its outer wall a continuous, undulating curtain of glass.

In 1969 SOM completed Chicago's 100-story John Hancock Tower. At 1,105 feet it dwarfed the surrounding buildings, though at its base it occupied just 40 percent of the site. It contained a mix of apartments, offices, and stores. Strapped from head to toe by a dozen pairs of cross-braces, it was one of the most fashionable monoliths of the decade. Its chief architect, Bruce Graham, went on to produce Chicago's 110-floor Sears headquarters, for many years the world's tallest building. □

▷ Chicago's John Hancock Tower soars above the famous 19th-century fire station. Finished in 1969, it is one of the most celebrated commercial buildings of the decade.

See Also: Design; Housing; Visual Arts

ARMS RACE

During the 1960s the United States and the Soviet Union were busy arming themselves to the teeth. Both claimed to be acting in self-defense, but critics questioned their logic.

Throughout the 1960s the rival U.S. and Soviet military establishments seemed to be engaged in a frantic competition. Each appeared to be trying to gain the upper hand over the other by designing and building more and more powerful and more and more numerous weapons. This process was known as the arms race. At its heart were nuclear weapons and the various methods of delivering these deadly objects to their potential targets. It

gradually became clear, however, that the nature of nuclear weapons meant that the arms race was a very unusual type of contest. It was one in which both sides could end up as losers, and it might even turn out to be self-defeating for either side to try to win.

Containing communism

The U.S. had been the first country to develop atomic weapons in the final stages of World War II. The U.S. in 1952 and the USSR in 1953 then exploded vastly more powerful atomic fusion weapons known as hydrogen bombs (or H-bombs). By the early

1960s both nations had tested H-bombs more than 1,000 times as powerful as the weapons that had destroyed the Japanese cities of Hiroshima and Nagasaki in 1945.

The U.S. and USSR had been allies during World War II, but their relationship soon became hostile as the so-called Cold War developed. From the end of World War II the Soviets had maintained a massive land army in their own country and Eastern Europe, but it had been counterbalanced by American nuclear superiority (which had been threatened but not overtaken by Soviet developments). During the 1950s U.S.

▽ The terrifying power unleashed during a U.S. H-bomb test in 1964. Both sides in the Cold War had a huge armory of such weapons.

Soviet MRBM

diminished in any way. American worries were still fueled by scare stories of communist infiltration of the U.S. government and other institutions, and by the provocative claims of Soviet leaders. For example, Soviet communist chief Nikita Khrushchev had boasted to Americans in 1959: "We will bury you... your grandchildren will grow up under communism." Furthermore, Soviet technologists seemed to have the power to back this boast. The Soviets launched the world's first successful satellite, the famous Sputnik, in October 1957. An American attempt to

◁ **Footage of Soviet missiles on parade in Moscow being studied at the Pentagon. Both sides strove for weapons superiority.**

foreign policy was based on the principle of "containment of communism," backed by the threat of "massive retaliation," including the use of nuclear weapons if the Soviets harmed key American interests.

Flexible response

By the start of the 1960s, however, the Soviets had substantial nuclear forces in service. For example, they had tested a 5,000-mile-range intercontinental ballistic missile (ICBM) in 1957. Faced by possible counterstrikes from weapons like these, it no longer made sense for the U.S. to threaten a huge nuclear strike in response to comparatively minor Soviet moves. The U.S. therefore changed to a new strategy known as "flexible response," which is still in operation today. Flexible response meant being able to reply to threats against the U.S. or its allies with appropriate force and at the highest level meant being able to launch a devastating nuclear strike to deter any serious aggression by the USSR.

The new strategy of flexible response did not mean that Americans thought the threat from the Soviet Union had

The view from Moscow

During the arms race of the 1960s Americans naturally looked at the situation from their own point of view. The U.S. had no intention of attacking the Soviet Union. On the contrary, it was the Soviet Union, with its massive Red Army, that threatened world peace by its proclaimed mission to spread the communist system to the four corners of the earth. The overwhelming U.S. military commitment was therefore defensive in nature, a bulwark against the spread of communism.

To Soviet analysts it all appeared quite differently. They disputed the charge that the Soviet forces were dangerously large and equipped for aggression, pointing out that the Red Army was concentrated in the USSR and in its allied countries in Eastern Europe to make sure that Germany could never attack the Soviet Union again. They said that Americans conveniently forgot that it was they rather than the Western Allies who had borne the brunt of the Nazi brutality and had suffered vastly greater losses.

As for the American charge that the Soviets undermined legitimate governments in countries on other continents, the Soviets could retort that the CIA was spending 80 percent of its budget on what it chose to call "covert action," and that Kennedy had established Green Beret units to fight in small-scale wars to help governments that the U.S. backed, regardless of how repressive such governments might be. What was the difference between the USSR backing its friends and the U.S backing its own?

On the question of nuclear weapons it was not the USSR but the U.S. that built the first atomic bomb, then the first H-bomb, and had the most powerful long-range bomber fleet. The U.S. had nuclear weapons in Turkey close to the USSR's southern border and sent submarines with more missiles to patrol all along the USSR's northern coast. So why, it could be argued, were Soviet missiles in Cuba a unique threat to world peace?

Soviets claimed that they were not aiming for nuclear supremacy but nuclear parity, that they wanted to be treated as an equal on the world stage and to be certain of their own security.

▷ President Kennedy puts his name to the Moscow Agreement banning atmospheric nuclear tests, agreed to by U.S., Soviet, and British diplomats in August 1963.

match the achievement a few weeks later blew up on the launchpad.

During the 1960 presidential campaign John F. Kennedy made much of a supposed "missile gap," alleging that the Soviets had a decisive lead in this type of weaponry. Kennedy was wrong about this. Even so, before he left office in 1961 President Eisenhower had already more than doubled the U.S. military's missile research budget. Later that year Kennedy increased the overall defense budget by more than 20 percent, to about 60 percent of total federal expenditure. Across the 1960s the U.S. defense budget rose from $45 billion to $78 billion by 1970, while it is estimated that Soviet expenditure kept pace, from $37 billion to $72 billion across the same period.

The domino theory

This massive increase included a planned tripling of the U.S. nuclear forces but also allowed for significant expansion of conventional forces. Flexible response meant building up enough forces to be able to compete with the Soviets all around the world. According to the "domino theory" widely accepted at the time, if the U.S. did not support a friendly government under threat from communism, then it would probably fall, causing its neighbors in turn to topple into the communist camp. It was this domino theory that caused the U.S. to become involved in the Vietnam War.

As well as deploying military forces when necessary, the U.S. was also prepared to use the Central Intelligence Agency (CIA) to oppose communist advances and support pro-American governments, even where they were undemocratic or repressive regimes. Most of the CIA's budget was spent on such secret work rather than on intelligence gathering.

In addition to the obviously military programs other new departures also

played a part in the arms race. Much of the research in the two sides' "peaceful" space programs was into such things as rocket fuels and guidance systems that were relevant to intercontinental missile systems. The American public heard most about the Atlas and Titan rockets in their roles as the respective launch vehicles for Mercury and Gemini space missions, but they had originally been designed and successfully tested in 1958 and 1959 as ICBMs and would serve in that form into the 1980s. In the early 1960s more than one-third of the scientific and engineering research conducted in U.S. universities was government-funded, most of it for the military.

Superpower confrontation

Around the start of the decade U.S. submarines made a number of well-publicized voyages under the Arctic ice to the North Pole. They were reported at the time as harmless feats of exploration, but they had a more sinister purpose as well. These missions were studying the problems involved in operating nuclear submarines in this

area in time of war, since the Arctic Ocean was the shortest route from U.S. waters to potential missile-firing positions off the Soviet coasts.

On the other side, Soviet scientific research and the Soviet economy generally were dominated by the needs of the military, leaving Soviet industry, agriculture, and the living standards of the Soviet people lagging far behind those of the West. Most of the Soviet Union's intimidating military forces remained based in Eastern Europe throughout the 1960s. Soviet land forces generally had roughly a two-to-one superiority in numbers of troops, tanks, and artillery weapons in comparison with the NATO ground forces in position to oppose a possible invasion.

Until this time the Soviet Navy had only had a short-range capability, but in the 1960s it also began developing new ships and weapons to challenge the U.S. Navy throughout the world's oceans. New antiship missiles fitted on both surface ships and submarines gave the Soviets a weapon to challenge American aircraft carriers for the first time, but the U.S. held a clear lead throughout the decade in the development of atomic submarines, which were widely seen as a decisive weapon in the event of all-out war (*see box*).

One area in which the Soviets are believed to have held a substantial superiority at the time is in chemical and bacteriological warfare. During World War II Germany had developed (but not used) a range of new and deadly weapons of this type. At the end of the war the German research laboratories and their staff were captured by the Soviets and helped give them a lead in this area. The U.S. also had a large capability in this field, however, though at the end of the 1960s President Nixon announced that the U.S. would destroy its stocks of such weapons.

Mutual assured destruction

As the decade went on, U.S. leaders came to recognize that they could not positively guarantee to prevent the Soviets from making a nuclear attack. But they believed that they could deter one from being made by the threat of "mutual assured destruction" (often abbreviated as MAD). Even if the Soviets made an all-out surprise nuclear

△ The launch of a Polaris submarine. In the open seas these nuclear-armed warships were undetectable and therefore certain to be able to retaliate against a Soviet first strike.

attack, the U.S. military planned for enough of its forces to survive to be able to kill more than a third of the Soviet population and destroy more than half of the USSR's cities and industries. This would be enough to prevent the Soviets attacking in the first place. Equally, U.S. leaders and Americans generally had to recognize in their turn that if they were so rash as to attack a vital interest of the Soviet Union, the Soviets would be able to destroy the United States just as assuredly.

A dangerous race to win

Thinking further along these lines led to the surprising conclusion that it might be a bad idea to develop or build more weapons or more effective ones. MAD only worked if both sides were certain that enough of their forces would survive an enemy attack to make a "second strike" of their own. If the U.S., for example, threatened to build weapons accurate enough or powerful enough to make a successful "first strike," knocking out the Soviet ability to retaliate, the situation would become very unstable. Faced with such a sce-

Polaris missile system

Polaris was the name of a missile system developed by the U.S. Navy for deployment in its nuclear-armed submarines. The first Polaris submarine came into service in 1960 and test-fired its first missile (with a range of over 1,200 miles) the same year. Each submarine carried 16 missiles combining more destructive power than all the bombs dropped in World War II. Longer-range versions of Polaris came into service later in the 1960s and in 1970 were joined by a new missile, Poseidon, with multiple warheads. The Soviets did not manage to build a system equivalent to Polaris until 1967–1968, by which time the U.S. Navy had 41 Polaris submarines in service.

Military strategists called submarine missiles like Polaris "second-strike" weapons. They could not be aimed quite accurately enough or carry the massive warheads needed to smash missile bases or other military installations on land; but because the ocean is so vast, they would be virtually impossible to hunt down and destroy before they had a chance to fire their missiles with incalculable effect in time of war. In the deadly calculations of mutual assured destruction Polaris was the ideal system. Polaris submarines would be guaranteed to survive an enemy "first strike" but could not themselves be used successfully in such an attack. They were designed for deterrence and, it was hoped, were never to be used.

nario the Soviets might decide to attack first, since that would be the only way to minimize their own losses. Stronger U.S. forces could therefore make a devastating nuclear attack on the U.S. more rather than less likely.

Limited nuclear war

Some military leaders and theorists on both sides looked at things quite differently. They said that nuclear weapons were like other military weapons, even though they were obviously more powerful. They argued that it would be quite possible to use nuclear weapons in fighting a war without it inevitably turning into an all-out nuclear attack by both sides. Americans who thought in this way said, for example, that the

U.S. could use nuclear weapons to halt a Soviet land attack in Europe without any nuclear attack being made on the USSR's own territory or in retaliation against the United States.

The possibility that the superpowers might devastate Europe while their own homelands remained unharmed had little appeal to Europeans. This was one reason why in 1960 the French tested their first atomic bomb and decided to keep independent control over whether to use nuclear weapons. Britain had built its own nuclear weapons in the 1950s and modernized them with U.S. help during the 1960s. China tested its first nuclear weapon in 1964. Such nuclear proliferation made it increasingly difficult for both the United

States and the USSR to work out sensible nuclear strategies for themselves.

Some people called MAD the balance of terror. They pointed out that since an intercontinental missile would take less than 30 minutes from its launch to reach its target, national leaders might be forced to make hasty and ill-considered decisions in a crisis that might easily lead to the destruction of world civilization. It was all too easy to imagine how, for example, a simple communication breakdown could lead to disaster, with missiles being launched by mistake. People who held views like this thought that mad was exactly the right thing to call a national strategy that might turn out to be suicidal. They also said that the fancy terminology used by the military to discuss nuclear warfare was a means of hiding the horrendous destruction and loss of life that would result from a nuclear war.

Test bans and SALT talks

Despite such doubts, both the U.S. and the USSR continued to develop and expand their nuclear capabilities throughout the 1960s. But at the same time, the first steps to control nuclear weapons also began. In 1958 the Soviets had announced that they would stop testing nuclear weapons above ground in response to fears of nuclear radiation fallout. The U.S. also suspended its tests in the atmosphere or under water, and the two countries agreed to a treaty to ban all such tests in 1963. This did not do much to halt the arms race since underground tests continued, but it was a first step toward the realization that survival might depend on cooperating with and talking to the other side.

Real progress in this direction came with the opening of the Strategic Arms Limitation Talks (SALT) in 1969. These discussions did not yield a treaty until 1972, but they began because of fears that the stability of the balance of

◁ On November 7, 1967, Soviets celebrated the 50th anniversary of the Russian Revolution with a huge military display in Moscow's Red Square, complete with nuclear missiles.

terror might be in danger. The Soviets had tested a "killer satellite," which could take out U.S. satellites, and both sides had begun work on antimissile systems that in time might have given protection against a "second strike" and so increased the risk of a "first strike." Once again developing better weapons might have the effect of encouraging rather than deterring an enemy attack.

Conflicting views on security

Some American military leaders looked at things differently. They knew that U.S. missiles were more accurate than Soviet ones and were becoming more accurate still as guidance systems were being improved. They said that the U.S. would soon be able to destroy most of the Soviet nuclear arsenal in a first "counterforce" strike and that having

▷ A nuclear reactor at Trombay, India. The purpose of the NPT was to prevent such facilities from being used to build nuclear weapons while encouraging their peaceful use.

The Non-Proliferation Treaty

The international Non-Proliferation Treaty (known as the NPT) was signed in 1968 and came into effect in 1970. It was designed to halt any possible spread of nuclear weapons to countries that did not already have them. It is still in operation. The U.S. remains committed to persuading more countries to agree to it, and to making sure that those countries that have already signed it obey its provisions.

When the treaty began, five countries (U.S., USSR, Britain, France, and China) possessed nuclear weapons. They agreed not to sell or give nuclear weapons' technology to any other countries but did say that they would share their expertise in the peaceful uses of nuclear power. Other countries that signed the treaty agreed not to try to buy or build their own nuclear weapons and not to allow any current or future nuclear power plants or similar installations they might build to be used for weapons research.

The NPT has not been completely successful. Some countries such as Israel, India, and Pakistan have never signed the agreement and have built nuclear weapons. Other countries like Iraq did sign it but have broken it by amassing nuclear technology and trying to build weapons in secret. Such countries often put the question "If the U.S. and the other 'old' nuclear powers need to have nuclear weapons for their national security, why is it so different for us?" Despite these inherent weaknesses, the NPT is valuable because it provides an international legal system that can be used to try to halt the reckless development of nuclear armaments, even if it has not always worked perfectly.

this capability and being prepared to use it in war was a far better guarantee of America's survival than the deterrent effect of a "countervalue" second strike against Soviet cities. They did not wish the U.S. to curb its missile program, as seemed the likely outcome of SALT.

Nuclear weapons and the arms race were therefore complicated issues for the U.S. military and political leadership, and in addition they had far-reaching effects on domestic political ideas. The dangers of the arms race and all it involved had the side-effect of making liberal social ideas unpopular with many Americans, since such ideas were seemingly similar to those espoused by the Soviets. On the other hand, there were many American conservatives who welcomed a strong U.S. military but were opposed to the build-up of federal power and authority that necessarily resulted from such a policy. In this and every other way nothing about the arms race was quite as simple as it seemed at first sight. □

See Also: Cold War; Deterrence; Missile Gap; Nuclear Fallout Shelters; Nuclear Weapons; Postwar World; SALT; Warsaw Pact

LOUIS ARMSTRONG 1900–1971

By the 1960s "Satchmo" had been a star jazz performer for four decades, but in the twilight of his career his music and personality captured the affections of millions beyond the world of jazz.

L ouis Armstrong was one of the pioneers of jazz in the 1920s. By the 1960s "Satchmo," as he was affectionately known, was a respected national and international figure whose enormous success with the single "What a Wonderful World" offered a vision of a unified, optimistic nation, something of an escape from the turmoil of riots in the black ghettos and protest against the Vietnam War.

Born in New Orleans, Armstrong spent some of his childhood in a home for delinquents. There he learned to play the cornet, and by the time he reached his midteens, he was an accomplished player in the New Orleans style. From 1918 to 1922 he was a leading musician in his hometown but then left for Chicago, to join the band of one of his former employers, Joe "King" Oliver. Armstrong now rose to national prominence as a musician and during the late 1920s made a series of recordings that changed jazz forever. In a set

of solos recorded with his own small groups or in duet with pianist Earl Hines, Armstrong demonstrated how a single instrument could cover a deep emotional range by exploiting the rhythmic, melodic, and harmonic possibilities of the jazz idiom. After these recordings jazz effectively became an art music in which reaching or appreciating such technical and musical heights became the holy grail for musicians and listeners.

After his artistic peak in the late 1920s Armstrong began playing in bigger orchestras, where his trumpet technique on high notes, his sense of swing, and his infectious personality made him a major entertainer. Then, in the 1940s he reverted to smaller groups again. With shifting personnel these groups were known as the "All Stars."

Although to some politically active blacks Armstrong sometimes seemed the image of the grinning entertainer, he made strong political statements in

△ **Louis Armstrong was the first great virtuoso performer in jazz history, and his popularity matched his critical reputation.**

the 1950s during the attempts to end segregation in southern schools. With his huge international following Armstrong was seen as an unofficial ambassador for the United States during this period, but once refused to tour the Soviet Union because of his distaste for what he considered President Eisenhower's insufficiently strong stand on the civil rights issue.

In the 1960s Armstrong was an internationally renowned figure, with a whole form of music as his progeny. He toured widely, to great acclaim, and represented a black America that could achieve both popular success and prestige and artistic greatness. In some ways his career had mirrored America's development during the 20th century, and he himself represented a positive side to the American Dream. □

See Also: Jazz

ARMY

The 1960s presented the U.S. Army with many challenges. While tasked with defending U.S. interests around the world, it was increasingly committed to fighting a major war in Southeast Asia.

The 1960s saw the recently strengthened and reorganized United States Army become embroiled in the Vietnam War, while at the same time having to maintain its commitments elsewhere in the world. In Europe American servicemen formed a key part of the NATO forces opposing the Soviet-dominated Warsaw Pact, and there was a significant U.S. presence in the Pacific, the Far East, and Central America. The army was expected to be able to respond to a crisis of any sort, wherever U.S. interests were at stake.

A key part of the fallout from the

▽ The heavily armed M60 tank came into service in 1960 and was a mainstay of the U.S. Army for more than 20 years.

Korean War (1951–1953) was a radical overhaul of U.S. defense policy and a reappraisal of military spending priorities. Korea had been an expensive and less-than-decisive war. The U.S. economy had felt the strain, and it was considered that defense spending could be cut in future without undermining U.S. security. Key to this was the Cold War strategy of massive retaliation based on air-delivered nuclear weapons. In other words, the overwhelming power of the USAF became the cornerstone of U.S. defense policy.

This major reappraisal had profound consequences for the U.S. Army. Its permanent overseas commitments were significantly cut back. The reduction in U.S. manpower was in part covered by local allies, in part replaced by a new,

highly mobile strategic reserve based in the United States and capable of being transported long distances at short notice. The strength of the army fell from 1.5 million men in 1953 to 859,000 by 1958. Its budget allocation was also reduced from $13 billion to $9 billion over the same period.

Flexible response

Several senior generals doubted the practicality of the new system. Some believed that, because of potentially heavy casualties in a limited nuclear war, more rather than less troops would be needed. Others warned that not all wars of the future would be nuclear and would require an army trained and flexible enough to fight under a wide range of circumstances. In the early 1960s

President Kennedy paid heed to these warnings, agreeing with the generals that the U.S. Army had to be flexible enough to fight a variety of wars, from full-scale nuclear conflict in Europe to counterinsurgency campaigns anywhere in the world. "Flexible response" became the new doctrine.

Enlarging the army

The army was therefore reorganized and enlarged; the number of combat-ready divisions rose by around 50 percent. Each of the 16 divisions was increased in strength to between 13,500 and 15,000 men. By 1965 the army had a strength of 963,000 men, although against that figure the Soviet Union's Red Army could muster two million men.

Individual U.S. divisions were also restructured in the early 1960s to carry out specific tasks—airborne, armored, infantry, and mechanized infantry—under a program known as ROAD (Reorganization Objective Army Divisions). Armored and mechanized divisions were primarily trained to fight

▷ A tank training maneuver in Italy in the early 1960s, as part of the major U.S. NATO commitment to the defense of Western Europe.

Hawks and doves

During the 1960s policy concerning the deployment of the U.S. military was ultimately dictated by the incumbent president. However, he relied to a large extent on advisors, many drawn from the U.S. Army. Some were termed "hawks"—senior officers who took a hard line in protecting U.S. interests, whether in Latin America, Southeast Asia, or Western Europe. All hawks backed a strong U.S. military presence to maintain a balance of power in Europe and more often than not advocated direct military intervention in U.S. spheres of influence.

For example, General Maxwell Taylor, President Kennedy's chairman of the Joint Chiefs of Staff, was strongly committed to U.S. involvement in Vietnam and direct confrontation with the Soviet Union in other international hotspots. During the Cuban Missile Crisis in October 1962, Taylor advocated a, invasion of Cuba to destroy the Soviet missiles and topple Cuban leader Fidel

Castro. Also in 1962, following a fact-finding mission to South Vietnam by Taylor Kennedy agreed to increase military assistance to South Vienam in the form of "advisors" despite his own reservations. Taylor, subsequently ambassador to Vietnam, convinced President Johnson to vastly increase the U.S. military commitment to the war in 1965.

Opposing the hawk" were those known as "doves." These men adopted a more measured approach to any threat, one of a graduated response based on clearly defined objectives and backed by political dialogue. For much of the 1960s presidents surrounded themselves with military hawks, although they did not always take their advice. Even after it became the stated policy of President Nixon to scale down U.S. involvement in Vietnam, many hawks were still strongly committed to a more full-blooded role. However, Nixon and his national security advisor Henry Kissinger had taken over the direct running of the war, and both were committed to withdrawal and a negotiated settlement.

a conventional war against the Warsaw Pact in Europe. The pure infantry units had a global role, either as conventional troops in Europe as part of the U.S. commitment to NATO or in limited wars elsewhere in the world The two airborne divisions were to be used as an international rapid-intervention force. Between 1963 and 1965 a fifth type of division was added, the helicopter-transported unit. The new formations began to receive state-of-the-art equipment, including the M60 tank and the M113 armored personnel carrier, which was amphibious as well as air-transportable.

In the early 1960s the ROAD concept was rarely put into practice. Most soldiers stayed in bases in the United States or were deployed to Europe as part of the country's NATO commitment. The army did, however, became embroiled in the civil rights struggles at home. In 1962, for example, 20,000 troops backed by 10,000 National Guardsmen oversaw the enrollment of an African American student at the University of Mississippi.

Some troops did see action overseas. In 1965 airborne forces intervened to stabilize the Dominican Republic, which was rent by political infighting that threatened U.S. interests. A second, and potentially more dangerous crisis had occurred a few years earlier, in August 1961, following the Soviet-sanctioned building of the Berlin Wall. President Kennedy sent 40,000 troops and 100,000 tons of equipment to bolster the defenses of Western Europe, and increased the regular army by 80,000 men. Kennedy also backed the creation of the Special Forces ("Green Berets"), who had two main roles: to organize guerrilla forces behind enemy lines during a conventional war and to aid local forces fighting counterinsurgency campaigns.

Vietnam and the draft

By the mid-1960s, therefore, the U.S. Army had been enlarged, reorganized, and become the key tool in the country's concept of flexible response. How effective it had actually become was to be tested in Vietnam, where the

U.S. commitment had been growing from a handful of advisors in 1961 to 23,000 men by November 1963. By 1969, the peak year of U.S. involvement, the army had some 444,000 men committed to Vietnam.

To meet its role in Vietnam while maintaining its presence in Europe and elsewhere, the Army's strength had to be increased. The raw manpower came from the draft, with each recruit likely to serve a year's duty in Vietnam before rotating home. A total of 8.7 million Americans served in Vietnam of which 4.4 million served in the army. However, to many the draft appeared far from fair. They felt that draftees were disproportionately drawn from a young base of rural and urban poor, both black and white, and that the better-off were avoiding military service.

There were statistics to back up such views. The average age of servicemen in Vietnam was only 19, as opposed to 26

▽ An M113 armored personnel carrier in South Vietnam in 1969. This versatile vehicle was extensively used during the war.

in World War II. In 1966 African Americans made up 10 percent of the forces in Vietnam but suffered 16 percent of total casualties, an indication they were disproportionately involved in actual combat. A total of 15 million of those eligible for the draft gained student or occupational deferments.

The Vietnam experience

For the ordinary soldier in Vietnam the war was a devastating experience. As the conflict dragged on with seemingly no end in sight, the draftees became increasingly embittered. Casualties grew and the troops were receiving an unprecedentedly bad press at home. Many frontline troops came to believe that they were laying down their lives for a cause few in the United States believed in. They also doubted that their generals had any clear idea of how to bring the war to a successful conclusion. The massacre of South Vietnamese peasants at My Lai in 1969 was revealed in 1970, and further

▷ **U.S. soldiers patrolling South Vietnam's Mekong Delta in 1968. Pitted against a determined enemy, many felt let down by growing antiwar sentiments back home.**

fueled antiwar sentiments in the U.S. Draft-dodging became an increasing problem at home, while in Vietnam morale plunged, and disobedience grew along with drug-taking. Reports of disillusioned soldiers attempting to kill overly enthusiastic officers ("fragging") also began to surface.

Aftermath of the war

The Vietnam War was a traumatic experience for the U.S. Army. It suffered a total of 130,000 combat casualties, roughly 60 percent of total U.S. casualties in the conflict. Of these casualties some 30,500 were killed. Vietnam was the first conflict in which the United States, if not defeated on the battlefield, did not prevail. This had a major impact on the relationship between the political and military establishments and severely shook the wider public's confidence in their political and military leaders. □

1st Cavalry Division (Airmobile)

The 1st Cavalry Divison (Airmobile) was the world's first unit of its size to rely solely on helicopters for its battlefield mobility. All of its troops and their equipment, including artillery, could be moved rapidly into action by air. It was a bold concept and one that some military traditionalists felt was overly ambitious, if not downright impracticable.

The division's origins dated back to the Howse Board in 1962, which was asked to examine the feasibility of the airmobile concept. Its report concluded that such a unit was "necessary and desirable." An evaluation unit, the 11th Air Assault Division (Test), was formed and approved the validity of the airmobile concept in a series of trials in 1965.

The division was now brought up to full strength with the addition of the 2nd Infantry Divison and was officially formed on July 1, 1965. Its initial strength totaled 16,000 troops, 400 fixed-wing aircraft and helicopters, and 1,600 vehicles. The 1st Cavalry Divison (airmobile) sailed to Vietnam a month later, establishing its first base at An Khe. The division had its first chance to put its training into practice in the fall of 1966, when it was ordered into action in the Ia Drang Valley. The 35-day action was fierce and bloody, but the division proved its mettle and the validity of airmobile warfare. It continued to play a frontline role for the remainder of the war.

See Also: Antiwar Movement; Cold War; Grunts; Tet Offensive; Vietnam War

ISAAC ASIMOV 1920–1992

A prolific and versatile writer, the Russian-born Isaac Asimov made a lasting impression on the world of science fiction, in particular with his highly praised and influential Foundation series.

During the 1960s Isaac Asimov came to prominence as a science fiction writer, which was ironic since in that decade his most significant work was not science fiction.

Asimov was born in Petrovichi in Russia in 1920, but his family moved to Brooklyn when he was three. He sold his first story to *Astounding Science Fiction* magazine when he was a chemistry student at Columbia in 1938.

Producing his famous Foundation trilogy in the early 1950s, Asimov supported himself as an academic until 1957. Then he was fired by Boston University School of Medicine, where he was associate professor of biochemistry, and became a full-time writer.

A writer of vision

As the 1960s dawned, Asimov's literary interests were no longer directed toward science fiction. The space program was revealing factual errors in his early work, and he felt out of touch with the new wave of science fiction writers. During the 1960s Asimov concentrated on nonfiction, completing his hundredth book in 1969. His nonfiction subjects included science, mathematics, history, Bible studies, humor, and satire, and he was lauded for his ability to make complicated scientific subjects understandable to the lay reader. Most notable are *The Intelligent Man's Guide to Science* and *Asimov's Encyclopedia of Science and Technology*, which stayed in print into the 1980s.

At the same time, the readership of Asimov's earlier works of science fiction continued to grow due to his speaking tours, appearances on TV chat shows, anthologies, and the regular series of science articles he wrote for *Fantasy and Science Fiction* magazine. They won him a special Hugo Award in 1962, and he won another Hugo—"best all-time

series"—for the Foundation trilogy in 1966. The Foundation series is seen as pivotal in science fiction, and Asimov himself as a visionary. It took the history of the rise of human civilization and retold it on a new and vaster canvas, set in the future and on a galactic scale. Asimov was seen as writing "psychohistory"—that is, his fiction dealt with the complex issues of sociology and psychology rather than ray guns and flying saucers. Critics claim that Asimov's Foundation series was, in part at least, the inspiration for George Lucas's *Star Wars* movies.

In 1965 Asimov landed the contract to produce a novelization of the science fiction movie *Fantastic Voyage*, which appeared in 1966. He also wrote a

△ **Asimov's remarkable range of interests included mathematics and humor as well as the science fiction that made him famous.**

handful of science fiction short stories during the decade. It was not until the 1970s, however, that Asimov returned to writing science fiction novels, with the Hugo and Nebula Award-winning book *The Gods Themselves*. Then in the 1980s Asimov returned to his celebrated Foundation series.

By the time he died in 1992, Asimov had written and edited a huge total of nearly 500 books, and along with Robert Heinlein, Arthur C. Clarke, and A. E. Van Vogt, he was considered one of the great science fiction writers of the mid-20th century. □

See Also: Literature; Science Fiction

AUTOMOBILE INDUSTRY

At the beginning of the 1960s Americans seemed very happy with the products being turned out in vast numbers by the U.S. car industry, but those days of uncritical acceptance were numbered.

The *Wall Street Journal* in 1971 said, "The novelty and status of car ownership are long gone." Instead, "People today look at their cars as appliances to get them economically from place to place and to be replaced when they wear out."

That view of America's falling out of love with the automobile, which since the 1920s had been so much a part of national social and economic life, is not quite true even at the beginning of the 21st century. What has been called the "car culture" is still fundamental, and cars still confer status. But there was a sea change in the significance of the automobile in America during the 1960s, when the nation's most distinctive and vibrant industry took a bumpy ride. At the same time as cars began to

lose much of their earlier romance, the industry was assailed for the first time by serious competition from abroad and critical appraisal at home.

The assembly lines roll

In the early days of the automobile industry American manufacturers like Henry Ford had taken the lead in mass producing cheap, serviceable vehicles. Up to 1923—when production finished—18 million Model-T Fords had been sold, and the price was down to a widely affordable $290. This contrasted sharply with Europe, where the automobile was a relatively rich person's toy developed to replace the horse-drawn carriages of the wealthier classes.

By 1929, when the Great Depression put a brake on the expanding industry,

△ **At the beginning of the 1960s Cadillac could advertise its limousine model as a vehicle for transforming the owner's life.**

over 26 million vehicles were registered, traveling 198 billion miles in the year. The manufacture of cars was worth over $3 billion, and the export of cars was ranked third in value of goods sold overseas. Motorists were spending $10 billion a year supporting huge industries from steel to petroleum. Half of American families owned cars. Government put vast amounts of money into road-building.

Economic depression first halted the spread of the automobile, and then the demands of war diverted the vast resources of the industry into the conflict in Europe and the Pacific: $29 billion went into making guns, tanks, machines, trucks, and aircraft. By the 1950s, therefore, there was a huge, pent-up demand for new automobiles in the U.S., which the industry was well-equipped to supply. In fact, it very soon faced a problem of overproduction despite the fact that America was the world's major exporter of cars.

Was bigger better?

There was fierce competition for market share, which was dominated by the Big Three—General Motors, Ford, and Chrysler. The variety of makes and models was dazzling, and the cars got larger and more powerful as the industry embarked on what was called the "horsepower race." The ordinary family car increasingly came equipped with all kinds of enticing new features such as power steering, power brakes, electric windows, automatic transmission, and later, air conditioning. Such luxury, once enjoyed, had a tendency to become part of normal expectations.

The price of automobiles began to rise steadily, and car dealers and salesmen, under pressure from manufacturers to take on more models and accompanying accessories than they could easily sell, evolved their notorious high-pressure sales pitches with customers. Their aim was to induce buyers to trade up to new models and accept lower prices on trade-ins of old cars. A whole language was developed to describe these sales techniques that one senator described as having the "morality of an Oriental bazaar."

By the early 1960s it was dawning on American commentators that something absurd was going on in the automobile industry. It insisted on making huge cars equipped with dozens of nonessential gadgets despite the fact that most journeys made were local, for which a smaller, more basic car would be adequate. Within the industry George K. Romney, president of American Motors, referred to these giant gas-guzzlers as the "dinosaur in the driveway."

Whereas even a thirsty Cadillac got 20 miles to the gallon in 1949, by the beginning of the 1970s the average American model managed less than 14 miles to the gallon. Because the cars were so cumbersome, more money had to be paid for wider roads, which pushed up vehicle taxes. And the emphasis on style took attention away from serviceability and safety. If a powerful "muscle car" of the late 1960s with its huge engine crashed, it was likely to fall apart in deadly manner.

▽ A typical 1960s car interior, gleaming with chrome that could turn lethal for unbelted occupants in the event of a crash.

Challenging the concept

In the heady days of the 1950s the American automobile industry reigned supreme and made cars that were large by international standards, equipped luxuriously, and produced in an astonishing range of ever-changing styles. There was no competition to speak of from abroad—despite the prestige associated with European luxury cars and a certain cult status enjoyed by jaunty little British sports cars. Gasoline was cheap, and the highways in which the government had invested billions were wide. There appeared to be little or no demand for smaller, more economical cars in this motoring wonderland, and small American models such as the Nash Rambler and Kaiser Henry J had not sold especially well.

The first sign that there was an American market for the small car came with the success of the odd-looking Volkswagen Beetle. From modest sales of 28,000 a year in the U.S. in the mid-1950s, the VW was selling 160,000 by 1960. It continued to be the leading imported model throughout the 1960s, achieving 62 percent of all import sales in 1968. By 1970, having earned an excellent reputation for reliability, the unprepossessing little Beetle had chalked up a remarkable 4 million sales in total.

The Big Three took note in the late 1950s and began to bring over modest-sized cars from their European subsidiaries to market themselves. General Motors, for example, imported Opels from Germany and Vauxhalls from Great Britain. But they did not begin to sell the "compacts" they had on their own drawing boards until 1959, when the Chevrolet Corvair, the Ford Falcon, and the Plymouth Valiant were launched. They were successful and for two years slowed the rate of foreign imports, which by then, ominously for the industry, included the first trickle of small cars from Japan.

The American compacts were not, however, in direct competition with the smaller foreign cars because buyers wanted them to have such features as power steering and automatic transmission, which raised their price. Research showed too that the biggest market for small cars was among families that already owned a standard car. By the beginning of the 1970s compacts were a feature of American highways, but full-size cars still had 60 percent of the market, with 23 percent going to American-made smaller cars, and the remainder to imports.

In order to sustain demand, manufacturers kept on producing new models with what critics called "built-in obsolescence"—they were designed to be replaced by the next new model. Whereas even in the mid-1950s more than 80 percent of cars made by the Big Three were still on the road nine years after they were sold, the figure had dropped to just 55 percent by 1967.

Glitz and profits

With no fewer than 370 new models on the market in 1967, the automobile industry had become to a large extent simply show, with practically nothing new in terms of basic design or increased safety. In fact, it was estimated that cars made by the Big Three had an average of 24 defects each on delivery to the customer, who then had to pay to make the vehicle roadworthy.

The automobile industry, however, was making huge profits: the bigger the

△ Road-building in Washington, D.C., in 1962. During the 1960s the road network expanded in line with the trend toward suburban living.

cars, the higher the return for both manufacturers and dealers. For the period 1950–1965 one study calculated that American car manufacturers were getting a return of over 13 percent on investment, far above that achieved in most other sectors of industry.

Coping with car culture

There were many criticisms of the industry in the late 1950s and 1960s, and serious attempts to regulate it. But overall it continued to boom. Government spent billions on interstate highways, and a large part of everyday life was restructured to accommodate the automobile. As car ownership rose from 59 percent of families in 1950 to nearly 80 percent at the end of the 1960s, "drive-in" movies, restaurants, banks, and churches multiplied. By 1972 the factories turned out

King car

According to the president of the United States, "The motor car has become an indispensable instrument in our political, social, and industrial life." So said President Warren G. Harding in 1921! At the time the automobile was seen as a replacement for the horse, but by the 1960s it had outlasted every other sort of transportation with the exception of air travel, now taking off with the jet age.

Many people saw the popularity of the automobile and its position at the center of American life in the 1960s as inevitable—it was what the people wanted. But the story is not as simple or as democratic as that. Cars are not much use without good roads to drive on, and the money for highways comes largely from governments that have a choice in how they spend public funds. And it was not just road-building. To create a car culture, much of the rest of life—for example, the positioning of schools and homes and businesses—has to be rearranged.

Already in the 1920s government was spending more than $2 billion annually on road-building. After the slowdown of the Great Depression and the World War II years road-building accelerated spectacularly. The Interstate Highway Act of 1956 committed the government to paying 90 percent of the cost of building 41,000 miles of toll-free expressways by the 1970s. The money was doled out through a Highway Trust Fund; and while it was earmarked for roads alone, there was no corresponding funding for other forms of transportation such as interstate railways. The fund was largely self-financing in that the money came from taxes on all kinds of motoring accessories, but it starved alternative forms of transportation. One estimate is that a staggering $249 billion was spent by local, state, and federal governments on all forms of road-building between 1947 and 1970.

The youth market

In 1950 only 7 percent of American families had more than one car. By 1960 this had doubled to 15 percent, and by the end of the decade nearly a third of all families had more than one car. This opened up entirely new markets for the automotive industry, which had been accustomed to turning out large, comfortable models that appealed primarily to the man of the house. Now many housewives had their own car, and what began to whet the industry's appetite, so did many teenagers.

It was recognized that one of the appeals of imported smaller cars like the Volkswagen Beetle was that they bestowed on the owner an air of "individuality." This, the stylists of the big manufacturers decided, was the key to success in the youth market. Claud McCammon, who worked on General Motor's styling staff, identified a new mass market, or more accurately, many markets. As he wittily put it: "These new mass markets are a reflection of a kind of mass individualism which makes everyone want to be different—exactly like everyone else is different."

Not only would cars be designed specifically to appeal to an age group, they would be offered with such a vast range of options that no two cars sold would be absolutely identical. To capture the new youth market, "Bunkie" Knudsen, who became general manager of Pontiac in 1956, set up a team of young managers and engineers who studied the amateur styling of 1950s "hot rod" enthusiasts. They came up with the GTO, named after a legendary Ferrari racing car. By taking existing parts and recombining them in a reworked body, they produced a powerful sports car—the compact Tempest model with a massive V-8 engine under the hood. To promote the car, a hit record called "Little GTO" was "manufactured" by Pontiac. This so-called "muscle car" sold 84,000 in three years at $3,200 apiece.

All the big manufacturers came up with variations on this theme—comparatively small cars that had huge engines and were offered with a range of options so that the buyer could get "individuality." Ford came up with the celebrated Mustang, designed specifically to appeal to the 16–24 age group. It was the brainchild of Ford Division president Lee Iacocca and was based on a proposed sports car model. The Mustang, which became known as a pony car, was built largely from existing components used for the Falcon and Fairline models. This meant that the Mustang could be mass-produced at a price within range of its young target market. "All we did was put a youth wrap around it," Iacocca said. Displayed on college campuses in 1965, the Mustang was a phenomenal success, selling 417,000 in its first year.

The pony car craze led on to General Motor's Pontiac Firebird and Chevrolet Camaro. Over time these long-snouted, short-bodied cars got bigger and heavier, and in 1971 Iacocca admitted that the Mustang had become more like a "fat pig" than a sleek horse.

▽ **The Mustang was an overnight sensation when it went on sale in 1965, and Ford's rivals hotly pursued it into the youth market.**

over eight million new cars, and there were 117.4 million private registrations of vehicles, which included campers, snowmobiles, and motor homes.

Though the car culture rolled on, the first attempts to deal with problems that are so familiar today came in the 1960s. Southern California, where the density of car ownership was highest, had experienced gasoline fume smogs in the 1950s and passed the first laws requiring manufacturers to modify cars in 1963. The industry itself was reluctant to comply with such regulations, but was eventually forced to do so when the federal government passed the Motor Vehicle Air Pollution Act of 1965 regulating emissions from cars. It was estimated in 1966 that in the country as a whole car exhausts pumped 86 million tons of pollutants into the atmosphere—in fact, by the late 1960s well over half of all pollutants in the air came from cars. Year by

▽ The traffic jam had become a chronic feature of American life by the 1960s, along with heavy pollution from car emissions.

year these emissions came under tighter control. Safety concerns as the death toll on the highways rose were a further setback to the industry's reputation.

Another aspect of the mounting disenchantment with the car culture in the 1960s was the realization that mass ownership was giving rise to new forms of social segregation between the increasingly affluent majority who could afford to live out of town in newly built suburbs, and the poorer segments of the population who were stuck in cities with declining public transportation services. There was an irony in this, because as late as the 1950s the car had been hailed as a boon to society because it allowed people to escape the overcrowding in the cities.

Living with traffic jams
The relentless spread of suburbia was not only a consequence of the car culture but itself added to the problems caused by the car. Sitting in traffic jams or crawling at a snail's pace along congested roads became an everyday event for suburbanites who commuted into

city centers. For all these interrelated reasons there was a growing realization that the automobile, which had been regarded as the servant of the American people, was becoming its master.

There were some efforts to combat the power of the big manufacturers, but the average motorist could do little to turn the tide until there was on offer an alternative kind of car to replace the gas-guzzlers made in America. This began to happen in the 1960s. Whereas only 5 percent of the new car sales were imports in 1963, that figure had risen to 16 percent by 1971.

Responding to new demands
Throughout the 1960s American manufacturers were being hammered both on the world market and at home. Belatedly they began to make smaller cars for both markets in response to the demands of a generation that was waking up to the fact that traditional big cars were impractical, unnecessarily polluting, unsafe, and wasteful. The oil crisis that followed in the 1970s would reinforce such attitudes. □

See Also: Car Safety; Consumer Society; Economy; Petroleum Industry; Suburbia; Transportation

BABY-BOOM GENERATION

In the years following World War II there was a surge in the birthrate, giving rise to an unprecedentedly large generation of children. During the 1960s this generation came of age.

The generation born between 1946 and 1964 is known as the postwar baby-boom generation, or baby boomers, sometimes abbreviated to boomers. It was called this because of the dramatic and sustained increase in the number of babies being born, making it the largest generation in American history (*see box p. 96*).

So many extra babies arrived so unexpectedly that the onslaught transformed America. GIs returning from World War II married and began having children at an unprecedented rate. The huge numbers of babies helped stimulate an economic growth that was creating the most affluent society in history. New schools and teachers were needed to house and educate millions of new school children. Their numbers also caused a home building boom and spread to other sectors of the economy. The sprawling suburbs that sprang up in the 1950s were designed to accommodate the growing numbers of young families.

Growing up in the suburbs

For a large part of this new generation of Americans the suburbs provided the formative environment. Many boomers grew up in planned, prefabricated suburbs of the type originated by William Levitt and called Levittowns. Levitt's genius was to standardize and mass produce prefabricated suburban homes. The planned communities offered Cape Cod houses for under $7,000, with just $100 down payment. That put them within the reach of most returning GIs. Later Levitt added ranch-style houses for under $10,000. Levittowns and similar schemes began a boom in suburban home construction

that stimulated the economy and led to a mass migration of the white middle class from the cities to new tract houses built in surrounding countryside.

Levitt and his imitators offered homes as a way for average Americans to roll up their sleeves and get to the business of producing a society in which every man had a good job and a decent place to live. In addition to the

△ A baby boomer's essential headgear in the mid-1950s, as a craze for backwoods hero Davy Crockett swept the country.

famously low price, the original Levitt design came with a kitchen, a living room with a fireplace, and two bedrooms sitting on a lot planted with fruit trees. These homes had central heating, built-in bookcases, closets, a washing machine, and a TV set (with an eight-inch screen). It could all be paid for with a 30-year mortgage. This provided a degree of affluence unprecedented for families just entering the middle class. Levitt thoughtfully put the kitchen beside the living room, so boomer mothers could keep an eye on their children as they sat on the floor in front of the TV set. "Everyone is so young that sometimes it's hard to remember how to get along with older people," one Levittown housewife remarked.

The first TV generation

In addition, the huge numbers of babies demanded new services and products, especially toys: from Hula-Hoops and Davy Crockett coonskin hats to Barbie dolls. With the economy flourishing and more and more families entering the middle class, indulgent boomer parents were eager to buy their children new products that appeared in the TV commercials on the children's programs and Saturday morning cartoon shows. The toy industry became big business.

Baby boomers became the first generation in history to grow up with television, which became an integral

▷ A fun way to learn the nation's geography— and still only 48 states to contend with—in a suburban primary school in the mid-1950s.

The baby boom

The 19-year baby boom produced 76 million American babies. During the first year of the boom 3.4 million were born. At the time it was a record number of births for one year. From January 1946 babies were being born at the rate of 338,000 a month, 100,000 more per month than the previous year, and many more than were predicted by the population trend.

In 1947 the annual birthrate increased by 400,000 to 3,834,000, and from 1954 on, over 4 million babies arrived each year until 1964, peaking in 1957, when 4.3 million babies were born. The boom exhausted itself in 1965, when births fell below 4 million, and a new generation began. By its end the baby boom accounted for 31 percent of the American population.

Making allowance for deaths and immigration, by 1990 there were 78 million baby boomers. Women accounted for a little over half of them (numbering 468,000 more than men). Sixty-one million were white, 9 million black, and about 6 million Hispanic, Asian, and Native American.

part of their lives almost from birth. Television served as an "electronic babysitter" during their formative years and exposed young boomers to the marvels of the world. There were, of course, terrors in the world too. There was no guarantee that the Cold War would stay "cold," and children were taught to "duck and cover" in the event of a nuclear attack while some worried parents invested in fallout shelters. Even if such concerns were at the back of their parents' minds, however, the boomer world remained the neighborhood, accessible by bicycle, always open, exciting, and safe. *Howdy Doody, Captain Kangaroo, I Love Lucy, Leave it to Beaver*, and other shows depicted a world that was whiter, more affluent, more Protestant, and safer than reality. But the other world was far away and had not penetrated baby boomers' lives. The future meant what would take place on "Anything Can Happen Day" on the *Mickey Mouse Club*, where Mouseketeer Annette Funicello was the personification of youthful beauty.

Boomers hit college

When baby boomers began to hit college in 1964, they had an impact that reached well beyond the college campuses. Americans had always put a high premium on a college education, but now there was a difference. The growing size of the middle class and generous governmental policies made college accessible to families that otherwise could not have afforded to send their children. The numbers coming into college were staggering. By 1960 there were already 24.6 million young of the ages 15–24. The teenage population itself amounted to about 21 million. Boomers were, as one historian put it, "a nation within a nation." Three million boomers reached college age in 1964, with 3 million following the next year. By the end of the decade 8 million boomers were in college.

A rude awakening

For first-year students university often came as a surprise, and not always a pleasant one. Universities characterized themselves as "multiversities" and "knowledge factories." Many boomers had come straight from secure suburban or small-town enclaves and were thrust into a situation where they felt lost in the campus crowd. They were processed, housed, and graded according to their social security number. At most universities registering for classes took two days or more. Classes of several hundred students were commonplace.

It was a rude awakening. They learned that the world did not consist of neighborhoods of plenty where

Dr. Spock's famous book

In June 1946 the pediatrician Benjamin Spock published the *Common Sense Book of Baby and Child Care*, and the book became a runaway bestseller. It is not too much of an exaggeration to say that the baby-boom generation was raised according to guidelines laid down by Dr. Spock. The liberal-minded Spock rejected earlier theories of child-rearing that laid heavy emphasis on discipline and routine. Instead, he encouraged parents to avoid rigidity and corporal punishment of their children. To a generation of expecting mothers Dr. Spock's book took the place of the Holy Bible on the nightstand and at the breakfast table. His message was somewhat new and so obvious now: "Trust yourself. You know more than you think you do." Above all, said Spock, "Hug your children." Spock also counseled to be friendly and encouraging rather than stern. If parents were successful, the result would be a generation of "idealistic children."

At an initial price of 35 cents this unassuming little paperback sold 4 million copies by 1952 and went on to sell a further million-plus a year for 18 straight years. By the 1990s the total came to over 50 million copies, translated into 39 languages, including Urdu and Catalan.

Spock became the first millionaire created by the baby-boom generation. Half a generation later he joined many youthful dissenters in the streets to protest against the war in Vietnam. By doing so, he alienated many of their parents' generation (his original readership), who came to identify the once-revered doctor as a symbol of permissiveness and revolution.

▽ **World-famous pediatrician and antiwar activist Dr. Benjamin Spock delivering an antiwar message to the Southern Christian Leadership Conference on August 17, 1967.**

everyone shared ethnicity and outlook. They were the first generation to confront America's new mass society (of which they were of course the most conspicuous feature), and they resented being treated like those ubiquitous IBM punch cards. They also resisted the strict rules that awaited them.

These rules were left over from the conformist 1950s, and they affected such areas as dating and socializing. The university officials felt it was their responsibility to assume a parental role and did not hesitate to impose curfews and dictate dress code. To take one example, which students ridiculed, there was a "three-foot rule" requiring three feet to be on the floor at all times during a coeducational dorm room visit. The door could be closed no more than the width of a textbook. While

this may have led to an imaginative search for slim volumes of poetry, it was arbitrary and insulting to people who might have risked their lives in support of the civil rights movement or might soon be asked to lay down their lives in the jungles of Southeast Asia.

Student protest

As it turned out, these sorts of rules had the opposite effect. Far from instilling obedience in the young, they triggered an aggressive response that took the form of demands for increased student freedoms. From there a more vocal element began to widen their attack to include restrictive attitudes and practices in society as a whole. That was how the student protest movement of the 1960s got started, and how it developed its wide-ranging agenda.

The first notable student protest was the Berkeley Free Speech Movement at the University of California at Berkeley, in 1964. Over several days of rioting, angry students virtually closed down the campus in defiance of administration attempts to restrict the scope of on-campus political discussion and activism among students. Inspired by the idealism and success of the civil rights movement, in which many students had participated, protests spread across the major campuses.

With the escalation of the war in Vietnam in 1965 protests grew in frequency and size. Because of their huge numbers on the major campuses disaffected students were able to make their voices heard across the nation.

Caught off guard by the ferocity and scope of the linked student and antiwar movements, college administrations complied with many if not most students' demands. Many campuses removed all the hated restrictions on dating and socializing, ending curfews and in some cases creating coed dormitories. Many also moderated at least for a time general education requirements that dictated which courses students must take as they set up black and women's studies programs in response to student demands.

Not all baby boomers went to college, of course. About a million baby boomers served in the armed forces in Vietnam, many of them military draftees, and it was widely remarked that college students showed much determination in avoiding the draft. This created a gulf among boomers that reflected a wider split in society between "hawks" who supported the war effort and "doves" who opposed it. This continued until the United States withdrew from Vietnam in 1973, and its echoes continue to the present time.

During the 1960s baby boomers revolutionized popular culture with the ideas and ideals of a counterculture, rock music, and general emphasis on being, looking, and acting young. This wide gulf in attitudes about sex, drugs, culture, and the Vietnam War became known as the Generation Gap.

Alternative lifestyles

The counterculture embraced a wide spectrum of attitudes and responses to existing American society, and young people moved to varying degrees across that spectrum. As the 1960s wore on, more and more young people adopted the flamboyant dress of the counterculture: long hair for both men and women, blue jeans, T-shirt and sandals, brightly colored headbands, and such paraphernalia—the look that was quickly dubbed the "hippie" style.

Outward appearances, however, could be misleading. In terms of committed political activism and the attempts to establish alternative lifestyles, such as communes, it has been estimated that fewer than one in four young people actively participated in the counterculture. On the other hand, youthful idealism (especially in relation to civil rights and the war) was widespread, and a great many did experiment with marijuana and psychedelic drugs, and rejected the strict sexual morality that characterized the preceding period. The fact that such terms as counterculture and hippie and youthful rebellion were imprecise and easily jumbled together was confusing because it ignored the great differences in the actual experiences of individuals.

The silent majority

Although the counterculture made a great impact on society in the late 1960s, for the majority of baby boomers it was not central to their lives. They might have grown their hair longer and listened avidly to loud rock music, but that did not make them political radicals still less revolution-

◁ The Vietnam War was a defining issue for many boomers. Opposition to the war was not confined to the young, but college students were in the vanguard of the protest movement.

Of more immediate importance was the political activism that emerged from the era. The student movement was to its critics misguided in many of its demands, but it undeniably produced a vastly less impersonal college environment. The antiwar movement certainly hastened the ending of an unpopular war. Not just the hugely important civil rights movement, but women's liberation, the Gray Panthers (senior rights), the Chicano and American Indian movements—all combined to make Americans conscious of gender, age, and ethnic discrimination. Concern for pollution and the condition of the environment today are a direct result of the efforts of the protest generation.

Youth generation grows up

Adult boomers tended to delay starting a family as women especially sought new opportunities created by political activism and social changes. When boomers did start families, they had to confront the moral complexities of drug use and rebellion by their children, when they might have participated in both themselves. □

△ Graduation Day at Columbia University in 1964. Far more boomers enjoyed a college education than had any earlier generation.

aries. Most either rejected or at least did not take part in the political activism and protest that convulsed the country and involved so many of their age. They simply got on with their lives.

The boomers' legacy

That does not change the fact that the baby-boom generation, if for no other reason than its large numbers, brought important changes to American society. No other generation has created so much change in the way people live. Informal attitudes about personal relationships and dress combined with an emphasis on hedonism, exercise, outdoor activities, and "natural" foods revolutionized much of the social scene. By the 1970s a huge variety of "self-improvement" gurus, encounter groups, religious cults, and even fundamentalist religious sects attracted a large following among boomers, many of whom turned from social activism to self-fulfillment with the same fervor that had put them in protest marches the previous decade.

Black baby boomers

In most African American families the more than nine million black baby boomers became the first of their race to enjoy the new freedoms won by the civil rights movement. Some of the earliest black boomers participated in the movement. During the 1960s and in the ensuing decades black boomers benefited from increased opportunity and affirmative action policies that sought out qualified applicants. Consequently, they entered college in unprecedented numbers and the mainstream workforce after that.

Although they still suffered from discrimination and the crisis of trying to be two things, American and black simultaneously, they came of age and had families under circumstances entirely new and different from their parents and grandparents. Today, two-thirds of Americans of African descent are solidly middle class, with many living in once white-only suburbia. The number of black elected officials has increased tenfold since the mid-1960s. Men such as Michael Jordan and Colin Powell enjoy opportunities unavailable if not unimaginable to previous generations. There are many successful black actresses and women writers, and female civil servants and politicians have served in high-ranking positions right across the spectrum of American political life, including numerous Congressional representatives and several United States senators.

See Also: Antiwar Movement; Berkeley Free Speech Movement; Counterculture; Feminist Movement; Generation Gap; Hippies; Schools and Universities; Sexual Revolution

JOAN BAEZ b. 1941

With her striking soprano voice, Joan Baez emerged as a star of the folk music scene in the early 1960s and went on to become a tireless campaigner for civil rights and against the Vietnam War.

Joan Chandos Baez was born in Staten Island, New York, on January 9, 1941, and brought up mainly in Palo Alto, California. She began her career singing in folk clubs and coffee houses in Greenwich Village, New York, and Boston, Massachusetts.

Baez first hit the headlines after her solo appearance at the 1960 Newport Folk Festival and the release of her first album later the same year. With her instantly recognizable, pure soprano voice she led the folk boom of the early 1960s, and several of her early recordings sold more than a million copies. In addition to material she wrote herself Joan Baez recorded many songs by Bob Dylan —her tenth album, *Any Day Now*, released in 1968, was a two-disk set of Dylan songs; the two were friends, collaborators, and for a time, lovers. "We Shall Overcome"—the song with which she is most readily associated—was written by veteran folksinger Pete Seeger and became an anthem of first the civil rights and then the antiwar movement.

Singer and political activist

A tireless activist for the causes she espoused, Baez made three concert tours of southern U.S. college campuses in 1962. Wherever she performed, she insisted that the audiences were not segregated. In November 1962 she appeared on the cover of *Time* magazine.

△ One of the finest folk singers of her generation, during the 1960s Joan Baez was equally well known for her antiwar activities.

In 1964 Baez began her long and highly publicized protest against U.S. involvement in the Vietnam War by withholding 60 percent of her income tax, the amount she claimed was used for military purposes. She took part in civil rights marches from Selma to Montgomery, Alabama, and through Grenada, Mississippi, with Martin Luther King, Jr., to protest against the flagrant violence committed against black children as schools were desegre-

gated. In 1965 Joan Baez founded the Institute for the Study of Non-Violence.

In 1967 the ultraconservative Daughters of the American Revolution blocked her plan to put on a concert at Constitution Hall in Washington, D.C. In response, Joan Baez appeared on Irv Kupcinet's Chicago talk show, where she and liberal Republican senator Chuck Percy humiliated the inarticulate DAR chairperson on air. Shortly afterward Baez held a free concert at the base of the Washington Monument in front of a crowd estimated to be 30,000. Later that year she served 10 days in prison for blocking the entrance to the Armed Forces Induction Center in Oakland, California. She obstructed the gateway again in December and was sentenced to a further 90 days, but she was let out after just a month because warders feared an uprising on her official release date.

In 1968 Joan Baez married David Harris, a leading draft-resister. They toured the country together and encouraged opposition to the Vietnam War. In July 1969 Harris was sentenced to three years in prison for draft resistance. He was released after serving 21 months of his sentence.

Joan Baez confirmed her status in the pop world when she became one of the stars of the 1969 Woodstock Festival. Over the succeeding three decades she has continued to tour successfully. □

See Also: Antiwar Movement; Civil Rights Movement; Dylan; Folk Music; Woodstock Festival

JAMES BALDWIN 1924–1987

As a writer with great insights into the experience of blacks in America, the novelist James Baldwin lent eloquent and impassioned voice to the civil rights movement of the 1960s.

James Baldwin published his first novel, *Go Tell It on the Mountain*, in 1949, but it was in the 1960s that his talent as a writer blossomed and that he came into prominence as a civil rights activist. Most of the 1950s Baldwin spent outside the United States in Paris, and though he met Martin Luther King, Jr., in 1958, it was not until 1961 that he met Malcolm X and Elijah Muhammad. Then in 1967 he met Eldridge Cleaver and Huey Newton. Baldwin marched from Selma to Montgomery with King in 1963, addressed civil rights meetings across the nation, and in 1967 undertook to write the screenplay for a film of Malcolm X's life. But he was foremost, as he insisted, a writer.

Holding himself aloof from black movements and organizations, Baldwin sounded his own articulate, independent voice of prophecy. Everything that he wrote was a distillation of his own expe-

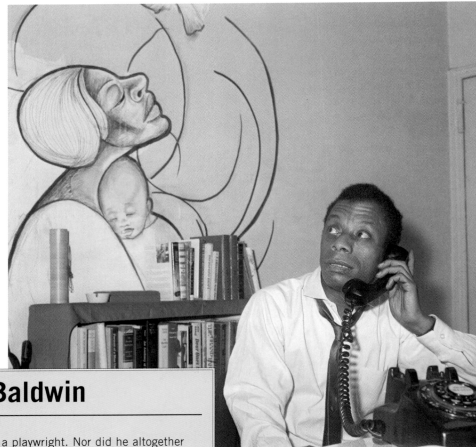

△ James Baldwin in his study in 1963. Baldwin returned to the U.S. from his home in France to get involved in the civil rights movement with Martin Luther King, Jr.

Blues for Mister Baldwin

Baldwin never achieved high fame as a playwright. Nor did he altogether master the craft of writing for the theater. But *Blues for Mister Charlie*, which opened on Broadway in April 1964, created a sensation. The English critic Kenneth Tynan wrote that "you could feel the shockwaves across the Atlantic." Howard Taubman of the *New York Times* praised it for bringing "eloquence and conviction to one of the momentous themes of our era." The play tells the story of a young Southern black man who goes north, discovers a different way of living there, and returns to the South, where he is unable to make his peace again with segregation. He is murdered by a beer-swilling redneck who is acquitted of the crime.

Blacks cheered the performances. Many whites were angered by the intense hatred depicted in the play and bewildered by its central message that the moral crisis of racism in America was in fact the white man's crisis. The play folded after a few weeks and failed to break even. It was subsequently taken to the World Theater Festival in London, where it was better received, and it remains one of the few plays by a black writer for a nearly all-black cast to have entered the repertoire.

rience, growing up in a country in which at the age of six, as he put it, he discovered that he was an Indian in a nation of Gary Coopers. As well, Baldwin's homosexuality further set him apart from the mainstream American society around him. The heightened language of his at times lyrical, although always highly disciplined, prose was rooted in his boyhood in Harlem. Baldwin was the son of a Baptist preacher and in his teens was a preacher himself at a local church.

In the early 1960s Baldwin wrote numerous articles for magazines such as *Harper's, Partisan Review, The Reporter,* and *Commentary,* and published three important works: a collection of essays, *Nobody Knows My Name* (1961), a novel, *Another Country* (1962), and *The Fire Next Time* (1963), an essay that was part autobiography, part polemic. He also had two plays produced on Broadway, *Blues for Mister Charlie* (1964) and *The Amen Corner* (1965, but written a decade earlier).

Baldwin's consistent text was that the so-called "Negro problem" could not be solved until an understanding of America's historical experience—what in *Another Country* he called the "unexamined pain"—had seeped into the American mind. The point of the title of *Nobody Knows My Name* was that slavery had robbed American blacks of their cultural identity by denying them a historical past of any importance. Whites therefore felt free to ignore what blacks did or said. A major element of such insidious oppression was to be left without a name.

A hatred of hatred

Baldwin's distance from Muhammad's Nation of Islam, with its advocacy of racial separateness, indeed, his distance from black power movements in general, stemmed from his objection to any program or strategy that exalted hatred. "The glorification of one race and the consequent debasement of another" was a "recipe for murder" that led to a "spiritual wasteland."

On the other hand, Baldwin had just as little regard for the idea of integration as he believed white liberals understood it, namely, that the black man had to be weaned on the milk of white civilization and raised to equality with the white man. Baldwin had reached the conclusion that desegregation itself would do little to improve the status of blacks in a systematically racist society. "Do I really want," he

▷ **Baldwin addressing a press conference on February 22, 1965, the day after the assassination of Malcolm X in Harlem.**

asked in *The Fire Next Time,* "to be integrated into a burning house?" King called integration "community"; Baldwin preferred to think of it as "the achievement of nationhood."

Baldwin's anger at injustice reached its height of literary intensity in *The Fire Next Time,* whose very title was arresting in its incendiary implications. Readers, blacks and white liberals alike, were alarmed by the assault on Christianity (Baldwin had left the Church 20 years earlier) and the author's suggestion that if God did not make Americans "larger, freer, and more loving," it was time to be rid of Him. Scarcely less provocative was the daring conclusion that the history of blacks in America was, from their suffering, "something very beautiful." As Baldwin saw it, the hour for redemption was at hand; America had but a short time to grow up or be lost. □

From the writings

"Freedom is not something that anybody can be given; freedom is something people take and people are as free as they want to be."
Nobody Knows My Name (1961)

"You can only be destroyed by believing that you really are what the white world calls a nigger."
The Fire Next Time (1963)

"The Negro's experience of the white world cannot possibly create in him any respect for the standards by which the white world claims to live. His own condition is overwhelming proof that white people do not live by these standards."
The Fire Next Time (1963)

"It is a terrible thing for an entire people to surrender to the notion that one-ninth of its population is beneath them. Until the moment comes when we, the Americans, are able to accept the fact that my ancestors are both black and white, that on this continent we are trying to forge a new identity, that we need each other, that I am not a ward of America, I am not an object of missionary charity, I am one of the people who built the country—until this moment comes there is scarcely any hope for the American dream."
"The American Dream and the American Negro" (1965)

See Also: Civil Rights Movement; Literature; Segregation

BALLET

The 1960s were years of innovation for American ballet, as a talented new generation of choreographers and dancers gained greater acceptance of their art within mainstream culture.

At the beginning of the 1960s ballet in the United States was in a dynamic phase and was able to draw on a wide range of traditions and innovations. Although professional opportunities for performers and choreographers were still relatively scarce, the 1950s had witnessed the development of the careers of a number of significant choreographers. Much of this progressive energy was focused on New York, although ballet companies were by now established in many regional centers, including San Francisco, Los Angeles, Chicago, and Boston.

One distinctive feature of U.S. dance at this time was the close relationship that existed between elements in the progressive modern dance scene and the commercial worlds of Broadway and Hollywood. Jerome Robbins was an established ballet choreographer in the 1950s, but he also created celebrated dances for musicals like *West Side Story*, thereby increasing the status of dance within the overall production. Robbins's versatile style incorporated elements of ballet, jazz dance, and realistic movement. One of his masterpieces of the 1960s was his classical *Dances at a Gathering*, created for the New York City Ballet in 1969 and danced to solo piano works by the 19th-century composer Chopin. He also created a version of *Les Noces* to the score by Igor Stravinsky for the American Ballet Theater in 1965.

Although the major companies presented established classics from the Russian repertoire, such as the versions of *The Nutcracker* and the one-act *Swan Lake* created by George Balanchine, for many in American ballet audiences the core repertoire in the 1960s was the recently created masterpieces of 20-century American dance. Two key but contrasting figures in this respect were Balanchine and Martha Graham.

Balanchine and Graham

Balanchine had danced in the Soviet Union in the 1920s and choreographed for Diaghilev's famous Ballets Russes. For him the starting point in making a new ballet was the rhythm, phrasing, and texture of the music itself rather than any psychological or cultural agenda. He continued to create narrative ballets such as *A Midsummer Night's Dream* (1963). However, his company, the New York City Ballet, consolidated its reputation through the 1960s for its performances of his plotless ballets, although they were still considered cold by some critics.

By contrast, Martha Graham was for some the central figure in modern American dance. Her innovative work was based on a concern to make dance provoking and emotionally engaging. Her themes were based both on the darker aspects of the human psyche, such as her recent full-length *Clytemnestra* (1959), and on aspects of American culture, for example, her *Appalachian Spring* (1944), which was revived regularly throughout the 1960s.

Graham's powerful dance technique was based on her theories of contraction and release, and of breath as the

◁ **Russian-born choreographer George Balanchine puts the dancers of the New York City Ballet through their paces in 1965.**

fundamental element in the work of the dancer. She herself continued to dance until 1969. Her impact around the world was strengthened at this time by the foundation of Graham-influenced companies such as the Batsheva Dance Company (Tel Aviv, 1963) and the London Contemporary Dance Company (London, 1967).

A new generation

It is perhaps the work of a younger generation of choreographers that created the greatest impact on American ballet in the 1960s. Merce Cunningham had danced in the first performance of Graham's *Appalachian Spring*, but evolved his own innovative approach in the 1950s, often in collaboration with the avant-garde composer John Cage.

Cunningham's work in the 1960s demonstrated his interest in indeterminacy and chance, which he perceived as conditions of actual life. In *Field Dances* (1963), for example, each dancer was given a number of relatively simple moves that they could execute in whatever order they chose.

Cunningham became interested in releasing dance from the confines of the

▷ After Nureyev defected to the West in 1961, he formed the most famous ballet partnership of modern times with Margot Fonteyn.

The defection of Nureyev

The 1960s began with the sensational defection to the West of Rudolph Nureyev during a tour of the Kirov Ballet to Paris in 1961. Nureyev believed that companies in the West would give him greater opportunities for freedom of artistic expression. This was a huge propaganda coup for the West at a time when tension with the Soviet Union was at a very high level. It also gave ballet newspaper headlines in the United States.

Nureyev had trained with the Kirov, a company that had an extraordinary tradition of performance in the classical repertoire dating back to the 19th century. Quite apart from his outstanding abilities as a dancer, Nureyev had a knowledge of the repertoire and style of the Kirov that was of great value to companies in the West. Although the Royal Ballet in London became his base for many years, he rapidly made an impact in the United States, with appearances in Chicago and on television that created a sensation. He established a precedent for later defections by artists like Natalia Makarova and Mikhail Baryshnikov, who worked extensively in the U.S.

proscenium so that it could be viewed from many different perspectives. In 1964 he initiated his Events, which took place in unconventional venues, such as museums or gymnasia, or on occasion even outdoors. Cunningham himself was not interested in communicating meaning as such. He believed that this was essentially created in the perception of the spectator. However, some of Cunningham's works, such as *Winterbranch* (1964), were powerfully evocative to those who saw them.

Another choreographer of the 1950s, Alwin Nikolais, continued his experiments with multimedia spectacle, for which he was often his own designer and composer. His dancers frequently wore masks or were even completely encased in bags. When accused of creating a depersonalized dance, Nikolais replied that he was interested in conveying "motion, not emotion." In *Tent* (1968), for example, the dancers ceremonially created a tent that ultimately swallowed them.

As a result of such work young American choreographers in the 1960s felt liberated from the necessity to tell a story or be self-expressive. The burgeoning of choreographic talent from this time includes Paul Taylor, Twyla Tharp, and Meredith Monk. Use of unconventional locations and modern technologies were key aspects of their

▽ **A performance of Martha Graham's** *Diversion of Angels* **performed at the Connecticut College Dance Festival in 1967.**

new works. Twyla Tharp's *Medley* (1969) was performed at dusk in New York's Central Park. Meredith Monk first used film in *16 Millimeter Earrings* (1966), at one point projecting inflated images of her face on a white drum concealing her head.

A new simplicity

Experimental dance in America was given a particular impetus after the first dance concert in 1962 at the Judson Memorial Church in New York, which became the home of the Judson Dance Group. Many of their choreographers rejected the idea that dance requires the acquisition of a special technique. Everyday movements were often the basis of their dances, for example, Steve Paxton's *Satisfyin Lover* (1967), in which performers simply walked across the floor in response to cues.

Paul Taylor was a dancer with both Merce Cunningham and Martha Graham before becoming a choreographer in his own right. His ballets often express a highly experimental quality, exposing the differences between appearance and reality, and having a tendency to disrupt the expectations of the viewer. Works created by Taylor in the 1960s include his plotless ballet *Aureole* (1962), which is set to music by Handel and is still performed by several companies today. In *Private Domain* (1969) portions of the stage are obscured by elements of the set design, so giving each spectator a unique view of the action, some of which is seen, some unseen.

Much of the more radical work of the 1960s, particularly by choreographers associated with the Judson Memorial Church, was concerned to reduce dance to its essentials. This purism of approach eradicated many of the theatrical qualities often associated with dance: the use of scenery and costumes, and the adoption of "characters" by the dancers, for example.

Avoiding the theatrical

Yvonne Rainer is an example of a choreographer from this group who rejected notions of the "magic" of theater and the need for virtuosic training for performers. Dance was simply people moving in a performing space. Rainer's key work *Trio A* (1966) has been performed by nondancers as well as dancers. In it the performers are encouraged to display to the audience their difficulty in executing the moves rather than as usual employing technique to disguise the effort.

Choreographers no longer felt the need to tell a story or to be expressive of emotion along the lines of Martha Graham. Their focus was often on the structure and the process of creating dances. One West Coast choreographer, Anna Halprin, used games and improvisations as the basis of her dances. In the work of Simone Forti, for example, her *Huddle* of 1961, the choreography often consisted simply of a set of movement-based rules for her performers

along the lines of a game, which they were then free to execute randomly during the performance.

This commitment to innovation by 1960s choreographers, building on the experiments of Cunningham and others in the preceding decade, may represent one of the most influential achievements in the history of dance.

African American dance

The diverse nature of American society was acknowledged at this time in companies such as the multiracial Alvin Ailey American Dance Theater, whose eclectic movement style incorporated African American and jazz dancing. His company's signature piece, *Revelations* (1960), was danced to Negro spirituals.

In the 1960s black and Hispanic dancers became associated predominantly with ethnic and modern dance techniques. However, in 1969, as a direct response to the assassination of Martin Luther King, Jr., Arthur Mitchell, who had previously been a dancer with Balanchine's New York City Ballet, created a school for black dancers. He wanted to prove that they could excel in classical ballet as well as in ethnic and modern dance. Within

▷ **Alvin Ailey performing** *Hermit Songs*, **set to the music of Samuel Barber, with his innovative American Dance Theater in 1964.**

Dancer as athlete

One major development in American ballet during the 1960s was the growing acceptance of the virility of male dancers. As early as 1958 Gene Kelly had presented *Dancing Is a Man's Game* on television in an attempt to counter the widespread prejudice against men in dance.

In the 1960s the televised performances by ballet superstar Rudolph Nureyev made audiences aware of the obvious strength and stamina displayed by many male ballet dancers. In 1966 the Joffrey Ballet staged the all-male Olympics as a showcase to reinforce the point that men were not present in ballet simply to lift the ballerinas.

Recognition was also achieved by Edward Villela of the New York City Ballet. Villela was a dancer of great power, which was celebrated in 1969 in a *Life* magazine article titled "Is This Man the Country's Best Athlete?"

As a result of this new awareness greater numbers of boys and men began to study dance and to enjoy this uniquely athletic form of artistic expression.

two years his students had created a sensation with their performances as the Dance Theater of Harlem.

The 1960s was also the decade when ballet became the subject of more media coverage than at any time previously. By the end of the 1960s national magazines such as *Newsweek* and *Saturday Review* began to feature dance reviews. Television shows, such as the *Bell Telephone Hour* and the *Ed Sullivan Show*, made dance available to many Americans who had no access to live performances. In 1968 Joffrey's sensational psychedelic ballet *Astarte* even appeared on the cover of *Time* magazine. By the end of the 1960s ballet had finally come of age as a part of mainstream American culture. □

See Also: Broadway; Classical Music

BARBIE DOLL

From 1959 to the present time one doll has stood out among all others as being an essential part of little girls' lives. Fashion-crazy Barbie first conquered the fashion-crazy world of the 1960s.

Barbie had an interesting ancestry. While visiting Switzerland in the middle 1950s, Ruth Handler, cofounder of Mattel Toys, came across a German doll called Lili. The blond, shapely Lili was modeled on a famous German cartoon character of the same name. Molded in hard plastic and wearing somewhat revealing outfits, Lili's appeal was dubious, but Handler was quick to see her potential.

Having obtained the rights to Lili, Handler toned down the doll's sexiness and began researching into its appeal. When mothers and their young daughters were shown the "respectable" version of Lili, the mothers generally expressed concern that she was too mature-looking for a child's toy. Their daughters simply wanted one immediately. What Handler had stumbled on was the fact that traditional baby dolls, however well liked, did not have the aspirational appeal to little girls that a confident teenager so obviously had.

The birth of Barbie

In 1958 the Barbie doll was patented and went on sale the following year. Named after Ruth Handler's daughter, the long-limbed Barbie stood just under a foot tall and was available with a variety of wardrobes. With perfect timing Barbie entered the 1960s as a teenage fashion model just as youth fashion was taking off. Barbie took off as well. In the first year of marketing more than 350,000 dolls were sold at a price of $3.

Barbie's entourage soon followed: boyfriend Ken (1960) was named after Handler's son; then came best friend Midge (1963), little sister Skipper (1964), and "mod" British cousin Francie, sporting go-go boots

△ **"Twist and turn" Barbie doll from 1966, when she was at the center of the "swinging sixties."**

and the latest "swinging London" gear (1966). Barbie's constantly evolving features included interchangeable wigs (1963), bendable legs (1965), and speech in English or Spanish (1968). Barbie cars, campers, and kitchens were soon a part of Barbie play. Throughout the "swinging sixties" Barbie kept abreast of the bewilderingly rapid changes in fashion, although her favorite color remained pink. This of course was very good news for Mattel, and by the end of the decade some $500 million worth of Barbie products had been sold. By the 1990s more than 60 additional friends and relations had made an appearance in the world of Barbie. She herself had had more than 75 careers. By the time of her 40th birthday in 1999 the Barbie industry was worth about $2 billion a year.

Enduring appeal

The immaculately turned-out Barbie attracted feminist criticism for conforming to gender stereotyping. But in her defense it could be argued that there were many sides to Barbie's character. While some of her earliest outfits included a wedding gown, Barbie's working girl ensembles in her first decade ranged from flight attendant to astronaut. And though it was true that Barbie endured the discomfort of feet molded for tiny high heels, (not flats or sneakers), the generation of girls who first played with Barbie dolls seemed not to be the worse for it.

The Barbie line encompassed not only changing fashions but also changing interests, emerging professions, and ethnic diversity. Her appeal has continued undiminished for successive generations of little girls, and Barbie dolls (especially early ones) are prized collectors' items. □

See Also: Fashion

BRIGITTE BARDOT b. 1934

The sensational French "sex kitten" had been world famous for nearly a decade when she visited the U.S. for the first time in 1965. She received a rapturous reception.

In the early 1960s the French film star Brigitte Bardot took over the mantle of America's "Sex Queen" from Marilyn Monroe. Eight years younger than Monroe, Bardot was born in Paris in 1934, the daughter of a successful industrialist. After a childhood in Nazi-occupied Paris she won a place at a leading dance school, but gave up that career when she was only 15 years old to become a model and was featured on the cover of the fashion magazine *Elle*.

Launching the "sex kitten"

When she was still only 16, Bardot was offered film parts and met the director Roger Vadim, who was to be her first husband and to turn her into the "sex kitten" of the 1950s. When her family opposed her marriage to Vadim, she attempted suicide by putting her head in a gas oven. It was the beginning of a stormy love life that was as much a part of Bardot's public persona as her ravishing, girlish looks and her spectacular film career.

One critic commented that Bardot "had a body which plunged the American male public into a great troubled state." Another said that she had a special relationship in her films with "the towel"—loosely draped, it was invariably discarded after much teasing to reveal much more of the female body than censorship had allowed in the Monroe years.

International stardom came with the film *And God Created*

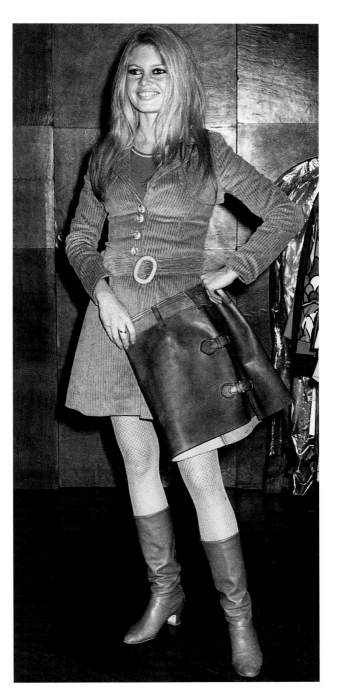

△ Bardot posing with a miniskirt in London's Carnaby Street in 1967. The French sex symbol's international appeal made her one of the most photographed and written about icons of the 1960s.

Woman, directed by Vadim in 1956. Bardot turned down offers to visit the United States until she was persuaded to make a trip in 1965 to promote the film *Viva Maria*.

When she landed at Kennedy Airport, Bardot was greeted by hundreds of reporters and won them over with her forthrightness and wit. The *World Telegraph and Sun* was ecstatic: "She is Miss World, Miss Universe, Miss Gemini 6 and 7. She is the Rose Bowl Queen, the Sugar Bowl Queen. She is Miss Everything."

That was the height of Bardot's fame in America, and by the end of the 1960s the sex-kitten image did not sit comfortably with the feminist movement's reappraisal of women's roles. She made her last film in 1973 and began to devote herself to the protection of animals, living a reclusive life in her native France. In 1976 she set up the Brigitte Bardot Foundation for the Protection of Distressed Animals, auctioning her jewelry and memorabilia to raise funds. From that time on she has been continuously in the news campaigning to stop the battery farming of chickens and the mistreatment of animals. The ex-sex kitten explained her change of priorities: "I gave my youth and beauty to men. Now I'm giving my wisdom and experience, the better part of me, to the animals." □

See Also: Foreign Movies; Hollywood

BASEBALL

The 1960s were turbulent years for major-league baseball, with expansion the most visible sign of the game's response to changing times. The decade also witnessed epic achievements on the field.

The national pastime entered the 1960s as popular as ever, as yet not seriously rivaled by such comparative upstarts as football and basketball. As had their fathers and grandfathers before them, men enjoyed the familiar ritual of taking their sons to the local ball game, and with TV now in almost every home they enjoyed too the excitement of major-league baseball in the comfort of their living rooms. With the exception of the welcome addition of a host of black players at the highest levels of the game, the world of baseball was little changed from what it had been before World War II. Change, however, was afoot.

At the beginning of the 1960s baseball owners and officials launched the game into the era of expansion. They took this bold step partly because they were faced with the threat of a new league to be called the Continental League, and also because they were impressed by the commercial success of the Los Angeles Dodgers and San Francisco Giants, who quit New York in 1958. Improved air travel made expansion to cities west of Chicago and St. Louis feasible, and there were large and rapidly growing urban markets to exploit in the South and West. Since its beginnings major-league baseball had stopped at the Mississippi. By the end of the 1960s there were five clubs in California alone, however.

In 1961 the Los Angeles Angels and Minnesota Twins were added to the American League; the Houston Astros and the New York Mets joined the National League in the following year. (The Mets immediately set a new benchmark for incompetence on the field by losing 120 games in their first season.) Each new franchise cost $2 million, and the established clubs were required to provide a pool of players to be drafted (and purchased) by the new franchises. Each new club had $20 million to spend on those players. The schedule in each league was increased from 154 to 162 games.

Optimism about the dawn of a new era was dampened when attendance figures, especially in the American League,

▽ **Fans mob the New York Mets after their 1969 World Series victory. By beating the Baltimore Orioles 4–1, they became the first expansion team to win the title.**

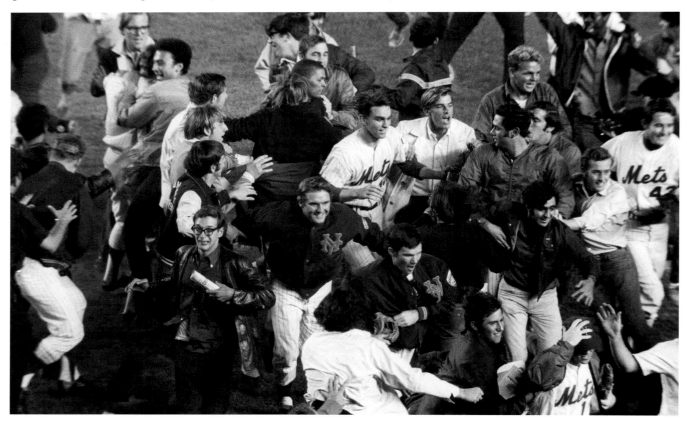

△ Bob Gibson of the St. Louis Cardinals pitching against the Detroit Tigers in the 1968 World Series. Althought the Cardinals lost, that year Gibson posted the lowest ERA ever to win both the MVP and Cy Young awards.

failed to meet expectations, partly, it was believed, because leagues of 10 teams contained too many players who did not belong in the majors. But in 1965 a new record for attendance was set, and it was broken the next year, when the total gate was over 25 million. For the rest of the decade, however, attendances fell steadily.

Continued expansion

In 1967, before the trend toward decreasing gate receipts became evident, both leagues announced that in the next four years they would expand from 10 teams to 12. One result of that second wave of expansion was that for the first time a franchise was granted to a city outside the United States, for the Montreal Expos.

The National League clubs led the way in modernizing their stadiums, eight new ones being erected during the decade. Each of those new ball parks had to conform to a regulation adopted in 1959—the first to attempt to standardize the size of the outfield—that the minimum distance down the foul lines be 325 feet and to centerfield, 400 feet. One other consequence of expansion was that in 1969 the two major leagues were, for the first time, split into divisions. Television moguls and baseball owners were eager to make the extra money, which flowed from postseason "championship" series. Purists, however, felt that divisional playoffs devalued the pennant race.

The decade also saw the first stirrings of "player power," a development in the game that would reverberate throughout the remainder of the 20th century. The Major League Players Association was revitalized under the leadership of the labor organizer Marvin Miller, who wrenched formal labor agreements from the owners that increased both minimum wages and pensions for the players.

Most established players quickly followed the precedent set by the Dodgers' star pitchers Sandy Koufax and Don Drysdale, who in 1966 engaged lawyers as agents to conduct their contract negotiations. In 1968 the minimum salary for a player was doubled to $10,000. By 1970 twenty players were earning more than $100,000 a year.

Owners' pockets were also hit by a requirement laid down in 1962 that each major-league franchise subsidize at least five minor-league clubs, whose numbers had been steadily declining

Astrodome

Texas gained its first major-league franchise, the Houston Astros, in 1962. Three years later the club opened for play in what its promoters boasted was the "Eighth Wonder of the World," the Astrodome. The first game was played there on April 12, 1965, when the Astros went down to the Philadelphia Phillies, 2–0.

The Astrodome, constructed at a cost of $31.6 million, was the world's first all-purpose, domed stadium and the world's largest indoor stadium—high enough to enclose an 18-story building. It was also the first to offer spectators luxury executive suites. The plastic roof contained 4,500 "lucite panels," or skylights. The temperature was to be kept at a constant 72°F.

For good or bad, the playing field was covered in a synthetic surface called "Astroturf," and in 1968, for the first time, the All-Star game was played, under the dome, on an artificial surface.

△ **The Houston Astrodome opened in 1965 as the world's first domed stadium. But its artificial surface was controversial.**

but were seen as essential to the future of the sport. The steadily increasing costs resulting from these developments were offset by rapidly rising revenues from television companies.

In 1969 the Players Association threatened to go on strike unless their pension benefits were improved. The players agreed not to report to spring training or to sign contracts until the dispute was settled. When spring training arrived, more than 90 percent of the players refused to report to their clubs. A settlement was reached early on, however, after an all-night meeting of the Players Association on February 24, at which the owners' offer to contribute $5.45 million annually to the players' pension fund was accepted.

Sport or business?

Despite the great volume of business that baseball was doing by the 1960s, in the eyes of the law it remained a sport, not a business. Although several court decisions of the mid-1950s ruled that boxing, football, and basketball were businesses subject to antitrust laws and laws regulating interstate commerce, baseball remained immune to the operation of such laws. When, in 1965, the owners of the Milwaukee Braves decided to move the franchise to Atlanta, the state of Wisconsin filed an antitrust action against the National League and the owners of all its teams on the grounds that they exercised a monopoly over major-league baseball. The litigants, who sought to force the defendants to organize and operate a major-league team in Milwaukee before moving the Braves out of the city, were upheld in a lower court, but judgment was found for the defendants in the Wisconsin Supreme Court. An appeal to the U.S. Supreme Court was refused

a hearing. Baseball thus remained (and has continued to remain) the only professional sport in the United States exempt from antitrust laws.

Great teams and players

On the field the decade was marked by the conclusion of a long era of dominance by the New York Yankees, who won five pennants in a row from 1960 to 1964 and two World Series. The Yankees did this without Casey Stengel, their legendary manager throughout the triumphant years after World War II, who was fired in 1960 and moved across town to manage the Mets in 1962. In 1965 the Yankees finished in the bottom half of the league for the first time since 1925. In 1969, the year in which each league was reorganized into two divisions, the Mets became the first expansion team to win the World Series.

The decade also witnessed both team and individual record-breaking achievements. In 1963 the Baltimore Orioles became the first club in history to make fewer than 100 errors in a season (they made 99). Then three years later they established another mark by holding the Dodgers scoreless for 33 consecutive innings in the World Series. The Dodgers' fine record in the first half of the decade would have been even better had they not (for the third time since 1946) lost the 1962 pennant in a tie-breaking playoff.

Outstanding among individual highlights was the breaking of Babe Ruth's record of 60 home runs in a season by Yankee outfielder Roger Maris, who hit 61 in 1961. (The team hit a record 240 home runs and six players hit 20 or more, also a record.) Maris's pleasure in his achievement was dimmed by Yankee fans' unconcealed disappointment that the record did not go to their hero Mickey Mantle, who hit 54 that year. Equally wounding for Maris was that so much play was made of the fact that Ruth had set his record in a 154-game season.

In 1962 the Dodgers' lightning-fast shortstop Maury Wills stole 104 bases, eclipsing the long-standing record of 96

▽ **Los Angeles Dodgers' Maury Wills steals third base. His anticipation and sprinting prowess gained Wills a record-breaking 104 stolen bases in 1962.**

Southpaw genius

Sandy Koufax, the left-handed pitcher for the Brooklyn and Los Angeles Dodgers from 1955 to 1966, was the dominant pitcher of his generation and one of the very best in history. His weapons were a superb fastball and a deceptive curve, combined with phenomenal control. Over his career Koufax struck out 2,396 batters (averaging more than nine a game) and walked only 817. His finest years came in the early 1960s when, despite a weak-hitting Dodger lineup, he led the team to three appearances in the World Series. In those years he compiled an extraordinary record: three Cy Young awards for Best Pitcher, one MVP, four no-hitters (including a perfect game against Cincinnati in 1965), more than 300 strikeouts (a record 382 in 1965), and 25 wins or more in 1963, 1965, and 1966. Each year from 1962 to 1966 Koufax led the NL in earned run average.

△ **The peerless Sandy Koufax, master of both fastball and curve, in action for the Dodgers against the Orioles in 1966.**

set by Detroit's Ty Cobb in 1915. In 1968 Detroit's Denny McLain (31–6) became the first pitcher to win 30 games in a season since St. Louis Cardinal Dizzy Dean in 1934. McLain also pitched 28 complete games, and he and Mickey Lolich (17–9) led the Tigers to their first pennant and World Series victory since 1945.

Bob Gibson's ERA of 1.12 for the Cardinals in 1968—the lowest since 1906—ranks as one of the most astonishing performances in the history of baseball. But it needs to be placed in perspective. The five leading pitchers in the American league that year all ended with ERAs under two runs a game. This highlights the fact that the 1960s were a pitchers' decade. The league batting averages for the decade were the lowest of the century: .245 for the AL, .253 for the NL. In 1966 only two AL batters hit over .290; in 1968, only one,

Carl Yastrzemski of the Boston Red Sox, who won the batting title with a paltry .301 average. In 1969, in an effort to redress the balance between pitching and batting, the strike zone, which had been enlarged in 1963 to the area from the top of the shoulder to the top of the knee, was returned to the boundaries set in 1950, from the armpit to the top of the knee. At the same time, the pitcher's mound was restricted to a height of 10 inches above the level of the playing field. The changes had an immediate effect. The average number of runs per game scored in both leagues rose from 6.84 in 1968 to 8.16 in 1969.

The 1960s saw a continuation of the the trend begun in 1947, when Jackie Robinson broke the color bar with the Brooklyn Dodgers. There were now so many African American stars prominent throughout the game that it was hard to believe major-league baseball had been an all-white preserve so recently in the past. Reflecting the transformation in attitudes, in 1966 Emmet Ashford, hired by the American League, became the first African American umpire to officiate in the major leagues. □

World Series

1960	Pittsburgh (NL) d. New York (AL) 4–3
1961	New York (AL) d. Cincinnati (NL) 4–1
1962	New York (AL) d. San Francisco (NL) 4–3
1963	Los Angeles (NL) d. New York (AL) 4–0
1964	St. Louis (NL) d. New York (AL) 4–3
1965	Los Angeles (NL) d. Minnesota (AL) 4–3
1966	Baltimore (AL) d. Los Angeles (NL) 4–0
1967	St. Louis (NL) d. Boston (AL) 4–3
1968	Detroit (AL) d. St. Louis (NL) 4–3
1969	New York (NL) d. Baltimore (AL) 4–1

Batting champions

	American League	National League
1960	P. Runnels (BOS) .320	D. Groat (PIT) .325
1961	N. Cash (DET) .361	R. Clemente (PIT) .351
1962	P. Runnels (BOS) .326	T. Davis (LA) .346
1963	C. Yastrzemski (BOS) .321	T. Davis (LA) .326
1964	T. Oliva (MIN) .323	R. Clemente (PIT) .339
1965	T. Oliva (MIN) .321	R. Clemente (PIT) .329
1966	F. Robinson (BAL) .316	M. Alou (PIT) .342
1967	C. Yastrzemski (BOS) .326	R. Clemente (PIT) .357
1968	C. Yastrzemski (BOS) .301	P. Rose (CIN) .335
1969	R. Carew (MIN) .332	P. Rose (CIN) .348

ERA leaders

	American League	National League
1960	F. Baumann (CHI) 2.67	M. McCormick (SF) 2.70
1961	D. Donovan (WAS) 2.40	W. Spahn (MIL) 3.02
1962	H. Aguirre (DET) 2.21	S. Koufax (LA) 2.54
1963	G. Peters (CHI) 2.33	S. Koufax (LA) 1.88
1964	D. Chance (LA) 1.65	S. Koufax (LA) 1.74
1965	S. McDowell (CLE) 2.18	S. Koufax (LA) 2.04
1966	G. Peters (CHI) 1.98	S. Koufax (LA) 1.73
1967	J. Horlen (CHI) 2.06	P. Niekro (ATL) 1.87
1968	L. Tiant (CLE) 1.60	B. Gibson (STL) 1.12
1969	D. Bosman (WAS) 2.19	J. Marichal (SF) 2.10

MVP winners

	American League	National League
1960	R. Maris (NY) (of)	D. Groat (PIT) (ss)
1961	R. Maris (NY) (of)	F. Robinson (CIN) (of)
1962	M. Mantle (NY) (of)	M. Wills (LA) (ss)
1963	E. Howard (NY) (c)	S. Koufax (LA) (p)
1964	B. Robinson (BAL) (3b)	K. Boyer (STL) (3b)
1965	Z. Versalles (MIN) (ss)	W. Mays (SF) (of)
1966	F. Robinson (Bal) (of)	R. Clemente (PIT) (of)
1967	C. Yastrzemski (BOS) (of)	O. Cepeda (STL) (1b)
1968	D. McLain (DET) (p)	B. Gibson (STL) (p)
1969	H. Killebrew (MIN) (3b)	W. McCovey (SF) (1b)

Cy Young Award (best pitcher)

1960	V. Law (PIT) (rh)
1961	W. Ford (NY) (lh)
1962	D. Drysdale (LA) (NL) (rh)
1963	S. Koufax (LA) (NL) (lh)
1964	D. Chance (LA) (AL) (rh)
1965	S. Koufax (LA) (lh)
1966	S. Koufax (LA) (lh)

	American League	National League
1967	J. Lonborg (BOS) (rh)	M. McCormick (SF) (lh)
1968	D. McLain (DET) (rh)	B. Gibson (STL) (rh)
1969	M. Cuellar (BAL) (lh)	T. Seaver (NY) (rh)
	D. McLain (DET) (rh)	

See Also: Aaron, Mantle, Mays

BASKETBALL

Basketball entered the 1960s far behind baseball and football in terms of popularity and profitability, but outstanding teams and superstar players were about to transform its fortunes.

At the end of the 20th century basketball was the fastest-growing sport in the world, with NBA games being carried on television to 180 countries around the world. Basketball was not such a major sport when the 1960s opened, however, not even in the United States, which, until the loss to the Soviet Union in a disputed cliffhanger at the 1972 Olympics, had never been beaten in international competition. Basketball could not yet rival the media attention given to baseball and football, nor did it have anything approaching the financial resources of those sports.

College basketball, like college football, was popular, but the professional game was really just coming of age. There had been a number of short-lived professional leagues since the beginning of the century, but the National Basketball Association was formed as late as 1949, more than a decade after the NCAA (National Collegiate Athletic Association) national championship had been introduced.

Basketball comes of age

Basketball had an inbuilt limitation. Being an indoor game, its arenas had far smaller seating capacities than the stadiums for football and baseball. Even at the end of the 1960s, when the professional game had taken a large stride forward, annual attendance figures never approached those for baseball and football. Players' salaries told a similar story: an average by 1970 of $10,000 for basketball players, against $15,000 in football and $20,000 in baseball.

The same imbalance could be seen in franchises. The owners of the Baltimore Bullets gained the franchise for $1 million in 1964, and even though a year later the Boston Celtics were sold for $3 million and the Los

Angeles Lakers for $5 million, those sums lagged behind the nearly $15 million that a baseball franchise was worth.

Critics said that the game was inherently less interesting than baseball or football, having little strategic variety. They also said that there was too high a frequency of scoring, especially since the introduction in 1954 of the rule that the attacking team must shoot within 24 seconds of getting the ball or relinquish possession. Against this there were signs that the game was entering a new era, notably the rapid rise in college scholarships offered to basketball players. A number of colleges, especially smaller ones, began to downgrade

△ **The 1960 NCAA final at San Francisco's Cow Palace. The Ohio State Buckeyes beat the University of California 75–55.**

football and place more emphasis on basketball. Scholarships increasingly brought African Americans into the game—at the beginning of the decade basketball was still largely a white man's sport. College basketball went from strength to strength. At the end of the 1960s the annual attendance was 22 million, nearly triple what it had been in the mid-1950s.

Attendance figures for professional basketball followed suit. The game in 1962 in which Wilt Chamberlain scored a record 100 points was watched by just over 4,000 spectators. In 1969 a doubleheader at the domed Houston Astrodome attracted a gate of 41,163—more than double the previous highest attendance for an NBA game.

New leagues and teams

Expansion of the NBA began to mirror the expansion in major-league baseball. In 1969 Milwaukee and Phoenix gained franchises, and by the mid-1970s the league had 18 franchises in two conferences, Eastern and Western, each with two divisions. In 1965 the first contract to televise NBA games—on Sunday afternoons—was signed for a reported sum of $1 million.

One consequence of the expansion of professional basketball and the doors that the game opened to black players was the decline of the all-black touring team, the Harlem Globetrotters. Their heyday was the 1950s. Thereafter their popularity gradually waned, and their clowning on court came to be seen as playing up to a racial stereotyping that in the age of civil rights movements and black power was distinctly out of date.

The money that was beginning to flow into the game persuaded promoters to attempt to found rival leagues to the NBA. The American Basketball League, which was the creation of Abe Saperstein, the founder of

△ **Wilt Chamberlain soars above Celtic defender Bill Russell in 1964. Their great rivalry spanned the decade.**

Wilt scores 100

Wilt Chamberlain was the greatest scoring machine in basketball history, at least until Michael Jordan came along. On March 4, 1962, he set a record unlikely to be broken—100 points in a single game. Chamberlain was playing for the Philadelphia Warriors against the New York Knicks at the Fairgrounds, Hershey, Pa. After the first quarter he had 23 points, at half-time, 42. As the final quarter started, with Wilt's total at 69, the Philadelphia coach, Frank McGuire, called a timeout and told his players that Wilt was to have every shot. The announcer, Dave Zinkoff, started to call out Chamberlain's point total every time he scored. The fans, on their feet for the whole quarter, kept up a steady chant of "Give it to Wilt! Give it to Wilt!" With 46 seconds remaining Chamberlain sent a short shot toward the basket—and there it was. Chamberlain had finished the night shooting 36 for 63 from the field and, despite not being the greatest of foul-shooters, a record 28 for 32 from the line.

the Harlem Globetrotters, folded only a season and a half after its formation in 1965. In its short existence, nevertheless, the ABL made a major impact by introducing a change in the scoring system. A basket sunk from outside a semicircle drawn beyond the key was awarded three points instead of two for a normal field goal. The change was adopted by the NBA in the 1979/80 season and by the NCAA in 1986/87.

Marginally more successful than the ABL was a league put together by a group of California businessmen in 1967. The new American Basketball Association had the biggest star of the 1950s, George Mikan, as its commissioner. With 10 teams in two divisions the ABA lasted until the 1974/75 season. The ABA struggled to find players among NBA castoffs, but the competition between the two leagues generated a sharp rise in the amount of money that professional clubs were willing to pay college players to sign up. It soon reached $1 million.

Superstar players

Basketball's rise in popularity and public esteem owed much to the emergence of two superstars, Bill Russell and Wilt Chamberlain. The first two superstars of the game, George Mikan of the Minneapolis Lakers and Bob Cousy of the Boston Celtics (who retired in 1964), were both white; Russell and Chamberlain were black. Russell joined the Celtics in 1957; Chamberlain, who played for the Harlem Globetrotters after creating a sensation at Kansas University, kickstarted his NBA career with the Philadelphia Warriors two years later.

For a decade these great stars outshone everyone else in the game, and a debate raged about which was the greater player. Russell and Chamberlain took salaries to new heights in 1964 when they each signed three-year contracts for $300,000. (In a comic moment that pinpointed the rivalry between the old and the new guard, Cousy signed a few days after Chamberlain for $300,000.03.)

The great rivalry

Chamberlain stood 7ft. 1in. tall and weighed about 275 pounds. Despite his great size, Chamberlain was no lumbering giant, and he disliked his nickname "Wilt the Stilt" because it implied that he had nothing to contribute but his height. He not only jumped higher than anyone else in the game, but he possessed the coordination of a much smaller man.

Chamberlain's statistical record remains unequaled: seven consecutive seasons as leading point scorer and 11 seasons as the leading rebounder. In a career that lasted from 1959 to 1973 Chamberlain scored a mammoth total of 31,419 points. No one has beaten the point total or average (50.4) he racked up during the 1961/62 season. He holds the top four places in the all-time list of single-game totals. Moreover, Chamberlain never once fouled out of a game in 1,045 NBA appearances, despite playing for the full 48 minutes in most of them. Because of Wilt's towering presence around the

basket the NBA introduced two rule changes: widening the foul lane and prohibiting "offensive goaltending" (knocking a shot away after it has started its downward arc to the basket).

Against the towering Chamberlain, his good friend as well as fierce rival Bill Russell was a mere 6ft. 9in., but his extraordinary reflexes and jumping ability provided him with defensive skills that revolutionized the way basketball was played. Russell moved

▽ Trials to pick the top amateur players to represent the U.S. in the 1964 Olympic Games in Tokyo, where the U.S. won the gold medal.

"Triple-Double" Robertson

Twenty years before Michael Jordan made the phrase "triple-double" known to every sports fan, Oscar Robertson regularly achieved double figures in each of the three statistical categories—scoring, assisting, rebounding—in a single game. Today it is considered an achievement if a player posts a dozen triple-double games in a season. But in 1961/62 Robertson became the first player to have a season triple-double, with averages of 30.8 for scoring, 12.5 for rebounds, and 11.4 for assists. That record has never been matched. Even more remarkable is that in his first five seasons with the Cincinnati Royals, from 1960/61 to 1964/65, he averaged 30.3 points, 10.4 rebounds, and 10.6 assists. And, although he was nicknamed the "Big O," Robertson was a quite modest 6ft. 5in. tall.

fast enough to block layups as they left the shooter's hands, thus making the traditional objective of the attacking team—to control the area directly beneath the basket—a more risky strategy. His control of rebounds enabled the Celtics to initiate lightning-fast breakouts from defense. It was because of Russell that blocked shots became a statistical category.

Until Michael Jordan equaled the record in 1997/98, Russell was the only player to have won the NBA's Most Valuable Player award five times. In 1966 Russell replaced Red Auerbach as coach of the Celtics, so becoming the first black person to be head coach or manager of any professional sports team in the United States.

Teams of the decade

The most successful NBA team of the decade was Boston. The Celtics won eight championships in a row from 1959 to 1966 and 11 in 13 years. UCLA was only slightly less dominant in college basketball. Under coach John Wooden, the Bruins won seven NCAA championships in a row from 1967 to 1973 and 10 in 12 years. In four of those seasons they went undefeated.

UCLA's star player was Lew Alcindor (later, as Kareem Abdul Jabbar, he had a long and high-scoring career in the NBA with the Milwaukee Bucks and the Los Angeles Lakers). Alcindor was fractionally taller than Chamberlain, and it was largely

▽ Lew Alcindor starred for UCLA in the late 1960s. In the 1970s, as Kareem Abdul Jabbar, he was equally successful in the NBA.

because of his prolific scoring that in 1968 the NCAA introduced a rule against dunking. The ban, however, was rescinded in 1976.

The rise of women's basketball

At the beginning of the 1960s basketball was still virtually a male preserve. Although by the 1920s women's basketball was being played all over the world, in the United States the game was held back largely because it was not considered "feminine." But in the 1950s and 1960s women's collegiate basketball finally began to move forward, thanks in great part to two small colleges, Wayland College, Texas, and Nashville Business College, Tennessee. The teams from those two colleges won every national AAU women's title from 1956

◁ Action in an Iowa girls tournament in 1968. Rule changes made women's basketball more popular and competitive by the early 1970s.

to 1969. In 1969 the first National Intercollegiate Women's Basketball Tournament was held, under new rules. In that year the old six-player team gave way to five players, and the restriction that, except for two "rovers," players had to remain in their designated sections of the court was abolished.

Those rules were officially adopted in 1971, and the game thereby became the same as that played by men. As it turned out, basketball proved to be the spearhead for the expansion of women's intercollegiate sports in general. In 1971 the Association of Intercollegiate Athletics for Women was formed. Its establishment filled a vacuum created because the NCAA shunned women's sports (and continued to do so until 1982) for fear that they might distract attention and money away from men's basketball and football. □

NBA champions

1960	Boston d. St. Louis	4–3
1961	Boston d. St Louis	4–1
1962	Boston d. Los Angeles	4–3
1963	Boston d. Los Angeles	4–2
1964	Boston d. San Francisco	4–2
1965	Boston d. Los Angeles	4–1
1966	Boston d. Los Angeles	4–3
1967	Philadelphia d. San Francisco	4–2
1968	Boston d. Los Angeles	4–2
1969	Boston d. Los Angeles	4–3

Rebound champions

1960	Wilt Chamberlain (PHI)	1,941
1961	Wilt Chamberlain (PHI)	2,149
1962	Wilt Chamberlain (PHI)	2,052
1963	Wilt Chamberlain (SF)	1,946
1964	Bill Russell (BOS)	1,930
1965	Bill Russell (BOS)	1,878
1966	Wilt Chamberlain (PHI)	1,943
1967	Wilt Chamberlain (PHI)	1,957
1968	Wilt Chamberlain (PHI)	1,952
1969	Wilt Chamberlain (LA)	1,712

Scoring champions

1960	Wilt Chamberlain (PHI)	2,707 pts
1961	Wilt Chamberlain (PHI)	3,033
1962	Wilt Chamberlain (PHI)	4,029
1963	Wilt Chamberlain (SF)	3,586
1964	Wilt Chamberlain (SF)	2,984
1965	Wilt Chamberlain (SF/PHI)	2,534
1966	Wilt Chamberlain (PHI)	2,649
1967	Rick Barry (SF)	2,775
1968	Dave Bing (DET)	2,142
1969	Elvin Hayes (SD)	2,327

NCAA champions

1960	Ohio State
1961	Cincinnati
1962	Cincinnati
1963	Loyola
1964	UCLA
1965	UCLA
1966	Texas Western
1967	UCLA
1968	UCLA
1969	UCLA

See Also: Olympic Games

BAY OF PIGS INVASION

When he entered office in 1961, President Kennedy inherited a plan to give covert U.S. support to an anti-Castro invasion of Cuba. His approval led to a humiliating fiasco.

◁ **Proof of U.S. complicity in the invasion: a Cuban soldier stands guard over the wreckage of a B-26 bomber, one of six that were shot down crudely disguised in Cuban colors.**

Eisenhower explained to Kennedy, he had authorized a covert CIA operation to topple the Cuban leader. The plan involved training a force made up of Cuban exiles who detested Castro in the jungles of Guatemala. These U.S.-trained paramilitaries would mount an amphibious landing to establish a bridgehead on the Cuban coast, following which it was expected by the CIA that the Cuban people would spontaneously rise up against Castro.

Kennedy approves the plan

Kennedy was not opposed to the scheme, which the CIA was urgently pressing him to authorize. But he was nervous about any U.S. involvement becoming known. Deniability was necessary whatever the outcome, but absolutely paramount in the event of failure. Despite the bullishness of CIA director Allen Dulles, and support from the Defense Department and the Joint Chiefs of Staff, it was impossible to rule out the possibility of failure. To his keen regret in hindsight, Kennedy faced both ways when it came to making the decision. He approved the invasion, scheduled for mid-April 1961, and then at a press conference just three days before it began he explicitly ruled out "under any conditions" intervention in Cuba by U.S. armed forces.

The invasion began when six U.S. B-26 bombers, disguised in Cuban colors so as to make it look as if they were flown by Cuban defectors, took off from Nicaragua and attacked Cuban airfields. This tiny bomber force caused minimal damage and provided no air cover for the amphibious landing force,

On January 19, 1961, the day before his inauguration, President-elect John F. Kennedy received the traditional personal briefing from his predecessor, the outgoing President Eisenhower. Among other topics, Eisenhower raised the issue of Cuba, where two years after leading his successful revolution, Fidel Castro had become a persistent thorn in U.S. flesh. Although initially Castro did not proclaim himself a Marxist, his program of economic reform involved nationalizing oil companies and sugar producers, which meant seizing American assets in Cuba. In retaliation,

△ Cuban troops move on the Bay of Pigs, where the invaders faced hopeless odds against Soviet-built tanks and a loyal army.

△ The Cuban Brigade embarked from Puerto Cabezas, Nicaragua, for Cuba's Bay of Pigs.

which crossed the Caribbean from the coast of Nicaragua in six ships. Despite that, 1,400 members of the anti-Castro Cuban Brigade managed to land at the Bay of Pigs on Cuba's south coast on April 17. There they came under fierce attack by Soviet-built Cuban artillery and tanks, and appealed desperately for U.S. air support. This was considered but rejected, not least because the anticipated anti-Castro uprising—crucial to the enterprise—failed to materialize.

Disaster and embarrassment

The invasion force was left to its own devices and after three days of hard fighting was forced to surrender, having lost over 100 dead. Meanwhile, the clumsy attempts to disguise the extent of the CIA's involvement had completely unraveled and the U.S. was made to look both deceitful and inept.

Kennedy accepted full responsibility for the Bay of Pigs fiasco and was privately furious with himself for his

Who was winning the Cold War?

The Bay of Pigs fiasco was the low point of Kennedy's presidency. He felt keenly a sense of personal and national humiliation over the bungled operation, but his concerns went deeper than that. The reason he had given the invasion his support, however foolish hindsight showed that to have been, was that Castro's Cuba represented an alarming development. Here was a charismatic leader who, if not in name a communist, was certainly a revolutionary socialist. With his long harangues about Yankee imperialism and his cosying up to the Soviet Union for military and economic aid, did this not foreshadow a communist presence right in America's backyard?

Kennedy's fears were reinforced two months after the Bay of Pigs invasion when he had a bruising encounter with Soviet premier Nikita Khrushchev at the Vienna summit. Khrushchev boasted that communism was in the ascendant, and that this could be seen in the developing world, where wars of liberation were overturning the old order. Kennedy privately conceded that Khrushchev's boast was not completely idle, and that if the Soviets, or at least their proxies, were winning the battle for hearts and minds in such widely separated parts of the world as Southeast Asia, Latin America, and southern Africa, did that not mean that the U.S. was losing the Cold War?

"stupidity." In particular, he blamed himself for not having questioned the CIA's false assumption about Castro's political weakness, and he vowed in the future to be less susceptible to the advice of such so-called experts. Embarrassment over the episode did not,

however, weaken the president's resolve to remove Castro one way or another. This was reinforced by Castro's pronouncement that in the face of such blatant American imperialism, he was determined to take Cuba down the path of socialist revolution. □

See Also: Castro; CIA; Cold War; Communism; Cuban Missile Crisis; Kennedy, J. F.; Khrushchev; Latin America

BEACH BOYS

The Beach Boys sang romantically about the delights of fast cars, pretty girls, and surfing in California. Their success was unrivaled by any other U.S. pop singer or group of the decade.

The Beach Boys were formed in 1961 in Hawthorne, California, by three brothers—Brian, Dennis, and Carl Wilson—with their cousin Mike Love and neighbor Al Jardine. (Jardine soon left, to be replaced by David Marks. He returned, taking Marks's place, in 1963.) The Wilsons' father, Murray, an amateur songwriter, was a domineering influence over the fledgling band. Their mother, Audree, occasionally sang backing vocals until Jardine rejoined the group.

The Beach Boys combined the tight harmonies of musically sophisticated groups like the Four Freshmen with the rock-'n'-roll rhythms of guitarists like Chuck Berry. When their parents went away, the young Wilsons used the food and housekeeping money to rent instruments. During this period they developed from simple two-part Everly Brothers sounds to a more complex and original style of their own. They formed a group known originally as Carl and the Passions, sometimes as the Pendletones, and eventually as the Beach Boys. Of the five, only Dennis Wilson was keen on surfing, but he persuaded his brothers to write songs about this stereotypical Californian pastime.

Rapid rise to the top

The Beach Boys played their first gig on the last day of 1961. Their first hit single, "Surfin'," issued on a local label in 1962, was popular in their home state and reached No. 75 nationally. Later that year the Beach Boys signed for Capitol, and their next release, "Surfin' Safari," became their first Top 40 hit. It was followed in October by a debut album, also called *Surfin' Safari*.

▷ The fresh-faced Beach Boys at the start of a glittering decade. By 1965 Brian Wilson (center) was shying from live performance.

In March 1963 "Surfin' USA" became the group's first Top 10 hit single. Its parent album, also called *Surfin' USA*, sold a million copies. The single "Surfer Girl" reached the Top 10 in July; the album of the same name, released in September, also went gold.

From the beginning the Beach Boys had always revolved around Brian Wilson, the eldest of the brothers, but by this time he was writing all the music and supervising production. The song lyrics were collaborations between himself, Mike Love, and others. The group also toured and made numerous television and celebrity appearances. This was an enormous workload, and the pressures on Brian were made worse

by the speed with which the group was expected to produce followup records. For example, the Beach Boys' fourth album, *Little Deuce Coupe*, was released less than a month after *Surfin' USA*; again, it sold a million.

The Beach Boys dominated the singles-led American charts in 1963, but in 1964 they began to be overshadowed by a phenomenal foreign group, the Beatles. Brian Wilson became obsessed with trying to match the British musicians. But at the same time, he was deeply inspired by them.

Despite the competition, the Beach Boys still had Top 10 hits with "Fun Fun Fun," "When I Grow Up (To Be A Man)," and "Dance, Dance, Dance," as

Good vibrations

Brian Wilson was downcast at the public reaction to the *Pet Sounds* album and determined that his next release would be a surefire success. After spending six months and an unprecedented $16,000 on experimentation, he came up with the monumental "Good Vibrations," which soon became the Beach Boys' biggest hit. Not only did it comprise dozens of overdubbed tracks, it was also the first pop record to make use of the theremin, an electronic synthesizer that creates music without being touched. The player moves his or her hands closer to or farther away from two antennae that control pitch and volume through radio frequency oscillators. The resulting signal is then amplified.

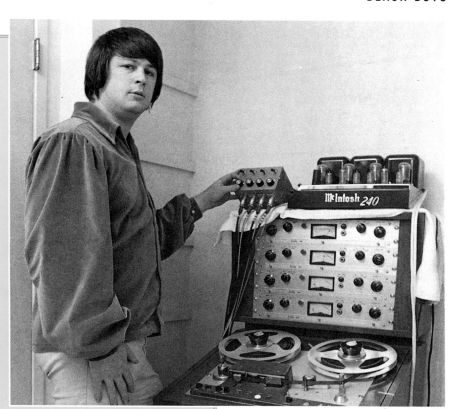

△ Brian Wilson immersed himself in the studio in 1966 after the lukewarm reception of *Pet Sounds*: the reult was "Good Vibrations."

well as their first No. 1 single, "I Get Around" and three more gold albums, including *All Summer Long*.

The strain of producing so much so quickly took its toll on Brian Wilson, whose use of LSD came to resemble a dependency. In 1964 he had a nervous breakdown and at the end of the year announced that he would not perform onstage again but concentrate on composition and production. The group originally replaced him on stage with Glen Campbell, then a session player and subsequently a successful solo performer, and later with Bruce Johnston.

The first fruit of this new lineup was the March 1965 album *The Beach Boys Today*, which carried "Help Me Rhonda," their next No. 1 single. Only four months later came *Summer Days (And Summer Nights)*, which spawned the Top 10 single "California Girls."

Brian Wilson's productions became ever more ambitious and slower in the making. He was fascinated by the "wall of sound" productions of Phil Spector, who had created lush records for girl groups and male groups such as the Righteous Brothers. Brian's increasingly

complex mid-1960s productions, many using session musicians rather than the band's instrumental skills, bear testament to Spector's influence.

Meanwhile, Capitol's demanding schedule still had to be met, accounting for the release of *The Beach Boys Party* album—something of a holding operation—in September 1965.

One of the great albums

May 1966 saw the release of *Pet Sounds*. This album yielded the Top 10 singles "Sloop John B" (at Capitol's insistence) and "Wouldn't It Be Nice." *Pet Sounds* initially peaked at No. 10 in the album charts—a failure by Beach Boys' standards. But it was a slow burner and came to be looked upon as one of the seminal albums of the decade. Paul McCartney later said that *Pet Sounds* "blew me out of the water. I love the album so much I've bought my kids each a copy of it for their education in life." It seems that the admiration was mutual, for *Pet Sounds* was heavily indebted to the Beatles' *Revolver* album and was itself an inspiration for *Sgt. Pepper's Lonely Hearts Club Band*.

In October 1966 Brian released the single "Good Vibrations," which went straight to No. 1 and sold over a million copies (*see box*). He was hailed as a genius, and the pop world awaited the new album, to be entitled *Smile*, on which he was currently working with lyricist Van Dyke Parks. The album never appeared, although a single from it, "Heroes and Villains," came out in July 1967. By this time the band was suffering internal disruptions. Brian gave up as leader, and the next album, *Smiley Smile* (September 1967), was produced by the group as a whole.

The Beach Boys saw out the decade with three fairly low-key albums: *Wild Honey* in December 1967, *Friends* in June 1968, and *20/20* in February 1969. Later years saw their careers hit highs and, just as often, tragic lows. Their early material not only haunted them—every audience would demand it—but also kept their legacy alive, preserving intact and timeless the spirit of California youth in the 1960s. □

See Also: Beatles; Pop Music; Rock Music

BEATLES

In late 1963 reports reached the U.S. of a new band that was taking Britain by storm. Very swiftly the Beatles conquered America and became the most successful and influential group ever.

△ **In February 1964 the Beatles arrived to a tumultuous reception at New York's JFK Airport. "Beatlemania" was launched.**

The Beatles were the most important and successful rock music group of the 1960s. They were a cultural landmark and a commercial phenomenon rolled into one. Without precedent, they appealed not only to the usual core market of adolescents, but also to connoisseurs of jazz and classical music, many of whom had never taken any serious interest in popular music before in their lives.

The Beatles originally formed around the nucleus of John Lennon and Paul McCartney, both guitarists and singers. The two shared an enthusiasm for American rock-'n'-roll and first performed together in 1957 under the name the Quarrymen in their native Liverpool. Both were largely self-

taught musicians who composed their own material from an early age. At the outset they played with many different people on a fairly casual basis, but by the end of 1957 they had acquired a third full-time member, lead guitarist George Harrison. From 1958 they appeared on stage with Stuart Sutcliffe, a friend of John Lennon who was good-looking but whose talents were artistic rather than musical (*see box, p. 127*). In 1959 the four of them formed the Silver Beetles—the name a playful allusion to Buddy Holly and the Crickets. In 1960 they dropped the "Silver" and

changed "Beetles" to "Beatles," and added a drummer, Pete Best. With that lineup they joined a small but booming beat music scene first at the Casbah, a club in the Best family's basement, then at the Cavern Club in Liverpool, and later in a series of clubs in Hamburg, West Germany (*see box p. 125*).

In the fall of 1961 Brian Epstein, the manager of the record department in his parents' Liverpool furniture store, saw the Beatles play at the Cavern and fell in love with them. (The group was now a quartet after the departure of Sutcliffe.) Epstein was unshakably convinced of their commercial potential and made it his mission to get them a recording deal. To this end he bombarded British music companies with letters and tapes of their work, eventually winning them a contract with Parlophone, a subsidiary of EMI. In the meantime, many labels had turned them down, including Decca, whose memorable judgment was that "guitar groups are on their way out."

At Parlophone the man put in charge of producing the Beatles was George Martin, a classically trained musician. Martin was enormously influential in nearly all aspects of their subsequent development and was sometimes dubbed "the fifth Beatle." He made his first mark on the group by persuading them to dispense with the services of Pete Best and hire a better drummer—they chose Ringo Starr, another Liverpudlian, whom they had got to know in Hamburg, where he was playing with Rory Storm and the Hurricanes. Next, Martin rearranged their second recorded song to turn it from a dirge into the upbeat "Love Me Do," which became their first UK hit, reaching No. 17 in October 1962.

Meteoric rise to fame

Throughout the winter of 1962 and the spring of 1963 the Beatles made steady progress along the road to fame by performing live on British radio a combination of their own songs and American rock-'n'-roll classics. Their second single, "Please Please Me," reached No. 2 in 1963, and by the end of that year they had had three consecutive UK Number Ones—"From Me To You," "She Loves You," and "I Want

△ **Appearances on British TV stoked up enthusiasm for the quartet, which by 1964 reached unprecedented heights.**

to Hold Your Hand." With the second of these chart-toppers the Beatles became the first act ever to knock itself off the No. 1 spot.

All the while the Beatles were being marketed with great flair and enterprise by Brian Epstein. Under his guidance they diversified into other areas, including collectible merchandise and, most notably, the feature films *A Hard Day's Night* (1964) and *Help!* (1965), both of which promoted records of the same names. The Beatles' carefully cultivated image was in many ways as important an ingredient of their popularity as their music. They had long hair, made flippant remarks to interviewers, and were devil-may-care in a challenging but still faintly respectable sort of way.

The Beatles in Hamburg

Before they hit the big time, the Beatles made four working trips to Hamburg in northern Germany, where they performed in several different nightclubs. During their first visit, which lasted for four months from August 1960, the group appeared at three venues—the Indra Club, the Kaiserkeller, and the Top 10 Club. After a period back in Liverpool they returned to Hamburg in April 1961 for another three-month stint. Then, from April 1962 they played seven weeks at the Star Club, the Hamburg venue with which they are most commonly associated. The Beatles were rebooked there for two weeks from December 18, 1962. By now they were becoming stars at home, and these were their last gigs at the Star Club.

All in all, they appeared pleasantly and articulately dissident rather than truculently subversive. This made them popular with the young and, just as importantly, enabled them to distance themselves from the parents without entirely alienating any but the most reactionary of the older generation.

During 1964 the fascination with the Beatles began to transcend the normal boundaries of taste, class, and age. Appearances on British television were newsworthy events, and there was a frenzy of public excitement. The Beatles could no longer appear in public without police protection in case they were mobbed by screaming fans. When the group appeared at the Royal Command Performance at the London Palladium, John Lennon invited the royals in the box to rattle their jewelry instead of applauding.

It was now America's turn to see what all the fuss was about. When the Beatles landed at Kennedy Airport on February 7, 1964, 50,000 screaming teenagers gathered to greet their plane. On February 9, 1964, they appeared on television on the *Ed Sullivan Show* and were seen by 73 million Americans.

The group's 1964 U.S. tour was greeted everywhere with mob adulation ("Beatlemania"). Their success came as a great embarrassment to Capitol, the U.S. arm of the EMI recording label. They had turned the Beatles down, and the group's first U.S. hits came out on the Swan and Vee-Jay labels.

The Beatles' early hits were pop songs, pure and simple. Their formative

▽ The *Ed Sullivan Show* proved the ideal showcase for the British group, which was viewed by 73 million on February 9, 1964.

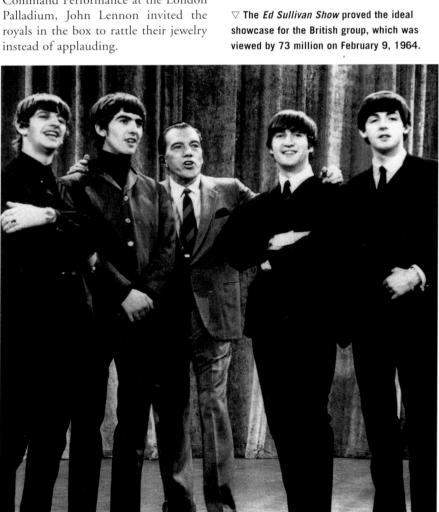

influences had been Chuck Berry, Little Richard, Fats Domino, Buddy Holly, and Elvis Presley. From about 1964 onward the Beatles also drew inspiration from Bob Dylan and Smokey Robinson, although by this time they themselves were having an enormous influence on rival American groups, such as the Beach Boys.

Songwriters supreme

By the middle 1960s the Beatles were composing nearly all their own material. Most of it was written by Lennon or McCartney—rather than by "Lennon and McCartney," as was always printed on the records. The two men set the standard and created a precedent for other rock groups to write their own music and lyrics.

Often experimenting with new forms, the Beatles were now beginning to produce an extraordinary variety of songs: McCartney's wistful, even bitter "Eleanor Rigby"; Lennon's witty folk song of unrequited love, "Norwegian Wood"; "Tomorrow Never Knows" and other hard rock numbers with drug-inspired lyrics; parodies of earlier pop styles, such as Lennon's Dylanesque "You've Got to Hide Your Love Away"; new electronic sounds and compositions scored for cellos, violins, trumpets, and sitars, as well as for conventional guitars and drums. The hugely successful and influential albums *Rubber Soul* (1965) and *Revolver* (1966) reveal a group expanding and developing creatively, rather than simply turning out enough material to fill two sides of vinyl.

The Beatles' enormous and sustained success bolstered the confidence of Lennon and McCartney as composers and encouraged them to branch out into even more ambitious forms of pop. One of the group's greatest achievements was the way it abandoned the safe and formulaic to experiment with more sophisticated music. They kept introducing new rhythms, melodic designs, and lyric conceptions and were at the forefront of a revolutionary epoch in popular music.

In 1966 the group announced its retirement from public performance in order to concentrate on the creation of more complicated studio material. The finest fruit of this development was the album *Sgt. Pepper's Lonely Hearts Club Band* (1967), a landmark in the history of pop and, many believe, the Beatles' finest hour. Among the startling innovations on this album were the hurdy-gurdy effect on "Being for the Benefit of Mr Kite," which was obtained by the random mixing of taped snippets of music from a steam organ. The last track, "A Day in the Life," ended with a 40-piece orchestra playing a long improvised chord that was followed by a 20,000-Hz sound that could be heard only by dogs. Throughout this album the influence of producer George Martin was again very much in evidence.

During this period the group members experimented with fashionable mind-bending drugs such as LSD and also became interested in transcendental meditation, a technique taught to them by the Maharishi Mahesh Yogi, an Indian guru. On both counts the Beatles came in for criticism.

The Beatles' swansong

In 1968 a wave of student protest engulfed France, seriously affected life in the U.S., and spread as far as Japan and Mexico. Increased political awareness and activism resulted in the Beatles' being superseded as leaders of youth culture, but the group remained in the forefront of pop music until the end of the decade. In 1968 they boldly

launched their own record label, Apple. In doing this they hoped to create a financially secure base for experimentation and to help struggling musicians.

The plan nearly worked—"Hey Jude," their first single on the label, sold three million copies, and they signed up Mary Hopkin and James Taylor, who quickly gained chart successes. But on the business side they just created administrative and financial chaos that wrecked the personal relationships of the band members.

△ The Beatles at EMI's Abbey Road studios on June 23, 1967, promoting the release of their latest hit single, "All You Need Is Love."

Apple was rotten: its boutique on London's Baker Street made no money because it was a shoplifter's paradise; another ill-fated Apple venture, Apple Electronics, was run by a supposed inventor who invented nothing.

Three of the Beatles wanted the ensuing mess to be sorted out by businessman Allen Klein, but Paul McCartney wanted the company to be run by New York lawyer John Eastman, who was soon to become his father-in-law. John Lennon, meanwhile, had come under the influence of Japanese performance artist Yoko Ono, a development the other Beatles viewed with suspicion. Even though the group was now falling apart, during this troubled period the Beatles still managed to cut and release *Abbey Road*, another best-selling album.

The Beatles formally disbanded in spring 1970, after the release of their final album *Let It Be*. □

The man who was nearly a Beatle

Stuart Sutcliffe was a promising painter who was persuaded by his friend John Lennon to join the Silver Beetles as bass guitarist. Although Sutcliffe could not play the instrument, Lennon figured that Sutcliffe's smoldering good looks outweighed the disadvantage. Sutcliffe sold one of his paintings and used the money to buy a bass guitar. He appeared on stage with his back turned so that the audience could not see how little he was doing. When the band finished their engagement in Hamburg in December 1960, he stayed on in Germany with his girlfriend. Paul McCartney took over on bass. Sutcliffe died in Hamburg of a brain hemorrhage in 1962, aged 21.

See Also: British Invasion; Pop Music; Rock Music

SAUL BELLOW b. 1915

With the publication of his novel Herzog *in 1964 Saul Bellow established himself as a leading literary voice, exploring the theme of the moral vacuum at the heart of contemporary life.*

Many writers of fiction in the United States in the 1960s directed their attention to what they perceived to be the meaninglessness and moral squalor of contemporary American life, especially life in the large cities. That theme was especially prominent in the work of a generation of influential Jewish writers that included Bernard Malamud, Philip Roth, and Saul Bellow. Bellow was actually born in Lachine, Quebec, and was raised in the Jewish quarter of Montreal (the district that also spawned novelist Mordecai Richler) until the age of nine, when he moved with his family to Chicago. Of his years as a student at the University of Chicago and Northwestern University he wrote movingly. "The dense atmosphere of learning, of cultural effort, heavily oppressed me; I felt that wisdom and culture were immense and that I was small." His fiction grew out of that sentiment.

Bellow's writing career began in 1944, with the appearance of his first novel, *Dangling Man*. By 1964, when he published *Herzog*, he was established in the front rank of American novelists. No novel of the 1960s gained greater critical acclaim. *Herzog* won the National Book Award, as one of his earlier novels, *The Adventures of Augie March*, had a decade before, and it was acclaimed by some as the long-awaited Great American Novel.

When Bellow was awarded the Nobel Prize for literature in 1976, he described his novel as a "sort of latter-day lean-to, a hovel in which the spirit

△ Saul Bellow had a huge critical and popular success with his novel *Herzog* in 1964 and won the Nobel Prize for literature in 1976.

takes shelter." *Herzog* can be read as a drawing out of Bellow's statement that in the 20th century our best conversations are with ourselves.

The book records the mental anguish of a twice-divorced, failed academic, a scholar of Romanticism whose life threatens to disintegrate into madness—characterized by obsessive letter writing (mostly in the mind) to friends, relatives, and almost anyone of intellectual or political renown. Madness looms for Herzog because there is no meeting place between the consciousness of the private individual (the

central point of interest for the Romantics) and the formlessness of an indifferent outside world. The malaise that afflicts Herzog is reflected in the apparent patternlessness of the novel's structure.

Herzog was followed, in 1970, by *Mr. Sammler's Planet*, an apocalyptic tale that arises from the social and moral crisis that was afflicting Vietnam-haunted and race-scarred America in the late 1960s. Like almost all of Bellow's heroes, Mr. Sammler lays himself open to the batterings of the world and becomes "a delicate recording instrument." Bellow's protagonists are both intellectuals and heroes, a combination somewhat rare in American literary tradition and one that allows Bellow to employ a high style of writing as he explores the deepest questions about the meaning of human life.

The novel as autobiography

Bellow once asked a prospective biographer, "What can you reveal about me that I haven't already revealed about myself?" *Herzog* is, indeed, a striking example of the retreat of the contemporary novel into the private world of self-inspection. In *Herzog* the autobiographical element is scarcely concealed. Storytelling takes second place to introspective musing. Bellow, in the words of the English novelist Martin Amis, "with all sorts of awkwardnesses and rough edges and extraordinary expansions, supremely well-equipped, erudite and humorous... has made his own experience resonate more memorably than any living writer." □

See Also: Literature

BERKELEY FREE SPEECH MOVEMENT

In 1964 a seemingly trivial incident at the Berkeley campus of the University of California gave birth to a new phenomenon in American society—widespread student protest and open revolt.

In the early 1960s the goals of student political activists lay outside the university. Many were involved in the civil rights movement, and in May 1960 students at Berkeley organized a well-publicized demonstration against the hearings of the House Un-American Activities Committee being held in San Francisco. The HUAC had long been a target for those who deplored its anticommunist "witch hunts" of the 1950s.

The incident that began the Free Speech Movement was trivial enough. On September 16, 1964, the university's administration announced that a 26-foot strip of land at the entrance to the campus was no longer to be used by off-campus political groups. This caused surprise, since up till then both students and faculty thought the area belonged to the City of Berkeley, and civil rights groups, in particular, used it to hand out leaflets and solicit funds.

The protest begins

However, the land in fact belonged to the university, and the administration was simply applying a long-unenforced rule on the grounds that tables manned by activists there impeded pedestrians. The students sought to negotiate the problem. They volunteered to make a survey of the flow of pedestrians and ban fund-raising, and offered to police the area themselves to ensure that no group broke the university regulations concerning posters. The administration would not listen.

For the rest of the month students held protest marches and all-night vigils, and picketed the chancellor. Five students deliberately violated the new rules, three others supported them, and

all eight were put on indefinite suspension. At this point the Free Speech Movement was born under the leadership of Mario Savio, one of the eight suspended students. On October 1 a nonstudent collecting money for the Congress of Racial Equality was arrested. The police car that arrived to take him away was surrounded by hundreds of angry students. It remained immobilized for 32 hours while FSM leaders climbed on it to make speeches.

△ **Mario Savio, leader of the Free Speech Movement, addressing a rally at Sproul Hall in late 1964 during the student occupation.**

(They later paid for the damage.) The crowd swelled to several thousand.

Protests continued throughout October, November, and December. Three sit-ins took place, and in the last 800 students occupied the university building Sproul Hall. Almost as many police were sent in to confront them,

and there were mass arrests. Both the students and faculty went on strike. One of America's most famous centers of learning had been brought to the verge of collapse, and students adopted the slogan familiar from the IBM punch cards then used to write computer programs: "UC student. Do not bend, fold, or mutilate."

The unrest was covered by the media, and many Americans felt that the police had no place on the campus,

△ In 1969 the Free Speech Movement came out in protest against plans to turn Berkeley's People's Park into a parking lot.

arresting their sons and daughters. Others deplored what they saw to be unruly student disobedience against legitimate authority. In the event, the chancellor took leave of absence, and President Clark Kerr left the next year. Concessions were offered, but Savio was jailed for 120 days and was later refused readmission to the university.

The rebellion spreads

Although the Berkeley student rebellion changed little in itself, it let the genie out of the bottle. Before the Free Speech Movement students had seen campus issues as trivial compared to the civil rights struggle. Afterward, students committed to social change saw the campus as the front line. They were no longer prepared to put up with paternalistic university authorities who even laid down the law on sexual morality. The spirit of the Berkeley rebellion quickly spread to other American campuses and then abroad to Europe, where it had a particularly dramatic effect in Paris in 1968. □

Vietnam Day

One of the most important consequences of the Berkeley Free Speech Movement was Vietnam Day. On May 21, 1965, more than 10,000 people gathered on the Berkeley campus of the University of California for a 24-hour carnival of antiwar protest. It was the brainchild of student activist Jerry Rubin, later one of the Chicago Eight charged in connection with the Chicago Democratic Party Convention riot in 1968.

In February 1965 President Johnson had ordered the bombing of North Vietnam. The FSM leaders were in jail at the time, and Rubin, the self-styled clown prince of the protest movement, stepped into the vacuum. He approached mathematics professor Stephen Smale, who suggested Rubin invite big-name guests, including the famous British philosopher and pacifist Bertrand Russell, and present the event to the university as a *fait accompli*. The strategy worked. Haunted by the specter of the FSM, the chancellor allowed Rubin to use the steps of Sproul Hall, the regular venue for medium-sized demonstrations. When the true size of the event became clear, the university took down a fence between the Student Union Plaza and the baseball field. Pediatrician Benjamin Spock, comedian Dick Gregory, and folk-singer Phil Ochs appeared. Bertrand Russell sent a recorded message. The protest was covered widely by the media, and there were no arrests.

See Also: Antiwar Movement; Baby-boom Generation; Civil Rights Movement; Counterculture; Paris Unrest in 1968; Schools and Universities

BERLIN WALL

By the summer of 1961 the exodus of East German refugees through a divided Berlin provoked a desperate response, as the Soviet-backed East German regime literally fenced its people in.

For most of the 1960s the Cold War between Soviet and Western interests found its most dramatic symbol in the German city of Berlin. Since the defeat of Nazi Germany in 1945 Berlin had been partitioned among the four victorious allies—the United States, Britain, France, and the Soviet Union. Berlin, however, lay deep inside communist East Germany, which had been under Soviet domination since the end of the war. West Germany, meanwhile, was an increasingly prosperous democracy and a staunch member of the Western alliance led by the United States.

East Germans enjoyed nothing like the living standard or political freedom of their West German counterparts, and by 1961 nearly three million had voted with their feet, crossing over into West Germany. Although the 900-mile border between the two states was mined and fortified to prevent this

△ A bleak winter view of the Berlin Wall, which cut right across the city street by street to prevent the escape of East Berliners.

△ The divided city of Berlin lay deep within Soviet-dominated East Germany.

migration, in Berlin itself movement was unrestricted, and East Germans could easily cross into the Western sectors. The loss of young skilled workers and professionals was a ruinous drain on the East German economy.

A desperate measure

Against this background, in June 1961 Soviet premier Nikita Khrushchev met the newly installed President Kennedy to demand that the Western powers end

their military occupation of West Berlin, which would have meant giving the East German authorities a free hand in stemming the flood of refugees. Kennedy responded with strong declarations of support for West Berlin and the announcement of a military buildup. Frustrated at having his bluff called, and afraid that East Germany could not indefinitely survive the hemorrhaging of its population, the Soviet leader gave his approval to a desperate remedy.

On the morning of Sunday, August 13, 1961, Berliners awoke to a chilling sight. All along the miles of streets that marked the border between East and West Berlin, East German workers under armed guard were tearing up cobblestones from the streets and piling them up to create makeshift barricades. Others were planting concrete pillars and stringing up barbed-wire fences from pillar to pillar. By nightfall the inhabitants of East Berlin, including some 60,000 who commuted daily to work in West Berlin, were fenced in.

A people walled in

Over the following weeks and months houses situated immediately at the border were forcibly evacuated and torn down. The makeshift barbed-wire fences were replaced by a solid concrete wall, with watchtowers and machine-gun emplacements. This was the real Berlin Wall. Its final extent was more

△ **Looking into East Berlin from Potsdamer Platz in 1967. This was one of a number of crossing points for permitted visitors.**

Better wall than war

Despite impassioned appeals by the mayor of West Berlin, Willy Brandt, Washington reacted cautiously to the erection of the Berlin Wall. Even graphic footage of desperate East Berliners being shot dead as they attempted to scale the wall provoked only routine protests. The reason for this tepid response was that it quickly became clear that the Soviets had no intention of either moving against West Berlin or interfering with access routes to the city. In other words, the wall, monstrosity though it was, did not pose a security threat to the West. It would have to be lived with, since the alternative was to risk nuclear war.

The potential danger of a confrontation over the wall was highlighted just two months after it went up, when a trivial dispute over passports at the famous border crossing, Checkpoint Charlie, escalated alarmingly. For 16 hours Soviet and American tanks, bristling with weaponry, stared at each other at a distance of a hundred yards. No one fired, and finally first the Soviet and then the American tanks slowly backed off. One nervous or trigger-happy act on behalf of a single soldier could have had incalculable consequences. Colonel Jim Atwood of the U.S. military mission in Berlin later expressed the opinion that this incident was "the closest that the Russians and the Allies came to going to war in the entire Cold War period." This would perhaps explain President Kennedy's seemingly flippant remark that "a wall is a hell of a lot better than a war."

than 60 miles, dividing the city and also cutting off West Berlin from surrounding East Germany. The wall itself was about 12 feet high, and behind it was a spotlit area overlooked by the watchtowers and known as the "death area." Behind that was a trench to stop vehicles from breaking through. Dogs and armed patrols were in evidence around the clock. Anyone making a run for it was shot without warning.

The first victim was 18-year-old Peter Fechter, who bled to death after being gunned down attempting to scale the wall on August 17, 1962. He was the first of at least a hundred to die trying to flee, while it is estimated that as many as 5,000 succeeded in escaping, some by tunneling under the wall. The dismantling of the wall in December 1989 symbolized the collapse of communism in Eastern Europe. □

See Also: Brandt; Cold War; Communism; Kennedy, J.F., Khrushchev; Postwar World

LEONARD BERNSTEIN 1918–1990

A composer of serious and complex works as well as Broadway smash hits, notably West Side Story, *during the 1960s Leonard Bernstein was at his peak as a spectacular conductor.*

Leonard Bernstein, as conductor and composer, was during the 1960s one of the best-known musical figures in the world. A handsome and flamboyant celebrity, he occupied a leading place in the worlds of both classical music and Broadway musicals. His classical compositions may not rank with the very greatest of the 20th century, but no one in his lifetime could match him for versatility. As principal conductor of the New York Philharmonic from 1958 to 1969—the first American-born composer to hold such a position with a major symphony orchestra—Bernstein brought to the podium an athletic, all-motion style. The intensity of his emotions was openly betrayed by kaleidoscopic facial movements; sweat would pour from him when he turned to the audience after conducting a major work. He was the composer of the path-breaking musical *West Side Story* (1957) and other hit Broadway shows, and a prolific composer of symphonies, ballets, chamber music, and choral works.

Musical celebrity

Bernstein was openly left-wing in his political sympathies. In the early 1950s he was one of a host of artists who, because of the anticommunist hysteria whipped up by Senator Joseph McCarthy, found it difficult to get air time on radio or television. By the end of the 1950s, however, he had become a familiar and hugely popular figure on TV, and the highly successful film of *West Side Story* (1961) made his music known to a wide public. Bernstein was a leading member of the artistic fraternity that paid court to the Kennedy White House in the early 1960s, and for the remainder of his life "Lenny" Bernstein was the most instantly recognizable classical musician in America.

△ As conductor of the New York Philharmonic Leonard Bernstein conveyed his great enthusiasm to musicians and audiences alike.

Bernstein was a compelling communicator and a witty and charming music educator. People listened to him—and watched him—because he was able to bridge the worlds of popular and classical music without condescension. He could describe Elvis Presley as "the greatest cultural force in the 20th century" and at the same time make it his burning determination to open the high arts to ordinary people.

Bernstein broadcast his message not only on American television and radio, but to people throughout the world. On a tour of Latin America in 1959, as part of an American goodwill mission, he was rapturously received while Vice President Richard Nixon was booed and stoned. Audiences in the Soviet Union, to whom he introduced the work of American composers such as Charles Ives, were delighted when, off the cuff, he repeated performances of works they had cheered. And they loved

the spontaneity of the casual remarks he would make to them during concerts—a previously unheard of practice that was characteristic of Bernstein's inability to be stuffy or pompous.

Bernstein's major compositions of the 1960s were a reflection of his cultural and musical breadth. One was the Jewish-inspired *Kaddish Symphony* (1963), the other the Christian *Chichester Psalms* (1965). The symphony, regarded by many critics as his finest work, has not entered the standard orchestral repertoire. (The composer David Diamond dismissed it as "Lenny being arrogant enough to think he can have a conversation with God.") The *Chichester Psalms*, however, has become one of his most frequently performed works. □

See Also: Ballet; Broadway; Classical Music

BIRTH-CONTROL PILL

The arrival of the contraceptive pill at the beginning of the 1960s revolutionized birth control—providing women with a convenient and reliable method of preventing unwanted pregnancies.

Of the many changes that affected day-to-day life in the United States in the 1960s, perhaps none was more profound, talked about, and written about than the arrival on the market of the first contraceptive pill for women. The drug Enovid had been developed and put on trial in the 1950s and proved to be the most effective and easily used method of birth control ever devised.

The research and development behind the female contraceptive pill was based on the observation that one of the first effects of pregnancy is to suppress ovulation in women. All women have a lifetime supply of eggs (or ova) that are released in a monthly cycle. Early in pregnancy women naturally produce hormones that prevent the release of the next egg—ovulation.

△ **Convenient packaging with clearly marked days helped women remember to take the pill for a set number of days during their menstrual cycle.**

Roman Catholics and the pill

While use of the birth-control pill was encouraged by the organization Planned Parenthood, it presented many American Roman Catholics with a dilemma. In 1951 Pope Pius XII had reaffirmed the Church's view that all forms of birth control were a grave sin with the exception of periodic abstinence. However, the Second Vatican Council, sitting between 1962 and 1965, appeared to redefine the nature of marriage, and a strong movement within the Church argued for a liberalization of the edicts on contraception.

A commission was set up to examine the issue and to report to Pope Paul VI. It included doctors and cardinals. The medical members voted overwhelmingly for the liberalization of Catholic views on birth control, as did a narrow majority of cardinals (nine to six in favor). Pope Paul received the report in 1966. But two years later he reaffirmed the traditional view forbidding artificial contraception.

It appears that on the whole Roman Catholics in the U.S. took little notice. By the early 1970s their average family size was only slightly higher than that of the general population at just over two children. In fact, it has been argued that the contraceptive pill was especially appealing to Roman Catholics because it artificially induced infertility in women, which was similar to the natural infertility that occurred between menstrual cycles and was the basis of the approved "rhythm method" of birth control.

By simulating the early symptoms of pregnancy, the contraceptive pill inhibited ovulation in women.

Although it had been available on prescription from 1957 as a remedy for various ailments, Enovid was not approved as a contraceptive by the Food and Drug Administration (FDA) until 1960 and not advertised as such by the makers G. D. Searle and Company until 1961.

In promoting the birth-control pill Searle had no doubts about what it would mean to American women. Its advertisements showed the Greek goddess Andromeda breaking free from her chains, with the caption "unfettered." The freedom implied was not just freedom from unwanted pregnancy itself but from the fear of such pregnancy, which was perceived as psychologically as well as physically liberating.

Among American married women who had had to live with more traditional forms of birth control in the 1950s—diaphragm, condoms, coitus interruptus (withdrawal), and plain abstinence—the advantages of "the pill" hardly needed advertising. They flocked to their doctors to ask for prescriptions. Some wrote to Gregory Pincus, who, at the Worcester Foundation, had developed Enovid. For example, one woman pleaded: "Will you please send me some of these birth-control pills. We have seven children, we are both 30 years old. And we can't have children every year. So please send me these pills c.o.d."

Why women chose the pill

Within five years of Enovid's approval by the FDA it had become the most popular form of contraceptive in the U.S. Nearly all doctors prescribed it, and by 1965 six and a half million women had chosen it. Among married women under the age of 45 one-quarter used the pill as opposed to other forms of contraception.

Although the advocates of birth control hoped that working-class women who already had large families, or were likely to have them, would be enthusi-

astic about the pill, it was young, middle-class American women who had the biggest adoption rate. Cost was probably a factor here, as well as better access to information and to the medical profession. One survey claimed that an astonishing 80 percent of non-Catholic married college graduates aged 20–24 had tried the pill by 1965.

By the end of the 1960s the National Fertility Study of 1970 confirmed that the pill was the most popular contraceptive of the decade. Among married women under the age of 45 one-third were pill users. Next in popularity was sterilization (16 percent), then the condom (14 percent), the intrauterine

△ The pill facilitated planned parenthood for many women who found other forms of birth control unreliable or inconvenient.

device (7 percent), and the diaphragm (6 percent). In 1969 the FDA estimated that every month 8.5 million American women used the pill.

Although some early pill users reported nausea and weight gain, modifications reduced these problems, and the issue of harmful side-effects had a low profile in the 1960s. It was not until the end of the decade that more serious problems came to light, such as abnormal blood clotting in some users that led to concerns about possible thrombosis. What troubled some was the moral consequences of a contraceptive that might induce young women, released from the fear of pregnancy, to embark on a sexual spree (*see box*). The fact that the pill arrived just as a sexual revolution was reportedly taking off encouraged the view in many newspaper and magazine articles that it was the pill that was largely responsible.

A myth about the pill in the 1960s is that it caused the birthrate to fall. It is true that the postwar baby boom was now past its peak, but in fact birthrates had leveled off in 1957, before the pill was available. Even with the advent of the pill birthrates did not fall to the very low levels of the 1930s. The true significance of the pill in the 1960s was in its transformation of the lifestyle of many married women who no longer feared unwanted pregnancy. □

Teenagers and the pill

The oft-repeated claim that the pill encouraged promiscuity among teenagers in the 1960s was never verifiable because no studies or statistics in that decade provided information on the sexual behavior of unmarried women. What evidence there is suggests that the appearance of the pill was probably of very little significance to teenagers. It was hard for an unmarried woman, especially a teenager, to get a prescription from a doctor. And as a general rule teenagers had a less thoughtful approach to contraception than more mature women.

Finally, in 1971 a study was made of the sexual and contraceptive practices of never-married women aged 15 to 19. Of the 4,000 women interviewed only 28 percent said they had had sexual intercourse. Within that minority most had tried some form of contraception, but not consistently. In fact, half of them had "forgotten" to use anything the last time they had been at risk. Only one-fifth had used the pill as their most recent form of contraception. Partly because of the problem of getting the pill, condoms and withdrawal were more popular.

See Also: Feminist Movement; Health and Healthcare; Sexual Revolution

BLACK PANTHER PARTY

In 1966 the civil rights movement took a decisive turn as militant young blacks lost patience with Martin Luther King, Jr.'s, strategy of nonviolence and equipped themselves for confrontation.

△ **Bobby Seale (left) and Huey P. Newton at the San Francisco headquarters of the Black Panther Party in July 1967.**

The starting point for the Panthers was their rejection of Martin Luther King, Jr.'s, strategy of nonviolent protest as the means to end racial injustice in the United States. In their view African Americans had no choice but to arm themselves for a showdown with their racist oppressors, represented at street level by the police. In their frequent manifestos the Panthers claimed that their armed patrols were purely defensive in nature, but their increasingly violent rhetoric suggested otherwise. For example, after a shootout in Oakland in April 1968 between Panthers and police Newton went on record as saying that "every time you go execute a white racist Gestapo cop, you are defending yourself." Eldridge Cleaver, the Panther's most articulate spokesman, was equally inflammatory: "A black pig, a white pig, a yellow pig, a pink pig—a dead pig is the best pig of all."

Gaining support

Such language, and much-publicized violent encounters with the police, attracted widespread fear and loathing to the Black Panthers. From tiny beginnings in 1966, however, the party's membership grew within two years to a claimed 5,000 in more than 40 branches across the country. And support for the Panthers was much greater than any membership figures. This was partly because it was not difficult for African Americans to see evidence of police racism and brutality on the streets around them and to sympathize with young men who were putting their lives on the line to fight it. The race riots that swept so many cities during the late 1960s were clear evidence that the Panthers' call for militancy fell on receptive ears. Also, while it was the taunting of "the pigs,"

The Black Panther Party was founded in 1966 by militant activists Huey P. Newton and Bobby Seale in Oakland, California. It rapidly became the most radical and most visible expression of the black power movement. The Black Panthers advocated armed struggle in support of their aims, and they were taken at their word by the forces of "law and order." They were persistently confronted by the police and harassed by the FBI.

Creating the image

The movement got its name and striking imagery from an incident far away from the streets of West Oakland, in Lowndes County, Alabama. Stokely Carmichael of the Student Nonviolent Coordinating Committee (SNCC) was leading a voter registration drive there in 1965, when he had the inspiration to choose a black panther as the symbol to put on the ballot.

It was such a striking image that Newton and Seale adopted it for their new movement, with Carmichael's permission. With the panther emblem emerged the guerrilla uniforms, black berets, and brazenly displayed firearms. The conspicuous physical presence, along with the inflammatory language that accompanied it, conveyed extreme menace to the movement's enemies, of whom there were many—African American as well as white.

the paramilitary uniforms, and the occasional gunfight that captured national headlines, there was another side to the Black Panther program.

From the beginning Newton and Seale stressed the need for self-help in the community. This took a number of forms in Oakland, including free meals and public health programs, cooperative housing, and transportation for seniors. In one celebrated incident the Panther leaders could claim credit for getting traffic lights installed at a notoriously dangerous crossing in Oakland. Newton and Seale would simply go out and direct traffic. The police would hurry to the scene, at which point the two would melt away, only to return when the police left. There was no bloodshed, and lights finally went up.

Violent confrontation

The Black Panthers pursued their goals in the teeth of fierce opposition: on the street from the police, and behind the scenes from the FBI. An FBI report

▽ **Black Panthers at the Federal Courthouse in New York, on May 1, 1969, in support of members charged with an alleged bomb plot.**

Life after the revolution

Following the decline in influence and eventual demise of the Black Panther Party in the early 1970s, the careers of its cofounders Huey Newton and Bobby Seale took different directions.

In 1974, three years after his manslaughter conviction was overturned on appeal, Newton was again implicated in violent crimes, including the murder of a prostitute. He fled into exile in Cuba, but returned to the U.S. in 1977 and spent the next decade battling the charges, which were eventually reduced to being an ex-felon in possession of a firearm. Convicted on this charge in 1987, he served a short prison sentence, but drugs and alcohol increasingly plagued his life. In 1989 Newton was gunned to death in a drug-infested area of West Oakland.

Seale remained as chairman of the Black Panther Party during Newton's imprisonment in the late 1960s and was one of those charged in connection with the riots at the Chicago Democratic Party Convention in 1968. He was gagged and chained in court for interrupting proceedings and eventually removed and convicted of contempt of court. Seale made an unorthodox bid to become mayor of Oakland in 1973 and later took to the lecture circuit and to writing, including a soul-food cookbook.

made public in 1976 gave details of illegal wiretaps, false arrests, and attempts to provoke confrontations with the police. However provoked, some of the confrontations were lethal. In 1967 there was a gun battle in

Oakland in which a policeman was shot dead. Newton was convicted of manslaughter, a conviction that was overturned in 1971. By then, however, the Black Panthers were no longer a force to be reckoned with. □

See Also: Black Power; Carmichael; Civil Rights Movement; Cleaver; FBI; King

BLACK POWER

In 1966 the civil rights movement's commitment to nonviolence was overtaken by more radical forces armed with a slogan that put a chill into the hearts of many white people—"black power."

△ **Floyd McKissick, national director of CORE, displays the militant new message at an antiwar demonstration in Harlem in July 1966.**

In June 1966 James Meredith, who had found fame in 1962 as the first African American to enroll at the University of Mississippi, set out on a one-man "March Against Fear" through Mississippi. On the second day of the march Meredith was ambushed and shot twice by an unemployed white hardware clerk who was waiting in the bushes along the highway.

Martin Luther King, Jr., Floyd McKissick, national director of the Congress of Racial Equality, Whitney Young, executive secretary of the National Urban League (*see box p. 141*), and Stokely Carmichael, leader of the Student Nonviolent Coordinating Committee (SNCC), rushed to his bedside. All but Young agreed to march in his stead.

Out on the road Carmichael soon made it clear that his views were very different from those of King. He was not for that "nonviolence stuff any more," he said. And he thought that whites should be excluded from the march. On June 17 Carmichael addressed a mass meeting in Greenwood, Mississippi. "Today's the 27th time I've been arrested and I ain't going to jail no more," he said. "The only way we gonna stop them white men from whuppin' us is to take over. We been saying 'freedom' for six years and we ain't got nothing. What we gonna start saying now is 'black power!'"

The crowd echoed: "Black power!"

"Ain't nothing wrong with anything all black," Carmichael continued, "cause I'm all black and I'm all good. And from now on, when they ask you what you want, you know what to tell them."

"Black power," the crowd roared.

A divided movement

ogan divided the civil rights movement. It was adopted by SNCC (called "Snik") and the Congress of Racial Equality (CORE), but King took Carmichael and McKissick aside and pleaded with them for five hours to abandon the slogan. "Black power," he cautioned, carried connotations of violence and separatism. "We are seeking to share power with whites," King said. Carmichael was resolute. A coalition with white people, he maintained, was undesirable. African American people had to act for themselves. This fundamental idea of black power, that it was up to African Americans themselves to fight back against the injustices they experienced, resonated deeply, especially among young African Americans.

When talking to the press, Carmichael would emphasize that black power was not antiwhite, and that he was not advocating violence. But on other occasions he urged every African American to come home from Vietnam "and fight here because here is where the fight is." By April 1967 he was telling African Americans: "If a white man tries to walk over you, kill him. One match and you can retaliate. Burn, baby, burn."

In July 1967 race riots erupted in Newark, New Jersey. Five days of

Black on black

△ At the end of July 1967 four days of rioting in Detroit left 42 dead. Racial violence swept some 70 U.S. cities that month alone.

In the early 1960s African Americans were usually called either Negroes or colored people. Stokely Carmichael changed all that. Within SNCC he began to use the term "black." When he used the termed publicly for the first time in his Greenwood speech, it was a revelation. African Americans suddenly saw themselves in a new way—as something distinct and different. Soul singer James Brown, although a political moderate, caught the ethos perfectly with the song "Say It Loud, I'm Black and Proud."

Explaining their rejection of the term "Negro," Carmichael and Hamilton drew attention to its origins: "This term is the invention of our oppressor; it is his image of us that he describes. Many blacks are calling themselves African Americans, Afro-Americans, or black people because that is our image of ourselves. From now on we shall view ourselves as African Americans and as black people, who are in fact energetic, determined, intelligent, beautiful, and peace-loving."

The term "black" was the preferred designation for the rest of the 1960s. It was only in the 1990s that it was superseded by "African American," although this term has caused difficulties with black people in other parts of the world to whom it may suggest a lack of identification with all blacks.

rioting left 26 dead, 1,004 injured, and 1,397 in jail. Next Detroit exploded. Forty-two were killed, 386 injured, and 5,557 arrested. In the smoldering ruins of Newark a national conference of African American leaders was held to explore the implications. The tone of the conference was militant. Even King came around. "The black power slogan did not spring full-blown from the head of some philosophical Zeus," he said. "It was born from the wounds of despair and disappointment. It is a cry of our daily hurt and persistent pain."

In the fall of 1967 Carmichael and Charles V. Hamilton, chairman of the Department of Political Science at Roosevelt University in Chicago, spelled out what they meant by black power in

Black Power: The Politics of Liberation in America. They explained that the call for black power was "the last reasonable opportunity for this society to work out its racial problems short of prolonged destructive guerrilla warfare."

White people had systematically excluded any meaningful mention of black contributions to history and the African American heritage from schools, textbooks, movies, and mass media, they argued. This was "cultural terrorism," which deprived African Americans of any knowledge of their past or pride in their race. It enabled white people to define the meaning of black, to stigmatize black as inferior, and to justify discrimination and oppression. The first step forward was to create a "black consciousness" where African Americans reclaimed their his-

△ H. Rap Brown, Stokely Carmichaels's successor, addressing a crowd in front of SNCC headquarters in July 1967.

H. Rap Brown and "cherry pie"

"You'll be happy to have me back when you hear from him. He's a bad man," said Stokely Carmichael when he introduced H. Rap Brown as his successor as chairman of SNCC in 1967. At first, though, Brown failed to impress. He was very different from Carmichael in appearance, unprepossessing and wearing a blue blazer and glasses. Soon, however, Brown was seen as a firebrand. Following the riots in Newark and Detroit, Brown went to Cambridge, Maryland, where he told a crowd of around 300 people: "Black folks built America. If America don't come around, we're going to burn America down, brother."

A few hours later the whole of the black section of town was ablaze. A policeman had been shot, and white volunteer firefighters refused to turn out. The following day Brown was arrested. Released on a $10,000 bond, he told the African American press: "You better get yourself a gun; the honky don't respect nothing but guns."

Then, in another of the memorable catchphrases of the black power movement, he said: "Violence is necessary. It is as American as cherry pie!" That night in a Washington church he told his audience that African Americans should "do more shooting than looting when they riot. If you are going to loot, loot yourself a gunstore. You got to arm yourself, brother!"

Brown was instrumental in forging a coalition between SNCC and the Black Panther Party. In 1968 Eldridge Cleaver announced that Brown had been drafted into the Black Panthers as minister of justice. In response Brown praised Huey Newton, who was in jail charged with murder at the time, as "our only living revolutionary in this country." However, SNCC found it difficult to go along with the Panthers' violent schemes, and after an alleged death threat from Eldridge Cleaver, Brown quit. He turned to Islam, took the name Jamal Abdullah Al-Amin, and became the proprietor of a small convenience store in Atlanta, Georgia.

tory and culture. It was up to black people to define what being black was.

Black power rejected integration because integration absorbed the African American middle class into white society, leaving the rest of the African American community behind, impoverished. To achieve power, the African American community had to hang together. Instead of delivering African American votes to the white political machines, the aim of black power was to get more black leaders elected.

From moderate to militant

After the assassination of King in April 1968 black power was seen by a growing number of activists as the only way ahead. Even Whitney Young of the National Urban League, who had long held out against the advocates of black

Whitney Young

During the early 1960s Whitney Young headed the National Urban League, the most conservative of the African American organizations. By the end of the decade, however, he found himself allied with the call for black power.

Born in 1921, in Lincoln Ridge, Kentucky, Young was the son of the president of Lincoln Institute, an African American college. His mother was a school teacher. In 1942 he joined the army and rose to the rank of sergeant in the all-black 369th Anti-Aircraft Artillery Group. After leaving the army in 1946, Young studied social work at the University of Minnesota. His first field placement was with the Minnesota chapter of the Urban League, where he sought to improve employment prospects for African American workers. In 1950 he became director of the Urban League's chapter in Omaha, Nebraska. Then he moved to Atlanta, Georgia, where he became dean of the School of Social Work at Atlanta University and a prominent leader of the local African American community.

△ Whitney Young (second row, left) joins other African American leaders for the March on Washington on August 28, 1963, the high-water mark of nonviolent civil rights protest.

In 1961 Young was appointed executive director of the National Urban League. The first wave of sit-ins was in progress, and Young sought to forge an alliance between the traditionally conservative League and other civil rights organizations without jeopardizing the League's powerful contacts with the white power structure that reached right into the Kennedy White House. In 1963 Young joined the March on Washington and became a member of the Council for United Civil Rights Leadership set up by the Kennedy administration. After President Kennedy's assassination Young forged even stronger ties with President Johnson. His call for a "domestic Marshall Plan," outlined in his 1964 book *To Be Equal*, was reflected in Johnson's War on Poverty program.

Disturbed by the drift toward militancy, by 1966 the Urban League had split away from the civil rights coalition Young had been instrumental in forging in 1961. Young refused to sign a manifesto drafted by other civil rights leaders and did not join them to continue James Meredith's march through Mississippi in 1966. He shunned the black power activists in CORE and SNCC, and sided with President Johnson against Martin Luther King, Jr.'s, stand against the war in Vietnam. He went to South Vietnam to review the troops there twice at Johnson's request. Before leaving office in 1969, Johnson rewarded Young with the Medal of Freedom, the nation's highest civilian award.

However, even a moderate such as Young could not resist the militant tide. After the assassination of King and the Poor People's March on Washington in 1968 he too embraced the black power movement. When President Nixon took office in 1969, Young found he no longer had powerful friends in the administration. He turned against the Vietnam War and concentrated the Urban League's resources on the inner-city young black underclass. He used his influence with the banks and foundations to funnel money into the ghettos in an attempt to give African Americans the economic power the militants were demanding. In March 1971 Young attended a conference in Lagos, Nigeria. While swimming, he suffered either a heart attack or a brain hemorrhage and drowned.

power, capitulated. Appearing at CORE's convention in July 1968 in Columbus, Ohio, he said: "America does not respond to people who beg." African Americans "were no longer enchanted with being near white people." Then Young called for "black power." The convention went wild.

SNCC, meanwhile, formed a coalition with the Black Panthers. Carmichael quit as chairman of SNCC to be replaced by H. Rap Brown (*see*

box p. 140) and joined the Panthers. Carmichael soon fell out with Eldridge Cleaver and Bobby Seale, however, and quit the Panthers. In his resignation letter he wrote: "I cannot support the present tactics and methods which the party is using to coerce and force everyone to submit to the party."

Carmichael married the South African singer Miriam Makeba and moved to Ghana. SNCC faded into oblivion and dissolved in the early

△ **"Integration stinks," reads one placard at this march in 1963. White supremacists resisted black civil rights at every stage.**

1970s, by which time the Black Panthers had been hounded almost out of existence by the police and FBI.

Although the organizations that made up the black power movement foundered, because African Americans became increasingly represented at every level of government the movement itself could be judged a success. It was also successful in raising the consciousness and the self-image of African Americans generally. Black power implied black worth. Carmichael, however, thought black power still had some way to go in America a generation later. In 1993 he told New York radio station WLIB: "[African Americans] have more elected officials in the Democratic Party than any other ethnic group in this country. Yet we have no power at all in the Democratic Party. That's why racism continues to run rampant and will continue to run rampant until we get power to stop it." □

The Olympic protests

The demand for Black Power reached a world audience at the 1968 Olympic Games. African American basketball stars Alvin Hayes, Westley Unseld, and Bob Lanier refused to try out for the U.S. team. Lee Evans, Larry James, and Ron Freeman, who won gold, silver, and bronze medals in the 400 meters, wore black berets in a black power protest. But the enduring image of the games was provided by Tommie Smith and John Carlos, who won gold and bronze medals in the 200-meter sprint. On the winners' rostrum they wore black scarves and black gloves raised in a clenched-fist black power salute while the national anthem played. For their pains they were suspended from the games and excluded from the Olympic village.

See Also: Black Panthers; Carmichael; Civil Rights Movement; Cleaver; Detroit Race Riot; Ghettos; Malcolm X; SNCC

BLACK STUDIES

Through widespread student demonstrations and even armed protest African American students succeeded in forcing the educational establishment to broaden its curriculum in their favor.

Black Studies is the study of human affairs from a black or African perspective. It is multidisciplinary in approach, with an emphasis on the humanities, sciences, and the arts. Black Studies—also known as Africana Studies, African American Studies, Pan-African Studies, and other titles—consciously blurs the distinctions between traditional academic departments.

Black Studies has a long history, but its formal existence within American colleges and universities was a product of the turbulent 1950s and 1960s. It was the culmination of the civil rights, black power, and free speech movements, and the organized resistance to the Vietnam War. Black Studies turned out to be the forerunner of women's studies, Chicano Studies, Asian American Studies, Native American Studies, and gay and lesbian studies.

The struggle for recognition

Although the first Department of Black Studies was established in the fall of 1968 at San Francisco State University, it would be a mistake to localize the origin of Black Studies to any specific institution. Instead, Black Studies was the product of a social movement that transcended state and national boundaries.

Widespread protest movements produced an awareness among students that collective struggle and resistance could produce dramatic changes. Colleges and universities were viewed as the microcosm of everything that was wrong in the world: the pervasive ideology of white supremacy, the abuse of power, and indifference to racial inequality. The struggle against the wrongs of society was therefore waged within the "brain" or "intellectual factory" that produced those wrongs.

By the mid-1960s African Americans had changed their group name

△ **A seminar on black literature at Cornell University in 1969, following the occupation of a university building by armed students.**

from Negroes to blacks. In 1966, for example, the Negro Student Association at San Francisco State University changed its name to the Black Students' Union (BSU). Simultaneous with this name change was the demand by the BSU for a department in Black Studies and for black faculty to offer courses in

black arts and culture. This program was closely connected with a community tutorial program, so Black Studies, from its conception, embraced the idea of what was called a "communiversity."

It took two years of demonstrations and strikes at SFSU before the university appointed Dr. Nathan Hare as coordinator of Black Studies. What happened at San Francisco State University was mirrored around the nation. At Howard University in Washington, D.C., stu-

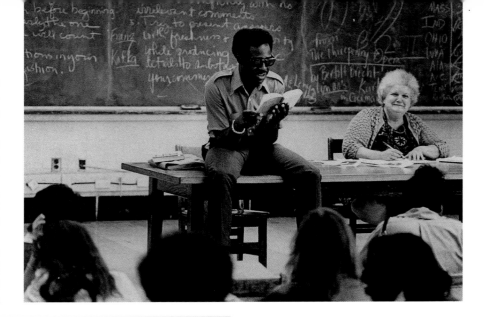

dent takeovers of the administration building in the spring of 1968 ultimately resulted in the university's acquiescence to student demands.

Perhaps the most memorable image from this era was the student takeover of Willard Straight Hall at Cornell University in the spring of 1969 (*see box*), where students issued the declaration: "We are not an act of goodwill, we are a reality that has to be dealt with!"

By the end of the decade most American colleges and universities had established Black Studies programs or departments. The goals of Black

△ **New perspectives: black history being taught to high-school students in Durham, North Carolina, in the early 1970s.**

Guns on campus

By early 1969 students at Willard Straight Hall at Cornell University had been demonstrating for a year for an autonomous black college, financed by the university, where students would have a voice in the curriculum, the hiring and firing of faculty, and student admissions. These demonstrations were followed by incidents in which black students received anonymous threatening phone calls.

On April 18, 1969, a rock was thrown through the window of a residence of a dozen black female students, and a cross was burned on their front steps. The next morning Willard Straight Hall was seized by black activists to protest the disciplinary actions that had been taken against students for their involvement in previous protests. Edward L. Whitfield, the 19-year-old sophomore chairman of Cornell's Afro-American Society, declared the takeover a protest of Cornell's "racist practices." The drama was heightened by the fact that it was Parents' Weekend, and about 30 parents and 40 university staff members were roused from their beds during the takeover.

Later that day a group of white men from Delta Upsilon fraternity raided the building, resulting in a physical confrontation and four students being treated for minor wounds. Rumors circulated that several carloads of whites—with guns—were on the way to Willard Straight Hall. That night black students began delivering guns, ammunition, and machetes to the students inside the building.

The university's response was to call for negotiations with the students, which ended peacefully the next day. The students marched from Willard Straight Hall, triumphantly holding their loaded weapons. Eric Evans, a senior from Chicago, was photographed with a rifle and bandoliers of ammunition across his chest. The students had wrested an agreement from the university for full amnesty for those involved in the takeover, the nullification of previous disciplinary actions against students for other demonstrations, police protection for the black students, and a full investigation into the cross-burning incident.

The armed takeover at Cornell sent a chilling message to other colleges and universities, resulting in an escalation of police/student confrontations and the ultimate acquiescence by university officials to diversify the students, faculty, and curriculum throughout American higher education. As one Cornell faculty member put it, "Guns work."

Studies were to authentically research and teach the historical and contemporary black experience, to engage in the struggle for intellectual and political emancipation of black people, to develop a commitment to community service, and to establish Black Studies as a legitimate scholarly discipline.

A wide-ranging agenda

Early courses in Black Studies emphasized history and literature, but some embraced the political motives of the protestors. At Berkeley, for example, the curriculum in Black Studies included Social Welfare 298: American Racism, Ethnic and Racial Groups; and also Psychology 191C: Psychological Aspects of Black Identity.

Critics viewed Black Studies as a political capitulation to violence and the threat of violence, and as a "feel-good" exercise in black separatism. Scholars also criticized the developments in Black Studies as eroding the faculty's control of hiring and firing and the determination of curricular directions. Many critics felt that Black Studies, and the admission of less prepared students, eroded the quality of the institutions of higher learning. To its supporters Black Studies programs played—and continue to play—an important role in the broader struggle for black liberation. □

See Also: Civil Rights Movement; Schools and Universities

BLACKOUT OF 1965

On the night of November 9–10, 1965, a power failure blacked out the northeastern states, plunging 30 million people, one-sixth of the population of the United States, into darkness.

The blackout began with a generator fault on the Canadian side of the border near Niagara Falls. It spread quickly across New York State, Connecticut, Rhode Island, Massachusetts, Vermont, New Hampshire, and northern Pennsylvania.

The blackout hit New York City at 5:27 P.M., the height of the evening rush hour. Some 800,000 people were trapped in subway tunnels or trains for up to five hours. Commuters spent the night in railroad stations, hotel lobbies, and bars. Traffic signals failed, causing massive traffic jams. People trapped in the elevator between the 24th and 25th floors of the Empire State Building waited five hours for rescuers to break through a concrete wall. It was the city's biggest ever peace-time emergency.

Few people panicked, however. Hospitals, the Strategic Air Command, and other defense installations switched over to auxiliary power and continued to operate as normal. Aircraft were diverted from New York's airports to airports outside the affected area, resulting in backlogs and delays.

Power was restored by 2:00 A.M. in Brooklyn, 4:20 in Queens, 6:58 in Manhattan, and 7:00 in the Bronx. Subways were running by 8:30.

Some 90 minutes after the lights went out New York's radio stations began broadcasting a message telling people to stay off the streets. About a dozen stores were looted, and 60 arrests were made, but this was low compared to a 1964 average of 380 arrests during a similar 16-hour period. However, police had to rush to a prison near Boston where rioting broke out.

President Lyndon Johnson ordered the FBI and other government agencies to investigate the causes of what the newspapers called "the biggest short circuit in history." However, it was soon clear that nothing sinister had occurred. A malfunction in the Ontario Hydro generating system on the Niagara River had caused an inrush of power into the upstate New York systems. They collapsed under the overload, which triggered a domino effect of overloads throughout the entire system.

Nine months after the blackout there was a sharp increase in the birthrate in the affected areas. New York's Mount Sinai hospital, which averaged 11 births daily, delivered 28 babies on August 8, 1966—a record for the hospital. Five other city hospitals also recorded more births than usual that day. □

◁ The eerie sight of downtown Manhattan blacked out by the massive power failure on the night of November 9–10, 1965.

BLUES

Developments in popular music during the 1960s led to a renaissance for one of America's oldest music forms.

American youth appeared to have turned their backs on the blues forever at the dawn of the 1960s. To many young African Americans, especially, the music was redundant, harking back to past times. As the new decade began, the slick, urban sounds of soul in the shape of Stax and black pop in the shape of Motown proved more engaging to the young. Unknown to many listeners—although not performers—the blues was an essential component in this new music. Even on a practical level its influence was pervasive. The first songs penned by Motown founder Berry Gordy had been released on the Chess record label, famous for its groundbreaking, postwar blues releases. In the face of changing fashion, however, such facts counted for little.

The legendary Muddy Waters

It was impossible, though, to lose the blues in Chicago. Amplified blues had developed in that city during the years following World War II through the inventiveness primarily of the legendary Muddy Waters. During the late 1940s and throughout the 1950s almost every great bluesman of the era had passed through Muddy's band. One such individual, guitarist Buddy Guy, had been on the verge of returning home to Louisiana when Waters heard him playing at a club in the late 1950s and recognized a unique talent. In 1960 the 23-year-old Guy became a member of the Chess house band. That year he recorded "First Time I Met the Blues," his debut on Chess, a startling combination of anguished vocals and heavily amplified, screaming guitar. It epitomized the new West Side sound, which

△ **Muddy Waters, elder statesman of the blues and inspiration to musicians of the 1950s, found a still wider audience in the 1960s.**

would encapsulate the frustrations of young men in that part of Chicago. It would also set the tone for much of the new blues of the 1960s and beyond.

Alongside Guy, distinguished practitioners of this sound included 26-year-old Otis Rush and Magic Sam, 22 at the the start of the decade (*see box p. 147*). Without the backing of a major record label, however, commercial success for such blues artists remained elusive. It seemed as if only a freakish development could revive the blues and bring it to the forefront of popular consciousness—and that is exactly what happened.

The birth of British blues

The impetus for a blues revival would come from a most surprising source—Great Britain. Young people in that

country, seeking relief from the bland, boring pop that filled their record charts, had turned to American music. For some, rock-'n'-roll was enough. For others a more exotic brew was required, and they slaked their collective thirst on deep drafts of blues. These records were like nothing they had heard before. Among those who made the transition from listeners to players were guitarist Eric Clapton, as part of John Mayall's Bluesbreakers and the Yardbirds, Van Morrison, vocalist with Them, and the Rolling Stones, a group with roots so deep in the blues that they took their name from a Muddy Waters song, "Rollin' Stone Blues." Mick Jagger summed up his band's ability to mix tradition with innovation when he said, "We were blues purists who liked ever-so-commercial things."

Such was the reverence of the Stones for the blues that in the earliest days after their formation in 1962, they would play concerts seated on high stools to ensure that no movement would distract their listeners from the purity of their blues sound. By 1964 this evangelical approach bore fruit with a previously unimaginable development—a No. 1 blues record on the British pop chart. That song, "Little Red Rooster," was among many written by Chess's Willie Dixon. It had been recorded in 1961 by Howlin' Wolf, but his down-home growl had been too gruff for it to be any sort of a hit in the early 1960s. In the hands of hip, young white groups such as the Stones this and other blues-based songs would become readily acceptable to a young white audience both in Europe and, more surprisingly, in the United States.

Transatlantic trade

The Stones had recorded "Little Red Rooster" and other blues covers at Chess Studios during visits there in 1964 (the young Englishmen were amazed to see Muddy Waters painting

△ Mississippi-born guitarist and vocalist Otis Rush was a leading exponent of the Chicago-style amplified blues during the 1960s.

Magic Sam

At a time when the blues was crying out for new stars, Magic Sam was ready to answer the call. More than any of his contemporaries, he revived Chicago blues and gave it soul. An expert exponent of the new Chicago West Side sound, Sam—born Samuel Maghett in the Mississippi Delta in 1937—spent the first half of the 1960s honing to perfection his inventive finger-picking, electric blues guitar in the clubs of the West Side of his adopted home city. Recording opportunities had been sparse for Sam, whose stage performances matched his music for flamboyance and style, but an alliance with the Delmark record label saw him create two stunning albums: *West Side Soul* (1968) and *Black Magic* (1969). As the title of the first of those hinted, Sam, an accomplished songwriter, was not afraid to mingle the sounds of blues and soul. The impact of those albums, together with a show-stopping performance at the 1969 Ann Arbor Festival, saw Sam set for popular acclaim. He was offered a contract with Stax, a joint venture that promised to take blues in new directions. But he died of a heart attack at the age of 32, depriving the blues of one of its major modern talents.

the ceiling when they walked into Chess). Soon, an exchange program was underway, with white British groups playing blues-based material to American audiences while American blues musicians found a warm welcome in Europe that often contrasted sharply with their treatment, musically and socially, at home. A notable development was the American Folk Blues Festival, an annual event in the 1960s, in which an entourage of leading blues musicians would tour together, playing dates in Europe's major cities.

The blues now had recognition from the coolest sources. Ironically, the popularity of the new blues-based British

B. B. King

△ B. B. King's unique playing style enabled him to expand the musical and emotional range of the blues guitar. Celebrated for his live performances, King easily adapted to 1960s blues-rock.

Harmonica and slide guitar were among the principal props white audiences of the 1960s expected to be in the armory of an "authentic" bluesman. Yet although neither slide nor harmonica featured in B.B. King's seminal work, that decade saw him grow quickly in stature to become one of the most celebrated bluesmen of the 20th century.

Unable to use a slide, King instead gave his guitar playing distinction by carefully bending and shaping every individual note he played, dwelling on each one to achieve a lasting effect. The finger vibrato evolved to make his music a subtle synthesis of jazz and blues forms, although the feeling with which B. B. delivered his music placed him firmly in the blues camp. His guitar solos were works of distinction, while his lyrics were more sophisticated than those of more down-home bluesmen. He dealt in subtle fashion with the complicated nuances of relationships, while such subjects as drug use were out of bounds as B. B. strove to make the blues respectable. Wry humor, delivered with superb timing, helped ease along many a B. B. song.

King was in his mid-30s as the 1960s began, and he was already well established among the African American listening public thanks to a series of R&B hits from the late 1940s on, as well as a punishing commitment to making live appearances. The Mississippi-born bluesman had first made his name on Memphis radio shows, where he had acquired the nickname "The Beale Street Blues Boy." The nickname was soon modified to "Blues Boy" and by the beginning of the 1960s had become further refined into the more stylish appendage "B. B."

In 1960 he ended his 10-year association with Modern Records to join ABC, but it was not until the middle of the decade that B. B. began to enjoy nationwide success in a unique niche between blues and rock. A hint of his potential came in 1964 with his first notable pop-chart hit "Rock Me Baby," which reached No. 34. Late that year a concert at the Regal Theater, Chicago, was recorded to become the album *Live at the Regal*, released in 1965. It captured B. B. in exceptional form and was one of the first recordings to showcase a blues artist performing at the peak of his powers.

By the end of the decade B. B.'s stock had risen to its highest point, and he was acknowledged by Buddy Guy and Eric Clapton as a major influence on their guitar work. The summer of 1969 saw him invited to appear at major festivals, notably the Atlantic City Pop Festival, where he joined the Byrds, Jefferson Airplane, and Creedence Clearwater Revival to entertain an audience of 110,000. In November 1969 King enlisted as the opening act on the Rolling Stones' sixth tour of the U.S. He crowned the decade majestically with *Completely Well*, the album that finally won him widespread recognition, and which yielded "The Thrill is Gone," his highest-ranking pop single.

rock groups ensured the end of the little chart success American bluesmen had enjoyed in the early 1960s.

Soon, young Americans were playing blues-based rock. The music of Jimi Hendrix, Janis Joplin, and Canned Heat was heavily indebted to the blues. Yet while the music was enjoying widespread respect, for straightforward bluesmen themselves times could still be hard. Buddy Guy, for example, had a day job throughout the 1960s. In 1968 Muddy Waters attempted a crossover into rock by recording *Electric Mud*, a less than successful attempt at a psychedelic album. While Muddy and other elder statesmen of the blues could count on unprecedented demand for concert and festival appearances in the wake of the success of blues-based rock, their record sales remained negligible.

Bringing the blues home

Three decades earlier, in San Antonio and Dallas, blues guitarist Robert Johnson had recorded 45 sides for the American Record Company in the most basic circumstances. In the dying days of 1969, at Madison Square Garden the clamor of a Stones concert melted into silence as singer Mick

△ Howlin' Wolf, in his fifties when the decade began, was a major influence on the younger bluesmen and rock musicians of the 1960s, in particular the Rolling Stones and the Yardbirds.

Blues festivals

The idea of a blues festival was an alien one as the 1960s began. The best a blues artist could do was obtain a booking at a jazz or a folk festival. Even then, problems of classification arose. In 1960, for example, the Newport Folk Festival could not countenance the electric blues of Muddy Waters for fear of upsetting acoustic folk purists. It proved their loss. Instead, Muddy was accommodated at the Newport Jazz Festival, where he recorded one of the most influential blues albums of the 1960s—*Muddy Waters at Newport*. Three years later times had changed sufficiently for Muddy and other electrified Chicago-style bands to be accepted as part of the Newport Folk Festival. Progress continued in Europe with the American Folk Blues Festival, an all-blues traveling show, despite its equivocal title. By the end of the decade there was enough interest in the blues—chiefly among the young, white audience—for it to launch its own festivals. One of the earliest and best took place in August 1969, when an audience of approximately 10,000 gathered for the first festival at Ann Arbor, Michigan. The novelty of playing at such an event attracted an exceptional gathering of blues luminaries, including B. B. King, John Lee Hooker, Lightnin' Hopkins, Muddy Waters, Magic Sam, Howlin' Wolf, and T-Bone Walker.

Jagger lingered lovingly over every note of Johnson's "Love In Vain," now re-recorded for their best-selling album *Let It Bleed* (the title a sideswipe at the Beatles *Let It Be*). No blues artist could command the drawing power or record sales of such musicians, who had integrated blues into rock. Some American bluesmen were bitter. After working with the Yardbirds and the Animals, Sonny Boy Williamson sarcastically remarked: "Those English boys want to play the blues so bad. And they play it so bad." Despite such reservations, the music now had a wider audience than ever before—more than even an optimist might have expected at the beginning of the decade. □

See Also: British Invasion; Rock Music; Rolling Stones

BOOK PUBLISHING

Although many worried that the book-reading habit was threatened by the medium of television, the 1960s saw a rising demand for books and an industry well able to satisfy it.

Television came to dominate the domestic lives and free time of Americans in the 1960s, and so it is often assumed that older forms of communication such as newspapers and radio lost much of their significance, and that the oldest medium—book publishing—was more or less on the way out. Media guru Marshall McLuhan said as much, when he announced that the age of print, which had begun with the Gutenberg printing press in the 15th century, was over.

A premature obituary

Though this seemed to be an inevitable consequence of the power of television to draw huge audiences far greater than the readership of most books, McLuhan's obituary for book publishing was not only premature, he was dismissing a U.S. industry that experienced a real boom during the 1960s. In the course of the decade 6,500 publishing houses were engaged in a wide-ranging business that included book clubs and highly specialized texts on law and medicine, as well as best-selling novels. By 1970 publishers were producing nearly 40,000 books a year worth nearly $3 billion.

The biggest slice of the annual publishing cake went not to bestsellers but to textbooks for college students and others studying specialized subjects. This was fueled by government drives for education that brought something like a quarter of the entire population into some involvement with learning in any one year. U.S. publishers benefited too from a worldwide explosion in education as new schools and universities were established in developing countries. Much of what was produced was

△ **The folding department at Kingswood Press in Kingswood, Tennessee, in 1967. Big presses encouraged large print runs.**

not new work but classics such as the Greek poet Homer's *Iliad* and *Odyssey*, written centuries before the development of the printing press. In addition to the demand for classics there was a thirst for knowledge about emerging subjects in science and technology.

The sale of books had always been limited by their cost, but a paperback revolution in the 1950s brought a vast literature within the grasp of millions of people. Old and expensive printing by hand was replaced by photocomposition—reproduction by a photographic process—and new offset printing machines that were capable of mass production with print runs of 300,000.

Two different kinds of paperback had sizeable shares of the market. The so-called trade paperbacks were soft-

Boom years for books

It is not easy to calculate total sales of books of various kinds and their value in any one year, but by combining information from various sources it is possible to show that publishing flourished in the age of television.

The total number of books published in the U.S. in 1960 was 15,012 and expenditure by consumers $1.139 billion (excluding purchases by government and businesses). This rose steadily to a 1965 figure of 28,595 books and expenditure by consumers of $1.68 billion. By 1970 the equivalent figures were 36,071 and $2.9 billion.

cover editions of books that were bought chiefly by libraries in their hardback, and more durable, editions. These paperbacks had a significant share of the market, bringing in around $50 million a year in the 1960s.

Catering to a diverse market

Then there were the bestsellers such as Jacqueline Susann's lurid *Beyond the Valley of the Dolls* (1966), books scorned by critics but which sold in their millions in cheap paperback versions. They were sold not only in bookstores but also on stands in supermarkets, airports, and many other outlets. By the end of the 1960s these pot-boilers, as they were sometimes disparagingly referred to, had a total annual sale of over $250 million.

Conventional hardback books, as well as those written for children, religious texts, dictionaries, encyclopedias, and reference works—the kinds of publications that conventionally line the

△ The co-op bookstore at the University of Oregon in 1969. The 1960s boom in higher education was reflected in book sales.

The knowledge industry

Book publishing remained in the 1960s a significant part of what has been called the "knowledge industry"—the sum total of all the activities of schools, colleges, government, television, radio, magazines, newspapers, and so on, the primary purpose of which is to keep a modern society informed. The communication media within that industry, which include advertising, telephone services, and photography as well as books, publications of all kinds, and broadcasting, was worth nearly $49 billion in 1963, had risen to $67 billion by 1967, and more than $100 billion by 1972.

Printed materials had three times the value of radio and television broadcasting in 1963—$15 billion as against $4.5 billion. By 1967 print was valued at over $20 billion and broadcasting at $7.4 billion.

The $2.9 billion value of book publishing in 1970 was therefore quite modest within the totality of the knowledge industry in purely financial terms. But it remained strong throughout the 1960s chiefly because of the growing demand for nonfiction publications. In 1963 just under 15 percent of books sold were defined as "practical"—they were about home economics or farming or medicine or anything technical. By far the largest share went to books defined as "intellectual," which covered everything from the arts to music, history, science, geography, and travel. Just under 20 percent were "pastime" books, fiction, games and sports, and children's books.

The share of pastime books fell in the 1960s—down to 14 percent by 1972, while intellectual books were up to 62 percent and practical books to 16 percent. Spiritual books, that is religious publications of all kinds, fell from just under 8 percent in 1963 to less than 5 per cent in 1972.

shelves of booksellers—brought in around $500 million a year in sales.

In addition book clubs expanded to cater to those with special interests and hobbies such as cooking and gardening and popular history. Publishers sold cheaply to the clubs in return for a guaranteed order, and there were profits to be made. The book-club trade was worth around $250 million by 1970.

Most publishers remained small in the 1960s, and many were specialized. Universities began to move into book publishing more and more, with small print runs of specialized works. And there were some familiar names that stood out, such as Harper and Row, McGraw-Hill, and Doubleday. So, in fact, much in the buoyant world of publishing was untouched by the challenge of television. TV provided no substitute for texts on law or medicine or technology, and perhaps served only to fuel an appetite for knowledge that could only be satisfied by reading. □

See Also: Literature; Schools and Universities

BOXING

Television provided a global audience for boxing in the 1960s, and despite the confusion caused by rival governing bodies, the decade witnessed epic battles between outstanding fighters.

During the 1960s professional boxing continued to follow trends that had been well established in the United States for decades. As a spectator sport it had wide appeal across all classes, and the big title fights were watched by millions on TV. With rare exceptions, however, boxers themselves came from tough backgrounds. They grew up in poor inner-city neighborhoods whose populations were predominantly African American or ethnic, and success in the boxing ring was seen as one of the few avenues of escape. Increasingly in the 1960s African Americans came to dom-inate the heavier divisons, and this may have had the effect of reinforcing racial stereotyping. At the same time, the per-formances of superb African American boxers was a source of pride to many. This was particularly so in the case of Muhammad Ali.

Although the public perception of boxing during the 1960s was domi-nated by Ali's exploits inside and outside the ring, the decade produced a number of notable boxers who would have been outstanding in any era. As well as Joe Frazier, who won the vacant heavyweight title in March 1968, after Ali had been stripped of it the previous year for refusing to accept the draft, there was also a wealth of talent fighting in the lower weight divisions.

Even as the influence of television helped boxing grow into a truly global spectacle, the sport was riven by internal conflict. The establishment of the New York-based World Boxing Council (WBC) in 1963 in opposition to the World Boxing Association (WBA) meant that boxing had two governing bodies. For much of the decade the heavyweight division would have two world champions, and before the 1960s ended, this confusion would spread to other weight divisions.

Ali and other legends of the era

The dominant heavyweight in the early years of the decade was the fearsome Charles "Sonny" Liston. After annihi-lating Floyd Patterson in September 1962 to claim the title, Liston looked set for a long reign. However, Liston's sur-prise defeat at the hands of Cassius Clay (he became Muhammad Ali following the fight) in 1964 brought about a period of turmoil for heavyweight boxing. In March 1965 Ernie Terrell won the WBA version of the title, while two months later Ali knocked out Liston in the first round of their rematch to consolidate his hold on the WBC title. Although Ali would reunify the champi-onship in February 1967, the title would be split again that same year, with Joe Frazier becoming new WBC champion and Jimmy Ellis taking the WBA crown.

At light heavyweight the skillful Puerto Rican Jose Torres succeeded Americans Archie Moore, Harold Johnson, and Willie Pastrano as world champion in 1965. Torres held the title

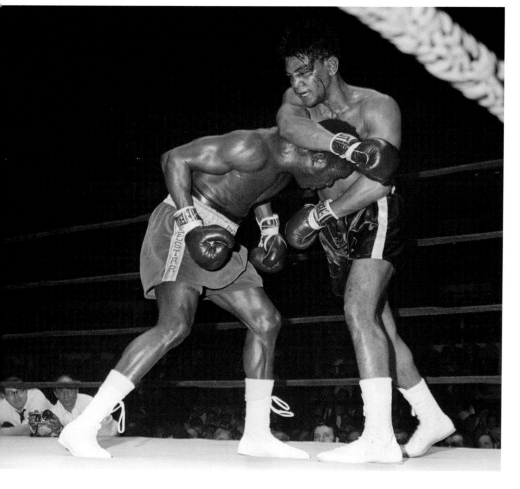

◁ **The great middleweight Emile Griffith ducks under the arm of battered opponent Stanley Hayward on the way to victory in May 1969.**

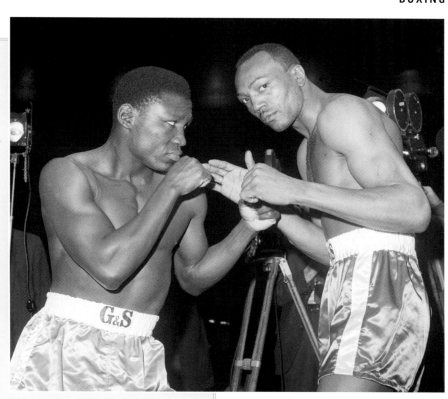

An unsung hero

The superb light-heavyweight champion Bob Foster's achievements were often overshadowed by fighters in the more glamorous heavyweight division. However, during his long reign as king of the light heavyweights Foster was involved in a number of epic battles that have entered into boxing folklore.

After a glittering career as an amateur Foster turned pro in 1961 and won his first nine fights before losing to top heavyweight contender Doug Jones. This was one of many unsuccessful attempts by Foster to compete at the top of the more lucrative heavyweight division.

In 1968, having won 30 contests at light heavyweight, Foster was rewarded with a shot at champion Dick Tiger. Born in Nigeria in 1929, Tiger had earlier held a world title in the middleweight division. His silky boxing skills had earned Tiger wide admiration; in 1962 and 1965 he was named "Fighter of the Year" by the respected *Ring* magazine. Tiger was almost 40 years old when he stepped into the ring on May 24, 1968, at Madison Square Gardens to face Bob Foster before a crowd of 11,547. Although he was seven inches shorter and nine years older than his challenger, Tiger was installed as the prefight favorite and dominated the first round of the contest. In the next two rounds, however, Foster took over. Using his eight-inch reach advantage, the younger man peppered his opponent with left jabs. In the fourth round Foster caught Tiger with a right hook followed by a left hook for a knockout; this sensational sequence was named "Round of the Year" by *Ring* magazine.

For the rest of the 1960s and well into the 1970s Foster was peerless at light heavyweight. He held the title for six years and is remembered as one of boxing most accomplished champions, a stylish boxer and terrific puncher.

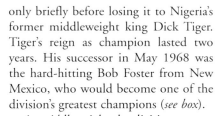

△ Bob Foster (right) and Nigeria's Dick Tiger square up at the weigh-in before Foster won their title clash by a knockout in May 1968.

only briefly before losing it to Nigeria's former middleweight king Dick Tiger. Tiger's reign as champion lasted two years. His successor in May 1968 was the hard-hitting Bob Foster from New Mexico, who would become one of the division's greatest champions (*see box*).

At middleweight the division was no less fiercely contested. In all, the title would change hands 11 times during the decade, with Boston's Paul Pender and Utah's Gene Fullmer being the dominant fighters of the opening years. Their intense rivalry was superseded in 1967 by the stylish former welterweight champion Emile Griffith from the Virgin Islands and the Italian slugger Nino Benvenuti. Benvenuti fought the Virgin Islander three times before establishing his superiority and defended his title until 1970. Other brief holders of the title included American Joey Giardello and England's Terry Downs.

Although he held the middleweight title for two years, it was as a welterweight that Emile Griffith truly excelled. The boxer kept a tenacious grip on the title for the early part of the decade, losing and regaining the championship on two separate occasions. Griffith relinquished his crown in December 1965, having registered 10 successful title defenses. His successor as champion was Dallas's Curtis Cokes, who gained the vacant title in August 1966 with a bruising win over New York's Manuel Gonzalez. Cokes's reign lasted for three years before he was succeeded by the brilliant Cuban Jose Napoles, who would dominate the division for the next five years.

In 1962 a new weight category was introduced. With a 154-lb. limit, the light-middleweight division was for boxers who had outgrown welterweight yet were not large enough to compete at middleweight. Relatively unpopular at the time, the division's champions during the 1960s were largely undistinguished. In June 1965, however, the future middleweight champion Nino Benvenuti afforded the fledgling weight category some credibility when he held the crown for seven months before moving up to middleweight.

Dominant at lightweight during the period was Puerto Rico's Carlos Ortiz. An excellent stand-up boxer, Ortiz held the title for five years, defending his crown 11 times. Ortiz eventually lost his title to Carlos Teo Cruz, an aggressive Dominican fighter whose reign as champion would last less than a year when he was beaten in February 1969 by California's Mando Ramos.

Although the junior-lightweight division had been in existence since 1921, it was during the 1960s that the weight category became fully accepted. The decade's most distinguished performer was Gabriel "Flash" Elorde. Born in the Philippines, Elorde held the title he won in March 1960 for seven years, making 11 successful defenses in the process. His eventual conqueror was Japan's Yoshiaki Numata, the first of a succession of Asian world champions at this weight.

The lighter weights

Equally outstanding in the featherweight division was Mexico's Vicente Saldivar. Saldivar captured the title in September 1964 with a surprise points win over Cuba's Ultiminio "Sugar" Ramos and reigned for four years before retiring as undefeated champion. After Salvidar's retirement the WBA

and the WBC followed the example of the heavyweight division in nominating their own separate contenders for the featherweight championship. In January 1968 Welshman Howard Winstone became the new WBC champion, but he held the title for only six months before being knocked out in the fifth round by Cuba's Jose Legra.

The new featherweight champion of the WBA was California's Raul Rojas. However, Rojas's reign as champion was almost as fleeting as Winstone's. In September 1968 he lost a points decision to Japan's Shozo Saijyo. The title confusion at this weight continued in 1969 when Jose Legra's WBC crown was taken from him by Australia's tal-

△ George Foreman at the beginning of his career, waving the flag after winning the Olympic heavyweight title in Mexico in 1968.

ented Johnny Famechon. A year later Famechon completed this game of boxing musical chairs when he surrendered his belt to the durable former champion Vicente Saldivar, who had come out of retirement.

At bantamweight Brazil's Eder Jofre and Japan's Masahiko Harada were the division's leading exponents. Jofre held the title for four years and defended it eight times before losing an epic contest

Amateur boxing

Although the United States dominated professional boxing during the 1960s, in the amateur ranks it was Europeans who gained the majority of the honors. Over the course of three Olympic tournaments staged in the decade European boxers picked up a total of 22 gold medals out of a possible 30. Among the outstanding medalists who would go on to make their mark on the professional stage was Italy's Nino Benvenuti, a future world champion at light middleweight and middleweight, who took the gold medal at welterweight in the Rome 1960 games. Champion that year at light heavyweight was an exciting young American boxer named Cassius Clay.

However, in the heavyweight division the Americans proved themselves a class above the rest. In Tokyo in 1964 Joe Frazier took the heavyweight gold medal. Four years later the giant American boxer George Foreman emulated this feat in Mexico City. Both men would go on to win the professional heavyweight title and take part in epic battles with Muhammad Ali.

World champions in the 1960s

Title Holder	Birthplace	Tenure	Status
Heavyweight			
Ingemar Johansson	Sweden	1960	undisputed
Floyd Patterson	U.S.	1960–62	undisputed
Sonny Liston	U.S.	1962–64	undisputed
Muhammad Ali	U.S.	1964–67	undis/WBC
Ernie Terrell	U.S.	1965–67	WBA
Joe Frazier	U.S.	1968–70	WBC
Jimmy Ellis	U.S.	1968–70	WBA
Light heavyweight			
Archie Moore	U.S.	1960–62	undisputed
Harold Johnson	U.S.	1962–63	undisputed
Willie Pastrano	U.S.	1963–65	undisputed
Jose Torres	Puerto Rico	1965–66	undisputed
Dick Tiger	Nigeria	1966–68	undisputed
Bob Foster	U.S.	1968–70	undisputed
Middleweight			
Gene Fullmer	U.S.	1960–62	WBA
Paul Pender	U.S.	1960–61	WBC
Terry Downes	England	1961–62	WBC
Paul Pender	U.S.	1962	WBC
Dick Tiger	Nigeria	1962–63	undisputed
Joey Giardello	U.S.	1963–65	undisputed
Dick Tiger	Nigeria	1965–66	undisputed
Emile Griffith	Virgin I.	1966–67	undisputed
Nino Benvenuti	Italy	1967	undisputed
Emile Griffith	Virgin I.	1967–68	undisputed
Nino Benvenuti	Italy	1968–70	undisputed
Welterweight			
Don Jordan	U.S.	1960	undisputed
Benny Kid Paret	Cuba	1960–61	undisputed
Emile Griffith	Virgin I.	1961	undisputed
Benny Kid Paret	Cuba	1961–62	undisputed
Emile Griffith	Virgin I.	1962–63	undisputed
Louis Rodriguez	Cuba	1963	undisputed
Emile Griffith	Virgin I.	1963–65	undisputed
Curtis Cokes	U.S.	1966–69	undisputed
Jose Napoles	Cuba	1969–70	undisputed

Title Holder	Birthplace	Tenure	Status
Lightweight			
Joe Brown	U.S.	1960–62	undisputed
Carlos Ortiz	Puerto Rico	1962-65	undisputed
Ismael Laguna	Panama	1965	undisputed
Carlos Ortiz	Puerto Rico	1965–68	undisputed
Carlos Teo Cruz	Dom. Rep.	1968–69	undisputed
Mando Ramos	U.S.	1969–70	undisputed
Featherweight			
Davey Moore	U.S.	1960–63	undisputed
Sugar Ramos	Cuba	1963–64	undisputed
Vicente Saldivar	Mexico	1964–67	undisputed
Howard Winstone	Wales	1968	WBC
Paul Rojas	U.S.	1968	WBA
Jose Legra	Cuba	1968–69	WBC
Shozo Saijyo	Japan	1968–70	WBA
Johnny Famechon	Australia	1969–70	WBC
Bantamweight			
Joe Becerra	Mexico	1960	undisputed
Eder Jofre	Brazil	1960–65	undisputed
Masahiko Harada	Japan	1965–68	undisputed
Lionel Rose	Australia	1968–69	undisputed
Ruben Olivares	Mexico	1969–70	undisputed
Flyweight			
Pascuel Perez	Argentina	1960	undisputed
Pone Kingpetch	Thailand	1960–62	undisputed
Masahiko Harada	Japan	1962–63	undisputed
Pone Kingpetch	Thailand	1963	undisputed
Hiroyuki Ebihara	Japan	1963–64	undisputed
Pone Kingpetch	Thailand	1964–65	undisputed
Salvatore Burruni	Italy	1965–66	undisputed
Horacio Accavallo	Argentina	1966–68	WBA
Walter McGowan	Scotland	1966	WBC
Chartchai Chionoi	Thailand	1966–69	WBC
Efren Torres	Mexico	1969–70	WBC
Hiroyuki Ebihara	Japan	1969	WBA
Bernabe Villacampo	Philippines	1969–70	WBA

with Harada. His conqueror, who styled himself "Fighting" Harada, would hold the bantamweight crown for two years before surrendering it to Australia's Lionel Rose.

After Italy's Salvatore Burruni failed to defend his title against Argentina's Horacio Accavallo, the flyweight crown, in common with the featherweight and heavyweight divisions, had two versions of the title. With Burruni forfeiting WBA recognition, the WBC title was contested by Accavallo and Japan's Katsuyoshi Takayama, with the South American taking the points verdict in December 1965. Prior to this the division had been dominated by Thailand's Pone Kingpetch, who held the title on and off from 1960 to 1965 before losing it to Italy's Salvatore Burruni. Burruni is the last boxer to be recognized as undisputed flyweight champion, a division that remains fragmented to the present day. □

See Also: Ali; Olympic Games

WILLY BRANDT 1913–1992

Willy Brandt was forced to flee Nazi Germany before World War II, but returned after the war to become mayor of West Berlin, chancellor of West Germany, and a leading international statesman.

◁ **During his time as West German chancellor (1969–1974) Willy Brandt was a leading proponent of détente with the Soviet bloc.**

when, after a spy scandal in his administration, he resigned from office.

Brandt's years in office were notable chiefly for his policy of *Ostpolitik* ("Eastern politics"), which was a sustained effort to break down barriers with the Soviet bloc and, especially, to normalize relations with East Germany. Although that policy was in tune with the thawing of Cold War tensions—détente—in those years it aroused fierce opposition from anticommunist cold warriors, who believed that it represented a permanent acceptance of the division of Germany into East and West. Brandt rode that storm. After being enthusiastically received by the East German public on a visit in March 1970, he signed nonaggression treaties with the Soviet Union and Poland later in the year. His reward was to lead his party to victory in the 1972 elections, when, for the first time since World War II, the Social Democrats emerged as the largest party in parliament.

Elder statesman

For his work in the international field, including support for the nonproliferation of nuclear weapons and for the expansion of the European Common Market, Brandt was awarded the Nobel Peace Prize in 1971. For the rest of his career he continued to seek ways of promoting international cooperation, his most notable contribution being the influential Brandt Report of 1980, which called attention to the economic gap between the northern and southern hemispheres. The report recommended a reform of the international monetary system and a substantial increase in Western aid to developing countries. □

Willy Brandt, who was one of the great internationalists of the 1960s, did more than any other politician to break the hold on power after 1945 of the Christian Democratic right in West Germany. Brandt served his political apprenticeship, after fleeing Nazi Germany in 1933 to escape arrest for his socialist activities, in the anti-Nazi underground movement in Norway. He returned to Germany at the end of World War II in 1945 and made his name as the most popular politician in Germany as mayor of West Berlin from 1959 to 1966.

It was as mayor of that troubled city that Brandt gained international prominence by staunchly resisting Soviet attempts to gain control of West Berlin. When the Berlin Wall was erected in August 1961, a moment of high drama in the Cold War, Brandt called unsuccessfully for a tougher U.S. response. He also used the Berlin crisis to castigate the aging German chancellor, Konrad Adenauer, and to raise his own political profile by appearing hour after hour on German television.

Party leader and chancellor

In 1964 Brandt was elected leader of the Social Democratic Party, and he held office in the federal government as the foreign minister from 1966 to 1969, and then as chancellor (the head of government) from 1969 to 1974,

See Also: Berlin Wall; Cold War; U.S.–European Relations

LEONID BREZHNEV 1906–1982

When Nikita Khrushchev was deposed as Soviet leader in 1964, his successor Brezhnev brought a very different personal style to the job—but an equal determination to further Soviet interests.

Leonid Ilyich Brezhnev became the leader of the Soviet Union in October 1964 when he succeeded Nikita Khrushchev. Although as First Secretary of the Communist Party he officially shared power with the prime minister, Alexei Kosygin, in fact Brezhnev followed in the footsteps of Stalin and Khrushchev by making himself the sole ruler in what was theoretically an elected, collective leadership. He remained effectively the dictator of the Soviet Union until his death in 1982, which meant that for nearly two decades he was the man a succession of U.S. presidents sat opposite in the councils of the world.

Rise to the top

Brezhnev owed much to his fellow Ukrainian, Nikita Khrushchev, for his rise through the ranks of the party. It was Khrushchev who appointed him President of the Presidium of the Supreme Soviet in 1960, in which post he came to gain control of the party machine. In domestic affairs, after the de-Stalinization of the Khrushchev years, Brezhnev was rather a throwback. He maintained a rigid public adherence to Marxism-Leninism, silenced the critics of Stalin, and maintained a severe censorship of ideas. His years in office, though marked by continued mismanagement of the agricultural economy, saw the rapid growth of the industrial economy and a steady rise in the standard of living of the people.

After the unpredictable Khrushchev, Brezhnev brought a less adventurous style to the Kremlin, making him an easier man for Washington to deal with. Brezhnev lent his weight to the pursuit of détente between the Soviet bloc and the West. He signed the first treaty for the nonproliferation of nuclear arms with the United States and Great

△ Leonid Brezhnev, ruler of the USSR from 1964 to 1982, addresses the Communist Party conference in Moscow in 1966.

Britain in 1968, and the first SALT (Strategic Arms Limitation Talks) treaty with the U.S. in 1972.

By détente Brezhnev did not mean to imply any weakening of Moscow's control of the communist world. He made his position clear in a speech in Moscow in March 1968: "An acute ideological struggle is now in progress. The front line of this struggle... lies between socialism and capitalism. Imperialism has attempted to weaken the ideological-political unity of the working people in the socialist countries..."

That speech was a clear warning to Czech president Alexander Dubček, whose attempt to liberalize the communist regime in his country was known as the "Prague Spring." This was at a time

of widespead political unrest in many parts of Europe (most notably the student riots in Paris) and at the height of the anti-Vietnam War protests in the U.S. In August 1968 Brezhnev sent Soviet and other Warsaw Pact troops to crush the "Prague Spring." This action gave rise to the so-called "Brezhnev doctrine," that the Soviet bloc would use force if necessary to maintain the communist system within its own sphere. The failure of the West to come to Dubček's aid demonstrated that the West accepted the USSR's free hand inside the Soviet bloc. □

See Also: Cold War; Communism; Khrushchev; Prague Spring; SALT; Warsaw Pact

BRITISH INVASION

When Americans succumbed to Beatlemania in 1964, it was the start of a major trend in popular music, with a host of British bands crossing the Atlantic to be acclaimed in the U.S.

The British Invasion is the term used to refer to the many British pop groups that became famous and successful in the mid-1960s in the U.S., where popular music had previously been dominated by home-grown performers.

Although the invasion itself was by British performers, almost all of the musical material the young hopefuls brought with them was at least partly American in origin. British teenagers had been deeply influenced in the late 1950s by popular American musicians such as Chuck Berry, Elvis Presley, Little Richard, Eddie Cochran, and Buddy Holly, and it was from them that they got their first real feel for the idiom of rock-'n'-roll. Additionally, the raucous tunes of these British invaders that America's youth so eagerly devoured were very often covers of hits performed originally by U.S. bluesmen, crooners, and girl-bands.

Stifled in the conformist 1950s, the earliest British pop music had been poor. Writers and performers alike seemed too inhibited and stuffy to swing, and their songs were certainly not exportable. But then pop music in the United Kingdom was suddenly energized by a craze known as skiffle. Skiffle groups were very similar to jug bands—drummerless ensembles that featured acoustic guitars and banjos and often sang traditional American folk songs. They were generally more remarkable for their spirit and enthusiasm than their virtuosity and polish, but one of the main exceptions to this general rule was Lonnie Donegan.

The undisputed "King of Skiffle" and one of the earliest and greatest exponents of the form, Donegan was a Scotsman who reached No. 8 on both sides of the Atlantic in 1956 with the American blues number "Rock Island Line." Many of his subsequent hits were skiffle versions of other U.S. material, including "The Battle of New Orleans" and "Pick a Bale of Cotton." His first hit album in 1957 was called *An Englishman Sings American Folk Songs*. Although Donegan remains little

The Tornados

The Tornados burst onto the British pop scene in August 1962 with their huge instrumental hit "Telstar." The record took its title from the name of the U.S. telecommunications satellite that had been launched from Cape Canaveral on July 10, 1962. The group topped the Billboard chart after spending five weeks at No. 1 in the U.K. The Tornados were initially three guitarists, two saxophonists, and a drummer, but keyboard was sometimes substituted for the saxophones for live performances. Bassist Heinz Burt (the blond) had a solo hit the following year with "Just Like Eddie," a homage to American rock-'n'-roller Eddie Cochran, who had been killed in a car crash in Britain in 1960.

△ **The Tornados in quintet formation, with keyboard instead of saxophones. The group topped the U.S. charts in July 1962, a full 18 months before the explosion of Beatlemania.**

The Beatles at Shea Stadium

▽ The Beatles at Shea Stadium for the second time, on August 23, 1965.

After their storming success on the *Ed Sullivan Show* in February 1964, the Beatles returned to the U.S. later the same year for a full-scale, coast-to-coast tour that opened on August 19 at the Cow Palace, San Francisco, and ended on September 20 with a charity concert in New York. When the Beatles returned to the U.S. the following year, they played Shea Stadium, New York, on August 15, 1965. They were rapturously received by a crowd of 56,000—a new outdoor attendance record for a concert. The Beatles further capitalized on their unprecedented appeal by playing Shea Stadium a second time a year later, on August 23, 1966. The last ever Beatles concert in the U.S. was at Candlestick Park, San Francisco, on August 29, 1966.

known outside the British Isles, his influence is readily acknowledged by almost every British performer and writer of the next wave of pop music.

By 1960 a whole generation of British teenage musicians had been inspired by the anyone-can-play populism of skiffle. They taught themselves the music of the American greats and became increasingly confident in their own material. They started to draw on local traditions such as dance hall and pop and from all these influences formulated an original style that they could claim as their own, and therefore play and sing with conviction. Young British groups with electric guitars began writing and performing up-tempo pop, rock-'n'-roll, and even Chicago-style electric blues.

Beatlemania sweeps the nation

This new movement was about to cross the Atlantic and make an enormous impact on the U.S. Although the most successful group in the British Invasion

was the Beatles, they were not the earliest. That distinction belongs to the Tornados, who became the first British group to reach No. 1 on the Billboard chart in 1962 with their instrumental "Telstar" (*see box p. 158*). But it was the Beatles who began the true invasion.

The Beatles were very much more than their songs—their attitudes, their language (English, but not American), and even their clothes and hairstyles were all new and enormously attractive to American youth. But amidst all the hype their music clearly marked them out as original talents. The group had started out in the mid-1950s playing the popular skiffle music, and their early material had been influenced by the greats of American rock-'n'-roll. Not content with slavish imitation, however, they had infused tired musical forms with their own vitality and wit, both musical and verbal.

With perfect timing the Beatles' songs came out in the U.S. shortly before they arrived in the flesh. After

having turned down their first three U.S. singles, Capitol released "I Want to Hold Your Hand" the day after Christmas 1963. Within three days 250,000 copies had been sold. By January 10, 1964, sales had passed the million mark. In New York City there were unconfirmed reports that the record was selling 10,000 copies an hour. This and the band's arrival in the country in February 1964 unleashed the tidal wave known as "Beatlemania" across the United States.

The floodgates open

The Beatles' first tour of the country aroused widespread mob adulation. Thousands flocked to see them in every city. Their concerts were scenes of mass hysteria and behavior resembling acts of worship. Not only did their records sell in millions—souvenirs and related merchandise such as plastic wigs, picture cards, and replica guitars were stacked high in shops and sold in unprecedentedly large quantities.

The Beatles' first film, the innovative *A Hard Day's Night*, directed by Richard Lester, was released in the same year. It was received enthusiastically by a wide audience that included many who had never before paid any attention to rock music. The film reinforced the image of the British capital as "Swinging London," the world's hippest city.

The Beatles also awakened Americans to the existence and distinctiveness of their native city, Liverpool, and partly as a result of interest in them this seaport in northwest England became the first hotbed of a new beat boom. Other quartets such as the Searchers, the Fourmost, and Gerry and the Pacemakers, together with the quintet Billy J. Kramer and the Dakotas, launched the phenomenon known as Merseybeat after the river that runs through Liverpool.

▽ **The youthful Rolling Stones performing on British television in the mid-1960s. "Satisfaction" hit No. 1 in the U.S. in 1965.**

The John Mayall school

Several British musicians who went on to success in the U.S. got their big break by their association with English blues guitarist John Mayall. A devoted follower of the American blues tradition, Mayall has fronted a band called the Bluesbreakers since the early 1960s. The fluid make-up of his band led to an immense turnover of personnel, some of whom have since become household names. In 1966 Mayall hired Eric Clapton, thus enabling the former Yardbird to enhance his reputation and become the first pop guitar hero. Clapton's departure—to form Cream with another ex-Mayall man, Jack Bruce—created a vacancy which was filled by Peter Green, the founding father of Fleetwood Mac. Other Mayall stars have included Fleetwood Mac's John McVie; Andy Fraser, who left Mayall after only two months to form his own band, Free; and Mick Taylor of the Rolling Stones, a band once described by its lead singer, Mick Jagger, as "The John Mayall School."

The British Invasion of the U.S. was not confined to Liverpudlians. There was an almost inexhaustible demand for anyone British. Among the groups from the south of England that first made it in the U.S. on the back of the Beatles' suc-

cess were the Rolling Stones. Offering a ruder, more louche sound than the inherently respectable Beatles, they topped the Billboard chart with "(I Can't Get No) Satisfaction" in 1965. Other British U.S. No. 1 hits of the period included "A

△ The Animals' 1964 hit "House of the Rising Sun" was an old New Orleans blues number, but the new British rendition made U.S. No. 1.

World without Love" by Peter and Gordon, "Do Wah Diddy Diddy" by Manfred Mann, and "Downtown" by the long-established solo singer Petula Clark. Further U.S. hits were scored by the British groups the Yardbirds, the Who, the Kinks, the Pretty Things, the Small Faces, and the Dave Clark Five, as well as by the solo singer Dusty Springfield.

These acts first surfaced in London, but many other British towns spawned groups destined to make it in America. Manchester, for example, yielded Donovan with "Sunshine Superman," Wayne Fontana and the Mindbenders with "Game of Love," Freddie and the Dreamers with "I'm Telling You Now," Herman's Hermits with "Mrs. Brown You've Got a Lovely Daughter," and the Hollies with "Look through Any Window." From Newcastle-upon-Tyne came the Animals; their "House of the Rising Sun," another American song, reached No. 1 and became an instant classic as young bands everywhere tried

to pick out its rolling guitar arpeggios. Birmingham in the Midlands of England spawned the Spencer Davis Group, the Moody Blues, and the Move. There was even a band from Belfast, Northern Ireland—Them— whose lead singer was Van Morrison. The last wave of the British Invasion featured the Troggs, whose biggest U.S. hit, "Wild Thing," was written by an American, Chip Taylor.

Cashing in on Britishness

To fledgling bands in Britain the new American market seemed to promise vast riches (which few in fact made). Hundreds of British bands sprang up overnight, most of them boasting little talent but plenty of the raucous enthusiasm that flowed from the more successful acts. It was in fact the sheer energy and volume of the minor British acts, rather than their musicianship, that carried them into an America that was hooked on the Beatles. Virtual

unknowns in Britain found overnight celebrity in the U.S. Take, for example, Chad and Jeremy and Ian Whitcomb. Actors turned guitarists, Chad and Jeremy sang a folk-based pop like that of the more successful British duo Peter and Gordon. They owed their success in the U.S. to several appearances on the *Hullabaloo* show. Ian Whitcomb had a 1965 Top 10 hit with "You Turn Me On (Turn On Song)" and settled in California. An eccentric, he wore a deerstalker on stage and sang in a voice that has been described as "a camp falsetto with panting."

Such slender acts as these were easily forgotten, but the most innovative British groups—above all the Beatles and the durable Rolling Stones—had a profound influence on the directions taken by American rock and pop. □

See Also: Beatles; Blues; Pop Music; Rock Music; Rolling Stones

BROADWAY

The showcase of American theater entered the 1960s in good shape, but the new decade confronted Broadway producers with changing tastes and some harsh economic realities.

In the course of the 1960s Broadway had to contend with rapidly moving developments in society that made its traditional output seem dated to many. At the same time, Broadway's traditional audience had clear expectations of what it wanted from a Broadway show. Attempts to meet the challenge took many forms and resulted in sharp differences between the types of theatrical fare on offer.

The 1960s followed a period of 15 years after World War II in which Broadway theater had enjoyed something of a golden age. The musical genre had been reinvigorated by such varied successes as *Oklahoma!*, *South Pacific*, and *West Side Story*. In 1959 alone had come the premières of two classic musicals, *Gypsy* and *The Sound of Music*. During this same period a new generation of serious playwrights, including Tennessee Williams and Arthur Miller, had enjoyed triumphs.

Dramatic themes

Williams and Miller continued to produce fine plays in the 1960s but with more mixed commercial success. Tennessee Williams's major 1960s success was *The Night of the Iguana* (1961), in which the central character was a defrocked minister. The play continued Williams's use of rich poetic language, theatricality, and compassion for his marginalized characters.

Although Williams wrote other plays during the 1960s, they all failed to repeat his earlier artistic and commercial success. Williams himself was later to explain that the 1960s was a period of almost continuous mental and emotional breakdown for him, made worse by escape into alcohol and drugs and repeated failures in the theater. His decline deprived the theater of one of its most exciting creative voices.

△ **Uta Hagen and Arthur Hill slug it out verbally in the 1962 Broadway production of Edward Albee's searing domestic drama *Who's Afraid of Virginia Woolf?***

Miller chose not to write for theater at all for nine years after *The View from the Bridge* (1955). His semiautobiographical *After the Fall* (1964), which critics believed to be a fictionalized treatment of Miller's own highly publicized marriage to the recently deceased movie star Marilyn Monroe, attracted largely hostile comment.

Miller did not consider the commercial environment of Broadway to be conducive to the production of challenging new work, and he participated in the short-lived experiment to create a repertory theater at Lincoln Center. He returned to commercial Broadway in 1968 with *The Price*.

Miller's writing at this time shifted its focus from the clash between the individual and society that had characterized earlier plays like *The Crucible* (1953). His emphasis now was on the journey his characters made through emotional and moral crises.

The outstanding new serious dramatist of 1960s Broadway was Edward Albee, whose searing and highly theatrical dissection of a marriage, *Who's Afraid of Virginia Woolf?*, was acclaimed in 1962. Albee's determination to probe the unhappiness and lack of communication in modern American life was also demonstrated in *A Delicate Balance* (1966), in which the central characters are forced to confront the pain and fear in their apparently successful lives.

These plays have a broadly realistic quality, but Albee was eager to experiment stylistically in his writing.

However, the more confused allegory of *Tiny Alice* (1965) appealed less to Broadway audiences.

The most commercially successful playwright to emerge from Broadway during the 1960s was the erstwhile television gag-writer Neil Simon, whose *Barefoot in the Park* (1963) and *The Odd Couple* (1966) launched a career that has lasted over 30 years. Although they lack the psychological depth of Simon's later, more autobiographical plays, his early successes thrived on one-liner gags that kept their audiences in stitches. Both *Barefoot in the Park* and *The Odd Couple* were turned into highly successful movies.

Imports and musicals

Serious drama on Broadway was regularly enlivened in the 1960s by imports from London's West End. They often featured big-name stars such as Paul Scofield, who had a great success as Sir Thomas More in Robert Bolt's *A Man for All Seasons* (1961), and Albert Finney, who played the title role in John Osborne's *Luther* (1963). As the decade progressed, there were examples of cross-fertilization between the two great centers of English-language theater. For example, U.S. playwright Arthur Kopit's *Indians* was put on first in London by the Royal Shakespeare

△ Mary Martin in the title role of *Hello, Dolly!* on Broadway in 1965. The musical was a great star vehicle and an excuse for lavish sets and costumes that audiences adored.

A crafty producer

As a purely commercial enterprise Broadway theater has always been dependent on producers of vision and resourcefulness. One example who had a huge impact in the 1960s was the remarkable David Merrick, who had begun producing on Broadway in 1949. Merrick was interested in producing risky new plays as well as more surefire successes. By 1959 he had established a tax-exempt foundation that enabled him to transfer funds from commercial hits to less successful ventures.

Merrick's record is an honorable one. In 1963/64 alone he produced five enterprising choices of play, including Jean Anouilh's *The Rehearsal*, Bertholt Brecht's *Arturo Ui*, and Williams's *The Milk Train Doesn't Stop Here Any More*, as well as three new musicals, including the smash hit *Hello, Dolly!*

Merrick was a notable publicist of his shows. In 1961 his production *Subways Are for Sleeping* was panned by the critics. He retaliated by finding members of the public with the same names as the critics. He then quoted their favorable reviews in an advertisement.

Company and then transferred successfully to Broadway in 1969.

The Broadway musical suffered some loss of energy and direction in the early years of the 1960s. The death of Oscar Hammerstein in 1960 brought to an end his innovative partnership with Richard Rodgers. New writing partnerships enjoyed some success (such as Jerry Bock and Sheldon Harnick with *Fiddler on the Roof* in 1964 and John Kander and Fred Ebb with *Cabaret* in 1966), but some critics said that the Broadway musical was becoming formulaic. In 1967 the veteran Broadway conductor Lehman Engel even produced a guide to writing musicals according to a set of rules.

One key Broadway figure of the period was the director/choreographer Bob Fosse, who achieved great success with his productions of shows such as *Little Me* (1962) and *Sweet Charity* (1966). These shows were characterized by Fosse's flair for innovative and spectacular staging. They were the result of his long experience as a dancer and choreographer and his hardworking quest for perfection.

Jerry Herman's *Hello, Dolly!* (1964) was in some ways a typical musical of the time. Based on *The Matchmaker*, Thornton Wilder's comedy of 1955, it supplied a glamorous and entertaining evening in the theater with its witty lines, its scope for stylish period sets and costumes, and the opportunities it provided for a star performer such as Carol Channing or Mary Martin in the central role. Its score was uneven, but it had at least one memorable song (the title number) that audiences could hum as they left the theater.

Other musicals of the period also achieved success with audiences, even if critics complained about a slightly old-fashioned quality. They included

▽ **Zero Mostel starring in** *Fiddler on the Roof* **in 1964. A sentimental tale,** *Fiddler* **captivated audiences with its catchy melodies.**

Fiddler on the Roof and a musical treatment of the Don Quixote story, *Man of La Mancha* by Mitch Leigh and Joe Darion, first presented in 1965.

By contrast with such essentially lightweight or at least undemanding entertainments, *Cabaret* was one of the more innovative Broadway musical successes of the 1960s (and has subsequently achieved even greater impact in a film version directed by Bob Fosse). It was based on the autobiographical stories of the English writer Christopher Isherwood and set in Berlin around the year 1930, when the Nazis had not yet gained power in Germany but were on the rise.

Cabaret was quite unconventional for its time in its choice of material, its structure, and its antiromantic conclusion. It has three major threads: the story of a young writer, Cliff (who is changed from an Englishman to an American in this stage version), and his involvement with the nightclub singer Sally Bowles; that of the older Fraulein Schneider, who rejects her admirer Herr Schultz out of fear of the increasingly menacing Nazis when she learns he is Jewish; and the decadent song and dance routines of the Kit-Kat nightclub where Sally works.

During the course of the show the audience becomes aware of the sinister rise of the Nazis in the background as the performances of the Kit-Kat's Master of Ceremonies become disturbingly anti-Semitic, and Cliff feels compelled to flee the repressive and hostile city. The show's sophistication, its political edge, and the ambivalent sexuality of its club performers have ensured *Cabaret* a more lasting success in subsequent decades than most Broadway musicals of the 1960s.

Box office blues

Successful shows in the 1960s often had long runs, but the failure rate was high. With increased production costs, even a run of over 500 performances might not guarantee that a show's investors would get a return on their money. In the 1967/68 season, which boasted the highest gross ticket sales in the history of Broadway, 10 out of 11 new musicals were commercial failures (*Hair* was the lone success), with a loss of over $3 million. Even the traditional inclusion of star names was no guarantee of commercial success.

The closing years of the 1960s saw a decline in ticket sales on Broadway, in the average length of a run, and in the number of new shows. Explanations have been offered for this trend: the rising costs of production, including the increased cost of unionized labor, and the flight from Manhattan to the suburbs of the middle classes who had been the mainstay of the Broadway audience. That segment of the New York population dropped by an estimated 900,000 across the decade. Ticket prices also began to increase: top price for a musical was $9.90 in 1965, but $15 in 1969.

It was also believed that the collapse or merger of several New York newspapers during the 1960s contributed to the problem. The *New York Times* was the

only remaining newspaper for the upscale market, and it appeared that its reviewer could make or break any new show.

Looking for a new audience

From the mid-1960s Broadway theaters realized they needed to make changes to woo back audiences. Producers placed a greater emphasis on spectacle to make shows more attractive, although this also added to the costs.

The licensing laws were revised in 1964 to allow bars in theaters. In 1967 a special bus service was inaugurated between Times Square and the East Side neighborhood where many of the ticket-buyers lived. The traditional curtain-up time of 8:40 was changed to 7:30 (and later back to 8 o'clock) to make it easier for audiences to travel back to the suburbs after the show.

Broadway producers began to look beyond the traditional audiences to boost their box-office returns. In 1967 David Merrick revived the ailing *Hello, Dolly!*, which had been running for four years, by installing an all-black cast, starring Pearl Bailey. This in turn led to the success of later all-black musicals such as *The Wiz* (1975).

△ **The exuberant *Hair* playing to a Broadway audience in 1970. *Hair* was a radical departure from the usual Broadway fare, capturing the hippie mood of the late 1960s.**

Producers also increasingly looked elsewhere for the hit shows they could no longer create themselves. The 1968 success *Hair* was a transfer from the New York Shakespeare Festival. Its rock-music score, its graphic representation of sexual matters, its celebration of drugs and hippie culture (not to mention its devastating critique of the Vietnam War) introduced a new energy and social focus to the Broadway stage, as well as bringing in a new audience.

By the end of the decade Broadway had surrendered much of its earlier energy and spirit of enterprise to the smaller theaters off-Broadway, which during the 1960s had increasingly become places to try out shows pre-Broadway. It had even spawned off-off-Broadway, a term coined by *Village Voice* critic Jerry Tallmer in 1960 to describe the diverse range of alternative performance activities springing up in Manhattan. Off-off-Broadway was to become a major source of energy and innovation as the 1960s went on. □

The financial side of Broadway

By the 1960s Broadway was a smaller operation than it had been a few decades earlier. Back in 1927/28 more than 260 shows were given during the course of the season, and 47 were running during any given week; by the 1960s this last figure averaged 23.

On the other hand, it would seem that a higher percentage of shows in the 1960s were strong: the average run for a musical doubled between 1927 and 1960 and that for a straight play increased on average by 50 percent.

Production costs increased significantly during the 1960s, even allowing for inflation. The average musical cost $500,000 to produce in 1960. By the end of the decade this figure had more than doubled.

See Also: Experimental Theater; Theater

HELEN GURLEY BROWN b. 1922

The original "Cosmo Girl," Helen Gurley Brown had a huge influence on women's journalism by attacking the sexual double standard and promoting the pleasures of recreational sex.

Born in Green Forest, Arkansas, Helen Gurley Brown was a 40-year-old advertising copywriter when she wrote her 1962 bestseller *Sex and the Single Girl*, which celebrated the pleasures of recreational sex for unmarried women—a highly controversial message at the time. It remained on the bestseller list well into 1963 and was made into a movie starring Tony Curtis and Natalie Wood.

The book was a prefeminist tract and dealt with the strategy of pursuing men, capturing them, and then keeping them happy. It gave advice on where to meet men, how to attract them, how to pick them up, how to handle relationships, how to end affairs, and how to have a fulfilling sex life. Practical issues like money, housing, clothes, work, eating, drinking, staying fit, and keeping other people in a woman's life happy were covered as well.

There had been books for women explaining how to ensnare a marriage partner before. The difference with *Sex and the Single Girl* was that it showed that the fun was in the chase, not just the outcome. The woman became proactive. The other provocative idea was that having an affair with a married man was advanced as an option.

Brown followed the book's success with *Sex and the Office*—also a bestseller—in 1965, *The Outrageous Opinions of Helen Gurley Brown* in 1967, *Helen Gurley Brown's Single Girl's Cook Book* in 1969, and *Sex and the New Single Girl* in 1970.

In tune with the times

Cosmopolitan, then a rather staid magazine with conventional views, was on the brink of collapse when Brown took over as editor in 1965. She opened its pages to frank discussions of sex and relationships, bringing *Cosmopolitan* into line with the new mood of the times. She managed to embrace the new militancy that was abroad among women while keeping the magazine mainstream. She claimed to possess "great common sense" rather than great intelligence. Circulation soared to three million, turning Brown into a publishing icon. She remained the editor of *Cosmopolitan* until 1997, though her promotion of sexual freedom and dismissive attitude to the issue of sexual harassment became dated in the age of AIDS and equality in the workplace.

The charge of hypocrisy was leveled at Helen Gurley Brown because she did not live the swinging single lifestyle she advocated. Her marriage to Broadway producer David Brown in 1959 has endured for over 40 years. But she answered her critics with her 1983 book *Having It All*. In her own words Brown is "a health nut, a feminist, an irredeemable but contented workaholic and passionately interested in the relationship between men and women." □

▽ Helen Gurley Brown at her typewriter in her Park Avenue apartment in 1965, the year she began her long editorship of *Cosmopolitan*.

See Also: Feminist Movement; Magazine Publishing; Sexual Revolution

JAMES BROWN b. 1928 or 1933

The most successful soul singer of the 1960s, James Brown's appeal transcended race, while at the same time he took often controversial stands on the social and political issues of the time.

Self-proclaimed "Soul Brother Number One," James Brown was a powerful force in reshaping dance music during the 1960s. His success was a symbol of the triumph of courage over racism, and with songs such as "Say It Loud, I'm Black and Proud" Brown voiced the new spirit of African Americans.

Born in poverty in the Deep South during the Great Depression, Brown picked cotton before being sentenced to three years in a juvenile detention institution for armed robbery at the age of 16. On his release he earned his living as a semipro boxer and a baseball pitcher before becoming a professional gospel singer.

Turning to rhythm and blues, Brown had a No. 1 R&B hit with "Try Me" in 1958. At the turn of the decade he formed the James Brown Revue, whose energetic dance routines earned him the title "The Hardest Working Man in Show Business." *Live at the Apollo*, recorded in 1962, sold a million copies, unprecedented for a black music album.

△ Soul singer James Brown developed a huge following among both black and white audiences in the 1960s.

International stardom

With "Papa's Got a Brand New Bag" in 1965 Brown gained a big following among white audiences. A string of hits followed, as Brown's raw lyrics and raucous delivery moved soul music closer to the harsher sounds of rock. As the first black artist to maintain complete control over his career, he could continue to be musically innovative without interference from managers, producers, or record companies. He became a major star in Europe in the mid-1960s and a draw for a young white audience on network TV variety shows.

James Brown took a keen interest in politics, and generally adopted a moderate, progovernment line. He was one of the few African American stars to entertain the troops in Vietnam, for example. And when he did a show in Tupelo, Mississippi, for James Meredith's "March Against Fear" in June 1966, Stokely Carmichael confronted him. He was, said Carmichael, a threat to the black power movement because African Americans listened to his moderate views instead of following the new militant line. Soon after, Brown pressed the record "Don't Be a Drop-Out" and presented the first copy to Vice President Hubert Humphrey in the White House as part of a campaign to get young African Americans to stay in school. When Martin Luther King, Jr., was assassinated in 1968, Brown went on television, calling for a restrained response to the outrage. He was accused by some of being an "Uncle Tom," but answered his critics in 1969 with "Say It Loud, I'm Black and Proud."

James Brown's career continued long after the end of the decade. In 1985 he had an international hit with "Living in America." His influence continued into the 1990s since his 1960s tracks contained the breaks most often sampled by young hip-hop artists. ☐

See Also: Soul Music

JIM BROWN b. 1936

One of the outstanding athletes of the 20th century, Jim Brown was a star in several sports at Syracuse University before going on to enjoy unprecedented success in professional football.

James Nathaniel Brown was born in Georgia in 1936, and his all-round athletic ability made him an outstanding star at Syracuse University in the middle 1950s. He made football All-American in both his junior and senior years, while regularly starting as a forward with the basketball team. However, his best sport may have been lacrosse, at which some experts claimed that he was the greatest player ever. In 1957 Brown was the first draft choice of the Cleveland Browns, and from then on he devoted himself to pro football.

Jim Brown became one of the greatest running backs in the history of the NFL. Standing 6ft. 2in. tall and weighing 235lbs., he was swift enough to run around defenders and powerful enough to run over them. He had an unusually high-stepping gait that enabled him to evade low tackles and leave defenders strewn in his wake.

Breaking all records

Brown played his entire professional career, nine seasons from 1957 to 1965, with the Cleveland Browns. The dominant team of the mid-1950s, the Browns were thought to be on the slide when Jim Brown arrived. With him, however, they reached three NFL championship games, winning in 1964, losing in 1957 and 1965.

In every season he played except 1962 Brown led the NFL in yards gained rushing, in seven of them rushing for more than 1,000 yards. He set the record for a 12-game schedule of 1,527 yards in 1958 and for a 14-game schedule of 1,863 yards in 1963. Over his career he scored 126 touchdowns, including 21 in his final season. Of this touchdown total 106 were scored rushing, 20 receiving. He scored 18 touchdowns in 1958 to lead the NFL in scoring. Brown's lifetime NFL records

See Also: Football

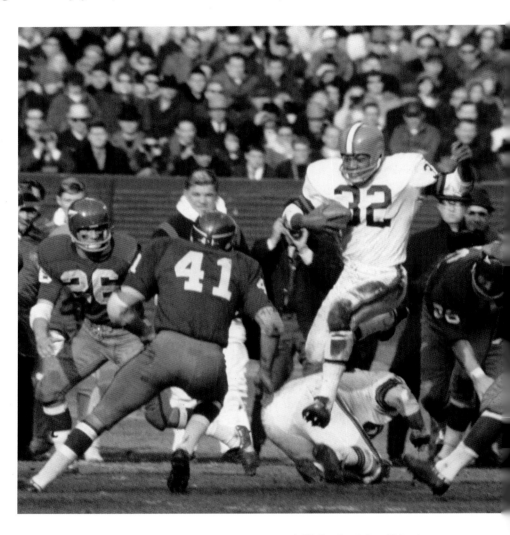

△ **The Washington defense closes in on Jim Brown during a game between the Redskins and the Cleveland Browns in 1965.**

of 12,312 yards rushing—at an average of 5.22—and 15,459 yards combined rushing and pass-receiving stood until 1984, when both were surpassed by Walter Payton of the Chicago Bears. Brown's rushing average remained unbeaten at the end of the century.

Throughout his career Brown never missed a game through injury, and only once was he knocked out of a game. He was voted All-Pro in eight of his nine seasons (1962 was his "poor" year) and three times named Cleveland's MVP. He was elected to the Hall of Fame in 1971, his first year of eligibility.

There were few black players in the NFL when Brown began his career, but his enormous success opened the door for many who followed. When he retired, Brown was taken up by Hollywood producers eager to cash in on his good looks and celebrity. He was cast in small parts in a number of films, most notably *The Dirty Dozen* (1967). □

DAVE BRUBECK b. 1920

The music of the Dave Brubeck Quartet provided the background to many of the parties of the early 1960s, and the tune "Take Five" is still one of the most instantly recognized jazz melodies.

Dave Brubeck was born in 1920 in California. He played jazz piano from an early age and in the mid-1940s studied with the French composer Darius Milhaud, who was resident for much of the year in California. This classical background was to have considerable influence on Brubeck's music. In the late 1940s he founded an octet, explicitly trying to play in the then new "cool" style that was popular on the West Coast. This octet soon became a quartet, with Brubeck partnered up front by alto sax player Paul Desmond. In the early to mid-1950s, this quartet toured widely and made some memorable recordings (notably *Jazz at Oberlin*, 1954).

Brubeck's smash hit

By the late 1950s the group comprised Brubeck, Desmond, Gene Wright on bass, and Joe Morello on drums. On tours to the Middle East and South Asia members of the group had listened to time signatures that were unusual in jazz and in 1959 recorded *Time Out*, an album that included the track "Take Five" (so-called because it was in 5/4 time). "Take Five" was written by Paul Desmond, who later confessed he first thought of the melody as the introduction to a drum feature; indeed, the track is largely taken up with Morello's drum solo. At this point in its history almost all jazz was in 4/4 time, and so the album, which featured tunes in 3/4 (for which there were some precedents), 5/4, 6/4, and 9/8 represented a considerable challenge to the musicians of the quartet. However, they managed to make the difficult time signatures seem quite natural, and the album reached a wide audience.

Interestingly, the album was given a hostile reception by many jazz critics, but "Take Five" became a huge hit

See Also: Jazz

△ **The Dave Brubeck Quartet plays a jam session for blind children at the Jewish Guild for the Blind in New York in 1962.**

when released as a single the following year. Jazz fans and musicians alike were fascinated by the introduction of unusual time signatures, and the album was soon on the shelves of every self-respecting sophisticate.

Up to the late 1960s the group was very successful: the combination of Desmond's lyrical sound with interesting musical explorations that could be understood by nonspecialists proved irresistible. However, Joe Morello's sight began to fail, and he found touring tough; cool jazz began to sound old-fashioned when set against rock; and in 1967 Desmond himself left the group to pursue a successful solo career.

Jazz critics were generally ambivalent in their attitude to Brubeck's groups

throughout the 1950s and 1960s. They could not deny the intellectual weight of Brubeck's music, most clearly shown in the harmonic progressions in his solos and in such compositions as "The Duke," his tribute to Duke Ellington; nor could they deny that Desmond's alto sax was one of the most distinctive voices in jazz; nor that Morello was a fine drummer who opened up new time signatures for later percussionists. Brubeck's piano style, however, was sometimes condemned as bombastic and lacking swing, while Desmond's playing was said to lack weight.

After the 1960s Brubeck continued to play in other quartets (including one with baritone player Gerry Mulligan) and in groups featuring his sons, and he also wrote several works in the classical tradition. But he never again reached the household renown he enjoyed with his early 1960s quartet. □

LENNY BRUCE 1925–1966

Dubbed the "sickest of the sick," Lenny Bruce introduced obscenity and profanity into stand-up comedy to drive home his contempt for the accepted values and morality of the time.

△ **Lenny Bruce being frisked by police in October 1962 in Hollywood. He was arrested on suspicion of possessing heroin.**

Bruce hated the label "sick" being attached to his brand of humor, but it stuck to him throughout his career. He saw himself as a satirist. His ad-libbed assaults on organized religion, racial hypocrisy, cultural myths, and the law, he argued, required the use of stereotypical and taboo terms. "All my humor is based on destruction and despair," he said.

Born Leonard Alfred Schneider in Mineola, New York, he was doted on by his well-read father and his mother, who worked as a stand-up comedian under the name Boots Malloy. His parents divorced when Bruce was a child. At 16 he dropped out of school and joined the Navy, serving during World War II.

Dishonorably discharged in 1946 for falsely claiming to be homosexual, Bruce studied acting under the GI Bill. To support himself, he became a stand-up comedian in burlesque houses. In 1949 he won first prize on *Arthur Godfrey's Talent Scouts,* a top-rated television show, impersonating James Cagney, Edward G. Robinson, and Peter Lorre. This sort of standard fare was a far cry from the kind of material that would later gain Bruce notoriety. In 1951 he married a stripper and was arrested for impersonating a Father Mathias, a priest who claimed to be collecting for African lepers.

By the 1960s Bruce had developed a following as a "hipster" comic. His records and word-of-mouth spread his reputation across the country.

In trouble with the law

Lenny Bruce's irreverent and scatological style incurred the wrath of both the religious and civil authorities. His shows were raided, and he was frequently arrested for both obscenity and the possession of narcotics. In 1964 he was convicted for obscenity after a performance in a Greenwich village nightclub. Mobilized by beat poet Allen Ginsberg, nearly a hundred figures prominent in artistic and intellectual life signed a statement describing Bruce as a "popular and controversial performer in the field of social satire in the tradition of Swift, Rabelais, and Twain. Although Bruce makes use of the vernacular in his nightclub performances, he does so within the context of his satirical intent and not to arouse the prurient interest of his listeners." Bruce declaimed in his own defense: "I would rather my child see a stag [porn] film than the *Ten Commandments* or *King of Kings*—because I don't want my kids to kill Christ when he comes back. That's what they see in those films—that violence."

Bruce died of a drug overdose in his Hollywood Hills home at the age of 40. Eighteen months later his obscenity conviction was overturned. The year before he died he published his autobiography *How to Talk Dirty and Influence People*, a swipe at Dale Carnegie's perennial bestseller *How to Win Friends and Influence People*. □

See Also: Satire

MᶜGEORGE BUNDY 1919–1996

McGeorge Bundy was one of President Kennedy's closest advisors, and he continued to advise President Johnson on international affairs after Kennedy's death.

President John F. Kennedy made McGeorge Bundy special assistant for national security in 1961. In that capacity Bundy advised on key policy matters during the Cuban Missile Crisis in 1962 and the early years of U.S. involvement in Vietnam.

Following Kennedy's assassination, Bundy continued in the same post under Lyndon Johnson. He was closely involved in the decision to intervene in the Dominican Republic in 1965 and to send ground troops to Vietnam that same year. It was Bundy who had briefed Johnson on the situation in Vietnam when he took over the presidency in 1963, and he was a key player in the decisions that took America into the war in Vietnam.

Bundy gradually turned against the war, though he never became an outright critic. In 1971, when GIs were "fragging"—that is, attacking their own officers with fragmentation grenades and other weapons—Bundy made the unemotional but devastating comment: "Extrication from Vietnam is now the necessary precondition of the renewal of the U.S. Army as an institution."

An establishment figure

By then Bundy was long removed from the situation. In 1966 he had quit the government to head the Ford Foundation, where he built up its public service role. He produced reports on the future of educational television and the use of communications satellites, and intervened to help out New York's failing public school system. Under Mayor John Lindsay Bundy came up with a plan to transfer the control of public schools from the central Board of Education to local school boards, which could be more responsive to the needs of the community they served. Bundy set up pilot boards in the worst areas of

△ **McGeorge Bundy was a key figure in the Kennedy and Johnson administrations and later headed the Ford Foundation.**

Brooklyn, Harlem, and the South Bronx. They were funded by the Ford Foundation, and community workers, paid by the foundation, rounded up voters to elect members.

Bundy was one of the many Harvard men Kennedy brought into his administration. He had taught at Harvard, becoming Associate Professor of Government in 1951 and Dean of the Faculty of Arts and Sciences in 1953.

He was very much part of the Eastern establishment that had so much influence during and after World War II. His father was assistant to Henry Stimson, secretary of war. Bundy first made his name editing Stimson's memoirs. His brother William was married to the daughter of former Secretary of State Dean Acheson.

When he quit teaching his course on the U.S. in world affairs to join the administration, Bundy was replaced by Henry Kissinger, who became national security advisor and then secretary of state under President Richard Nixon. □

See Also: Cuban Missile Crisis; Dominican Republic Intervention; Politics and Government; Vietnam War

ELLSWORTH BUNKER 1894–1984

Diplomat Ellsworth Bunker was U.S. ambassador to South Vietnam for six years of the Vietnam War and played a major role in pushing through a negotiated settlement to end the war.

△ **Ellsworth Bunker had a long career in public service, culminating in his role in extricating the U.S. from the Vietnam War.**

By the time Ellsworth Bunker was posted to Saigon in 1967, he had a wealth of business and diplomatic experience. After graduating from Yale, he went to work in the family firm, the National Sugar Refining Company, which had extensive interests in Latin America. This gave him experience in dealing with non-Americans that would set him in good stead in his diplomatic career.

When Bunker retired in 1950, President Truman named him ambassador to Argentina. Following a posting to Italy and stints at the American Red Cross and the United Nations, Bunker entered the 1960s as ambassador to India. In 1962, at the request of the United Nations, he negotiated the handover of western New Guinea by the Netherlands to Indonesia. The two countries had been at loggerheads for 12 years, and war seemed inevitable, but the "Bunker Plan" was accepted by both sides. Then, in 1963 he was sent by President John F. Kennedy to the Middle East, where he persuaded Saudi Arabia and Egypt to withdraw from the civil war in Yemen.

Bunker became U.S. delegate to the Organization of American States, then chairman of its council. As such, he arranged the appointment of a provisional civilian president in the Dominican Republic following the assassination of the country's dictator Rafael Trujillo. Despite the cynicism of other OAS members, thanks to Bunker's negotiating skills the Dominican Republic successfully returned to democracy.

At the height of the Vietnam War in 1967 Bunker replaced Henry Cabot Lodge as ambassador to South Vietnam, where he served as principal advisor and paymaster to the regime. He spent six years in Saigon, the longest tour served by any U.S. ambassador there. With the weight of his office behind him Bunker managed to persuade Premier Nguyen Cao Ky to withdraw from the 1967 presidential election after he had been accused of illegal campaign practices. This left Bunker open to the accusation that he was under the thumb of President Nguyen Van Thieu, whom he supported in both the 1967 and 1971 elections. Bunker defended his position, saying that it was part of his job to support America's ally and to halt North Vietnamese incursions.

Bunker believed that the Vietnam War could only end in a negotiated settlement and backed the Paris peace talks that began in 1968. He also backed Richard Nixon's "Vietnamization" plan and persuaded a reluctant President Nguyen Van Thieu to sign the Paris Peace Accords of 1973, which ended U.S. involvement in the war. □

See Also: Paris Peace Talks; United Nations; Vietnam War

BUREAU OF INDIAN AFFAIRS

The Bureau of Indian Affairs had never been popular with Native Americans, but the 1960s saw increased strife between a truly reforming Bureau and a new Indian militancy.

By the beginning of the 1960s Native Americans had grown deeply suspicious of the intentions of the federal government. This was brought on by the policy of "termination" introduced by Congress under the Eisenhower administration. The policy called for the absorption of Native Americans into the mainstream of society as private individuals by terminating the federal supervision of individual tribes.

Commissioner Nash

Seven tribes had already been terminated or faced imminent termination when John F. Kennedy entered the White House in 1961, and the new administration inherited a legacy of mistrust. Anthropologist and former lieutenant-governor of Wisconsin Philleo Nash was appointed Commissioner of Indian Affairs.

Nash had previously served as secretary to the Yale–Toronto International Conference on Indian Welfare, as a director of the Association on American Indian Affairs, and as vice-chairman of the Menominee Indian Tribal Trust. Despite (or perhaps because of) his great experience, Nash was an unpopular choice with Congress since many feared that he would be too sympathetic to Native Americans. Nash was indeed well liked by Native Americans and began rebuilding the bridges between the Bureau and those he sought to serve.

"There will be no more termination," Nash declared in the fall of 1962. Instead, he planned to create viable tribal economies by persuading major companies to establish factories on the reservations. However, this proved

harder than he anticipated. The oldest Bureau schools were remodeled to meet modern needs, and the Institute of American Indian Art was established at Santa Fé in 1962. Native Americans' college enrolment soared—but so, too, did their dropout rate as their raised expectations failed to be met. The continuing poverty among Native Americans was seen to be at odds with the aims of President Johnson's Great Society, and Nash was ousted in 1966, a move that was vehemently opposed by Native Americans.

△ **Robert L. Bennett became Commissioner of Indian Affairs in 1966 and attempted to represent the Indian cause in Washington.**

Nash was replaced by Robert L. Bennett, a member of the Oneida tribe and only the second Native American to head up the Bureau. He had been born on a reservation in Wisconsin and joined the Office of Indian Affairs at the Ute Agency in Utah at the age of 21. A career civil servant, Bennett had worked his way up from the lowest levels of the Bureau and was well posi-

△ **Armed Native Americans block the road to protest against the violation of their fishing rights on the Columbia River in 1971.**

tioned to implement radical changes. Bennett believed that the Bureau was there to act as an advocate for the Indians rather then impose government policies on them. He tried to squeeze out the paternalism that was rife in the Bureau and avoided giving a categorical "no" to any tribal request.

In March 1968 President Johnson promised self-determination to Native Americans. Despite opposition from Congress, Bennett tried to put this policy into action. However, the American Indian Movement and the growth of "Red Power" outdistanced Bennett's reforms, while the Indians' involvement with the Office of Economic Opportunity and other Great Society agencies increasingly marginalized the Bureau.

In 1969 the Nixon administration appointed Louis R. Bruce to head the Bureau. Although he was a Native American—half-Mohawk, half-Oglala Sioux—he was quickly denounced by Indian activists. Nixon continued the policy of self-determination for Native Americans, but again, the Bureau was not seen to be moving fast enough for the militants. This resulted in the occupation of the island of Alcatraz off San Francisco in 1969 and the Bureau's Washington headquarters in 1972.

Although Native Americans were far from satisfied with the Bureau of Indian Affairs at the end of the 1960s, during the decade it had nevertheless reversed the policy of assimilation, ended termination, and overseen the growth of self-determination and economic independence. □

The end of termination

In June 1961 some 500 Native Americans from 67 tribes convened in Chicago to protest against termination and to urge greater Indian participation in federal programs. The result was the "Declaration of Indian Purpose." It represented a new beginning. Indian spokesman Vine Deloria, Jr., pointed out that when Indians had opposed termination in the 1950s, "no one had listened." But when the Chicago conference called for its abandonment, it was reported all over the country. Members of the Kennedy Task Force on Indian Affairs attended the Chicago conference. Less than three weeks later, they recommended that the federal government shift its emphasis from "termination of federal supervision and benefits to spurring the development of Indian-owned resources."

A member of that Task Force was Philleo Nash, who was nominated as Commissioner of Indian Affairs on July 31, 1961. Sworn in on September 26, 1961, he promised to overcome "termination psychosis." During his five years in office he visited every reservation in the country. And he gained the respect of the leaders of the National Congress of American Indians by staying up all night singing and playing the drums at their annual conference.

See Also: American Indian Movement; Native Americans

WARREN BURGER 1907–1995

Appointed Chief Justice of the Supreme Court by President Nixon in 1969, Warren E. Burger only partly fulfilled the president's desire to see conservative principles reflected in the Court's decisions.

Warren E. Burger, as Chief Justice of the United States Supreme Court from 1969 until 1986, presided over what was known as the "Nixon Court" from the number of President Nixon's appointees who sat on it. It was Nixon's intention to appoint conservative-minded judges who would shift the Court away from the liberal tendencies it had exhibited during the long tenure of Burger's predecessor, Earl Warren.

After graduating from St. Paul College of Law in Minnesota, Burger took an active part in Republican politics. In 1953 President Eisenhower appointed him assistant attorney general. Two years later he was raised to the second-highest court of appeals in the land, the U.S. Court of Appeals for the District of Columbia. Burger gained notice for attacking judicial decisions that afforded defendants in criminal cases the protection of their constitutional rights. Especially controversial was his opposition to the so-called "suppressionary rule," which rendered police evidence gained by unconstitutional means inadmissible in court. He was regarded as a "strict constructionist," that is, one who took a narrow view of judges' ability to interpret the constitution and therefore looked with suspicion on judicial decisions that in effect made new law.

The Burger court

President Nixon and conservative elements in the United States generally were disappointed by early decisions of the Burger Court. One concerned completing the process of desegregating the nation's schools. The Johnson administration had set the beginning of the school year in the autumn of 1969 as the deadline for an end to the dual system of education. When that did not

△ **Warren E. Burger being sworn in as Chief Justice of the Supreme Court by President Nixon on May 21, 1969.**

happen in Mississippi, where delay was encouraged by Nixon and upheld by a district court, the National Association for the Advancement of Colored People (NAACP) took the issue to the Supreme Court.

To Nixon's dismay, Burger and his fellow judges came to the unanimous decision that desegregation must be implemented at once. Equally alarming from the conservative point of view were several decisions of the early 1970s. In 1972, by a unanimous ruling, the Supreme Court came down in favor of busing students outside their neighborhoods in order to achieve racially mixed schools. In another ruling that year it found that capital punishment

was a "cruel and unusual punishment" in violation of the Eighth Amendment (loopholes allowed states to get around the ruling). Then, in 1973 came the landmark ruling in *Wade v. Roe* in which the "right to privacy" argument enunciated in striking down a Connecticut law against contraception was used to give women the constitutional right to abortion. By such decisions the Burger Court seemed not to be stemming radical and liberationist trends of the 1960s, but giving them its seal of approval. □

See Also: Busing; Politics and Government; Supreme Court

WILLIAM BURROUGHS 1914–1997

A founder member of the 1950s "beat generation," novelist William Burroughs continued his personal and literary crusade against respectable society throughout the turbulent 1960s.

William Burroughs formed, with Allen Ginsberg and Jack Kerouac, a literary triumvirate at the head of the "beat generation" that was at odds with the material prosperity and social conformity of the 1950s. In promoting an antiestablishment, free-thinking lifestyle they were the forebears of the hippie movement of the 1960s.

The lifelong rebel

A morphine-user from 1944 to 1959, Burroughs both celebrated and satirized the life of drug-addiction in his first novel *Junky* (1953). That novel also announced a recurrent theme in his writing, the explicit treatment of homosexual encounters, then illegal.

Burroughs gained national attention in 1959 with the publication of *Naked Lunch*, which covered the same territory in a new, brutal literary language that went beyond the stream-of-consciousness style of Kerouac's *On the Road*. In a series of novels published in the 1960s—*The Soft Machine* (1961), *The Ticket That Exploded* (1962), *Dead Fingers Talk* (1963), *Nova Express* (1964)—Burroughs developed an extreme surrealism that included what became known as his "collage style." His own paragraphs, meshed with quotations from other sources, were cut up and shifted in position in a seemingly random fashion. By that method Burroughs broke away from the linear narrative progress of the traditional novel, thus appearing to subvert authorial control and striking a literary blow against the great target of the "beats," the mind control they believed was exercised by persons of authority throughout society.

That remained the target in the last book that Burroughs wrote in the 1960s. Commissioned by *Esquire* mag-

△ **William Burroughs broke new literary ground with his graphic depictions of drug-taking and homosexual encounters.**

azine to cover the Democratic Party convention in Chicago in 1968, Burroughs took little interest—he never did—in the political turmoil surrounding him. But in the street drama of the youth riots that accompanied the convention he found inspiration for *The Wild Ones*. The novel marked a departure from the helter-skelter style of earlier works and a return to narrative and character study.

What drives the novel is the irreconcilable conflict between the unqualified hedonism and sexuality of its heroes and the deadening conformity of respectable society. "We intend to march on the police machine everywhere," proclaim the homosexual wild ones, as if participating in the Stonewall riots in which gays did battle against police officers in New York that very year. "We don't want to hear any more family talk, mother talk, father talk, cop talk, priest talk, country talk, or party talk. To put it country simple we have heard enough bullshit." □

See Also: Chicago Convention Riot; Counterculture; Hippies; Literature

BUSING

Until the 1960s the yellow school bus was one of the most innocuous symbols of American life. By the end of the decade it had become the center of a political storm.

The school bus had long been necessary to get children to rural schools. Riding the bus had also become routine for suburban and inner-city students by the 1950s. By the early 1970s just over half of all primary and secondary school students rode buses to class.

However, busing became hugely controversial when the federal courts began to use it as a way to desegregate urban schools. To engineer racial equality in education, African American and Hispanic children were bused to schools in predominately white areas, while white children were bused to schools in predominately African American and Hispanic areas.

Engineering a racial mix

Those who opposed busing said that it represented an infringement on personal choice and resulted in the destruction of neighborhood schools. People who had moved so their children would be in the enrollment area of a good school claimed they were being disadvantaged. In turn, they were accused of being racist. Civil rights leader Jesse Jackson summed up the black perception of the furor over busing when he claimed, "It's not the bus, it's us." The resulting conflict became a fundamental debate over the meaning of American values.

In 1954 the U.S. Supreme Court had ruled that the segregation of schools was unconstitutional. The following year the justices instructed lower federal courts that they should use their powers to end segregation with all deliberate speed. However,

△ **White students being bused into an African American neighborhood in Berkeley, California, in November 1971.**

courts and school boards in the South dragged their feet—so much so that in 1963 the Supreme Court pointed out that all deliberate speed did not mean indefinite delay.

The Civil Rights Act of 1964 cut federal funds from segregated schools and allowed federal attorneys to sue them. By 1968 the percentage of African American school children attending desegregated schools in the South increased tenfold. However, in rural Virginia, for example, students were given the choice of attending a traditionally African American school or a traditionally white school. Most students chose to attend the school identified with their race.

In the landmark ruling *Green v. New Kent County* in 1968 the Supreme Court held that freedom of choice in student assignment plans that did not result in substantial racial mixing violated the Fourteenth Amendment, which guaranteed equal protection under the law. In other words, individual choice was not paramount, and all local school boards had the duty to take affirmative action to eliminate segregation in schools.

In Alabama in 1968 Judge Herbert Christenberry ordered Montgomery

County school administrators to alter the bus routes, as well as to desegregate staff. The school bus came to be seen to be the vehicle of segregation's demise.

Although these rulings were primarily aimed at southern states, it soon became apparent that because of residential patterns there was de facto segregation in other parts of the country. Black children in all-black neighborhoods would inevitably end up in all-black schools. In the view of the courts this was just as discriminatory as enforced segregation in the South. As a result, a succession of court orders insisted that students be transported, by bus, from one neighborhood to another to achieve racial balance. These busing rulings aroused nearly as much controversy as earlier desegregation decisions.

The 1968 election put Richard Nixon, an avowed opponent of busing, in the White House (*see box p. 179*).

◁ **Children surge up the stairs at a primary school in Berkeley, California, on September 11, 1968, the first day of enforced busing.**

The case for busing

When the Supreme Court considered the case for busing in 1970, Chief Justice Warren Burger asked that four essential questions be borne in mind:
1. Whether the Constitution authorizes courts to require a particular racial balance in each school with a previously segregated system.
2. Whether every all-Negro and all-white school must be eliminated as part of a remedial process of desegregation.
3. What the limits are, if any, on the arrangement of school districts and attendance zones as a remedial measure.
4. What the limits are, if any, on the use of transportation facilities to correct state-enforced racial school segregation.

When spelled out that way, the implementation of busing was inevitable. In 1954 the Supreme Court had already decided that "separate but equal" meant "separate and unequal." The Constitution required that all citizens receive equal treatment, so the courts were empowered to require a racial mix in previously segregated school systems. As a consequence, all-African American and all-white schools had to be eliminated. During the

passing of the 1964 Civil Rights Act Senator Hubert Humphrey complained in the Senate that southern school boards gerrymandered school districts to maintain segregation. This meant that if all American school children were to receive equal treatment, they would have to be bused among school districts.

However, the Supreme Court never defined how far it was permissible to bus students to produce a proper racial mix. One federal district court set a limit of seven miles. Another said the journey should take "not over 35 minutes at the most." Likewise, the federal court of appeals juggled with the terms "reasonable," "feasible," "workable," "effective," and "realistic."

The courts found themselves in further difficulties because of the mobility of American society, so that once the grossest excesses of segregation were removed, it was difficult to assess the situation. Black and white people moved around, and neither the school authorities nor the district courts were required to make annual adjustments to the provision of busing to maintain racial quotas. The federal courts did not rule out future action, but in the 1970s they decided that in the absence of proof that school or state authorities had tried to fix the ethnic mix of a school, the courts should not intervene any further.

△ Students in Columbus, Georgia, on the first day of school, September 7, 1971, following a court order to ensure integrated schools.

most vociferous in the northern cities of Detroit, Chicago, and particularly, Boston. Yellow school buses escorted by police motorcyclists being greeted by howling mobs became a regular feature on the evening news. Sometimes anti-busing protesters were moved to violence. There was turmoil in freshly integrated classrooms. In Boston Senator Edward Kennedy, a probusing liberal, was punched and kicked by an antibusing mob. "Why don't you let them shoot you like they shot your two brothers?" railed one of the protesters.

For all the passions aroused, according to the Department of Transportation less than 1 percent of the increase in school busing between 1954 and 1975 was a consequence of desegregation. Even so, it was enough to accelerate the movement of whites to the suburbs, a process that had been going on for years. Sometimes called "white flight," it enabled parents to put their children in predominantly white neighborhood schools. The number of white children enrolling at inner-city public schools dropped significantly. □

Nixon argued that money spent transporting young children miles away from their neighborhoods would be better spent on improving their local schools and the curriculum. With his support the House passed a bill that would have permitted southern school districts to retain freedom of choice within their desegregation plans despite the Supreme Court ruling. The legislation failed in the Senate.

Meanwhile, the federal courts stuck to their guns. In North Carolina in 1971 Judge James McMillan ordered the Charlotte-Mecklenburg school district to undertake substantial busing, a judgment subsequently upheld by the Supreme Court.

The battle between the Supreme Court, the legislature, and the administration rumbled on throughout the 1970s. However, the opposition was

The case against busing

President Nixon characterized busing as taking children out of the schools they would normally attend and forcing them to attend others more distant, often in strange or even hostile neighborhoods. He spelled out the case against it in an eight-point statement in 1970.

1. There were inconsistencies between federal and state laws on busing, and the Supreme Court's position was extreme.
2. Desegregation should not disrupt students' education and did not require precise racial balancing or sending students beyond normal school zones.
3. The Constitution only prohibited de jure segregation—that is, segregation enforced as public policy—not de facto segregation, which resulted in this case from the fact that a neighborhood might be solidly black or white.
4. Assuming that all-black schools were necessarily substandard was racist; their students did not do well because they were poor, not because they were black.
5. It was unfair to expect schools to build a multiracial society that the adult world has failed to achieve for itself.
6. Tension caused by involuntary school desegregation might create psychic injury to sensitive children.
7. Too much desegregation would accelerate white flight to the suburbs.
8. A pluralistic society did not require complete racial integration. "It is natural that people with a common heritage retain special ties; it is natural and right that we have Italian or Irish or Negro or Norwegian neighborhoods."

See Also: Civil Rights Movement; Schools and Universities; Segregation

MARIA CALLAS 1923–1977

During the 1950s and 1960s the dramatic soprano Maria Callas created a sensation in the opera world—and was equally well known to the general public for her off-stage dramas.

Maria Callas was born in New York City in 1923. Her parents were Greek immigrants, and at the age of 13 she accompanied her mother back to Greece. At this age she already showed promise as a singer, and in Athens she had the good fortune to study under the Spanish soprano Elvira de Hidalgo, who recognized her extraordinary potential. By her own admission the adolescent Maria was awkward in her appearance (overweight and very short-sighted), but, perhaps to compensate, a most tenacious student. During the German occupation of Greece in World War II she made her first professional appearances.

After the war Callas returned briefly to the United States, but first rose to prominence in Verona, Italy, in 1947. After appearing in a number of Italian opera houses, she made her debut at the famous La Scala opera house in 1951 in Verdi's *I vespri siciliani*. She had a string of triumphs at La Scala over the next few seasons, and there was a great demand for her to appear at opera houses around the world.

Callas conquers America

Callas made her American debut in 1954 in Chicago, singing the title role in Bellini's *Norma*, one of many tragic roles that perfectly suited her vocal and dramatic qualities. Her soprano voice was not as effortlessly beautiful as some, but none could match it for emotional intensity and sheer musical expressiveness. Throughout the remainder of the 1950s and early 1960s Maria Callas thrilled audiences in all the great European and American opera houses. At the same time, recordings of her performances sold in great numbers. Her farewell performance in the United States was at the Metropolitan Opera House in 1965, in Puccini's *Tosca*.

See Also: Opera

△ **Maria Callas and baritone Tito Gobbi in Franco Zefferelli's production of *Tosca*, the final opera she sang at the Met in 1965.**

In parallel with her triumphant onstage career, Callas's offstage life was conducted in the spotlight of publicity. Having shed her excess weight, she was a striking beauty and was pursued by photographers as relentlessly as any Hollywood star. Her at times tempestuous behavior and public quarrels seemed to be quite in keeping with the public's expectations for a great opera diva (a prima donna). The public was also fascinated by her relationship with Greek shipping tycoon Aristotle Onassis, who abandoned her to marry the widowed Jacqueline Kennedy in 1968. Callas died in Paris in 1977.

Although her singing career was comparatively short, Maria Callas made an indelible impression on opera enthusiasts of her time, and her fame and reputation have outlived her. Her extensive recordings are as much in demand today as they were in her lifetime, and many critics acknowledge her as the greatest interpreter of operatic music ever recorded. □

FURTHER READING

BOOKS

Breuer, William B. **Vendetta! Fidel Castro and the Kennedy Brothers.** *New York: John Wiley, 1997.*

Carmichael, Stokely. **Stokely Speaks, Black Power Back to Pan-Africanism.** *New York: Random House, 1971.*

Carson, Claybourne. **In Struggle: SNCC and the Black Awakening of the 1960s.** *Cambridge, Mass: Harvard University Press, 1981.*

Ceruzzi, Paul E. **A History of Modern Computing.** *Cambridge, Mass: MIT Press, 1998.*

Churchill, Ward. **Agents of Repression: The FBI's Secret Wars against the Black Panther Party and the American Indian Movement.** *Boston: South End Press, 1988.*

Davis, James K. **Assault on the Left: the FBI and the Sixties Antiwar Movement.** *Westport: Praeger, 1997.*

Duiker, William J. **The Communist Road to Power in Vietnam.** *Boulder: Westview Press, 1981.*

Fine, Sydney. **Violence in the Model City: The Cavanagh Administration, Race Relations, and the Detroit Riot of 1967.** *Ann Arbor: University of Michigan Press, 1989.*

Gentry, Curt. **J. Edgar Hoover: The Man and the Secrets.** *New York: Norton, 1991.*

Gitlin, Todd. **The Sixties: Years of Hope, Days of Rage.** *New York: Bantam, 1987.*

Harrington, Michael. **The Other America: Poverty in the United States.** *New York: Macmillan, 1962.*

Hershey, Gerri. **Nowhere to Run: The Story of Soul Music.** *New York: Da Capo Press, 1985.*

Hodgson, Godfrey. **In Our Time: America from World War II to Nixon.** *Garden City, N.Y.: Doubleday, 1976.*

Karnow, Stanley. **Vietnam: A History.** *New York: Viking, 1983.*

Miller, Jim, ed. **The Rolling Stone Illustrated History of Rock & Roll.** *New York: Random House, 1976.*

Patterson, James T. **Grand Expectations: The United States 1945–1974.** *New York: Oxford University Press, 1996.*

Perkus, Cathy, ed. **Cointelpro: The FBI's Secret War on Political Freedom.** *New York: Monad Press, 1975.*

Pichaske, David. **A Generation in Motion: Popular Music and Culture in the Sixties.** *New York: Schirmer, 1979.*

Pollock, Bruce. **When the Music Mattered: Rock in the 60s.** *New York: Holt, Rinehart and Winston, 1983.*

Robbins, Natalie. **Alien Ink: The FBI's War on Freedom of Expression.** *New York: Morrow, 1992.*

Sheehan, Neil, ed. **The Pentagon Papers.** *Chicago: Quadrangle Books, 1971.*

Spector, Ronald H. **After Tet: The Bloodiest Year in Vietnam.** *New York: Free Press, 1993.*

Viorst, Milton. **Fire in the Streets: America in the 1960s.** *New York: Simon & Schuster, 1981.*

Whitcomb, Ian. **Rock Odyssey: A Chronicle of the Sixties.** *New York: Doubleday, 1984.*

Williams, Juan. **Eyes on the Prize.** *New York: Viking, 1987.*

Wirtz, James J. **The Tet Offensive: Intelligence Failure in War.** *Ithaca: Cornell University Press, 1991.*

USEFUL WEBSITES

African American Journey
http://www.worldbook.com/fun/aajourny/html/

American Indian Movement
http://www.aimovement.org

American women's histories
http://web.uccs.edu/~history/index/women

Baby-boom generation and its culture
http://bbhq.com/sixties.htm
http://hippy.com/glossary.htm
http://www.lib.virginia.edu/exhibits/sixties/
http://www.suite101.com/welcome.cfm/baby_boomers

Black Panther Party
http://www.blackpanther.org

Computer History Museum Center
http://www.computerhistory.org/

Martin Luther King
http://www.stanford.edu/group/King/

Music of the 1960s
http://www.rockument.com/links.html
http://www.woodstock69.com

NAACP (National Association for the Advancement of Colored People)
http://www.naacp.org

NASA (National Aeronautics and Space Administration)
http://www.nasa.gov

Stanford Linear Accelerator Center
http://www.slac.stanford.edu

Vietnam veterans home page
http://grunt.space.swri.edu

Vietnam War
http://www.pbs.org/wgbh/amex/vietnam/index.html
http://www.vietquoc.com

PICTURE CREDITS

PRE1960

1945
August 6, 8 American atomic bombs at Hiroshima and Nagasaki kill 120,000 civilians instantly. On September 2 Japan surrenders, bringing about end of World War II.

1947
October 14 Chuck Yeager breaks sound barrier in rocket-powered Bell X-1 airplane.
December 16 John Bardeen, Walter Brattain, and William Shockley invent transistor.

1948
May 14 State of Israel founded.
November 2 Harry S Truman wins full term.

1949
July 21 North Atlantic Treaty Organization (NATO) ratified in Washington, D.C.
September 23 Soviets detonate first atomic bomb, precipitating arms race.
October 1 Communist Party takes over China.

1950
June 30 U.S. commits troops to South Korea. War against North Korea rages until July 1953, claiming some 35,000 U.S. casualties.

1951
May 12 United States detonates first hydrogen bomb.

1952
November 5 Dwight D. Eisenhower elected president.

1954
April 7 Eisenhower warns of "domino effect"—wave of communism threatening to sweep across Southeast Asia.
April 12 Salk polio vaccine licensed.
May 7 Communists overrun French colonial forces at Dien Bien Phu, Vietnam.
May 17 Supreme Court in *Brown v. Board of Education of Topeka, Kansas*, rules against segregated schooling.

1955
February 23 U.S. sends military advisors to South Vietnam.
December 1 African American Rosa Parks sits at the front of a bus in Montgomery, Alabama, and refuses to move to "colored" seats.

1956
January 10 Elvis Presley records "Heartbreak Hotel" in Nashville.
November 6 Eisenhower reelected.
November 13 Supreme Court rules bus segregation unconstitutional.

1957
September 25 Troops and National Guardsmen enforce desegregation in Little Rock, Arkansas.
October 4 Soviets launch Sputnik, first satellite, precipitating space race.

1959
January 3 Alaska becomes 49th state, followed on August 21 by Hawaii.
February 3 Rock-'n'-roll star Buddy Holly dies in plane crash.

1960

January
1 U.S. population at the start of the decade is 179 million.

February
1 Four African American students sit down in the "whites only" section of the lunch counter of Woolworth in Greensboro, North Carolina, and refuse to be moved to the "colored" section. Sit-ins spread across the South as the civil rights movement gathers momentum.

March
At the Winter Olympics the U.S. hockey team defeats Canada (2–1) and the USSR (3–2) to take gold medal.

April
1 NASA launches Tiros 1, the first weather satellite.
5 *Ben Hur*, starring Charlton Heston, wins a record 10 Oscars.
17 Civil rights activists form the Student Nonviolent Coordinating Committee in Raleigh, North Carolina, to organize sit-ins and African American voter registration.

May
1 An American U-2 spy plane, piloted by Gary Powers, is shot down while flying over Soviet air space. President Eisenhower refuses to apologize, and the Paris Summit, scheduled for that month between the U.S., the Soviet Union, Great Britain, and France, is derailed.
2 Controversial execution of Caryl Chessman, who admitted then denied charges of multiple rape and burglary, rekindles debate over death penalty.
9 Food and Drug Administration approves the use of birth-control pills, which are to be put on sale the following year.
15 First working laser is operated by Theodore Maiman at the Hughes Aircraft Company.

August
12 NASA launches Echo 1, the first communications satellite.

September
At the Rome Olympics Cassius Clay takes gold medal for light heavyweight, and Wilma Rudolph runs 100-meter final in 11 seconds. Fidel Castro denounces U.S. "imperialists" and praises the Soviet Union.
24 Launch of *USS Enterprise*, the world's first nuclear-powered aircraft carrier and largest vessel.
26 First televised debate between presidential candidates Richard M. Nixon and John F. Kennedy.

October
19 Martin Luther King, Jr., arrested along with several other protesters after taking part in a sit-in in Atlanta. Robert Kennedy obtains his release.

November
9 John F. Kennedy wins the presidential election by the narrowest margin ever—49.7 percent of the popular vote over Nixon's 49.6 percent.

1961

January
3 President Eisenhower severs diplomatic relations with Cuba.
17 In farewell speech Eisenhower draws attention to the growing influence of the "military-industrial complex."
20 In inaugural address President Kennedy exhorts every American to "ask what you can do for your country."
21 Robert Kennedy sworn in as attorney general.

March
1 President Kennedy sets up the Peace Corps, an initiative to provide U.S. aid and manpower for developing nations.

April
11 Adolf Eichmann stands trial in Jerusalem for crimes against Jews during World War II. He is executed in Israel on May 31, 1962.
12 Soviet cosmonaut Yuri Gagarin becomes first human in space when he circles Earth in orbital flight.
17 CIA-backed forces land at the Bay of Pigs, Cuba, in an attempt to topple Fidel Castro. Within a week they are crushed: a humiliating setback for Kennedy.

May
4 "Freedom Rides," organized by CORE, leave Washington to test abolition of Jim Crow laws in the South. First bus is torched in Anniston, Alabama, and other Freedom Riders are attacked in Birmingham and Montgomery. Attorney General Robert Kennedy sends in 500 federal marshals.
5 Alan B. Shepard, Jr., becomes the first American in space after a suborbital flight 115 miles above Earth's surface.
11 President Kennedy dispatches 100 military advisors and 400 Special Forces soldiers to South Vietnam. (An estimated 2,000 advisors are already there.)
25 Kennedy pledges to put a man on the moon before the decade is out.

June
3–4 During his five-day tour of Europe Kennedy meets Soviet premier Nikita Khrushchev at Vienna summit.

August
13 Berlin divided overnight, penning East Germans behind the Iron Curtain.
17 Latin American nations (excluding Cuba) subscribe to Kennedy's Alliance for Progress.

September
5 U.S. follows USSR in resuming nuclear weapons testing after 34-month informal moratorium.

October
Joseph Heller's novel *Catch-22* published.
1 New York Yankee Roger Maris hits 61 home runs in 162 games, breaking Babe Ruth's 34-year record.

December
14 Kennedy appoints Eleanor Roosevelt, former first lady, head of his new President's Committee on the Status of Women.

1962

January
3 NASA unveils Gemini program.

February
20 John Glenn becomes first American astronaut to circle Earth, making three orbits in Friendship 7 before a safe splashdown.
26 Supreme Court rules against segregation in state transportation services.

March
22 U.S. Army personnel commence Operation Sunrise in South Vietnam, in which peasants are removed from known communist regions.

April
13 Kennedy faces down attempt by steel unions to raise price of steel.

May
17 Kennedy sends a small group of U.S. Navy and ground personnel to Laos.

June
16 *New Yorker* magazine publishes first of three installments of *Silent Spring*, a new book by Rachel Carson that warns of the effect of pesticides on nature. The full book, an early milestone of the environmental movement, is published in the fall.
25 In *Engel v. Vitale* Supreme Court judges recitation of prayer in state schools to be in violation of the First Amendment.

July
11 Telstar communications satellite transmits the first satellite television signals.

August
5 Marilyn Monroe dies after an apparent overdose of barbiturates.

October
1 James Meredith braves a violent mob to become the first African American student enrolled at the University of Mississippi.
2 Johnny Carson hosts his first *Tonight Show*.
10 President Kennedy signs legislation banning thalidomide in the U.S. after it is revealed that use of the drug in Europe has led to birth defects.
14 A U.S. spy plane brings back images of a Soviet nuclear missile launch site on Cuban soil, less than 100 miles off the U.S. coast. Six days later Kennedy imposes a naval blockade around Cuba. On October 28 Soviet premier Khrushchev agrees to dismantle the missile site on Cuba, ending the tensest superpower confrontation of the Cold War era.

November
7 Richard Nixon, defeated in the gubernatorial races in California, announces his retirement from politics.

1963

January
14 Alabama Governor George Wallace vows to uphold "segregation now, segregation tomorrow, segregation forever."
18 Supreme Court judgment in *Gideon v. Wainwright* secures defendant's right to counsel.

April
10 Nuclear submarine *Thresher* sinks in the Atlantic, taking crew of 129 with it.
12 Martin Luther King, Jr., jailed after leading a civil rights march in Birmingham, Alabama.

May
3 Eugene "Bull" Connor, police chief of Birmingham, Alabama, orders his men to turn fire hoses and dogs on African Americans—children included—protesting against local Jim Crow laws.
8 *Dr. No*, first James Bond movie, opens in the United States.

June
10 Equal Pay Act signed.
11 Buddhist monk in Saigon self-immolates in protest against the repressive regime of Vietnamese premier Ngo Dinh Diem.
12 Medgar Evers, an NAACP field worker, shot dead in Jackson, Mississippi.
26 President Kennedy, addressing the people of West Berlin, proclaims "Ich bin ein Berliner" ("I am a Berliner").

July
28 More than 40,000 attend folk festival in Newport, R.I., to hear Joan Baez, Bob Dylan, Pete Seeger, and others.

August
5 Americans, Soviets, and British sign Limited Nuclear Test Ban Treaty, in which they pledge not to test nuclear weapons in the atmosphere, in outer space, or underwater (underground tests remain permissible). The treaty takes effect from October 10.
28 More than 200,000 civil rights protesters march on Washington, D.C., where Martin Luther King, Jr., delivers his "I have a dream" speech.
30 "Hot line" installed between White House and Kremlin in the wake of the 1962 Cuban Missile Crisis.

September
15 Segregationists bomb Sixteenth Street Baptist Church in Birmingham, Alabama, killing four young African American girls.

October
28 With his 545th goal Gordie "Mr. Hockey" Howe breaks Maurice Richard's all-time record.

November
2 South Vietnamese premier Ngo Dinh Diem and his brother assassinated amid rising tensions.
22 President Kennedy assassinated by Lee Harvey Oswald in Dallas, Texas. Lyndon B. Johnson sworn in as president. Two days later Oswald shot dead, on live TV, by Jack Ruby.
25 Funeral of Kennedy in Arlington, Virginia.

1964

January
11 Surgeon General Luther L. Terry reports that cigarette smoking is a serious health hazard.
23 Twenty-fourth Amendment outlaws poll taxes, a discriminatory practice in South.
29 *Dr. Strangelove*, Cold War black comedy, opens in U.S.

February
9 Beatles play on *Ed Sullivan Show*.
25 Cassius Clay upsets Sonny Liston to win world heavyweight boxing title, then announces conversion to Islam, taking the name Muhammad Ali.

March
3 Launch of an unmanned Gemini spacecraft, which makes 64 Earth orbits over four days.
16 President Johnson requests nearly $1 billion from Congress for his War on Poverty. Poverty Act signed later that year.

May
22 At a speech in Ann Arbor, Michigan, Johnson calls for the creation of a "Great Society."

June
21 Civil rights activists James Chaney, Andrew Goodman, and Michael Schwerner murdered by racists in Mississippi.

July
3 Johnson signs Civil Rights Act.
16–24 Riots tear through Harlem, New York, as racial tension boils over. One killed, 141 injured.
24 Teamsters president Jimmy Hoffa found guilty of jury tampering, fraud, and conspiracy. Jailed in 1967, he serves four years of 13-year sentence.

August
2, 4 Navy reports attack on two U.S. warships in Gulf of Tonkin by North Vietnamese gunboats. Johnson retaliates with bombing raids. On August 7 Gulf of Tonkin Resolution gives him a virtually free hand to wage war in Vietnam.

September
27 Warren Report finds no evidence of conspiracy in assassination of President Kennedy.

October
1 Students demonstrate on the University of California campus at Berkeley, home of newly founded Free Speech Movement.
14 With Nikita Khrushchev ousted from office, Leonid Brezhnev takes over as Soviet premier.
16 China conducts its first nuclear bomb test.
24 Swimmer Don Schollander brings home four gold medals from Tokyo Summer Olympics.
30 Viet Cong attack Bien Hoa, largest American air base in Vietnam, killing four U.S. servicemen.

November
3 Johnson retains office after landslide victory over his Republican challenger, Barry Goldwater.

December
10 Martin Luther King, Jr., is awarded the Nobel Prize for Peace.
24 Viet Cong blow up Brinks Hotel, Saigon, killing two Americans.

1965

February

13 President Johnson gives the order for Operation Rolling Thunder, a heavy bombing campaign against North Vietnam, which starts on March 2 and marks major escalation in U.S. involvement in Vietnam conflict.
21 Militant black activist Malcolm X shot dead in New York by members of Nation of Islam.

March

7–25 In the face of overwhelming police brutality, Martin Luther King, Jr., leads civil rights march from Selma to Montgomery, Alabama.
8 U.S. Marines storm the beaches at Da Nang, South Vietnam.
17 Alice Hertz, a 72-year-old, burns herself to death in a Detroit street in protest of U.S. involvement in Vietnam.
23 Virgil "Gus" Grissom and John Young orbit Earth three times during Gemini 3 mission.

April

11 Tornadoes kill 271 in the Midwest.
17 Fifteen thousand students stage antiwar rally in Washington, D.C.
24 President Johnson declares Vietnam a war zone and steps up bombing of North.
28 Johnson sends marines to Dominican Republic to quell unrest.

June

3 During Gemini 4 mission Edward White conducts first American space walk.

July

25 Bob Dylan offends purist folk fans with his electric "folk-rock" set at the Newport, Rhode Island, festival.
30 President Johnson signs Medicare and Medicaid into existence to provide care for elderly and poor.

August

6 Johnson signs Voting Rights Act.
11 Five days of rioting break out in Watts, a black ghetto in Los Angeles.
18–24 Marines crush 1st Viet Cong Regiment in Quang Ngai Province during Operation Starlite.

September

16 California grape-pickers strike over wages.

October

David Millar is first American to burn draft-card, inspiring others to follow suit throughout decade.
3 Johnson signs Immigration Act, easing restrictions for immigrants into the U.S.

November

9–10 Blackout strikes Northeast as electricity fails, plunging 30 million into darkness.

December

15 Gemini 6A and 7 conduct rendezvous in space.
25 Johnson suspends bombing of North Vietnam in an attempt to draw communists into negotiation but without success. Bombing is resumed on January 31.

1966

January

U.S. forces step up search-and-destroy missions in Mekong Delta.
1 Health warnings appear on cigarette packs.
17 In Spain a B-52 bomber, carrying four hydrogen bombs, crashes after colliding with refueling plane.
20–21 Trips festival, a celebration of LSD featuring a performance by the Grateful Dead, takes place in San Francisco.

March

22 General Motors admits having conducted a smear campaign against Ralph Nader, the consumer activist who rocked the motoring industry with his November 1965 book *Unsafe at Any Speed*, and publicly apologizes to him.

May

Antiwar protests sweep the country; in Washington protesters surround the White House.
16 Beach Boys' *Pet Sounds* album released.

June

6 James Meredith, first black graduate of the University of Mississippi, shot and wounded in Hernando, Miss.
13 In *Miranda v. Arizona* the Supreme Court rules that police must inform accused of their legal rights.
29 For the first time in the Vietnam War waves of B-52 bombers pound Hanoi and Haiphong Harbor in North Vietnam.
30 National Organization for Women founded by women, including Betty Friedan, whose book *The Feminine Mystique*, now acknowledged to be a milestone in feminist thought, was published in spring 1963.

July

19 Richard Speck arrested in Chicago for murder of eight student nurses.

September

9 Johnson signs National Traffic and Motor Vehicle Safety Act and Highway Safety Act.
10 Race riots erupt in Atlanta.

October

6 Hippies hold "Love Pageant Rally" in Haight-Ashbury, San Francisco.
10 Department of Transportation established.
25 Johnson begins talks with South Vietnam's prime minister, Nguyen Cao Ky, in Manila.

November

Bobby Seale and Huey P. Newton form the Black Panthers in West Oakland, California.
11 Launch of Gemini 12, manned by Edwin "Buzz" Aldrin and James Lovell. Aldrin sets extravehicular activity record of 5 hours 30 minutes.

December

15 Walt Disney, creator of Mickey Mouse, Donald Duck, and Disneyland, dies in Hollywood from lung cancer.
31 Boeing and General Electric win contract for design and study phase of the supersonic transport (SST) development program.

1967

January

8–26 Supported by South Vietnamese troops, U.S. First and 25th Infantry Divisions attack communist bases north of Saigon in Operation Cedar Falls.
14 Hippies stage "Human Be-in" in San Francisco's Golden Gate Park.
27 Roger Chaffee, Virgil "Gus" Grissom, and Edward White die in fire in Apollo 1 space capsule during training exercise on Cape Kennedy launchpad.

February

22 Operation Junction City, involving 22 U.S. and 4 South Vietnamese battalions, pounds NVA forces in Tay Ninh Province.

April

30 Muhammad Ali stripped of his world heavyweight title after he vociferously refuses to be drafted for Vietnam: "I ain't got no quarrel with the Viet Cong."

June

2 *Sgt. Pepper's Lonely Hearts Club Band* by the Beatles is released in the U.S.
5–10 Six-Day War erupts between Israel and Arab States, resulting in a decisive victory for Israel.
16–18 Jimi Hendrix, the Grateful Dead, Janis Joplin, the Byrds, Jefferson Airplane, the Mamas and the Papas, and others play the Monterey pop festival in California, heralding the "Summer of Love."

July

17 John Coltrane, jazz saxophone player, dies from liver cancer.
23–27 Racial tension in Detroit explodes in citywide riots and looting, leaving 43 dead.

August

30 Thurgood Marshall becomes first African American to be appointed to Supreme Court.

October

9 Ché Guevara killed in Bolivia.
9 *Rolling Stone* magazine launched.
21 Fifty thousand antiwar protesters march on the Pentagon, clashing with military police.

November

29 Robert McNamara resigns from post as secretary of defense.
30 Senator Eugene McCarthy of Minnesota announces his intention to challenge President Johnson for the Democratic nomination the following year.

December

3 In South Africa Dr. Christiaan Barnard performs the world's first human heart transplant on Louis Washkansky (who survives for 18 days).

1968

January
16 Jerry Rubin and Abbie Hoffman found Youth International Party, or Yippies.
21 Marine base at Khe Sanh besieged by North Vietnamese Army until relieved on April 8.
23 Naval intelligence-gathering ship *Pueblo* captured by North Koreans. Freed December 23.
30 North Vietnam launches Tet Offensive. To many Americans at home the Vietnam War now seems unwinnable.
30 Clark Clifford appointed secretary of defense.
31 Suicide squad seizes compound of U.S. Embassy in Saigon and holds it for six hours.

February
24 Newsman Walter Cronkite forecasts "stalemate" in Vietnam after visiting the country.
28 Kerner Commission Report blames white neglect and racism for the riots that have swept America's cities in recent years.

March
12 Senator Eugene McCarthy unexpectedly wins 42 percent of vote in New Hampshire primary.
22 Arrest of six students sparks unrest in Paris that will escalate into violence in May and briefly threaten to topple the French government.
31 President Johnson rejects demand for 206,000 more troops in Vietnam and reduces bombing campaigns. He also announces that he will retire at the end of his term.

April
3 Hanoi agrees to begin peace negotiations.
4 Martin Luther King, Jr., assassinated in Memphis, Tennessee.
29 Hippie musical *Hair* opens on Broadway.
30 Police gain control of Columbia University after week-long occupation by antiwar protesters.

May
12 U.S. and North Vietnam commence Paris Peace Talks, an initiative to end war in Vietnam.

June
4 Senator Robert Kennedy shot dead in Los Angeles by Jordanian Sirhan Sirhan.
19 Congress passes Gun Control Act to curb firearm ownership.

July
1 Nuclear Non-Proliferation Treaty signed.

August
20 Warsaw Pact countries invade Czechoslovakia to stamp out program of liberalization.
26–29 World watches on TV as police brutally subdue antiwar protesters on streets outside Democratic convention in Chicago. Hubert Humphrey beats Eugene McCarthy for the party's presidential nomination.

October
27 At Mexico City Olympic Games Tommie Smith and John Carlos cause uproar when they raise fists on podium in black power salute.

November
5 Republican Richard M. Nixon wins slender victory over Humphrey to become president.
5 Shirley Chisholm becomes first African American woman to be elected to Congress.

1969

March
18 President Nixon begins secret bombing campaign against Cambodia.

June
8 Nixon announces that 25,000 U.S. troops will be withdrawn from Vietnam by end of July.
27–29 Rioting erupts at Stonewall Inn in New York after police raid on homosexuals. Lasting until July 2, the violence sparks gay liberation movement.

July
18 Senator Edward Kennedy escapes unharmed after driving off a bridge on Chappaquiddick Island, Massachusetts. His passenger, Mary Jo Kopechne, is drowned.
24 Apollo 11 astronaut Neil Armstrong becomes the first man to walk on the moon. He is followed shortly by Edwin "Buzz" Aldrin. Awaiting the two in the Command Vehicle is Michael Collins. The three splash down safely in the Pacific on July 24.

August
9, 10 Hippie "family" of Charles Manson murders seven Los Angeles residents, including actress Sharon Tate, the pregnant wife of film director Roman Polanski.
15–17 Crowd of nearly 450,000 gathers at Woodstock music festival in New York State to celebrate youth culture.

September
3 North Vietnamese leader Ho Chi Minh dies.
24 Trial of Chicago Seven, who include Tom Hayden, Jerry Rubin, and Abbie Hoffman, begins in Chicago before Judge Julius Hoffman.

November
15 Crowd of 250,000 antiwar protesters marches peacefully on Washington, D.C.
16 Defense Department officials reveal that U.S. troops massacred dozens of unarmed villagers at the My Lai hamlet in South Vietnam on March 16, 1968. Lt. William L. Calley, who ordered his men to kill, is charged with murder.

December
6 Two members of the Black Panthers, Fred Hampton and Mark Clark, are killed in police raid in Chicago.
6 Hell's Angels run amok at Altamont festival in California, where the Rolling Stones and Grateful Dead are performing. There are four fatalities, including a stabbing.

POST 1969

1970
January 1 U.S. population stands at 203 million.
February 18 Chicago Seven acquitted of conspiracy to derail 1968 Democratic convention in Chicago.
May 4 National Guardsmen kill four students during antiwar protests at Kent State, Ohio.

1971
March 29 Lieutenant William Calley found guilty of murdering 22 Vietnamese civilians in March 1968. Sentenced initially to life imprisonment, he is paroled in November 1974.
March 29 Charles Manson and three women from his "family" are sentenced to death for the 1969 Tate–LaBianca killings in Los Angeles. Their sentences are later commuted to life imprisonment.
June 30 *New York Times* publishes the Pentagon Papers, leaked top-secret Vietnam documents.

1972
February 28 President Nixon visits China.
June 1 Nixon and Leonid Brezhnev sign SALT at Washington summit.
June 17 Break-in at Democratic National Committee offices in Watergate complex, Washington. Nixon, initially denying involvement, is directly implicated in ensuing scandal.

1973
January 27 Paris Peace Accords end U.S. military involvement in Vietnam.
January 22 Supreme Court permits women's right to abortion in *Roe v. Wade*.

1974
August 8 Nixon resigns presidency in wake of Watergate scandal. Gerald Ford succeeds him.
October 29 Muhammad Ali regains world heavyweight title, knocking out George Foreman in the "Rumble in the Jungle."

1975
April 30 Helicopters evacuate last U.S. forces from South Vietnam via embassy rooftop.

1976
July 4 United States celebrates bicentenary of the Declaration of Independence.

SET INDEX

Volume numbers are in **bold**. Page numbers in **bold** refer to main articles; those in *italics* refer to picture captions.

A

Aaron, Hank **1**:5
ABC **4**:156, **5**:102, **6**:70
Abel, Rudolf **6**:105
Abernathy, Ralph **1**:6, **2**:17, 42–3, 46–7
abortion **1**:175, **3**:39, 40, 41, **6**:19
Abrams, Creighton **6**:175
absurd, the **3**:16
Abzug, Bella **3**:33
Academy Awards **3**:141
Acheson, Dean **2**:26, 63
Acid Tests **2**:111, **3**:108–9, 127, **5**:*92*, 93
Action Office **2**:148
Acuff Rose **2**:114
Adair, Paul "Red" **5**:37
Addams Family, The **6**:78–9
Adderley, "Cannonball" **2**:135, **3**:170
ADELA **4**:38
Adenauer, Konrad **1**:156
Adler, Kurt Herbert **5**:19
Adler, Lou **5**:67–8
advertising **1**:7–11, **2**:92, 104, **4**:68
    and Betty Friedan **1**:10, **3**:36
    political **1**:*10*, 11, **5**:54, 55
    tobacco **1**:11, 48, 49
aerospace industry **1**:12–18, **2**:172, **4**:100
affirmative action **2**:143, 144, **5**:114
Affluent Society, The **3**:64
AFL-CIO **4**:25–8, 31
Africa
    and the civil rights movement **2**:42, 50–1
    decolonization **2**:36, 81–2, 136–7
    wars of liberation **6**:170, 171
African-American Institute **5**:31
African Americans
    Afro-Caribbeans **3**:157–8
    baby boomers **1**:100
    boxers **1**:152
    dance **1**:107
    hairstyles **3**:26
    and music **6**:39
    on television **6**:74–5
    as a term for blacks **1**:139
    and Vietnam **1**:50–1, 88
    see also black power; civil rights movement; ghettos
African American Studies **1**:143–4
Africana Studies **1**:143–4
African National Congress **1**:58–9, **6**:171
Africare **5**:31
Afro-Caribbeans **3**:157–8
afro hairstyles **3**:26

After the Fall **1**:162
Agena space vehicles **3**:*68*, 69, 70, 71
Agency for International Development **2**:137
Agent Orange **6**:143, 144
Agnew, Spiro T. **1**:19, **2**:57, **4**:21, **5**:50, **6**:21
agribusiness **1**:26
agriculture **1**:20–6, **4**:51
    migrant camps **5**:79
    see also Green Revolution
aid, foreign **2**:173, *175*, **3**:*151*, 153, **4**:38
AIDS **3**:121
Ailey, Alvin **1**:*107*
AIR-2 Genie **1**:29–30
Air America **2**:36
aircraft **1**:12–18, **4**:87, 132–3
    reconnaissance **1**:31
    transport **1**:30, 31, **6**:98–9
    see also aerospace industry
Air Defense Command (ADC) **1**:29–30
Air Force **1**:14, 27–31, 85
    AGMs **1**:32–3
airlines **1**:35, **6**:98–9
airports **1**:36–7, 77
Air Quality Act (1967) **2**:61
air stewardesses **4**:136
air traffic control **1**:37
air travel **1**:13–14, 18, 34–7
    supersonic transport **6**:64–5
    see also aerospace industry
Akira, Kurosawa **3**:59
Alabama, University of **2**:48, 49
Alaska **2**:*154*, **4**:139, **5**:35
Albania **2**:96, **5**:83, **6**:169
Albany, civil rights **2**:42–3, **4**:125
Albany Movement **6**:35
Albee, Edward **1**:162–3, **3**:16, **6**:95
Alcatraz Island **1**:45, 46–7, 174
Alcindor, Lew **1**:118, **5**:9
Aldon Music **5**:65–6
Aldrich, Robert **3**:56
Aldrin, Edwin "Buzz" **1**:68, 69, 70
    Gemini mission **3**:71
Al Fateh **4**:106–7
Alfred Hitchcock Presents **2**:91
Ali, Muhammad **1**:38–9, 152, 154, **4**:74, **5**:6, 7
Allende, Salvador **1**:42, **4**:179
Allen, Donald **4**:63–4
Allen, James A. **2**:57
Allen, Woody **1**:40, **3**:16, **5**:154
Alliance for Progress **1**:41–2, **2**:80, **3**:151, **4**:34, 38
All Volunteer Force **2**:167
Almanacs **3**:44, 45, **5**:90
Altamont Festival **1**:43–4, **3**:88, 128, **6**:177
aluminum **3**:167
American Cancer Society (ACS) **1**:49
American Conservatory Theater **6**:93
American Dream **3**:145, **5**:71
American Dream, An **4**:72–3
American Express **2**:120, 121, **6**:97
American Folk Blues Festival **1**:147

American Independent Party **2**:143; **5**:52
American Indian Movement **1**:45–7
American Medical Association **1**:49, **5**:58
American Mind, The **5**:45
Americans for Democratic Action **3**:64, 154
Americans, The **2**:104
Amish **5**:*111*
Amtrak **6**:100, 101, 130
amusement parks **2**:160
Andean Group **4**:38–9
Anders, Bill **1**:65
Andre, Carl **6**:*163*, 164
Andrews, Julie **2**:163, **3**:138, 139
Anger, Kenneth **3**:137
Angleton, James Jesus **2**:35
Angola **2**:137, **6**:170
angst **3**:16
Animals **1**:161
Another Side of Bob Dylan **2**:168
antibiotics **3**:118, 121
antismoking campaign **1**:48–9
antitrust laws, and baseball **1**:112
antiwar movement **1**:50–7, **2**:110–11, **3**:73
    and Benjamin Spock **1**:51, 52, 97, **5**:152
    and the FBI **3**:28, 30
    and Joan Baez **1**:101
    and Muhammad Ali **1**:39
    and Noam Chomsky **2**:33
    student protest **1**:51, 56, 57, 98–9, 130, **2**:108, 110, **6**:*54*
    see also Chicago Convention riot
Antonioni, Michelangelo **3**:57–8, 140
Anuszkiewicz, Richard **5**:14, 15
ANZUS treaty **4**:145
apartheid **1**:58–9, **5**:6, **6**:109
Apollo program **1**:14, 60–71, **2**:91, **4**:131, **6**:46–7
Appalachia, poverty **5**:78
Arafat, Yasir **6**:30
Arber, Werner **3**:120
Arbus, Diane **5**:41
Archies **5**:67
architecture **1**:72–7, **2**:145, 146
    building with steel **3**:163–4
    theater **6**:95
    see also design; housing
Arecibo telescope **5**:166
Arendt, Hannah **2**:180
Argentina **4**:38
Arkansas, jails **2**:124
armored personnel carriers **1**:87
arms race **1**:78–83, **4**:110–11
    see also Cold War; deterrence; missile gap
Armstrong, Louis **1**:84
Armstrong, Neil **1**:68–9, 70, **6**:47
    Gemini mission **3**:70, 71
Army **1**:85–8
    grunts **3**:100–1
    and mind control **2**:38
    Special Forces *see* green berets
    Vietnam War **1**:87–8, **4**:95
    see also draft; Vietnam War
Artaud, Antonin **3**:17

art-rock **5**:89
arts **4**:52–3, **5**:57, 72
    black **6**:94–5
    and education **5**:158
    see also theater; visual arts
ASEAN **6**:7
Asia
    Green Revolution **3**:98–9
    immigrants from **3**:*156*, 157, 161
Asimov, Isaac **1**:89, **5**:175
Astrodome **1**:112, **3**:164
astronauts
    first Soviet **1**:61, **3**:63, 67
    first U.S. **1**:16, **2**:87, *172*, **3**:63, 67, 4:97
astronomy **5**:165–8
Aswan High Dam **4**:*104*, 105, 134
AT&T **2**:91, **6**:133
Atkins, Chet **2**:115
Atkins, Susan **4**:76, 77
Atlantic City, Democratic Convention (1964) **2**:*52*, 53
Atlas rockets/ICBMs **1**:28, 80, **4**:96, 98, 113, **5**:125–6
atomic bombs **4**:174
    Chinese **2**:28, 29
Atomic Energy Commission (AEC) **2**:65
Atoms for Peace **6**:106, 131
audion tubes **3**:9
Auschwitz **2**:*180*
automobile industry **1**:90–4, **3**:167
    advertising **1**:8, *9*, 10
    assembly lines **2**:103, 105
    strikes **2**:105
    see also cars
auto racing **4**:49
Avedon, Richard **5**:43
Avery, Margaret **4**:162

B

B-26 bombers **1**:120
B-52 *see* Boeing, B-52
B-70 bombers **6**:64, 65
Babbs, Ken **3**:127
baby-boom generation **1**:95–100
    and consumerism **2**:105
    and crime **2**:123
"back to the land" **2**:111–12
bacteriological warfare **1**:81
Baez, Joan **1**:**101**, **2**:*107*, 109, 168, **3**:44
Bahamas, casinos **5**:25
Bailey, David **3**:24, 140, **5**:43
Bailey report **2**:140
Bakara, Amiri **6**:94
Baker, Bobby **5**:50
Baker, Ella **6**:34, 36
Baker, LaVern **3**:87
Baker v. Carr (1962) **6**:69
Bakker, Jim **6**:72
Balaguer, Joaquin **2**:165
Baldwin, James **1**:102–3
ballet **1**:104–7
Ball, George **2**:63
Ball, Lucille **6**:*76*, 77
balloons **2**:88, **4**:52

Band 5:136, 143
bank cards 2:120–1
Barber, Samuel 2:58
Barbie doll 1:108
Bardot, Brigitte 1:109, 3:140
Barnard, Christiaan 3:115, 122
Barnett, Ross 2:43, 44
Barth, John 4:55, 56, 60
baseball 1:110–14, 4:49
    Aaron, Hank 1:5
    Mantle, Mickey 1:113, 4:78
    Mays, Willie 1:5, 4:90
    novels 4:61
basketball 1:115–19, 4:49, 50
    1968 Olympics 1:142
Batista, Fulgencio 2:12
Bauhaus school 2:145
Bay of Pigs invasion see Cuba
Beach Boys 1:122–3, 5:86, 131–2
Beamon, Bob 5:10
Beatles 1:124–7, 2:118, 3:48, 5:69,
    93, 139–40, 142
    and fashion 3:22, 24, 27
    films 3:141, 5:139
    Sgt. Pepper's Lonely Hearts Club
        Band 1:127, 2:169, 3:27, 43,
        5:86, 139, 6:48, 61
    in the U.S. 1:126, 159–60, 5:66,
        67, 129, 130
beatniks 2:107, 5:72–3
Beau Brummels 5:131
Beauvoir, Simone de 3:15, 33–4
Bee Gees 2:159
beepers 2:92
Be-ins 3:109, 128, 6:32, 33, 60
Belli, Melvin 1:43
Bellow, Saul 1:128, 3:16, 4:55,
    56–7
Bell Telephone Company 2:88, 91
Bell X-1 5:126
Ben-Gurion, David 2:180, 4:93,
    6:30–1
Bennett, Elijah 2:8
Bennett, Robert L. 1:173–4
Bennett, Tony 2:115–17
Bergman, Ingmar 3:57
Berkeley see California, University of
Berkeley Free Speech Movement
    (FSM) 1:98, 2:109, 110, 3:18,
    73, 128
Berlin Wall 1:87, 131–2, 156, 2:72,
    4:16, 153
Berman, Shelley 5:153
Bernbach, William 1:10, 3:79
Bernstein, Leonard 1:133, 2:60,
    3:178
Bertolucci, Bernardo 3:58
Best, Pete 1:124, 125
Betts v. Brady (1942) 3:77
Beverly Hillbillys 2:116, 6:71, 78
Bewitched 6:78
Biba 3:20, 23, 27
big bang 5:167–8
Big Brother and the Holding
    Company 3:109, 175
Bilingual Education Act (1968)
    3:157
billboards (N.Y.) 1:11
Billy Jack 1:47
Binh Xuyen 4:94, 135

John Birch Society 2:97, 5:96–7
Birmingham, and civil rights
    2:45–8, 4:22–3
birth-control pill 1:134–5, 3:40,
    6:15
birthrate 1:96, 135, 145, 6:14
Bitches Brew 2:135, 3:172
Blackboard Jungle, The 5:71
"black consciousness" 2:8
black holes 5:166
Black, Hugo L. 2:43
Black Muslims see Nation of Islam
blackout (Nov. 1965) 1:145
Black Panther Party 1:136–7, 140,
    142, 2:43, 56, 6:13
    and the Chicago Convention riot
        2:21
    and Eldridge Cleaver 2:62
    end 1:137, 2:57
    and the FBI 3:31
    and Stokely Carmichael 1:142,
        2:8, 6:37
black power 1:138–42, 167, 2:56,
    4:127
    and Angela Davis 2:134
    and Eldridge Cleaver 2:62
    see also Black Panther Party
Black Power Conference (1968)
    2:56
Black Power, The Politics of
    Liberation 2:8
Black Studies 1:143–4
Blackwell, R. "Bumps" 3:86
Blake, Eugene C. 5:108–9
Bliss, Ray 5:114
Block, Herbert 5:156
Blonde on Blonde 2:169
Blood, Sweat, and Tears 5:141
Bloomfield, Mike 5:133
"Blowin' in the Wind" 2:168
"blue-collar blues" 2:105
bluegrass 2:116
blues 1:146–9
    to rock 5:132–3
Blues for Mister Charlie 1:102, 103
Blumberg, Baruch 3:119, 5:171
Boeing 1:17
    377 Stratocruiser 1:13, 34, 63
    707 1:13–14, 34
    747 1:18
    B-52 Stratofortress 1:17, 27–8,
        29, 2:155, 178, 4:175
Bohan, Marc 3:24
Bomarc missiles 6:115
"bomber gap" 4:114
Bonanza 2:86, 91, 92, 6:71
Bond, James 2:36, 3:140
Bond, Julian 6:35
Bonnie and Clyde 2:116, 3:136
book clubs 1:151
book publishing 1:150–1
Boone, Pat 6:81
Pat Boone Show 6:81
Boorstin, Daniel 2:104
Borlaug, Norman 3:98
Borman, Frank 1:65, 66, 68, 3:69,
    70
Bosch, Juan 2:164, 3:152, 4:180
bossa nova 3:169
Boulez, Pierre 2:59

Boutwell, Albert 2:45, 46
bowling, ten-pin 4:50
boxing 1:152–5, 5:9
    see also Ali, Muhammad
Boyer, Paul 5:110
Boyle, Tony 2:66
Boys in the Band, The 3:66
Bracero Program 1:25, 3:158
Bradbury, Ray 5:175
Bradford, Alex 3:86
Bradley, Owen 2:115
Branco, Humberto Castello 4:36–7
Brandt Report (1980) 1:156
Brandt, Willy 1:132, 156
Branunwald, Nina 3:114
bras 3:22–3
    "burning" 3:35
Braun, Wernher von 1:14–15, 62,
    5:124, 126
Brazil 3:151, 153, 4:36–7
Breuer, Marcel 2:145–6
Brewster, Kingman 2:167
Brezhnev Doctrine 1:157, 2:29, 79,
    5:83
Brezhnev, Leonid 1:157, 2:77, 95
Brig, The 3:18
Brill Building 5:65
Bringing It All Back Home 2:169,
    3:48
Brinkley, David 4:157–8
British Invasion 1:158–61, 3:47,
    5:67
    the Beatles 1:126, 159–60, 5:66,
        67, 129, 130
    the blues 1:146–9
    and discotheques 2:158
Broadway 1:162–5, 3:16, 4:53
Brooklyn, riot (July 1964) 3:112
Brooks, Mel 3:138
Brotherhood of Sleeping Porters
    2:50
Brown, Edmund "Pat" 4:164; 5:47
Brown, Helen Gurley 1:166, 6:83
Brown, H. Rap 1:140, 142, 6:37
Brown, James (singer) 1:139, 167,
    3:84, 6:38, 40–1
Brown, Jim (athlete) 1:168
Brownlee, Archie 3:84
Brown, Norman O. 2:112
Brown, Sam 1:57
Brown v. the Board of Education of
    Topeka, Kansas (1954) 2:41,
    4:124, 6:69
Brubeck, Dave 1:169, 3:169
Bruce, Lenny 1:170, 5:153
Bruce, Louis R. 1:174
Brutalism 1:77
bubblegum music 5:67
Buchwald, Art 5:154–5
Buckley, James 5:99
Buckley, W. F., Jr. 5:98–9
Buddhist monk, self-immolation
    1:51, 5:148
Buffalo Springfield 3:49, 5:90, 91,
    131
Bui Tin 3:129, 6:156
Bullpup missiles 1:33, 5:125
Bundy, McGeorge 1:171, 2:63, 129,
    3:177–8
Bunker, Ellsworth 1:172, 2:165

Bunker Plan 1:172
Bureau of Indian Affairs 1:173–4,
    4:139
Bureau of Mines, U.S. 2:65
Burger, Warren E. 1:175, 178, 6:66,
    69
Burns, Hayden 2:161
Burroughs, William 1:176, 2:22,
    4:56, 59
Burt, Heinz 1:158
Burton, Gary 3:171, 172
Burton, James 2:118
Bury My Heart at Wounded Knee
    1:47
buses 1:35, 6:98, 99
    see also Freedom Riders;
        Montgomery bus boycott
Busicum 2:100
busing 1:175, 177–9
Butterfield, Paul 5:133
Byrds 2:119, 3:47, 48–9, 5:143

C

Cabaret (musical) 1:164
Caesar, Shirley 3:85
Cafe LaMama (company) 3:18
Cage, John 1:105, 2:58–9, 5:14
Calexico 2:17
California
    air pollution 2:61
    Disneyland 2:160–3
    grape-pickers' strike 2:17, 4:24
    population explosion 5:75
    Silicon Valley 3:8, 9, 6:58–9
    water provision 6:129–30
California, University of (at
    Berkeley)
    antiwar movement 1:51
    Black Studies 1:144
    hippies and People's Park
        2:111–12
    radical students 2:108, 109–10
Callas, Maria 1:180, 5:17
Calley, William L. 4:123, 6:146,
    147, 150
Cambodia see Vietnam War
"Camelot" 3:178
Camorra 5:20
Campbell, Glen 1:123
Canada
    health insurance 3:116–17
    hockey 3:132, 133
    Quebec separatism 5:95
    U.S. relations with 6:112–15
cancer 3:120–1, 5:171
Canned Heat 5:133
Cao Dai sect 4:94, 135
Cape Canaveral (Cape Kennedy)
    1:60, 64, 65, 66, 71
capital punishment 1:175, 2:125,
    127, 128, 3:150–1
Capote, Truman 2:5, 4:56, 70, 112
Captain Beefheart 5:89
Cardin, Pierre 3:25, 26
Carey, Gordon 6:27
Carlos, John 1:142, 5:9
Carmichael, Stokely 1:136, 142,
    2:8, 43, 6:37
    and the Black Panthers 1:142,

2:8, 6:37
and black power 1:138, 139–40, 2:8
and James Brown 1:167
and the term "black" 1:139, 2:8
Carnaby Street 3:*19*, 24–5
Carnegie Hall 2:60
Carpenter, M. Scott 1:16, 4:*96*, 97, *100*, 101
cars 1:8, 10, 6:57, 98
culture 1:92–4
imported *see* imports
safety 2:6–7, 3:126
see also automobile industry
Carson, Johnny 1:52, 2:9, 5:154, 6:81–2
Carson, Rachel 2:10, 3:11
Carter, Elliot 2:59
Carter, June 2:11
Cash, Johnny 2:11, 117, 118
Johnny Cash Show 2:11
Cassady, Neal 3:127
Cassidy, David 5:69
Castaneda, Carlos 2:112, 5:93
Castro, Fidel 1:41, 120, 2:12–13, 72, 4:179
attempts to remove 2:13, 36, 129, 3:151
and communism 2:97
and the Cuban Missile Crisis 2:13, 129
Catch-22 2:14, 4:59, 60, 5:154
Catcher in the Rye 3:72
CAT scans 5:173
Dick Cavett Show 6:82, *83*
CBN 6:72
CB radios 5:102, 103
CBS 2:85, 86, 4:156, 158, 5:47, 102, 155, 6:70
Ceausescu, Nicolae 2:29, 5:83
cemeteries 6:12
CENTO 4:145
Central American Common Market (CACM) 4:38, 179
Cernan, Eugene 1:67, 3:71
Cessna 1:35
Chabrol, Claude 3:56, 57
Chad and Jeremy 1:161
Chaffee, Roger 1:63, 64
Chaikin, Joseph 3:18
Chamberlain, Wilt 1:115–16, 117
Chaney, James 2:52, 53, 4:23
Chanh, Nguyen Thi 2:133
Chappaquiddick 2:15–16
Charles, Ray 3:84, 86, 6:38
Chavez, César 2:17, 4:24
Checker, Chubby 5:64, *65*
Chelomei, Vladimir 6:43
Chelsea Girls 6:166
chemical warfare 1:81, 3:117
Chessman, Caryl 2:127
Chiang Kai-shek 2:18, 26, 27, 4:79
Chicago 1:77, 3:*10*
ghettos 3:*75*
music 1:146, 5:18–19, 133
suburbs 6:56–7
Chicago Convention riot (1968) 1:56, 2:19–23, 111, 3:73, 6:180
see also Chicago Seven trial
Chicago Seven trial 1:130, 2:24–5

Chicano movement 1:100, 3:158, 6:95
Chile 1:42, 4:*39*
China
Chiang Kai-shek 2:18, 26, 27, 4:79
Chou En-lai 2:34, *96*
communism 2:27, 95, 96
Cultural Revolution 2:30–1, 34
Forbidden City 2:34
Great Leap Forward 2:30, 4:79
immigration from 3:157, 161
and Japan 6:122
Mao Zedong 2:26, 29, 30–1, 4:*79*
nuclear weapons 2:155, 4:172
and the Olympic Games 5:5–6
split with the Soviets *see* Soviet Union
U.S. relations with 2:**26–9**, 75, 95, 4:79
and wars of liberation 6:171
"China Lobby" 2:18
Chinese-American relations 2:**26–9**, 75, 95, 4:79
Chinese Cultural Revolution 2:**30–1**, 34
Chisholm, Shirley 2:32, 3:33
chlorofluorocarbons (CFCs) 3:13
Chomsky, Noam 1:52, 2:33
Chou En-lai 2:34, *96*
Chrysler (company) 1:91, 2:174
Church, Frank 3:153
CIA 2:**35–8**, 4:71
and the Alliance for Progress 1:42
and the arts 5:72, 6:159
and communism 2:77
and the Cuban Missile Crisis 1:31, 2:36, *37*
and decolonization 2:136
and the domino theory 1:80
and Fidel Castro 2:13, 36, 129
gadgets used by 2:37
in Laos 4:33, 6:151
and Latin America 2:80
and mind control 2:38
secret air force 2:36
and the U-2 incident 2:35, 6:104
and Vietnam 2:36, 77
cigarettes *see* antismoking campaign
Circus Maximus 5:88
cities
decay 3:145
Native Americans 4:140
regeneration 3:146
suburbs 6:56–7
see also ghettos; suburbia
Citizens' Commission to Investigate the FBI 3:31
Civil Rights Act (1875) 2:40
Civil Rights Act (1957) 2:41, 4:126, 6:12
Civil Rights Act (1960) 4:126
Civil Rights Act (1964) 1:177, 178, 2:49–50, 3:36–7, 4:126, 6:13
and Johnson 2:51, 3:92, 5:161
Civil Rights Act (1965) 3:14
Civil Rights Commission 6:12

civil rights movement 2:**39–57**
and the antiwar movement 1:50
and the Army 1:87
in Birmingham 2:45–8
and Christianity 5:109
and communism 2:76
and James Baldwin 1:102, 103
and Joan Baez 1:101
and labor unions 4:26–9
March on Washington *see* Washington, March on
organizations 2:43
and protest music 3:*47*, 5:91
Selma to Montgomery march 2:*47*, 55–6, 6:37
and soul music 6:40–1
and voting rights 2:54–6, 4:126–7
see also black power; CORE; King, Martin Luther, Jr.; NAACP; SCLC; segregation; SNCC
Clapton, Eric 1:146, 148, 160, 5:134–5, 138
Clarke, Arthur C. 2:89, 5:175
Clark, Larry 5:42
Clark, Ramsey 3:29, 4:40–7
class, and the generation gap 3:72
classical music 2:**58–60**
see also Bernstein, Leonard; opera
Clay, Cassius M. *see* Ali, Muhammad
Clean Air Acts 2:61
Cleaver, Eldridge 1:136, 140, 2:**62**, 4:56
Cleopatra 3:136
Clifford, Clark 2:63
Clifton, Bill 2:116
Cline, Patsy 2:115, 117
coal industry 2:**64–7**
Coates, Dorothy Love 3:85
Cobb, Ty 1:5, 113
Code of Federal Regulations 3:94
Cohen, Leonard 3:47
COINTELPRO 1:47, 2:126, 3:29, 143
and the New Left 3:31
Cold War 1:78, 85, 121, 2:**68–83**, 96, 4:174
Brezhnev Doctrine 1:157, 2:29, 79, 5:83
communism in Eastern Europe 2:78–80, 94–5, 5:82–3, 6:169
confrontations *see* Berlin Wall; Cuban Missile Crisis; U-2 incident
and deterrence 2:**151–5**
"flexible response" 1:79–80, 85–6, 4:67, 145
and human rights 3:151
and Japan 6:122–3
and McCarthyism 5:73–4
and the military-industrial complex 4:109
and missile attacks 1:29
and the Nonaligned Movement 2:71
nuclear fallout shelters 4:**170–1**
and the Olympic Games 5:6
reconnaissance aircraft 1:31;

6:104–5
and South Africa 1:58
Soviet military parades 2:*69*, *94*, 5:124
and suburbia 6:58
and U.S. radio broadcasts 2:77
and Vietnam 2:73–5, 6:139–40
see also arms race; communism; détente, U.S.–Soviet; deterrence; nuclear weapons; Soviet Union
Coleman, Ornette 3:168, 171
Cole, Nat "King" 2:45
Collins, Judy 3:46, 47
Collins, Mike 1:65, 66, 68, 69, 3:71
Colombia 1:*41*, 42
immigrants from 3:161
color television 2:85–6, 6:75
Coltrane, John 2:84, 135, 3:168, 171, 172
Columbia (shuttle) 1:69, 70
Columbia University SDS 6:55
Columbo, Joe 5:*23*, 24–5
COMECON 6:169
Commager, Henry 3:11, 5:45
Committee to Outlaw Entrapment 3:65
Common Sense Book of Baby and Child Care 1:97
communes 3:43, 5:110
Communication by Moon Relay 2:88
communications 2:**87–92**, 6:133
and Marshall McLuhan 4:66
communism 2:**93–7**
and the Brezhnev Doctrine 1:157, 2:29, 79
Chinese 2:27, 95, 96
and the civil rights movement 2:76
"communist monolith" 2:96
containment of 1:78–9, 2:26, 28–9
CPUSA 2:95
domestic effects 2:96–7
in Eastern Europe 2:78–80, 94–5, 5:82–3, 6:169
and folk music 3:44, 45
and human rights 3:151
and JFK 2:26–7
in Mexico 6:125
and nationalism 2:97
Soviet 2:68, 69–70, 94–5
U.S. views on 2:93, 96
see also Berlin Wall; Cold War; SEATO; Warsaw Pact
Community Service Organization (CSO) 2:17
computers 2:**98–101**, 5:164, 6:179
Comsat 2:89
Congo 2:136, 137, 6:109
Congress 5:45
and the presidency 2:77, 5:46–9
Congress of Racial Equality *see* CORE
Connection, The 3:18
Connor, T. E. "Bull" 2:45, 46, 48, 4:19
Conrad, C. "Pete" 1:*12*, 3:71

conscientious objectors 2:167
Conservative Party 5:99
"conspicuous consumption" 2:102
conspiracy theories about:
    the CIA 2:35, 38
    communism 2:97
    JFK's assassination 4:9, 6:167
consumer price index 2:170
Consumer's League 2:104
consumer society 2:102–5, 3:72,
    5:71
    and women 3:36
    see also advertising; automobile
        industry; credit cards; retail
        industry
Consumer's Union 2:104
contact lenses 2:106
containment see communism,
    containment of
Contemporary style 2:146
contraceptives 6:69
    see also birth-control pill
Cooke, Sam 3:84, 86, 6:38
Cooley, Denton 3:115, 123
Cooper, L. Gordon, Jr. 1:16, 4:96,
    97, 101
Coover, Robert 4:61
Copland, Aaron 2:58
CORE 2:43, 44, 46
    and black nationalism 1:138,
        2:44, 56
    and Freedom Rides 2:42, 3:60,
        61
    and sit-ins 6:26, 27
Corea, Chick 3:170, 172
Cornell University, armed takeover
    1:144
Cosby, Bill 2:36, 6:74
Cosmopolitan 1:166
cost of living 2:170
cotton, growing 1:23
Count Basie's Orchestra 3:169
counterculture 2:107–13
    and drugs 2:109, 111, 128,
        3:127
    and the FBI 2:126
    mystics 2:112–13
    radical 2:107–11, 113
    see also Haight-Ashbury; hippies;
        Woodstock; generation gap
country music 2:114–17
    Cash, Johnny 2:11, 117, 118
    see also country-rock
country-rock 2:118–19
Courrèges, André 3:21, 25–6
Cousins, Norman 5:152
Cox, Cortland 6:35
Crane, Les 6:82
Cream 1:160, 5:134–5
credit cards 2:120–1, 3:72
Creedence Clearwater Revival 5:137,
    143
Creeley, Robert 4:63
Creutzfeldt-Jakob disease 5:172
crime and punishment 2:122–8
    right-to-counsel 3:77
    see also drugs; fraud; gun control;
        law and order; Manson
        murders; organized crime
Cronkite, Walter 1:65, 4:157, 6:70

and Vietnam 1:55, 56, 4:156,
    157, 6:89, 145
Crosby, Bing 2:115–17
Crosby, Stills, and Nash (and Young)
    3:49, 5:139, 140
Cuba
    and the Alliance for Progress
        1:41
    Bay of Pigs invasion 1:120–1,
        2:13, 72, 129, 4:179–80
    economic embargo on 2:13, 72,
        3:151
    Guevara, Ché 2:80–1, 3:102
    immigration from 3:157,
        159–60
    and JFK's assassination 4:9
    see also Castro, Fidel; Cuban
        Missile Crisis
Cuban Missile Crisis 1:86, 2:13,
    72–3, 129–32, 154, 4:16, 154
    and the CIA 1:31, 2:36, 37
    and Congress 5:46–7
    and the "hot-line" 2:73, 153,
        4:177
    spy planes 1:31
Cuban People's Party 2:12
Cultural Revolution 2:30–1, 34
Cunningham, A. A. 4:87
Cunningham, Merce 1:105
Cutler, Sam 1:44
cyclists 3:12, 13
Czechoslovakia 2:79–80
    films 3:59
    Prague Spring 2:95, 5:82–3,
        6:169

D

Daley, Richard 2:21, 56, 4:21,
    5:51–2
    and the Chicago Convention riot
        2:20, 21, 23
    and Edward Kennedy 2:16
dams 6:128, 129
Da Nang 2:133, 3:149, 4:89, 6:142
Dance Theater of Harlem 1:107
Davidson, Bruce 5:42
Davis, Angela 2:134
Davis, Edward Mills 3:112
Davis, Marvin 2:162
Davis, Miles 2:84, 135, 3:168, 172
Davis, Rennie 2:20, 22, 24
Davis, Sammy, Jr. 4:127, 6:25
Davis Sisters 3:85
Dean, James 5:71
death, definition 3:123
"Death of the Hippie" 3:16, 42,
    6:61
death penalty see capital punishment
DeBakey, Michael 3:115
decolonization/independence
    2:81–2, 136–7, 4:104, 5:29
    and African Americans 2:42
    and the CIA 2:36
    and communism 2:71, 82, 97
    and nationalism 2:97
    see also wars of liberation
Deconstructionism 4:55
defense budget 1:80, 2:70, 174,
    4:111

see also military expenditure
de Gaulle, Charles 2:138, 3:74,
    4:146, 155, 172, 6:118–19
De La Beckwith, Byron 2:49
Dellinger, David 1:52, 2:20, 24,
    4:80
Delta rockets 5:126–7
Democratic Advisory Council 3:64
Democratic Party 2:139–44, 5:50,
    51, 112
    Convention (Atlantic City,
        1964) 2:52, 53, 144
    Convention (Chicago, 1968)
        2:142
    Convention riot (Chicago, 1968)
        see Chicago Convention riot
    and labor unions 4:29–31
    presidents see Johnson, Lyndon
        B.; Kennedy, John F.
    see also Goldwater, Barry;
        Humphrey, Hubert;
        Stevenson, Adlai
Demonstration Cities Bill 3:76
Deneuve, Catherine 3:59
Deng Xiaoping 2:31
DeNiro, Vince 5:22
Dennis, David 2:53
Department of Transportation
    6:102, 130
DePugh, Robert 5:97
desegregation
    in education 1:175, 2:41, 43, 44,
        49, 5:163, 6:12
    and James Baldwin 1:103
    in transportation 2:41, 42
    see also busing; segregation; civil
        rights movement
design 2:145–50
    see also architecture; housing;
        visual arts
détente, U.S.–Soviet 1:157, 2:71,
    75, 4:154
    and China 2:28
    and the Cuban Missile Crisis
        2:73
    see also arms race; Cold War;
        Non-Proliferation Treaty;
        Nuclear Test Ban Treaty; SALT
deterrence 2:151–5, 4:67, 174,
    5:150
    and MAD 1:81–2, 2:151
    see also arms race
Detroit
    inner-city decay 3:145, 146
    race riot (1967) 1:139, 2:156–7
    Renaissance Center 3:145
    suburbs 6:56–7
Diaz Ordaz, Gustavo 6:124
Dichter, Ernest 1:8
Dick, Philip K. 5:176
Diefenbaker, John 6:114
Diem, Ngo Dinh 3:6, 74, 4:94,
    6:139, 141
Dien Bien Phu 4:169, 6:138
Dillinger, John 3:29
DiMaggio, Joe 4:115, 116
Diners Club 2:120, 121, 3:72
Dionysus 68 3:18
Dior, Christian 3:24
Dirksen, Everett 3:92, 6:167

discotheques 2:158–9, 5:68
discount stores 5:118–19
disease, conquering 3:118–20
Disneyland 2:160–3
Disney, Roy 2:161, 162
Disney, Walt
    and Disneyland 2:160–1, 162
    movies 2:160, 161, 163, 3:141
Disney World 2:162, 163
Distant Early Warning (DEW) Line
    1:29
Divided Self, The 2:112
divorce 3:62, 6:17
Dixie Hummingbirds 3:84
DNA 3:120, 5:169–70
Dobrynin, Anatoly 2:131, 132
Doctorow, E. L. 4:57
doctors, numbers of 2:177
Dodd, Thomas 3:106–7
Dole, Robert 3:105
dollar, the 2:171, 172
Dolphy, Eric 3:171
domes, geodesic 1:76
Dominican Republic 1:172
    immigrants from 3:161
    U.S. intervention 1:87, 2:80,
        164–5, 3:151–2, 4:87, 178,
        180
domino theory 1:80, 2:73–4, 6:140
Donegan, Lonnie 1:158–9
Donora (Pa.) 2:61
Doors 5:140
Dorn, Edward 4:64
Douglas 1:17, 6:64
    DC-3 1:17
    DC-9 1:16
Douglas, Helen 4:164
Douglas, Mike 6:81
    Mike Douglas Show 6:81
Doyle Dane Bernbach 1:10
draft 1:87–8, 2:166–7, 6:142
    and African Americans 1:50
    evasion 1:39, 99, 2:167
    protests 1:52, 54, 2:166, 167,
        6:142
Dragnet 6:72, 79
drive-in retail 5:121
drop-outs 3:72–3
Dr. Strangelove 2:155, 3:139, 140,
    4:170
drugs 2:128, 3:73
    and crime 4:44–5
    drug laws 4:84–5
    and sport 3:54
    see also marijuana; psychedelic
        drugs
Drysdale, Don 1:111
Dr. Zhivago 3:139, 141
Dubček, Alexander 1:157, 2:79–80,
    5:83
Du Bois, W. E. B. 4:125
Duke Ellington Orchestra 3:169
Dulles Airport 1:37, 77
Dulles, Allen 1:120, 2:35, 36,
    6:167
Dulles, John Foster 2:26, 27, 68
Dundee, Angelo 1:38
Duplessis, Maurice 5:95
Duvalier, "Papa Doc" 3:152, 153,
    160–1

Dylan, Bob 2:118, **168–9**, 5:90, 130, 142
   and folk-rock 2:169, 3:47, 48
   and Johnny Cash 2:11

E

Eagle (lunar module) 1:68, 70
Eagles 2:119
Eames, Charles and Ray 2:150
Early Bird satellite 2:89–90, 3:69, 5:126, 165
Eastwood, Clint 3:138, *139*
Easy Rider 3:138
Echo 1 (balloon) 2:88
ecology *see* environmental movement
Economic Opportunity Act (1964) 5:78, 79
Economic Report of the President (1969) 2:170
economy 2:**170–8**, 4:155, 5:70
   see also Galbraith, J. K.
Ecuador 4:38
education *see* schools and universities
Education Act (1965) 5:159
Edwards, Eldon 4:22
Egypt 2:82–3, 4:*104*, 105, 134, 6:109
Ehrmann, Jacques 4:55
Eichmann, Adolf, trial 2:**179–80**
Eichmann in Jerusalem 2:180
Eisenhower Doctrine 4:105
Eisenhower, Dwight D. 3:**5–6**, 5:74, 112–13
   the arms race 1:80, 3:6
   the Bay of Pigs invasion 1:120, 2:72, 3:6
   civil rights 3:6, 6:8, 9
   the Cold War 4:16
   communications 2:88
   and communism 2:26, 3:6
   Cuba 1:41, 120, 2:13, 72, 3:6
   the economy 2:171–2, 174, 3:6
   and education 5:158
   and health insurance 4:91
   Middle East 4:105, 134, 6:109
   military-industrial complex 1:13, 17, 2:174, 3:6, 4:**108–11**
   Native Americans 1:173
   and Nixon 3:6
   nuclear power 6:106, 131
   the space program 1:60, 4:130
   the Third World 2:*80*
   the U-2 incident 3:6, 4:16, 6:105
   Vietnam 3:6
   welfare 3:5–6
Electric Flag 5:141
electricity 6:130–2, *133*
electronics 3:**7–9**; *see also* computers
electron tube 3:7
Ellington, Duke 3:*169*
Elliott, Jack 3:47
Ellsberg, Daniel 1:57, 2:38, 6:**150–1**
El Salvador 4:37
El Teatro Campesino 3:18
Emancipation Act (1863) 2:40
Emerging Republican Majority, The

6:21
Emerson, Lake, and Palmer 5:87
employment
   affirmative action 2:143, 144, 5:114
   and civil rights 3:14, 6:**10–11**, 12
   and the postindustrial society 2:173
   see also Equal Pay Act
Engel v. Vitale (1962) 5:105, 6:69
engineers, numbers of 2:173
ENIAC (computer) 2:98, 101
Enterprise, USS 4:*148*, 149, 6:123
environment, and Congress 5:51
environmental movement 3:**10–13**, 5:170–1
   Carson, Rachel 2:10, 3:11
   see also Clean Air Acts
Environmental Protection Agency 3:13
EPCOT city/theme park 2:161, 162
Epstein, Brian 1:124–5, 125
Epton, William 3:112–13
Equal Employment Opportunity Commission (EEOC) 3:37
Equal Pay Act (1963) 3:14, 36
Equal Rights Amendment (ERA) 3:38
Erikson, Erik 4:58
Escobedo v. Illinois (1964) 4:112
Eshkol, Levi 6:28, 31
Europe
   EEC 2:138, 6:116, 117, 118–19
   immigration from 3:156
   nuclear weapons 1:82
   tourism 6:96, 97
   U.S. forces in 1:30–1, 87
   U.S. relations with 2:138, 6:**116–19**
   see also communism
European Economic Community *see* Europe, EEC
Evans, Bill 2:135, 3:169, 171
Everly Brothers 2:118
Evers, Medgar 2:49, 4:125–6
ExComm 2:129–31, 132
Executive Committee of the National Security Council *see* ExComm
existentialism 3:**15–16**, 42
experimental theater 3:**17–18**
Explorer 1 satellite 1:15, 6:44
Expo '67 1:76
exports, agricultural 1:26
extraterrestrial life 5:166, 167

F

F-4 *see* McDonnell-Douglas
F-8 4:132
F-100 Super Sabre 1:32–3
F-105 *see* Republic
Faas, Horst 5:42
fabrics 3:20
"faction," TV documentary 2:5
Fairchild Camera and Instrument Company 3:8
Fair Housing Act (1968) 3:147,

4:126
Fairport Convention 3:49
Fantastic Voyage 1:89
"farm bloc, the" 1:24
Farmer, James 2:44, 46, 57
   a Freedom Rider 2:42, 46, 3:60
farming *see* agriculture
Farrakhan, Louis 4:75, 137
fashion 3:**19–27**, 5:72, 6:**15–17**
   hippie 1:*98*, 99
FBI 3:**28–31**
   illegal actions 2:77, 126
   and Native Americans 1:47
   racial bias in employment 6:11
   see also Hoover, J. Edgar
FBI, The 3:28
Federal-Aid Highway Act (1962) 6:103
Federal Bureau of Narcotics 2:128
Federal Communications Commission 2:85, 4:70–1, 6:133
Federal Trade Commission 1:11
Feldman, Morton 2:60
Fellini, Federico 3:57, 58
Fellowship of Reconciliation (FOR) 6:26, 27
Female Eunuch, The 3:40
Feminine Mystique, The see Friedan, Betty
feminist movement 3:**32–41**
   and equal pay 3:14, 36
   and the Equal Rights Amendment 3:38
   Redstockings 3:34, 37, 40, 6:36
   science fiction writers 5:176
   and sexual issues 3:40–1
   see also birth-control pill; Friedan, Betty; women
fertilizers 1:*22*, 23–4
films
   American Indians 1:47
   Beatles' 1:125, 160
   classification 3:137
   cop 3:138
   costume dramas 3:139
   crime 3:138
   depicting housewives 3:34
   Disney 2:160, 161, 163, 3:141
   drive-in 2:92
   Elvis Presley's 5:85
   foreign *see* foreign films
   Frank Sinatra's 6:24, 25
   gay 3:66
   in-flight 1:36
   James Bond (spy) 2:36, 3:140
   musicals 3:138
   and nuclear disaster 4:170, 172
   religious themes 5:104
   science fiction 5:177
   sexual themes 6:18–19
   war 3:138–9
   westerns 3:138, *139*
   see also Hollywood
Fire Next Time, The 1:103
First Amendment 2:95
fishing 4:51, *52*
Flatt, Lester 2:116
Flavin, Dan 6:159
flexible response *see* Cold War; deterrence; nuclear weapons

Flight Research Center 1:16–17
Florida, Disney World 2:162, 163
"Florida Paper" 3:40
flower power 3:**42–3**
Flying Burrito Brothers 2:118, 119
Flynn, Sean 5:39
FM radio 2:92, 5:102, 135
Foggy Mountain Boys 2:116
folk music 3:**44–7**
   folk-protest singers 2:110, 168, 3:*47*, 73
   and Joan Baez 1:101
   see also Dylan, Bob
folk-rock 2:169, 3:47, **48–9**, 5:67, 130–1
   and Bob Dylan 2:169, 3:47, 48
   progressive 5:87
   Simon and Garfunkel 3:48, 5:131, 6:**22–3**
   see also Byrds
Fonda, Jane 3:140
food stamps 5:52
Fool, The 3:27
football 3:**50–5**, 4:49–50
   Brown, Jim 1:**168**
   Super Bowl 6:**62–3**
footwear 3:21, 24
Ford (company) 1:91, 2:105, 174
   assembly lines 2:103
   and Detroit 3:145
Ford cars, advertising 1:10
Ford, Gerald 6:155, 167
Ford, Henry 2:103
Ford, Henry, II 3:145
Ford, John 3:138
Foreign Assistance Act (1961) 3:151, 152
foreign films 3:**56–9**
   see also Bardot, Brigitte
Foreman, George 1:39, 154
Forman, James 2:44, 5:109
Forman, Milos 3:59
Fortas, Abe 6:66, *67*
Forti, Simone 1:106–7
Fosbury flop 5:11
Fosse, Bob 1:163–4
Foss, Lukas 2:60
4'33" (musical work) 2:58
Fourteenth Amendment 2:40, 126
Four Tops 4:118, 120, 121
fragging 1:171, 3:**100–1**
France
   and NATO 2:138, 4:146, 147, 6:119
   nuclear weapons 2:155, 4:146, 147, 172, 6:119
   and SEATO 6:5–6
   and Vietnam 4:102–3, 6:138
   see also de Gaulle, Charles
Frankenheimer, John 3:137
Frankenthaler, Helen 6:160–1
Franklin, Aretha 3:86, 6:39
Fraser, Dawn 5:8
fraud, credit-card 2:121
Frazier, Joe 1:39, 152, 154
Freed, Alan 5:100
Freedom Riders 2:42, *43*, 45, 3:**60–1**, 4:22, 125
Freedom Schools 2:52, 6:37
Freedom Summer 2:52, 109, 6:**36–7**

Free Speech Movement *see* Berkeley Free Speech Movement
freight 6:99, 100–1
Frelimo 6:171
Friedan, Betty 3:32, 33, 34–6, **62**
  and the advertising industry 1:10, 3:36
  The Feminine Mystique 1:10, 3:33, 34, 62
  and NOW 3:38, 4:136
Friedkin, William 3:138
Friedlander, Lee 5:41, *42*
Friendly, Fred 4:157
Froines, John 2:24, 25
Frost, Robert 4:*62*
FSM *see* Berkeley Free Speech Movement
Fulbright, J. William 1:54–5, 57, 3:105, 4:26, 5:49, 6:145
Fuller, R. Buckminster 1:76
Fuller, Samuel 3:56
furniture 2:150

G

Gable, Clark 3:136, *138*, 4:*116*
Gagarin, Yuri 1:61, 3:*63*, 67, 4:99, 131, 6:*43*
Gaia Theory 3:11, 5:168
Galaxy *see* Lockheed, C-5A
Galbraith, J. K. 1:7–8, 2:175, 3:*64*, 4:26, 5:73, 160
gambling, and the Mafia 5:25
"garage bands" 5:129, 131
Garcia, Jerry 3:88, 4:*56*
Gargan, Joe 2:15
Garner, Errol 3:169
Garvey, Marcus 3:29
Garwood, Bobby 4:103
gas, natural 6:132–3
Gault, Gerald 2:126–8
Gay, Connie B. 2:114–15
Gaye, Marvin 4:118, 121
gay movement 3:65–6, 6:17
  Stonewall riot 3:65, *66*, 6:17, 51
  theater 6:95
Gell-Mann, Murray 5:169
Gemini program 1:17, 60, 63, 3:*67*–71, 4:131, 6:*73*
General Motors 1:91, 2:174, *176*
  and car safety 2:6–7, 104, 3:126
  strikes 2:105
generation gap 3:*72*–3
  see also fashion
genetic engineering 5:169–70
Genet, Jean 2:22, 4:56
Geneva Accords (1954) 3:74, 4:32; 6:138–9
Geneva Convention 5:80, 81
geology 5:173–4
George Washington (submarine) 2:*152*, 5:127
germanium 3:7
Germany
  and NATO 4:147
  see also Berlin Wall; Brandt, Willy
Gernreich, Rudi 3:20, 22, 23
Getz, Stan 3:169
Ghana 2:137

ghettos 3:75–6, 147
  see also Harlem race riot; Watts riot
Giancana, Sam 5:24
Giap, Vo Nguyen 4:89, 168, 169, 6:138
GI Bill of Rights (1944) 5:159
Gibson, Bob 1:*111*, 113
Gideon, Clarence 3:77
Gideon v. Wainright (1963) 3:77, 6:69
Gillespie, Dizzy 3:169, *170*
Gilligan's Island 6:79
Gilmore, Gary 2:127
Gilruth, Robert 3:68, 4:101
Ginsberg, Allen 1:176, 3:15, 4:63, 6:*32*
  and drugs 2:128, 3:127, 128
Glaser, Milton 2:149
Glass, Philip 2:60
Glenn, John H. 1:16, 62, 2:*87*, 4:*96*, 97, 99–101, 131
global warming 3:13
Glushko, Valentin 6:43
Godard, Jean-Luc 3:56, 57
Godoy, Hector García 2:165
go-go girls 2:158
Gogolak, Pete 3:51
gold reserves 2:171
Goldwater, Barry 1:*10*, 11, 2:140, 141, 3:78–9, 5:54, *57*, 113–14
  and Medicare 4:92
  and nuclear weapons 2:152, 3:78–9
  and radio 5:102
golf 3:*80*–3, 4:50
Golitsyn, Anatoly M. 2:35
Gonzales, Pancho 6:85
"gonzo" journalism 4:70
Goodman, Andrew 2:52, 53, 4:23
Good Neighbor policy 4:178–9
Gordon, Richard F. 3:71
Gordy, Berry 1:146, 4:117, 120, 121, 5:65, 6:38
Gospelaires 3:84
gospel music 3:84–7
Gould, Glenn 2:58
Gould, Jay 5:50–1
Graduate, The 3:136, 138, 5:154, 6:23
Graham, Bill 3:108
Graham, Billy 5:104, *110*
Graham, Martha 1:104–5
grape-pickers' strike (Calif.) 2:17, 4:24
Grateful Dead 2:111, 119, 3:*88*, 108, 109, 127, 5:93, *136*
Great Britain
  antiwar movement 1:52, 6:119
  and the blues 1:146–9
  and the EEC 6:118–19
  nuclear weapons 1:82, 2:155, 6:119
  pop music from *see* British Invasion
  rock music 5:128–30
  U.S. relations 6:118, 119
  and Vietnam 6:146, 156
Great Debates 2:90, 4:*12*–13

Great Depression 1:90
Great Society 2:123, 142–3, **3:89–94**
  and the Cold War 2:76, 77
  and education 5:161
  and healthcare 3:93, 114, 4:92
  and housing 3:145
  and immigration 3:156
Green Acres 6:71
Green berets (Special Forces) 1:79, 87, 3:*95*, 130, 4:33
Greenberg, Clement 6:159–60
green cards 1:25
greenhouse effect 3:13
Green, Rev. Al 6:41
Green Revolution 1:26, 3:*96*–9
Green v. New Kent County (1968) 1:177
Greer, Germaine 3:40
Gregory, Dick 1:130, 5:153–4, *156*
Griffin, Merv 6:80–1, 83
Merv Griffin Show 6:80–1, 83
Griffin, Rick 2:149, 3:88
Andy Griffith Show 6:79
Griffiths, Martha 3:14, 37
Griffiths, Philip Jones 5:40–1
Grissom, V. I. "Gus" 1:16, 63, 64, 3:*68*, 4:*96*, 97, *99*
Gromyko, Andrei 2:130, 131
Gropius, Walter 1:72, 75, 2:145
gross national product 2:176
Grotowski, Jerzy 3:18
Group, The 4:56
Growth of the American Republic, The 3:11
Gruen, Victor 1:*74*, 2:162
grunts **3:100**–1
Guatemala, Shigella infection 3:121
Guerrilla Warfare 3:102
Guevara, Ché 2:80–1, **3:102**
Guideline missiles 1:32
Guinea 2:82
gulags, Soviet 2:76
gun control **3:106**–7
Gunsmoke 2:86, 91, 6:71
Guthrie, Arlo 5:91
Guthrie, Woody 2:168, 3:44–5, 5:90
Guy, Buddy 1:146, 148, 149

H

Haber, Robert 6:52, 53
Haggard, Merle 2:117, 5:91
Haight-Ashbury 2:111, *112*, 3:42, **108–9**
Haiphong 3:**110**–11, 6:143, 152
Hair (musical) 1:165, 3:43, 128, 6:17, 95
hairstyles 3:26, 72
Haiti 3:152–3
  immigrants from 3:160–1
Haley, Alex 4:75
Hall, Gus 2:95, 3:30
Hamer, Fannie Lou 2:49, 53–4
Hamilton, Charles V. 1:139–40, 2:8
Hamilton, Richard 5:60–1
Hammarskjöld, Dag 6:108
Hammond, John 2:168
Hancock, Herbie 2:135, 3:170, 172

Hancock Tower 1:77, 3:164
Hansberry, Lorraine 6:95
happenings 3:17, 6:18, 164
hard bop 3:170
Harding, Warren G. 1:92
Hardin, Tim 5:130–1
Hargis, Billy James 5:97, 98
Harlem Globetrotters 1:116
Harlem race riot 3:76, 112–13, 4:*40, 42*
Harrington, Michael 2:97, 3:90
Harris, David 1:101
Harris, Emmylou 2:119
Harrison, Al 1:50
Harrison, George 1:124
Harrison, Wallace K. 1:*74*
Havana, March on (1959) 2:*12*
Hawkins, Coleman 3:170
hawks and doves 1:86, 99
Hawn, Goldie 2:158, 6:77
Hayato, Ikedo 6:123
Hayden, Tom 3:73, 94, 6:53, 54
  and the Chicago Convention riot 2:19, 20, 23
  and the Chicago Seven trial 2:24, 25
  and the March on Washington (1965) 1:50
Hayes, Bob 5:8
Haynsworth, Clement 6:68
Hayward, Stanley 3:*152*
health and healthcare 3:114–21
  antismoking campaign 1:48–9
  birth-control pill 1:134–5, 3:40, 6:15
  heart transplants 3:115, **122–3**
  thalidomide tragedy 6:90–1
  see also Medicare
heart transplants 3:115, **122–3**
Hefner, Hugh 6:14, 16
Heinlein, Robert 5:176–7
Heinz (company) 2:174
Heizer, Michael 6:160
helicopter carriers 4:88
helicopters 1:87, 88, 4:88
  in Vietnam 1:31, 88, 614, 2:*73*, 3:115, 6:*150*
Heller, Joseph *see Catch-22*
Hello Dolly! (musical) 1:*163*, 164, 165
Hell's Angels, and the Altamont Festival 1:43–4, 3:88
Helms, Richard 2:37–8
Help 2:118
Hendrix, Jimi 3:124–5, 5:135–6, 6:41
Henry, Aaron 4:126–7
hepatitis 3:118–20, 5:171
Herman, Jerry 1:164
Herreshoff, David 3:30
Herzog 1:128, 4:56–7
Hewlett-Packard (company) 3:9
Higgins, Marguerite 4:162
highways 6:57, 100–1, *102*
Highway Safety Act (1966) 3:**126**
Highway Trust Fund 6:57
Hill, Herbert 4:28–9
Hillman, Chris 2:119
hippies 1:*98*, 99–100, *165*, 2:*108*,

111–12, 113, **3**:72, **127–8**
clothes **3**:22, 26–7
Death of the Hippie **3**:*16*, 42, **6**:*61*
drugs **2**:109, 128, **3**:127, **5**:*93*
environmental interests **3**:11–12
flower power **3**:*42–3*
jewelry **3**:25
and people's parks **2**:111–12, **3**:12
posters **2**:149
"religious" **5**:110
and the sexual revolution **6**:17–18
Summer of Love **2**:111, **6**:*60–1*
the term "hippie" **6**:32
underground newspapers **2**:*110*
and William Burroughs **1**:176
see also existentialism; Haight-Ashbury
History of Decision Making Process on Vietnam, The (report) **1**:57
Hitchcock, Alfred **3**:56, 139
Hitchcock, Henry Russell **1**:73
HIV infection **3**:121
Hoa Hoa **4**:135
Ho Chi Minh **3**:74, 131, **4**:169, **6**:138
Ho Chi Minh Trail **1**:32, **3**:*129–31*, **4**:33, **6**:140
hockey **3**:*132–5*, **4**:50, **5**:12, **6**:113–14
Hoffa, Jimmy **4**:30
Hoffman, Abbie **2**:19, 20, **6**:180
Chicago Seven trial **2**:24
March on the Pentagon **3**:42, **4**:80, 81, **6**:18
Hoffman, Dustin **3**:136
Hoffman, Julius J. **2**:24, 25
Hoff, Marcian "Ted" **2**:100
Hogan's Heroes **6**:79
Holly, Buddy **2**:115, **5**:128
Hollywood **3**:*136–41*
see also films
Holocaust
and the Eichmann trial **2**:179–80
"industry" **6**:29
homosexuals *see* gay movement
Honduras **4**:35
Hoover, Herbert **2**:140
Hoover, J. Edgar **2**:24, 52, **3**:28, *142–3*, **4**:*41*
and organized crime **3**:29, **5**:20, 22
and Robert Kennedy **3**:29, 31, *142*, 143
Hoover's FBI **3**:29
Hopkins, John **3**:120
Horn, Daniel **1**:*49*
"hot-line", U.S.–Soviet **2**:73, 153, **3**:105, **4**:177
hot pants **3**:22, **6**:*15*
Hound Dog missiles **1**:29, **5**:125
House Un-American Activities Committee **1**:129, **2**:95, 108
housing **1**:72, **3**:*144–7*, **5**:70–1
ghetto **3**:76
segregation in **3**:76, 147, **6**:9
see also suburbia

Houston, population **6**:56
Howe, Gordie **3**:134
Howlin' Wolf **1**:149
Hoxha, Enver **5**:83
HPSCHD **2**:59
Hubbard, L. Ron **5**:179–80
Huber, Robert **3**:30
Huebler, Douglas **6**:165
Huerta, Dolores **2**:17
Hulanicki, Barbara **3**:20, 23
Hull, Bobby **3**:*133*, 134, 135
human rights **3**:*150–3*
Humphrey, Hubert **3**:*154–5*, **6**:*127*
and the Chicago Convention riot **2**:22, 23
and civil rights **1**:178, **2**:57, **3**:154
and labor unions **4**:31
and Native Americans **1**:45, **4**:140
presidential bids **1**:11, **2**:140, 141, 144, **3**:154, 155, **5**:56
and segregation **1**:178
and Vietnam **1**:56, **3**:155, **6**:147
Hunter, Meredith **1**:44
Huntley, Chet **4**:157–8
Hutton, Bobby **2**:62
Huxley, Aldous **5**:92
hydrogen bombs **1**:78, 79, **4**:174, **5**:*70*

I

IBM **2**:99, 100, 101, 174, **6**:179
ICBMs *see* missiles
IFP petitions **3**:77
immigration **1**:25, **3**:*156–61*, **6**:113
laws and quotas **2**:143, 144, **3**:156, 161
imports **2**:177
car **1**:93, **2**:174, *178*, **3**:126
oil **5**:34
steel **3**:164
In Cold Blood **2**:5, **4**:70, 112
independence *see* decolonization/independence
India, Green Revolution **3**:97, 98, 99
Indian Civil Rights Act (1968) **1**:46
Indians of All Tribes (IAT) **1**:46–7
Indonesia **2**:*80*, 81, **6**:171
industry
and suburbia **6**:56
see also coal industry; iron and steel industries; petroleum industry
In Persona **3**:57
In a Silent Way **2**:135, **3**:172
Institute of Design **2**:146
Institute for the Study of Non-Violence **1**:101
insurance, health **3**:116, **4**:91
integrated circuits **2**:87, 89, 91, 100–1, **3**:8, **5**:164
Intel Corporation **2**:100, **3**:9
intelligence community **2**:36
Intelsat **2**:90
satellites **2**:*89*, **5**:126, 165
Inter-American Music Festivals **2**:60
Inter-American Peace Force **2**:165

intermodal transportation **6**:100–1
International Biology Program **5**:171
International Style **1**:72–3, **2**:146
Interstate Highway Act (1956) **1**:92
Intertel **5**:25
Ionesco, Eugène **3**:16
Iron Curtain **2**:68
Iron Hand missions **1**:32–3
iron and steel industries **3**:*162–7*
and pollution **2**:*61*
Israel **4**:104–7
the Eichmann trial **2**:*179–80*
Meir, Golda **4**:93
see also Six-Day War
Itliong, Larry **4**:*24*
Ives, Charles **2**:58
Iwerks, Ub **2**:160

J

Jackson, Blyden **2**:44
Jackson, George **1**:58, **2**:134, **4**:56
Jackson, James **6**:12
Jackson, Jesse **1**:177, **3**:147
Jackson, Jimmy Lee **2**:54–5
Jackson, Mahalia **3**:85, **5**:91
Jackson Movement **2**:49
Jagger, Mick **1**:44, 146–7, 149, 160, **3**:24
Japan
cars from **2**:174
economy **4**:111
immigration from **3**:161
technology **2**:177, **3**:8–9, **6**:*122*
U.S. relations with **6**:116, **120–3**
Jarrett, Keith **3**:170
jazz **3**:*168–72*
Armstrong, Louis **1**:84
Brubeck, Dave **1**:*169*, **3**:169
Coltrane, John **2**:84
Davis, Miles **2**:135
and rock **3**:172
J. Edgar Hoover Building **3**:*28*, 29
Jennings, Waylon **2**:11
Jesus Christ Superstar **5**:89
Jet Propulsion Lab. **1**:14, 15
Jet Set **1**:34, 35, 37
Jetstar (jet) **1**:35
jewelry **3**:25
Jewison, Norman **3**:137
Jews **5**:104, *106*, 111
Jim Crow **2**:40, 42, 45, 56, **6**:8, 10, 13
and Nixon **2**:57
see also civil rights movement; segregation
Job Corps **3**:91, **5**:78
Johns, Jasper **5**:*60*, 61–2
Johnson, Lady Bird **3**:*92*, *169*, *174*, **4**:*9*, **5**:*77*
Johnson, Lyndon B. **3**:89, **173–4**
the aerospace industry **1**:13
American Indians **1**:45, 174
the antiwar movement **1**:50, 51, 52, 55
the arts **4**:52, **6**:92
becomes president **4**:6, *9*
China **2**:18, 27–8
civil rights **1**:175, **2**:51, 54, 55,

56, **3**:92, 173–4
and Clark Clifford **2**:63
and communications **2**:88
desegregation in schools **1**:175
détente **2**:*74*
the Dominican Republic **2**:164, 165, **4**:180
and education **1**:175, **3**:93–4, **5**:160–3
the environment **3**:12
Great Society program *see* Great Society
and health provision **3**:93, **4**:92
and housing **3**:145
and J. Edgar Hoover **3**:29, 143
the labor unions **4**:31
and McGeorge Bundy **1**:171
the Middle East **6**:29
and Native Americans **4**:140
presidential bid **5**:55
satirized **5**:155–6
the space race **1**:60–1, 63, **6**:*73*
Vietnam **1**:32, 86, 2:28, 63, 77, **3**:74, 94, 103–4, 105, **5**:26, 46–7, **6**:139–47, 156
and voting rights **2**:55, 56, **3**:174
war on crime **2**:123, 128
War on Poverty **1**:13, 141, **5**:76, 77, 78–9
"wise men" **2**:63
Johnson, Philip **1**:72, 73, 75
Johnson, Rafer **5**:7
Johnson, Robert **1**:149
Johnston, Bruce **1**:123
Joplin, Janis **3**:108, 175, **5**:141, **6**:*177*
Journey of Reconciliation **2**:46, **3**:60
Judd, Donald **6**:164
jug bands **5**:133
Jules and Jim **3**:56, 57
jumbo jets **1**:18
Junky **1**:176
Jupiter rockets **1**:15, **5**:*126*
Justice Department **4**:43

K

Kaiser, Ray **2**:150
Kameny, Frank **3**:66
Kantrowitz, Adrian **3**:122, 123
Kaprow, Allan **5**:43
Karl, Frederick **4**:57–8, 73
Kaufman, Irving **6**:68
Kearney, Michael **2**:*5*
Keating, Kenneth **5**:99
Kefauver, Estes **5**:74–5
Kelley, William M. **4**:57
Kellogg **1**:*7*
Kelly, Ellsworth **6**:162
Kelly, Gene **1**:107
Kelsey, Frances **6**:91
Kennedy (Idlewild) Airport **1**:18, 34, 77
Kennedy, Edward "Ted" **4**:*159*
and busing **1**:179
Chappaquiddick **2**:15–16
presidential hopeful **2**:16
Kennedy, Jacqueline **3**:176, *178*, **4**:5–6, *8*, *9*
Kennedy, John F. **2**:142, **3**:177–8,

179, 4:*108*
the Alliance for Progress 1:41,
  4:34, 152
the arms race 1:80, 4:113–14,
  153, 5:152
the Army 1:85–6, 87
assassination 2:51, 3:31, 54,
  179–80, **4:5–9**, 5:*38*, 6:67,
  167
Bay of Pigs invasion 1:120, 121,
  2:72, 4:152
Berlin/Berlin Wall 1:87, 131,
  132, 3:178, 4:153
"Camelot" 3:178
China 2:26–7
civil rights 2:41, 48, 49, 50,
  3:178, 4:154–5, 6:9–10
the Cold War 2:*71*, 72, 3:178,
  4:16, 170
communications 2:88
Cuban goods 2:13
Cuban Missile Crisis 2:129–31,
  3:178, 5:46–7
defense 4:87
détente 3:178, 4:*172*
domestic policy 4:155
the Dominican Republic
  3:151–2
the economy 2:172, 4:155
emerging nations 2:136–7
Europe 6:117–18
the FBI 3:29, *142*, 143
food stamps 5:52
funeral 2:90–1
the green berets 3:95
health insurance 4:91
and Johnson 3:174
Kennedy-Nixon debates 2:90,
  4:12–13
and the March on Washington
  4:82
Native Americans 4:138–9
New Frontier **4:152–5**
Peace Corps 2:137, 3:178,
  4:152, 5:29–30
presidential bid 1:11, 2:90,
  139–40, 142, 3:154, 177,
  4:12–13, 124–5, 5:47, 54
quotes from 4:154
sexual conduct 2:77, 3:178,
  4:116
space 1:*14*, 60, 61–2, 63, 4:153,
  6:*44*, 45
the steel industry 3:162–3
television 2:90
Vietnam 1:86, 4:154, 6:139, 140
women's rights 3:14, 36, 37
Kennedy, Robert F. **3:179–80**
assassination 4:10–11, 5:41
civil rights 2:41, 49, 57, 3:179,
  6:35
the Cuban Missile Crisis 2:129,
  130, 131, 3:179, 4:154
in Europe 6:*119*
the FBI 3:28–9, 31, *142*, 143
Freedom Riders 3:60, 61, 179
and Johnson 3:174, 180
and Martin Luther King, Jr.
  4:11, 19, 6:27
Native Americans 4:140, 141

presidential bid 4:65
and right-to-counsel 3:77
Vietnam 1:54–5, 3:180
war on organized crime 5:20–1,
  22
Kent State killings 1:57, 2:108, 113,
  6:148
Kepes, Gyorgy 2:*148*
Kerner Commission 2:157, 3:76,
  4:46, 6:173
Kerouac, Jack 1:176, 3:15
  On the Road 3:127, 5:72–3;
  6:125
Kesey, Ken 2:111, 3:127, 128, 4:59,
  5:93
Keynes, John Maynard 2:172
KGB, defections from 2:35
Khe Sanh 4:14–15, 89, 6:89,
  145–6, 175
Khrushchev, Nikita 2:*70*, 77, 94–5,
  4:16, 5:*46*
  the Berlin Wall 1:131–2
  the Cold War 1:121, 2:*71*, 72
  the Cuban Missile Crisis 2:72,
    94, *129*, 130, 132
  détente 4:*173*
  and Leonid Brezhnev 1:157
  "peaceful coexistence" 2:94, 96,
    6:171
  and Richard Nixon 2:102
  the space race 1:63
  the U-2 incident 4:16, 6:104,
    105
Kind of Blue 2:84, 135, 3:168
King, A. D. 2:46
King, B. B. 1:148, 149
King, Billie Jean **4:17**, 6:86
King, Carole 5:65, 69
King Crimson 5:86–7
King, Martin Luther, Jr. **4:18–19**,
  166
  and the antiwar movement 1:50,
    52, 2:56
  assassination 2:57, 62, 4:11,
    20–1
  and black power 1:138, 139, 140
  and civil rights in Birmingham
    2:45, 46–8
  funeral 3:85, 4:20–1
  and housing 3:147
  "I have a dream" speech 2:50,
    4:19, 82, 83
  jailed 2:42–3, 47, 54, 4:18
  and James Meredith 1:138
  and J. Edgar Hoover 3:29–30,
    143
  the March on Washington
    (1963) 2:50, 4:19, 82–3
  quoted on JFK's assassination
    2:51
  and Ralph Abernathy 1:6,
    2:46–7
  support for Johnson 2:51
Kingston Trio 3:*44*, 46
Kinks 5:134
Kinsey, Alfred 3:65, 6:14, 15
Kirk, Roland 3:171
Kishi, Nobusuke 6:122
Kissinger, Henry 1:171, 2:34, 83
  and Vietnam 1:86, 2:83, 5:27,

6:154, 155
KMart 5:119
Knight, Maria 3:86
Knights of the Clock 3:65
Knoll Associates 2:147
"knowledge industry" 1:151
Knowles, John 5:58
Komarov, Vladimir 6:46
Kopechne, Mary Jo 2:15
Korea, North, and the USS *Pueblo*
  2:81, 5:94
Korean War 1:85
Korea, South, and the UN 6:109
Korolev, Sergei 6:43, 44
Kosuth, Joseph 6:165
Kosygin, Alexei 1:157, 6:146
Koufax, Sandy 1:111, 113
Kubrick, Stanley 2:155, 3:139, 140
Ku Klux Klan 2:40, 48, 3:61,
  4:22–3
kuru 5:171–2
Ky, Nguyen Cao 1:172, 6:142, 143,
  147, 151, 156

L

labor, immigrant 1:25
labor relations **4:24–31**
  and the Bracero Program 1:25
  and the California grape-pickers'
    strike 2:17
  and discrimination 6:11
  steel unions 3:166
La Cosa Nostra (LCN) 5:22
La Dolce Vita 3:57, 58
Laing, R. D. 2:112
Landsat satellites 5:168
Lansky, Meyer 5:21, 25
Laos 2:36, 3:*130*, 131, **4:32–3**, 87,
  6:150
  MIAs 4:103
  Pathet Lao 2:36, 4:32, 33
  and SEATO 6:5
LaPorte, Roger Allen 1:51
Larkin, Philip 3:72
Larsen, Jack Lenor 2:147
Larson, Lance 5:7
lasers 5:174
Last Exit to Brooklyn 3:66
Latin America **4:34–9**
  Green Revolution 3:97–8
  and the OAS 4:179–80
  U.S. intervention in 2:80,
    164–5, 3:151–2, 4:*178*, 180
  see also Alliance for Progress;
    Cuba
Latin American Free Trade
  Association 4:38, 179
L'Avventura 3:57–8
Law Enforcement Assistance
  Administration (LEAA) 2:123,
  128, 4:44, 45
Lawford, Peter 6:25
law and order **4:40–7**
  see also crime and punishment;
    FBI; organized crime
Lawson, James 6:26, 27, 34
Leadbelly 3:44–5
League of Nations 6:106
Lean, David 3:139

Learjet 1:35
Lear, William P. 1:35
Leary, Timothy 2:62, 3:42, 4:58–9
  and drugs 2:111, 128, 3:128,
    4:85, 5:93
Leave It to Beaver 3:32
Lebanon 4:86–7
Le Duc Tho 5:27
Led Zeppelin 5:*141*, 142
Lee, Brenda 2:115
Le Guin, Ursula 5:176
Lehrer, Tom 5:153
Leinsdorf, Erich 2:59
leisure industry **4:48–53**
  see also Disneyland; tourism
LEMAR 2:128
Lennon, John 1:124, 126, 127,
  5:*140*, 6:81
Leno, Jay 2:9
Leonov, Aleksey 6:46
Lesage, Jean 5:95
Letterman, David 2:9
Levittowns 1:95–6, 6:57–8
Levitt, William 1:95, 3:145
Lewis, Jerry Lee 2:11
Lewis, John (SNCC leader) 2:42,
  50, 55, 3:60, 4:21, 82, 6:*34*, 36
Lewis, John L. (labor leader) 2:66,
  3:166
Library Awareness Program 3:28
Libya 2:82
Lichtenstein, Roy 5:63; 6:165, 166
Life 2:92, 4:70, 97
lifting bodies 4:132–3, 5:126
light artists 6:159
Lincoln Center 1:*74*, 4:52, 5:16,
  6:*92*, 95
Lindsay, John 1:171, 2:157, 6:21
Lindsey, Hal 5:110
linguistics, and Noam Chomsky
  2:33
Lipscomb, G. "Big Daddy" 3:54
Liston, C. "Sonny" 1:38–9, 152
literature **4:54–64**
  civil rights *see* Baldwin, James
  gay novels 3:66
  science fiction 1:89, 5:175–8
  and the sexual revolution 6:14,
    15
  spy novels 2:36
  see also Bellow, Saul; book
    publishing; Burroughs,
    William; Capote, Truman;
    Catch-22; Mailer, Norman;
    Updike, John
"Little Boxes" (song) 3:144
Little Red Book 2:30, 31, 4:79
Little Rock, desegregation in schools
  2:41, 4:124, 5:163, 6:9
Liu Shao-chi 2:30
Lloyd, Charles 3:172
Loan, Nguyen Ngoc 6:89
lobbyists, political 5:58
Lockheed 1:35, 4:111, 6:64
  C-5A Galaxy 1:30, 31
  C-130 6:5
  C-141 Starlifter 1:30, 31, 4:*110*
  Constellation 1:36
  Jetstar 1:35
  U-2 6:*104*

Locks, Seymour 3:109
Lodge, Henry Cabot 2:63, 4:16
Lomax, Alan 3:44, 46
Lomax, John Avery 3:44
Lombardi, Vince 3:53
London, fashion 3:19
Lon Nol 6:7, 153, 156
Look 2:92, 4:70
López Mateos, Adolfo 6:125
Loren, Sophia 3:140
Los Angeles
    the gay movement 3:65
    ghettos 3:75
    immigrants 3:161
    population 6:56
    smog 2:61
    suburbanization 6:59
    see also Watts riot
Louis, Morris 6:158, 161
Louis X 4:75
Louvin, Charlie and Iva 2:118
Lovell, James A. 1:65, 68, 3:69, 70, 71
Lovelock, James 3:11, 5:168
Love, Mike 1:122
Lovett, Willie Joe 2:49
Lovin' Spoonful 3:49, 5:132, 133
Lower, Richard 3:123
LSD 2:111, 149, 3:127
    experiments with mind control 2:38
    and Timothy Leary 2:111, 128, 3:128
Luce, Henry 4:70
Lucy Show, The 6:76, 77
Lumet, Sidney 3:136
Lumumba, Patrice 2:137
lunar modules 1:62, 63, 67, 68
Lunar Orbiter missions 4:133
Luna space probes 6:44, 46
Lynd, Staughton 2:25
Lyon, Danny 5:42

M

M60 tank 1:85, 87
M113 armored personnel carriers 1:87
MacArthur, Douglas 6:120, 121
McCain, John 5:81
McCarthy, Eugene 3:174, 4:65
    antiwar stance 1:55, 2:144, 4:65
    and the CIA 2:38
    and Edward Kennedy 2:16
    presidential bid 4:10, 65, 66, 5:52, 55
McCarthy, Joseph 1:133, 2:14
    anticommunism 2:26, 5:73–4
    and Robert Kennedy 3:179
McCarthy, Mary 4:55, 56
McCartney, Paul 1:123, 124, 126, 127, 3:125
McClellan, John 3:28–9, 5:20
McCone Commission 6:173
McCone, John 2:35, 36, 37, 129
McDermott, Terry 5:12, 13
McDivitt, James A. 1:67, 3:69
McDonald's 5:123
McDonnell (company) 1:17, 4:97
McDonnell-Douglas 1:17

A4 Skyhawk 2:151, 4:149, 162
F-4 Phantom 1:32–3, 2:177, 4:87
McDrew, Chuck 3:73
McGovern, George 2:23, 144, 4:165, 6:54
McGuinn, Roger 2:118
McGuire, Barry 2:110
McKissick, Floyd 1:138, 2:44, 54
McLaughlin, John 3:172
McLuhan, Marshall 4:54, 66
McMahon, Ed 2:9
Macmillan, Harold 2:136, 3:178, 6:118
McMillan, James 1:179
McNamara, Robert 3:177–8, 4:67, 81, 6:150
    and the Cuban Missile Crisis 2:129, 132
    and race riots 2:157
    and Vietnam 1:52, 53, 55, 4:67, 6:144–5
McQueen, Steve 3:138
Macy's (New York) 2:170
Maddox, USS 3:103, 104, 105, 4:148, 6:141
Mafia
    and JFK's assassination 4:9
    see also organized crime
magazine publishing 1:166, 4:68–71
    and the sexual revolution 6:14, 16, 19
"Magic Bus" 3:127, 5:93
magic mushrooms 5:93
Magic Sam 1:146, 147, 149
Mahesh Yogi, Maharishi 2:112
Mailer, Norman 2:5, 4:55, 59, 70, 72–3
    antiwar movement 1:52, 53–4
    Chicago Convention riot 2:22
makeup 3:23, 27
Malamud, Bernard 4:57
Malcolm X 1:58, 2:43, 4:74–5, 6:172
    quoted 2:50, 51, 54, 4:74
Mamas and the Papas 3:49
Mandela, Nelson 1:58, 59, 6:171
Man for All Seasons, A 1:163, 3:141
"Man in the Hathaway Shirt, The" 1:9, 10
Manila Treaty 6:5, 7
Mann, Herbie 3:171
Manson murders 3:43, 128, 4:76–7
Mantle, Mickey 1:113, 4:78
Mantovani 6:48
Maoism, in America 2:31
Mao Zedong 2:26, 29, 30–1, 4:79
Marburg fever 3:121
"March against Fear" 1:138, 167, 2:8
March on the Pentagon see Pentagon, March on
March on Washington see Washington, March on
Marcuse, Herbert 2:134
Margold Report 6:10
marijuana 2:109, 128, 3:73, 4:84–5
Mariner probes 4:133, 5:168
Marines 4:86–9
    in Vietnam 4:14, 15, 89, 95

Maris, Roger 1:113, 4:78
Markham, Paul 2:15
marriage
    divorce 3:62, 6:17
    interracial 6:9
Marshall, Burke 2:48
Marshall Plan 6:116
Marshall, Thurgood 4:41, 126
Martin, Agnes 6:162
Martin, Dean 6:25
Martin, George 1:125, 127
Maslow, Abraham 2:112
mass media 2:87
Masters and Johnson 6:15
Mastroianni, Marcello 3:58
Matsu 2:27
Mattachine Society 3:65, 66, 6:51
Matus, Don Juan 2:112
Mayall, John 1:160; 5:138
May, Elaine 5:154
Mayfield, Curtis 6:41
Mays, Willie 1:5, 4:90
Means, Russell 1:45
Meany, George 4:26, 27
Medicaid 3:93, 114, 115–16, 4:92
medical research, unethical 3:119
Medicare 3:93, 114, 115–16, 4:91–2
Medina, Ernest L. 4:122, 123
Mehta, Zubin 2:59–60
Mei-ling Soong 2:18
Meir, Golda 4:93
Mekong Delta 4:94–5, 150
Melman, Seymour 2:177
Mercury program 1:16, 17, 60, 62, 4:96–101, 131, 6:44–5
Meredith, James 1:138, 2:43, 44, 4:126, 6:9–10
Merry Pranksters 3:108, 109, 127, 5:92, 93
Merseybeat 1:160
mescaline 5:92, 93
Method acting 6:93
Metropolitan Opera Association 5:17
Mexico
    Green Revolution 3:97–8
    illegal immigrants from 1:25, 3:159
    migrant workers from 1:25, 3:158
    U.S. relations with 6:124–7
MIAs 4:102–3, 5:81
Michoud 1:62, 63
microprocessors 2:100
microscopes 5:168
microsurgery 3:115
Mid-Canada Line 1:29
Middle East 4:104–7, 5:34
    see also Israel; Nasser, Gamal Abdul
Mies van der Rohe, L. 1:72, 2:145, 6:159
Mighty Clouds of Joy 3:84
military expenditure 2:174–5, 177, 178, 4:110, 111, 153
military-industrial complex 1:13, 17, 2:174, 3:6, 4:108–11
Military Sales Act (1968) 3:153
Millar, David 1:51–2

Millenarianism 5:110
Miller, Arthur 1:162, 4:115
Miller, Steve 3:109
Steve Miller Band 5:137
Millett, Kate 3:36, 4:72
"Million Dollar Quartet" 2:11
Mills, Billy 5:8
Mills, C. Wright 2:19
Mills, Wilbur 4:92
mind control 2:38
Mine Safety Act (1969) 2:65
Minh, Duong Van 6:156
minimalism 2:60, 6:162–4
mining, coal see coal industry
miniskirts 3:19, 72
Minuteman ICBMs 1:28, 4:113, 146, 175, 177, 5:124–5
Miranda v. Arizona (1966) 4:112, 6:68
missile gap 4:113–14, 153, 5:151
missiles
    air-to-air 1:29–30
    air-to-ground (AGMs) 1:32–3
    antiaircraft 2:153, 6:115
    antiballistic (ABMs) 5:127, 150, 151
    antiship 1:80–1
    cruise 1:28, 29
    intercontinental ballistic (ICBMs) 1:27, 28, 29, 79, 4:113, 145, 175, 5:124–6, 127
    missile-warning stations 2:154
    submarine-launched ballistic (SLBMs) 4:175
    surface-to-air (SAMs) 1:32–3, 5:125
    see also Cuban Missile Crisis
Mississippi
    civil rights protests 2:42, 51–3
    Freedom Summer 2:52, 109, 6:36–7
Mississippi Freedom Democratic Party 2:53, 6:36, 37
Mississippi University, black student enrolment 1:87, 2:43, 44
Mister Rogers' Neighborhood 6:74
Mitchell, Arthur 1:107
Mitchell, Charlene 2:95
Mitchell, Clarence 4:125, 126
Mitchell, John 2:57, 4:47, 6:83
Mob see organized crime
Mobe 4:80
Mobilization for Youth 3:94
Moby Grape 2:111, 5:141
modernism 1:72–3, 2:145–8, 6:158–9
"mod" style 3:24
Moholy-Nagy, László 2:145, 146
Mondale, Walter 2:17
Monessen (Pa.) 3:165
monetarists 2:173
Monkees 5:67, 68, 6:72, 73
Monroe Doctrine 2:79, 4:178
Monroe, Marilyn 3:136, 138, 178, 4:115–16
Monterey Festival 3:125, 5:136–7, 6:60
Montgomery bus boycott 1:6, 2:41, 4:18, 124, 6:27

Moody Blues 5:86
moon
    first journeys to 1:64–9, 6:46–7
    landings 1:68–9, 2:90, 91, 6:47
    radio signals bounced off 2:88
    robotic missions to 4:133
moonscooper launches 6:47
Moore, Charles 1:75–6
Moore School of Engineering 2:98
Mormons 5:108
Morris, Esther 3:34
Morrison, Jim 2:112
Morrison, Norman 1:51
Morse, Wayne 3:103, 105, 153
Moscoso, Victor 2:149
Moses, Bob 2:42
Moses, Robert 6:179
Mosk, Stanley 3:82
Motivational Research, Institute for 1:8
Motor Vehicle Air Pollution Act (1965) 1:94
Motown 4:117–21, 5:65, 6:38–9
Mouse, Stanley 2:149, 3:88
movies see films
movie theaters 2:91–2, 5:121
Moynihan, Daniel P. 5:116, 117
Mozambique 6:171
Mr. Tambourine Man 3:47
Ms. 3:33
Muhammad, Elijah 3:30, 4:74, 137
Muhammad, Fard 4:137
Mulligan, Gerry 1:169
multinational corporations 2:174
Murdoch, Rupert 2:16
Murrow, Edward R. 4:157
Muscle Shoals 6:39–40
Museum of Modern Art (New York) 2:146, 147
music see under different categories of music
Musicircus 2:59
Muskie, Edmund 2:144, 3:155
Muslims 5:109
mutual assured destruction 1:81–2, 2:151
My Fair Lady 3:138, 141
My Lai massacre 1:88, 4:122–3, 6:146, 147, 150
mystics 2:112–13

N

NAACP 2:39–40, 43, 4:124–7, 6:11
    and capital punishment 2:127
    and sit-ins 4:124, 6:26
    and Vietnam 2:56
NACA 1:12–13, 4:130
Nader, Ralph 2:6–7, 104, 3:126
Naked Lunch 1:176
Namath, Joe 6:63
Namibia 1:58
napalm 4:128–9
NASA 4:130–3, 5:168, 6:44–5
    and communications 2:88–9
    first astronauts 1:16, 3:63, 4:97
    and research 1:15
    see also Apollo program; Gemini program; Mercury program;

space race
Nash, Diane 6:35
Nash, Philleo 1:173, 174
Nashville, and civil rights 2:40, 6:27, 35
Nashville Sound 2:115, 117
    and country-rock 2:119
Nasser, Gamal Abdul 4:105, 107, 134, 6:28–9
Nathans, Daniel 3:120
National Advisory Committee for Aeronautics 1:12–13, 4:130
National Committee for Equal Pay 3:14
National Defense Education Act (1958) 1:15, 4:110, 5:158, 159
National Fertility Study 1:135
National Highway Safety Bureau 2:7
National Institutes of Health 3:114, 117
nationalism 2:97
National Liberation Front 4:135, 6:134, 140
National Moratorium 1:57, 2:110
National Organization for Women 3:38–9, 41, 4:136, 6:18
national parks 3:11
National Political Congress of Black Women 2:32
National Review 5:98–9
National Security Act (1947) 2:38
National Security Agency 4:102
National States Rights Party 2:52
National Television System Committee (NTSC) 2:85, 86
National Traffic and Motor Vehicle Safety Act (1966) 2:7, 3:126
National Urban League 1:141, 2:43
    and Vietnam 2:56
National Women's Party 3:38
National Women's Political Caucus 3:33, 39
Nation of Islam 2:43, 44, 4:137, 6:13
    and Malcolm X 4:74, 137
    and Muhammad Ali 1:39, 4:137
Native Americans 4:138–43
    and Alcatraz 1:45, 46–7, 174
    American Indian Movement 1:45–7, 100
    Bureau of Indian Affairs 1:173–4, 4:139
    poverty 5:76, 77
    "termination" 1:173, 4:138, 140
NATO 2:69, 82, 4:144–7, 6:169
    aircraft 1:30–1
    and France 2:138, 4:146, 147, 6:119
    and the U.S. Army 1:86, 87
Navy 4:95, 148–51
    see also Marines; submarines
NBC 4:156, 5:102, 6:70
"Negro," rejection of 1:139, 143
Negro American Labor Council 4:26–7
Nelson, Ricky 2:118, 5:65
neocolonialism 2:82, 6:171
Newark, race riots (1967) 1:138–9
Newark Community Union Project (NCUP) 3:94

New Bauhaus 2:146
New Country 2:119
New Criticism 4:54
New Frontier 4:152–5
New Hamphire primaries 5:55
Newhart, Bob 5:153
New Haven (Conn.), sit-outs 2:43–4
New Industrial State, The 2:175, 3:64
New Journalism 4:70
New Left 2:19, 20, 23, 4:24
    and the counterculture 2:108
    and the FBI 3:30–1
    and flower power 3:42
New Look style 2:146, 147
    of Christian Dior 3:24
New Lost City Ramblers 3:47
Newman, Barnett 6:160–1
Newport Folk Festival 2:169, 3:44, 47, 48
Newport Jazz Festival 1:149, 3:170, 171
New Right 2:23
news and current affairs 4:156–9
newspapers 1:19, 164–5, 4:160–3
Newton, Huey P. 1:136, 137, 140, 2:8
New Wave 3:56, 57–8, 59
New York City
    antiwar demonstrations 1:52–3
    architecture 1:73–7, 2:146
    blackout (1965) 1:145
    immigrants 3:161
    organized crime 5:23–5
    population 6:56, 57
    slums 3:90
    smog 2:61
    World's Fair 6:178–9
New York City Opera 5:17–18
New York Review of Books 4:58
New York Times 4:160, 162–3, 6:150
Nicaragua 4:180
Nice 5:87
Nichols, Mike 3:136, 5:154
Nicklaus, Jack 3:81
Nigeria, oil reserves 5:34
Night of the Iguana, The 1:162
Nikolais, Alwin 1:105–6
Nixon Doctrine 2:82, 6:7, 147
Nixon, Richard M. 4:164–5, 5:48, 49, 113
    the antiwar movement 1:55, 6:20, 21
    "Checkers" speech 4:165
    China 2:29, 95, 155, 6:151
    and civil rights 1:175, 2:56, 57, 5:114, 115
    and communism 2:97
    and desegregation 1:175, 178–9
    and Eisenhower 3:6
    extols virtues of consumer society 2:102
    and Henry Kissinger 2:83
    Japan 6:123
    and J. Edgar Hoover 3:29, 143
    Kennedy–Nixon debates 2:90, 4:12–13, 5:54
    and law-and-order 4:40, 42–3,

47, 5:115
Native Americans 1:47, 174, 4:138, 140, 143
    and poverty 5:79, 117
    presidential bid (1960) 2:90, 139, 141, 3:177, 4:12–13, 5:47, 53–4
    presidential bid (1968) 2:142, 3:155, 5:58, 115–17
    satirized 5:156
    the Silent Majority 6:20–1
    southern Africa 2:137
    Soviet Union visit 3:102
    and Spiro Agnew 1:19
    and student rebellion 2:24
    the suburbs 5:116
    supersonic transport 6:65
    the Supreme Court 1:175, 4:47, 6:66, 68, 69
    use of the veto 5:49, 117
    Vietnam 1:56–7, 86, 2:74–5, 3:105, 4:165, 5:27, 115–16, 6:147–55
    war on drugs 2:128
    see also Watergate affair
Nkrumah, Kwame 2:82, 5:32
Nobel Prizes 4:166–7
Nobody Knows My Name 1:103
Noland, Kenneth 6:161–2, 163
Nonaligned Movement 2:71
Non-Proliferation Treaty (1968) 1:83, 2:74, 4:173, 177, 5:150
NORAD 1:29, 6:112
North American (company) 1:17
    XB-70 Valkyrie 1:28–9
North Atlantic Treaty Organization see NATO
North Vietnamese Army 4:14–15, 94, 168–9, 6:152
Nosenko, Yuri I. 2:35
Nova (rocket) 3:67
NOW see National Organization for Women
Noyes, Eliot 2:146
nuclear fallout shelters 4:170–1
nuclear physics 5:168–9
nuclear power 5:170, 6:106, 131
Nuclear Test Ban Treaty (1963) 2:78, 96, 4:171, 172–3, 177, 5:150
nuclear weapons 4:174–7
    and the Cuban Missile Crisis 2:73
    dropped from aircraft 1:27–8
    and effects on health 3:121, 4:172, 5:152
    missiles 1:28, 29–30, 2:69, 5:125, 127
    and NATO 4:144–7
    "nuclear triad" 2:152
    Soviet 1:82, 2:69, 70, 151, 4:113, 114, 175, 176
    test bans 1:80, 82–3, 2:78, 96, 4:154, 172–3
    triggering 2:154
    United States 2:151–2, 152, 174
    see also arms race; atomic bombs; détente, U.S.–Soviet; deterrence; hydrogen bombs

nudity 3:23, 6:*14*, 17, 18
Numbers 3:66
Nureyev, Rudolph 1:105, 107

O

Oaks, Richard 1:46–7
OAS *see* Organization of American States
Oates, Joyce Carol 4:*58*, 60–1
obscenity 6:14–15
Ochs, Phil 2:110, 3:47, 179, 5:91
O'Dell, Jack 2:44
Oerter, Al 5:10–11
Office of Economic Opportunity 1:45, 5:78–9
Office of Law Enforcement Assistance 2:123
Office of Public Safety (OPS) 3:153
offices, open-plan 2:148
Ogdensburg Agreement 6:112
Ogilvy, David 1:10
oil *see* petroleum industry
Okinawa 6:123
Oklahoma, Native Americans 4:140
Oklahoma City, and sonic booms 6:65
Oldenburg, Claes 5:62–3
Oldham, Andrew Loog 5:145
Olympic Games 5:5–13
    and black power 1:142, 5:9
Omnibus Crime Control and Safe Streets Act (1968) 2:128, 3:29, 4:43–4
Onassis, Aristotle 1:180, 3:176
One Day in the Life of Ivan Denisovich 2:76
One Flew over the Cuckoo's Nest 3:127, 4:59, 5:93
Ono, Yoko 3:17, 5:*140*, 6:81
On the Road 3:127, 5:73
Op Art 3:20, 5:14–15, 6:163
OPEC 5:33, 35
Open Theater 3:18
opera 5:16–19
    Callas, Maria 1:**180**, 5:17
Operation Abolition 2:108
Operations, military
    CHAOS 2:38
    Eagle Pull 6:157
    Flaming Dart 4:149–50
    Frequent Wind 6:157
    Game Warden 4:150
    Homecoming 5:81, 6:154
    Market Time 4:150
    Mongoose 2:36
    Pan America 1:41
    Rolling Thunder 1:32, 4:150, 6:142
    Shu-Fly 4:95
Organization of Afro-American Unity 2:43, 4:75
Organization of American States (OAS) 4:**178–80**
    and the Dominican Republic 2:165, 6:109
    and Ellsworth Bunker 1:172
organized crime 3:29, 5:20–5
Ormandy, Eugene 2:59, 60
Oroville Dam 6:129

Orth, Franklin 3:107
Osborne Brothers 2:116
Oswald, Lee Harvey 2:92, 3:31, 4:5, 6–9, 5:*38*, 39, 6:167
Other America, The 2:97, 3:90
Other Voices, Other Rooms 2:5
Our Depleted Society 2:177
Owens, Buck 2:117
Oz 2:149
Ozzie and Harriet 3:32, 5:*65*, 68, 71

P

Paar, Jack 2:9, 6:*80*, 81
pacemakers, heart 3:114, 115, 5:172
Pacifica Radio 4:159, 5:103
Packard, Vance 1:8
Pageos (satellite) 2:88
painting *see* visual arts
Palestine Liberation Organization 4:106, 107, 6:28, 30
Palestinians 4:104, 6:30
Palmer, Arnold 3:80–1, 82
Pan-African Congress 1:59
Pan-African Studies *see* Black Studies
Pan Am 1:34, 35
    building (N.Y.C.) 1:75
Panama 4:36
Panetta, Leon E. 2:57
pantyhose 3:22
paperbacks 1:150–1
Paradise Now 3:18
Paraguay 2:80, 4:37
Paris Peace Accords (1973) 4:103, 169, 5:27, 6:154
Paris Peace Talks 1:172, 4:103, 5:26–7, 6:152, 153
Paris, unrest (1968) 1:130, 2:138, 5:28
Parker, Col. T. 5:84, 85
Parker, William H. 6:173, 174
Parks, Rosa 2:41, 4:18, 124, 5:75
Parks, Van Dyke 5:88–9
Parsons, Gram 2:118, 119
particle accelerators 5:169
Pasarell, Charlie 6:75
Pasolini, Pier Paolo 3:58
Passaro, Alan 1:44
Patterson, John 3:60–1, 4:124–5
Patton, George S. 2:*41*
Paul, Alice 3:38
Pauling, Linus 4:166
Paul VI, Pope 1:134
Pawnbroker, The 3:136–7
Paxton, Tom 3:47
payola scandal 5:64, 100, 128
Peace Corps 2:137, 3:151, 154, 178, 4:152, 5:29–32
Peace and Freedom Party 2:62
Peace of San Francisco 6:121
Peale, Norman V. 5:108
Pearl 3:175
Pei, I.M. 1:*72*, 73
Penitentiary Study Commission 2:124
Penkovsky, Oleg 2:35
Penn, Arthur 3:141
Pentagon, March on (1967) 1:*51*, 52, 53–4, 3:42, 4:*43*, 80–1, 6:18
Pentagon Papers 1:57, 2:38, 4:163,

6:149, 150–1
people's parks 2:111–12, 3:12
Percy, Walker 4:61–2
Performance Group 3:18
Perkins, Carl 2:11, 118
permissiveness 5:75
Peru 4:*37*, 38
pesticides 1:*21*, 23–4
    and *Silent Spring* 2:10, 3:11, 5:170
Peter, Paul, and Mary 3:*47*, 48, 73, 5:91
petrochemical industry 5:36
petroleum industry 5:33–7
    oil reserves 3:11, 5:34–6
    oil spills 3:12, 5:37
Pet Sounds 1:123, 2:169
peyote 5:92
Pfizer (company) 2:174
Phantom *see* McDonnell-Douglas
Philadelphia Plan 5:114
Philby, Kim 2:35
Philippines
    Green Revolution 3:97, 98, 99
    immigration from 3:157, 161
    and SEATO 6:6, *7*
Phillips, Kevin 6:21
Philly records 6:41
photography 5:38–43
photorealism 6:165
Phoumi Nosavan 4:33
"piggyback service" 6:100–1
pill, birth-control *see* birth-control pill
Pincus, George 1:135
Pine Tree Line 1:29
"pink economy" 1:10
Pink Floyd 5:87, 6:48
Pioneer probes 6:44
Planet of the Apes 5:178
Planned Parenthood 1:134, *135*
Plante, Jacques 3:*134*, 135
plants, hybrid 1:22–3
plasmids 3:121
plate tectonics 5:174
Plath, Sylvia 4:63
Playboy 6:14, 16, 19
Playboy Clubs 6:16, 18
Player, Gary 3:81
Plessy v. Ferguson (1896) 2:40, 41, 6:8, 10
"plumbers," White House 1:57
pneumonia 3:121
Poco 2:119
poetry 4:62–4
Poitier, Sidney 3:137
Polanski, Roman 3:59, 139
Polaris missiles 1:81, 4:113, *145*, 150, 5:127
    in Britain 6:119
pole-houses 3:146
police 4:112
Politics of Experience, The 2:112
politics and government 5:44–59
    and advertising 1:*10*, 11
    "homophile politics" 3:65–6
    the presidency 2:77, 3:89, 5:46–9
    and satire 5:155–6

and television 1:19, 2:90, 5:53–4, 6:70
    see also Democratic Party; Republican Party
Pollock, Jackson 5:72
pollution, air 2:61, 67, 3:10, 5:37
    and cars 1:94, 2:61
    and cyclists 3:12
pollution, water 3:*12*
Pol Pot 4:169, 6:153
Poons, Larry 5:14, 15
Poor People's March (1968) 2:57, 3:30
Pop art 3:20, 5:60–3, 6:160, 164
    see also Warhol, Andy
pop music 5:64–9, 6:48
    Beach Boys 1:*122–3*, 5:86, 131–2
    see also Beatles; British Invasion; discotheques; Motown; rock music
Popular Front for the Liberation of Palestine 6:30
population, explosion 3:10, 11
Port Huron Statement 2:108, 6:53–5
Poseidon missiles 1:81, 5:127
posters, design 2:148, 149
postindustrial society 2:173
postmodernism 2:148–50
postwar world 5:70–5
    economy 2:170–1, 5:70
    Eichmann trial 2:**179–80**
    ghettos 3:75
    and punishment of crime 2:125
    women 3:34, 36, 5:74, 6:18
    see also NATO
poverty 1:21, 2:97, 5:76–9
    see also ghettos; Great Society
Poverty Act (1964) 3:91
Powell, Michael 3:139
"power elite" 6:53
Powers, Gary 1:31, 3:6, 5:125, 6:104, 105
POWs 5:80–1, 6:154
Prague Spring see 2:95, 5:82–3, 6:169
presidency 2:77, 3:89, 5:46–9
    elections 5:54–8, 74–5, 106
Presidential Commission on Marihuana and Drug Abuse 2:128
Presidential Commission on the Status of Women 3:14, 36
Presidential Papers, The 4:73
Presley, Elvis 2:11, 114, 118, 5:84–5, 128, 142–3
    gospel music 3:87
Price, Cecil 2:52, 53
Price, Leontyne 5:18, 19
primaries 5:52, 74–5
printing 4:68–9, 161
prisons 2:124, 128, 4:46–7
    black prison writers 4:56
    experiments on prisoners 3:119
Process Church 4:77
Procul Harum 5:87
production lines 2:103, 105
Progressive Labor Movement 3:113
progressive rock 5:86–9, 135
Protestants 5:106–11

protest music **2**:110, 168, **3**:*47*, 73, **5**:**90–1**, 140
psychedelic drugs **2**:109, 111, 128, **3**:127, **5**:**92–3**
and mind control **2**:38
psychedelic movement **2**:148, 149, **3**:88
bands **5**:140
clothes **3**:27
light shows **3**:109
Psychedelitype **2**:149
Public Broadcasting Act (1967) **5**:103
Public Broadcasting Service **6**:74, 83
publishing *see* book publishing; magazine publishing
Pueblo incident **2**:81, **5**:94
Puerto Rico, immigrants from **3**:159
pulsars **5**:165–6

Q

Qaddafi, Muammar **2**:82
Quant, Mary **3**:19–20, 21–2, 23–4
quasars **5**:165
Quebec, separatism **5**:95
Quemoy **2**:27

R

Rabanne, Paco **3**:25–6
Rabbit, Run **6**:111
Raborn, William **2**:37
radar-directed missiles **1**:32
radar system, SAGE **1**:29
radiation **3**:119, 121
radical right **5**:**96–9**
radio(s) **2**:92, **5**:**100–3**, **6**:133
and country music **2**:114
FM **2**:92, **5**:102, 135
news/current affairs **4**:156–9
stereo **2**:92
transistor **3**:9, **5**:*101*, 102
Voice of America **2**:77
rail travel **1**:35, **6**:99–100, *101*
"rainbow coalition" *see* New Left
Rainer, Yvonne **1**:106
Ramparts **4**:71
Rand, Ayn **5**:97
RAND Corporation **1**:14
Randolph, A. Philip **2**:50, **4**:26, 27–8, 82
Rand, Paul **2**:147
Ranger missions **4**:133
Rascals **5**:130
Rat Pack **6**:25
Ratterman, George **5**:21–2
Rauschenberg, Robert **5**:43, 61
Ray, James Earl **4**:20, *21*
RCA **2**:85
Reader's Digest **2**:97, **4**:70
Reagan, Ronald **2**:112, **4**:25, **5**:46, *59*, 114
Real Majority, The **6**:21
recessions **2**:172
Rechy, John **3**:66, **4**:59
Reconstruction **2**:40
Redding, Otis **6**:39
Red Light Bandit **2**:127
redlining **3**:147

Redstockings **3**:34, 37, 40, **6**:36
Reeves, Jim **2**:117
"Reforger" exercises **1**:31
refugees **3**:156, 159, 160
rehabilitation **4**:46–7
Reich, Steve **2**:60
Reinhardt, Ad **6**:163, 164
religion **5**:**104–11**, **6**:72
Republican Party **5**:56, **112–17**
presidents *see* Eisenhower, Dwight D.; Nixon, Richard M.
voters **2**:139
see also Goldwater, Barry; radical right
Republic F-105 Thunderchief **1**:32–3
Resnais, Alain **3**:57
retail industry **5**:**118–23**
Reunion **3**:73, **6**:53
Reuther, Walter **4**:26, 27
rhesus system **5**:171
Rhodesia **6**:110
rhythm and blues **5**:132
Ribicoff, Abraham **2**:6, 10, 23
Rice, Thomas "Daddy" **6**:8
Richards, Keith **1**:44
Richardson, Tony **3**:59
Ridenhour, Ronald **4**:123
Riesman, David **4**:58
Riggs, Bobby **4**:17
Riley, Bridget **5**:14, 15, **6**:163
Rio Pact **4**:145
riots (1964–8) **2**:56, **3**:76, 147, **4**:21
Detroit **1**:139, **2**:**156–7**
Harlem **3**:76, **112–13**, **4**:*40*, *42*
see also Kerner Commission
Rise and Fall of Great Powers, The **2**:176
Rive Gauche (boutique chain) **3**:24
ROAD divisions **1**:86
roads *see* highways
Robbins, Jerome **1**:104
Robbins, Marty **2**:117
Robertson, Marion "Pat" **6**:72
Robertson, Oscar **1**:118
Robertson, Robert **1**:47
Roberts, Oral **5**:104–5, 110
Robinson, Jackie **1**:114, **4**:124, **5**:75
Robinson, W. "Smokey" **4**:119
rockabilly acts **2**:118
Rockefeller Foundation **3**:97, 98
Rockefeller, Nelson **3**:78, **4**:36, **5**:54, 55
rocket technology **1**:15, 16–17, 80, **5**:**124–7**, **6**:42
X-15 program **1**:17, **4**:**131–2**
rock music **5**:69, **128–43**
acid-rock **5**:**136–7**
country-rock **2**:**118–19**
festivals *see* Altamont Festival; Woodstock
and jazz **3**:172
progressive/art **5**:**86–9**, 135
see also Beatles; British Invasion; Grateful Dead; Hendrix, Jimi; Joplin, Janis; pop music
rock-'n'-roll **2**:114, 118, **3**:72, **5**:71–2, 137
eclipse **5**:128
and the sexual revolution **6**:14

Rockwell, George Lincoln **5**:97
Rockwell, Norman **4**:69, **6**:159
Roessel, Robert A. **4**:141–2
Roe v. Wade (1973) **1**:175, **3**:41, **6**:19
Rohmer, Eric **3**:56, 57
Rolling Stone **4**:69, 71, **5**:86, 139
Rolling Stones **1**:149, 160–1, **5**:86, *131*, 132, 140, 143, **144–5**
and the Altamont Festival **1**:43, 44, **6**:177
and the blues **1**:146–7
and Gram Parsons **2**:119
hairstyles **3**:26
Rollins, Sonny **3**:170, *172*
Roman Catholics **5**:98, 106, 107–8, 109, 111
and contraception **1**:134, **5**:108
schools **3**:93, **5**:158
Romania **5**:83, **6**:169
Romney, George K. **1**:91, **5**:55
Ronstadt, Linda **2**:119
Roosevelt, Eleanor **3**:14, 36, **5**:74, **6**:50
Roosevelt, Franklin D. **4**:82, 178–9
Rose, Wesley **2**:114–15
Ross, Diana **4**:*117*, 120, 121
Rothko, Mark **5**:146, **6**:158, 160–1
Roth, Philip **4**:*54*, 56, 57, 59
Roth, Samuel **6**:14
Rowan and Martin's Laugh-In **2**:158, **6**:33, 71, 76, 77
Rozelle, Pete **3**:51, 54
rubella, vaccine **3**:118, **5**:171
Rubin, Jerry **4**:80, 81, **6**:180
Chicago Convention riot **2**:19, 20, 21
Chicago Seven trial **2**:24
and Vietnam Day **1**:130
Ruby, Jack **2**:92, **4**:5, 8, 9, **5**:*38*, 39
Rudolph, Paul **1**:77, **2**:*145*
Rudolph, Wilma **5**:5, 7
Rush, Otis **1**:146, *147*
Rusk, Dean **2**:*74*, **3**:*64*, 152, **4**:*34*, **5**:147
and the Cuban Missile Crisis **2**:129, 131, 132
Russell, Bill **1**:*116*, 117–18
Russ, Joanna **5**:176
Russo, Anthony J. **1**:57, **6**:151
Rustin, Bayard **4**:82, **6**:174
Ruth, G.H. "Babe" **1**:5, 113
Ryman, Robert **6**:164

S

7-Eleven stores **5**:121–2
700 Club **6**:72
SA-2 Guideline missiles **1**:32
Saarinen, Eero **1**:76–7, **2**:150
Sabah **6**:6
Sabin, Albert B. **3**:118
Safdie, Moshe **1**:76
Sagan, Carl **5**:172
Sahl, Mort **5**:153, 156
Saigon **1**:55, 56, **5**:**148–9**, **6**:*88*, 89, *134*, 138, *142*, 145, 157
Saint Laurent, Yves **3**:24, 25
St. Lawrence Seaway **6**:114, *115*
St. Louis, inner-city decay **3**:146

Salinger, J.D. **3**:72, **4**:56–7
Salisbury, Harrison **4**:162
SALT **1**:82–3, **4**:114, 173, 177, **5**:**150–1**
Samos satellite **1**:15
Samuelson, Paul **2**:174
SANE **1**:51, **5**:**152**
San Francisco **3**:108
see also Haight-Ashbury
San Quentin, jail **2**:124, *127*
San Rafael, Hall of Justice shootout **2**:134
Santa Fe Opera **5**:19
Sartre, Jean-Paul **3**:15, 16, **6**:146
Sassoon, Vidal **3**:*21*, 26
satellites **1**:15, 60, 61, **2**:70, **5**:165, **6**:42, 44
communications **2**:87–8, 89–91, **4**:133, **5**:164
"killer" **1**:83
navigation **5**:165
satire **5**:**153–6**, **6**:79
Bruce, Lenny **1**:170, **5**:153
and *Catch-22* **2**:14, **5**:154
SAT tests **5**:162
Saturday Evening Post **2**:92, **4**:68, 69
Saturday Night Fever (movie) **2**:159
Saturn rockets **1**:*61*, 62–3, 64, 65, 66, **5**:*126*, 127
Savio, Mario **1**:129, 130, **2**:109, 110
Scarp missiles **4**:175
Schaffner, Frank J. **3**:137
Schechner, Richard **3**:18
Schirra, Walter M., Jr. **1**:16, **3**:70, **4**:*96*, 97, 101
Schlafly, Phyllis **3**:38
Schlesinger, Arthur, Jr. **1**:7–8, **3**:*177–8*
schools and universities **1**:97–8, *100*, **5**:**157–63**
and the antiwar movement **1**:51, *56*, 57, 98–9
basketball **1**:115
bilingual education **3**:157
Black Studies **1**:143–4
and books **1**:150, 151
"duck-and-cover" practice **4**:170
federal aid **3**:93–4, **5**:158–9
and the military **4**:110
Native American education **4**:140–2, **5**:77
numbers of teachers **2**:173
photography studies **5**:40
recreation studies **4**:49
school buses **6**:98
school prayer **5**:105, **6**:69
segregation **6**:9–10
and war veterans **5**:159
Women's Studies **3**:41
see also desegregation, in education
Schwarz, Fred **5**:97–8
Schweickart, Rusty **1**:67
Schwerner, Michael **2**:52, 53, **4**:23
Schwerner, Rita **2**:53
science fiction **1**:89, **5**:**175–8**, **6**:74
science and technology **5**:**164–74**
and agriculture **1**:22–3
and education **5**:158
numbers of scientists **2**:173

see also aerospace industry; computers; electronics
scientology **5:179–80**
SCLC **1:**6, **2:**43, **4:**19, **6:**35–6
and formation of SNCC **2:**41
see also Abernathy, Ralph
Score (satellite) **2:**88
Scott, David R. **3:**70, 71
Scranton, William **3:**78
Scruggs, Earl **2:**116
sculpture **6:**164
SDS *see* Students for a Democratic Society
Seale, Bobby **1:**136, 137, **2:**8, 21, 24, 25
SEALS, Navy **4:**95
SEATO **4:**145, **6:**5–7
Second Sex, The **3:**33–4
Seeger, Pete **1:**101, **2:**169, **3:**44–5, **5:**90–1
SEEK **2:**32
Seekers, the **3:**49
segregation **2:**40–1, **6:8–13**
in education **6:**9–10
in housing **3:**76, 147, **6:**9
in transportation **2:**42
see also civil rights movement; desegregation; Freedom Riders; Jim Crow; Montgomery bus boycott
Seigenthaler, John **3:**60
Selby, Hubert **3:**66, **4:**59
self-actualization theory **2:**112
Sellers, Peter **3:**140–1
Sell, Evelyn **3:**30
Selma to Montgomery march **2:***47*, 55–6, **6:**37
Sesame Street **6:**74, 75
sewage **3:***12*
Sex and the Single Girl **1:**166
Sexton, Melvin **4:**23
Sexual Behavior in the Human Male **3:**65, **6:**15
Sexual Politics **3:**36, **4:**72
sexual revolution **3:**40, 72, 73, **6:14–19**
Brown, Helen Gurley **1:166**
see also birth-control pill
Shanghai Communiqué **6:**7
Shannon, Del **2:**118
Sharpville Massacre **1:**59
Shea, John **1:**64
Shelton, Robert **4:**22, 23
Shepard, Alan B., Jr. **1:**16, **2:***172*, **3:**67, **4:***96*, 98–9, 131, **6:**44–5
Shockley, William B. **3:**7, 8
shopping malls **1:**74, **4:**51, **5:**118, 122
see also retail industry
Shorter, Wayne **2:**135, **3:**170, 172
Shoup, David M. **4:**87–9
Shrike missiles **1:**33, **4:**151
Shrimpton, Jean **3:**24
Shriver, Sargent **3:**91, **5:**29
Shumway, Norman **3:**115, 122–3
shuttle services, air **1:**36
Shuttlewoth, Fred **2:**45, 46–7
Siegel, Don **3:**56
Sifford, Charlie **3:**81, 82
Sihanouk, Norodom **6:**153

Silent Majority **6:20–1**
Silent Spring **2:**10, **3:**11, **5:**170
silicon **3:**7–8
chips *see* integrated circuits
Silicon Valley **3:**8, 9, **6:**58–9
Simon and Garfunkel **3:**48, **5:**131, **6:22–3**
Simon, Neil **1:**163
Simon, Paul **3:**47, 48
Sinatra, Frank **6:24–5**
Sir Douglas Quintet **5:**131
Sirhan, Sirhan Bishara **4:**10
sit-ins **2:**39, 40, 108, **4:**124, **6:26–7**, 34
sit-outs **2:**44
Six-Day War **4:***105, 106*, 107, 134, **5:**40, **6:28–31**
postwar resolutions **6:**108
skiffle **1:**158–9, **5:**129
skiing **4:**51
Skinner, B. F. **2:**33
skyjackings **1:**37
skyscrapers **1:**72–3, *76*, 77, **3:**164
slang **3:**100, **6:32–3**
Slayton, "Deke" **1:**16, **4:***96*, 97
Sly and the Family Stone **5:**141, **6:***40*, 41
SM-62 Snark missiles **1:**28, 29
Small Faces **5:**141
"Smart" weapons **4:**151
Smiley, Glenn **6:**26, 27
Smith, Al **2:**140
Smith, Hamilton O. **3:**120
Smith, Howard W. **3:**14, 37
Smith, Margaret Chase **3:**14, 37, **5:**53
Smithson, Robert **6:**160
Smith, Tommie **1:**142, **5:**9
Smith, Tony **6:**164
smog **1:**94, **2:**61, **3:**10, **5:**37
smoking **3:**121, **5:**171
antismoking campaign **1:**48–9
unethical experiments **3:**119
Smothers Brothers **5:**154, 155
Snark missiles **1:**28, 29
SNCC **1:**138, **2:**44, 52, 108, **4:**125, **6:34–7**
and Africa **2:**50–1
against the Vietnam War **2:**56
and black nationalism **2:**56
and the Black Panthers **1:**140, 142
formation **2:**41, **4:**124, **6:**34
see also Carmichael, Stokely
"Soccer War" **4:**180
Socialist Realism **6:**159
Soleri, Paolo **1:**76
Solid Waste Disposal Act (1965) **6:**132
Solzhenitsyn, Aleksandr **2:**76
Somosa, Luis **4:**180
Song Cycle **5:**88–9
sonic booms **6:**65
Sontag, Susan **4:**54, 56
Sony (company) **3:**9
Sorensen, Theodore "Ted" **2:**129, 140, **3:**177–8
Soul on Ice **2:**62, **4:**56
soul music **5:**69, **6:38–41**
and gospel singers **3:**87

see also Brown, James; Motown
Sound of Music, The **3:**138, 141
Souphanouvong, Prince **4:**32, 33
South Africa, apartheid **1:**58–9, **5:**6, **6:**109
Southeast Asia Treaty Organization *see* SEATO
Southern Christian Leadership Conference *see* SCLC
South West Africa **1:**58
Souvanna Phouma **4:**32, 33
Soviet Russia in China **2:**18
Soviet Union
communism **2:**68, 69–70, 94–5
and the Cuban Missile Crisis **2:**72, 73
and Czechoslovakia **2:**94–5, **5:**82–3, **6:**169
dissidents **2:**76, 77–8
gulags **2:**76
"hot-line" **2:**73, 153, **4:**177
and Jews **2:**78
military parades **2:***69, 94*, **5:**124
nuclear weapons **2:***69*, 70, 151, **4:**113, 114, 175
Olympic Games **5:**6
post-Stalin **2:**77–8
racial clashes **2:**78
religion **2:**78
Solzhenitsyn, Aleksandr **2:**76
space program **1:**60–1, **3:**63, **4:**131, **6:**42–6
split with China **2:**27–8, 70, 78, 95, 96, 155
and the USAF's nuclear bombing strategy **1:**28–9
and wars of liberation **6:**170–1
see also arms race; Brezhnev, Leonid; Cold War; Khrushchev, Nikita; U-2 incident
Soyuz spacecraft **6:**43, 46
space race **1:**14–17, 61, **6:**42–7
and missile systems **1:**80
Soviet **1:**60–1, **3:**63, **4:**131, **6:**42–6
space rendezvous **3:**67, 69–70, 71
see also aerospace industry; NASA; satellites
spacewalks **3:**67, 69, **6:**46
Spano v. New York (1959) **4:**112
Spartan missiles **5:**151
Special Forces *see* Green Berets
Special Operations Group, CIA **2:**38
Spector, Phil **1:**123, **5:**65, 66
spies, depiction of **2:**36
Spock, Benjamin **1:**51, 52, 97, **5:**152
sports **4:**49–51, **6:**75
see also Olympic Games
Sprint missiles **4:***114*, **5:**151
Sproul Hall occupation **2:***107*, 109
Sputnik **1:**15, 60, 61, **2:**70, 88, **4:***96*, 130, **6:**42, 44
Stafford, Thomas P. **1:**67, **3:**70, 71
stagflation **2:**172
Stalin, Josef **2:**77, 94, 152
Standard 101 **2:**7
Standard missiles **1:**33

Standard Oil **2:**174, **5:**34
Staple Singers **3:**87
Starlifter *see* Lockheed, C-141
Starr, Albert **3:**115
Starr, Ringo **1:**125
Star Trek **2:**91, **5:**178, **6:**74–5
Stax Records **6:**39, 40
Steamboat Willie **2:**160
Steiger, Rod **3:**136, *137*
Steinbeck, John **4:**56
Steinberg, David **5:**155
Steinem, Gloria **3:**33, *40*
Steiner, Stan **1:**47
Stella, Frank **5:**14, **6:**163–4
Stephen, John **3:**25
stereo **2:**92, **6:**48
Stern, Isaac **2:**60
Stevenson, Adlai **3:**5, **6:**49–50
Stieglitz, William **2:**7
Stigwood, Robert **2:**159
Stockdale, Sybil **5:**81
Stone, Dana **5:**39
Stone, Edward Durrell **1:**73
Stone, I.F. **3:**92–3, **5:**30
Stonewall riot **3:**65, *66*, **6:**17, **51**
Stored Program Control **2:**91
Storms, Harrison **1:**64
Strasberg, Lee **6:**93
Strategic Air Command (SAC) **1:**27, 28, 29
Strategic Arms Limitation Talks *see* SALT
Stratocruiser *see* Boeing
Stratofortress *see* Boeing
Stravinsky, Igor **5:**19
Streisand, Barbra **3:**138
strikes **2:**105, **4:**24
Stroessner, Alfredo **2:**80, **4:**37
Structuralists **4:**55
Student League **6:**52
Student Nonviolent Coordinating Committee *see* SNCC
student rebellion **2:**24, 107–8, **5:**99
and the Democratic Party **2:**144
and ecology **3:**12
in Mexico **6:**127
and theater **3:**18
see also antiwar movement
Students for Civil Liberties **2:**108
Students for a Democratic Society (SDS) **2:**19, 108, **6:52–5**
antiwar **1:**50, 52, **6:**54
and the FBI **3:**30, 31
Styron, William **4:**61, *64*
submarines **1:**80, **4:**148
nuclear-armed **1:**81, **2:***152*, **4:***145*, 150, *151*, **5:**127
suburbia **1:**72, 94, **5:**116, **6:56–9**
and African Americans **2:**56
and credit cards **2:**120
housing **1:**95–6, **3:**145, **6:***56*, 57–8, *59*
"white flight" to **1:**179, **2:**144, **3:**144–5
women in **3:**34
Suez Crisis **4:**105, 134
Suharto, Thojib N.J. **2:**81
suicides, public, over Vietnam **1:**51
Sukarno, Achmad **2:***80*
Sullivan, Ed **2:**9

Ed Sullivan Show 1:126, 5:68, *145*, 6:72
Summer of Love 2:111, **6:60–1**
Super Bowl **6:62–3**
see also football
supercarriers 4:149
supermarkets 5:*118*, 119, 120
Super Sabre 1:32–3
supersonic transport (SST) **6:64–5**
superstores *see* retail industry
Supreme Court 5:46, **6:66–9**
    and the death penalty 2:127
    and desegregation 1:177, 178, 3:61, 6:8
    and the draft 2:167
    and justice 2:126–8
    and Nixon 1:175, 4:47, 6:66, 68, *69*
    and right to counsel 3:77
    and school prayer 5:105, 6:69
    see also Burger, Warren E
Supremes 4:120
Surveyor spacecraft 4:133, 5:126
Sutcliffe, Stuart 1:124, 127
Sutherland, Joan 5:19
Sweet Inspirations 3:*86*
swimsuits, topless 3:23
Symbionese Liberation Army 2:113
Syncom satellites 2:89, 5:165
Syntactic Structures 2:33
syphilis, and research 3:119
Szell, George 2:60

T

Taft, Robert 5:112
Tai, Nguyen Van 5:149
Taiwan 2:18, 3:103
"Take Five" (melody) 1:169
Take the Money and Run 1:40
tanks 1:*85*, 86, 87
Tartar missiles 2:*153*
Task Force on Indian Affairs 1:174
Taylor, Maxwell 1:86, 2:129, 130, 132
teachers 2:173, 3:30
Teamsters Union 2:17, 4:30
technology *see* science and technology
teenagers 1:135, 3:72, 5:71–2, 6:58
telephones 2:91
telescopes, radio 5:166
television 4:53, **6:70–5**
    and advertising 1:7, 9, 11
    and the baby-boom generation 1:96
    color 2:**85–6**, 6:75
    comedy **6:76–9**
    companies 4:156–7, 158
    Disney shows 2:161
    escapist entertainment 6:73–5
    evangelism 6:72
    FBI-based shows 3:28
    manufacturers 3:9
    music 6:72–3
    news and current affairs 4:156–9, 6:70–1
    and nuclear disaster 4:170, 172
    politics 1:19, 2:90, 5:53–4, 6:70
    pop music 5:68

portraying housewives 3:32
satellites 2:89, 90–1, 3:69
satire 5:154, 6:79
science fiction 5:178, 6:74
space achievements 1:69, 3:69
sport 3:50, 51, 52–3, 82, 4:50, 6:75
"spy" programs 2:36
talk shows 2:9, **6:80–3**
Telstar satellites 2:89, 4:133, 5:165, 6:75
Temptations 6:41
tennis 4:17, 50–1, **6:84–7**
Tereshkova, Valentina 6:45–6
Terman, Frederick 3:9
terrorists, Palestinian 6:30
Terry, Luther L. 1:48
Tet Offensive 2:133, 3:111, 4:135, 169, **6:88–9**, 145–6
    and Hue 3:148–9, 4:89, 6:89, 146, *149*
    and Saigon 1:55, 5:149, 6:*88*, 89, 145
    and the Viet Cong 3:148, 149, 6:89, 137
Texas Instruments 2:100, 3:8
Texas Proviso 3:159
textiles, and Jack Lenor Larsen 2:147
Thailand 4:87, 6:5, 7
thalidomide tragedy **6:90–1**
Thant, U 6:*50*
Tharpe, Sister Rosetta 3:85–6
theater 3:16, **6:92–5**
    experimental **3:17–18**
    see also Broadway
Theory of the Leisure Class, The 2:102–3
Thieu, Nguyen Van 1:172, 6:143–4, 151–2, *154*, 156
Third Stream music 3:171
Third World
    and the Cold War 2:80–1
    Green Revolution 1:26, **3:96–9**
    and the Peace Corps 5:29–30
    wars of liberation 6:171
Tho, Nguyen Huu 4:135
Thompson, Hunter S. 2:5, 4:70, 71, 5:156
Three-Fifths of a Man 2:54
Thunderchief 1:32–3
Thurmond, Strom 3:154
Ticonderoga (ship) 3:104, 105, 4:149
"tiger cages" 3:153
Time 4:69, 70
Time Out 1:169, 3:169
Times Magazine 4:71
Times They Are A-Changin', The 2:168
Tiros satellites 1:15, 5:126, 165
Titan rockets/ICBMs 1:80, 3:68, 4:*109*, 113, 5:124, 125
Tito, Josip 2:79
tobacco industry 1:11, 48, 49
Today 6:80
To Kill a Mockingbird 4:60, 61
Tolson, Clyde 3:142, 143
Tonight Show 1:52, 2:9
Tonkin, Gulf of incident **3:103–5**, 4:148–9; 6:141

Tonkin, Gulf of resolution 2:77, 3:94, 104, 105, 4:149, 5:46–7, 6:141, 148–9
Tornados, the 1:158, 159
Toscanini, Arturo 2:59
tourism **6:96–7**
Townshend, Pete 5:134
toys 1:96, 108
Trade Expansion Act (1962) 6:117–18
trade, international 2:173, 174, 177, 178
    see also exports; imports
Trafficante, Santo, Jr. 5:25
transistors 2:146, 158, 3:7
    and communications 2:87, 91, 92
    and computers 2:99–100
Transit satellites 5:165
transplants 3:122, 5:172
    heart 3:115, **122–3**
transportation 1:35, **6:98–103**, 130
    supersonic **6:64–5**
    see also cars
travelers checks 6:97
Travis, Jimmy 2:44
Tree, Penelope 3:24
triple-double 1:118
Troggs 1:161
trucks 6:99, *100*
Trudall, John 1:46–7
Truffaut, François 3:56, 57
Trujillo, Rafael 1:172, 2:164, 3:151, 4:180
Truman, Harry S 2:26, 3:162, 5:47
Tshombe, Moise 2:136, 3:102
Tureck, Rosalyn 2:58
Turkey, U.S. missiles 2:130, 132
Turner Joy (ship) 3:103, 105, 4:148
Turner, William 3:29
Twenty-fourth Amendment 2:51, 140
26th of July Movement 2:13
Twiggy 3:20, *22*, 23
Twist, the 5:64

U

U-2 incident 1:31, 2:35, *70*, 72, 3:6, 4:16, **6:104–5**
ultrasound 5:*171*, 172–3
Un-American Activities Committee of the House of Representatives 2:75, 93
unemployment, rate 2:170
Union Carbide (company) 2:174
Union of Mine Workers 2:66
unions *see* labor relations
United Arab Republic 4:106
United Fruit Company 4:35
United Mineworkers 3:166
United Nations 1:58, 3:13, **6:106–10**
    China's admission to 2:29
    Universal Declaration of Human Rights 3:150
UNIVAC computers 2:99
universities *see* schools and universities
Unsafe at Any Speed 2:6, 7, 3:126

Untouchables, The 3:28, 142
Updike, John 3:16, 4:55, 56, 57, **6:111**
Urban Mass Transportation Act (1964) **6:102**, 103
urban-renewal 3:146–7
Uruguay 4:38
U.S.–Canadian relations **6:112–15**
U.S.–Chinese relations 2:**26–9**, 75, 95, 4:79
U.S.–European relations 2:138, **6:116–19**
U.S.–Japanese relations 6:116, **120–3**
U.S.–Mexican relations **6:124–7**
    see also Alliance for Progress
U.S. v. Seeger (1965) 2:167
utilities **6:128–33**

V

V2 missiles 1:15
vacations 1:36, 4:48, *49*
vaccines 3:118, 5:171
Vadim, Roger 1:109, 3:140
Dick Van Dyke Show 6:78
Van Hamersveld, John 2:149
van Vogt, A.E. 5:175
Varèse, Edgar 2:58
V. 4:60
Veblen, Thorstein 2:102–3
Vehicle Equipment Safety Compact 2:7
vehicles, recreational 4:51–2
Vela satellites 1:15, 5:165
Velvet Underground 5:142, 143
Venera space probes 6:46
Venezuela 1:42
Venturi, Robert 1:73–5, 2:147–8
Venus 5:168, 6:46
Vidal, Gore 5:51
videophones 2:91
Vienna summit (June 1961) 2:*71*, 72
Viet Cong 4:168, **6:134–7**, 140
    Kit Carson Scouts 6:136
    and the Mekong Delta 4:94, 95
    and the My Lai massacre 4:122, 123
    National Liberation Front 4:135, 6:134, 140
    and POWs 5:80, 81
    as POWs 5:*81*, 6:*135*, *137*
    and the Tet Offensive 3:148, 149, 4:169, 5:149, 6:89
    tunnels of Cu-Chi 6:139
Vietminh 6:134, 138
Vietnam
    divided 6:139
    Green Revolution 3:*96*, 97
Vietnam Day 1:130
Vietnam Day Committee 1:51
Vietnam Moratorium Committee 1:57
Vietnam Veterans Against the War 1:55
Vietnam War 2:73–5, **6:138–57**
    and African Americans 1:50–1, 88

aftermath 1:88
aircraft 1:30, 31, 2:73
air-to-ground missiles 1:32–3
Ap Bac 6:140
Bien Hoa 6:141
and Cambodia 6:147, 148, 149, 153, 154, 156, 157
and China 2:28
and the CIA 2:36, 77
cost 2:176–8, 6:155
Da Nang 2:133, 3:149, 4:89, 6:142
defoliants 6:143, 144
draft 1:50, 52, 54, 87–8, 99, 2:166, 167
and Ellsworth Bunker 1:172
end see Paris Peace Talks
and Europe 6:119, 146
final U.S. evacuation 6:157
and fragging 1:171, 3:100–1
green berets 3:95, 130
grunts 3:100–1
Gulf of Tonkin incident 3:103–5, 4:148–9
Gulf of Tonkin resolution 2:77, 3:94, 104, 105, 4:149, 5:46–7, 6:141, 148–9
Haiphong 3:110–11, 6:143, 152
Hamburger Hill 6:151
Hanoi bombed 4:162, 6:143
Ho Chi Minh Trail 1:32, 3:129–31, 4:33, 6:140
Ia Drang 1:88, 6:142–3
and Japan 6:123
Khe Sanh 4:14–15, 89, 6:89, 145–6, 175
Kit Carson Scouts 6:136
and Laos see Laos
and McGeorge Bundy 1:171
McNamara Line 6:143
Marines 4:89
media reports 1:19, 4:129, 162–3
Mekong Delta 4:94–5, 150
MIAs 4:102–3, 5:81
and mind control 2:38
My Lai massacre 1:88, 4:122–3, 6:146, 147, 150
napalm 4:128–9
non-American troops 6:156
North Vietnamese Army 4:14–15, 94, 168–9, 6:152
Pentagon Papers 1:57, 2:38, 4:163, 6:149, 150–1
photography 4:129, 5:39–40
POWs 5:80–1, 6:154
public opinion 6:149
reasons for U.S. entering 1:80, 2:73–4, 97, 136, 6:139, 140
Saigon 1:55, 56, 5:148–9, 6:88, 89, 134, 142, 145, 157
search and destroy missions 6:142, 148
and self-immolation 1:51, 5:148
Shu-Fly operations 4:95
Son Tay raid 3:95, 6:149
and Spiro Agnew's attack on the media over 1:19
tropical warfare 6:152
tunnels of Cu-Chi 6:139

and the U.S. Army 1:87–8, 4:95
Vietnamese nationalism 2:97
Vietnamization 2:63, 82, 4:151, 6:147, 154
see also antiwar movement; draft; Geneva Accords; Tet Offensive; Viet Cong; Westmoreland, William
Viking probes 5:168
Villela, Edward 1:107
Vincent, Gene 2:114
viruses 3:121
VISTA 3:94, 5:79
visual arts 6:158–65
Rothko, Mark 5:146, 6:158
Warhol, Andy 5:60–3, 6:166, 164–5
see also design; Op Art; photography; Pop Art
Voice of America (VOA) 2:77
Volkswagen, Beetle 1:91, 93, 2:174
Von Braun, Wernher see Braun, Wernher von
Vonnegut, Kurt 5:177
Voskhod program 6:43, 46
Vostok spaceships 3:63, 67, 6:45
vote, black
effects of the 2:140–1
voting rights 2:54–6, 4:126–7, 6:8, 12–13, 35
Voting Rights Act (1965) 1:50, 2:46, 54, 140, 141, 3:93, 4:19, 126, 6:13
and Johnson 2:56, 3:174

W

Wagner, Robert 2:60, 3:113
Wahpepah, James 4:140
Wald, George 3:117, 118
Wallace, George 2:55, 143
presidential bids 2:57, 141, 143, 5:52–3
prosegregation 2:45, 49, 143, 4:19
Wallace, Mike 4:159
Wal-Mart 5:119
Walters, Barbara 6:82
Warhol, Andy 3:20, 23, 5:43, 6:164, 166
Warner, Jack 3:136
War on Poverty 1:13, 141, 5:76, 77, 78–9
Warren Court 4:47, 6:66, 67–8
Warren, Earl 3:77, 4:47, 112, 6:66–9, 167
Warren Report 3:31, 4:9, 6:167
Warren, Robert Penn 4:62
Warrior, Clyde 1:45
Warsaw Pact 1:30, 87, 6:168–9
wars of liberation 6:170–1
see also
decolonization/independence
Washington, Dinah 3:87
Washington, March on
antiwar 1:50, 51, 2:110, 112
civil rights (1963) 2:50–1, 168, 3:47, 154, 4:19, 82–3, 127, 6:34, 36
Poor People's March (1968)

2:57, 3:30
see also Pentagon, March on
waste disposal 6:132
water, provision 6:129–30
Watergate affair 2:77, 4:47, 165
and the CIA 2:38
Waters, Muddy 1:146, 147, 149
water sports 4:51
waterways 6:99
Watson, James 4:166
Watson, Tom, Jr. 2:99
Watts riot 3:75, 76, 147, 6:59, 172–4
weather forcasting, and satellites 1:15
Weather Report 3:172
Weather Underground 1:57, 2:113
Weaver, Robert 3:147
Weavers 3:45
Webb, James 3:63
Weinberg, Jack 2:109
Weiner, Lee 2:24, 25
Wein, George 3:171
Welch, Robert 5:96–7
Welles, Orson 3:56
Wells, Henry 6:97
"We Shall Overcome" 1:101, 2:42, 55, 109, 5:91
Western Union 6:133
West Indies, immigration from 3:157, 158
Westmoreland, William 1:55, 2:63, 6:88, 89, 142, 143, 146–7, 156, 175
and Khe Sanh 4:14, 15, 6:175
West Side Story 1:104, 133, 3:138, 141
"What's Happening in America?" (essay) 4:54
Where Do We Go from Here? 2:56
Whitcomb, Ian 1:161
White, Edmund 6:51
White, Edward H. 1:63, 64, 3:67, 69
"white flight" see suburbia
White House 3:176
White, Maud 3:30
White, Theodore 2:144, 5:52
Who's Afraid of Virginia Woolf? 3:16, 136, 6:95
Who, the 5:134, 141, 143
Why Are We in Vietnam? 1:54, 4:72–3
Wilder, Billy 2:150
Wild Ones, The 1:176
Wild Weasels (aircraft) 1:32–3
Wilkins, Roy 4:124–5, 127
Willard Straight Hall 1:144
Williams, Hank 2:114, 117, 118
Williams, John 4:61
Williams, Marion 3:84
Williamson, Sonny Boy 1:149
Williams, Tennessee 1:162
Williams, Tony 2:135, 3:172
Wilson, Brian 1:122, 123, 5:86
Wilson, Harold 6:119, 146
Wilson, Wes 2:149
Winogrand, Garry 5:41
Wolfe, Tom 2:5, 4:56, 70, 6:163
"Wolfman Jack" 5:101

women
and advertising 1:10
education 5:159
as housewives 3:32
journalists 4:162
rights 5:74
and TV talk shows 6:82–3
in the workforce 3:14
see also feminist movement
Women's Action Alliance 3:33
Women's Equity Action League 3:39, 4:136
Women's Liberation Movement 3:33, 39
see also feminist movement
Women's Strike for Equality 3:39
Woodstock 2:113, 3:49, 5:91, 6:176–7
nudity 6:14, 17
Woolworth, and civil rights protests 2:39, 40, 107, 4:124, 126, 6:26–7, 34
Worden, USS 4:151
World's Fair (1964) 6:178–9
World Trade Center 1:73, 76
World War II
aircraft 1:12, 13, 14
and the civil rights movement 2:41
and the coal industry 2:64
computers 2:98
and the economy 4:109
napalm 4:128
women's role 3:34
see also postwar world
World Wildlife Fund 5:170–1
Wright, Gene 1:169
Wright, Mickey 3:82–3
Wylie, Philip 4:170

X

X-15 program 1:17, 4:131–2
Xerox (company) 2:174
X-planes 5:126
X-rays 5:173

Y

Yablonski, Joseph "Jock" 2:66
Yamasaki, Minoru 1:73, 76
Yardbirds 5:134
Yarrow Roots 2:149
Yeager, Chuck 5:126
Yes 5:87
Yippies 2:19–22, 111, 6:180, 180
Young Americans for Freedom (YAF) 5:98–9
Young, John W. 3:68, 71
Young, La Monte 1:260, 3:17
Young, Neil 2:119, 3:49
Young Rascals 5:131
Young, Whitney 1:138, 140–2
Youth for Wallace 5:99
Yugoslavia 5:83

Z

Zappa, Frank 3:172, 5:88, 89
Zedong, Mao see Mao Zedong